The Underground Railroad
on the Western Frontier

ALSO BY
JAMES PATRICK MORGANS

Grenville Mellen Dodge in the Civil War: Union Spymaster, Railroad Builder and Organizer of the Fourth Iowa Volunteer Infantry (McFarland 2016)

John Todd and the Underground Railroad: Biography of an Iowa Abolitionist (McFarland, 2006)

The Underground Railroad on the Western Frontier

Escapes from Missouri, Arkansas, Iowa and the Territories of Kansas, Nebraska and the Indian Nations, 1840–1865

JAMES PATRICK MORGANS

McFarland & Company, Inc., Publishers
Jefferson, North Carolina

The present work is a reprint of the illustrated case bound edition of The Underground Railroad on the Western Frontier: Escapes from Missouri, Arkansas, Iowa and the Territories of Kansas, Nebraska and the Indian Nations, 1840–1865, *first published in 2010 by McFarland.*

LIBRARY OF CONGRESS CATALOGUING-IN-PUBLICATION DATA

Morgans, James Patrick.
The underground railroad on the western frontier : escapes from Missouri, Arkansas, Iowa and the territories of Kansas, Nebraska and the Indian nations, 1840–1865 / James Patrick Morgans.
p.   cm.
Includes bibliographical references and index.

ISBN 978-1-4766-7826-9
softcover : acid free paper ∞

1. Underground railroad.
2. Antislavery movements—United States—History.
3. Fugitive slaves—United States—History.
I. Title.
E450.M77   2019   973.7'115—dc22   2009054188

British Library cataloguing data are available

© 2010 James Patrick Morgans. All rights reserved

No part of this book may be reproduced or transmitted in any form or by any means, electronic or mechanical, including photocopying or recording, or by any information storage and retrieval system, without permission in writing from the publisher.

Front cover: General map of the United States & their territory between the Mississippi & the Pacific Ocean, 1859 (Library of Congress); lantern © 2019 Shutterstock

Printed in the United States of America

McFarland & Company, Inc., Publishers
Box 611, Jefferson, North Carolina 28640
www.mcfarlandpub.com

To my loving wife, Judith A. Morgans,
and my two children, Patrick James Morgans
and Meredith Joy Morgans Kuehler

Contents

Acknowledgments ix
Preface 1

1. Kansas 5
2. Missouri: Freedom Escapes 36
3. Missouri: Hemp and "Little Dixie" Empires 64
4. Iowa-Nebraska 90
5. Arkansas: Liberty Via Steamboats 119
6. Arkansas: Fleeing from Farms and Plantations 139
7. Western Frontier and the Indian Nations
   (Oklahoma) 162
8. Conclusions 186

Chapter Notes 199
Bibliography 213
Index 219

Acknowledgments

First of all, I would like to thank my son, Patrick James Morgans, for his hard work in finding and obtaining research materials for this book. Also, I would like to thank my daughter, Meredith Joy Morgans Kuehler, of Omaha, Nebraska, for looking up legal cases pertinent to this subject in her law books and legal software. I am indebted to J.V. Eckley of Cape Girardeau, Missouri, for his fine illustrations in the book.

I am grateful that Michael Irvin of Shenandoah, Iowa, read the manuscript and pointed out needed corrections. I appreciate Wanda Ewalt of Tabor, Iowa, for her kind words and encouragement.

I would like to thank James Hill and Diane Miller of the National Park Service's "National Underground Railroad Network to Freedom" program for allowing me to use their collection of Arkansas slave advertisements assembled by Dr. S. Charles Bolton of the University of Arkansas at Little Rock. I would also like to thank Dr. Sara Crook of Peru State College in Peru, Nebraska, for use of her Nebraska Territorial newspapers.

Eveleth Hill of Marshall, Missouri, has my gratitude for sharing her research on this subject for central Missouri. I would like to thank Lynn Handy of Percival, Iowa, for the material he sent to me. I would also like to thank the staffs at the Kansas State Historical Society in Topeka, Kansas, the State Historical Society of Missouri in Columbia, Missouri, and the State Historical Society of Iowa in Des Moines, Iowa, for their help in locating research materials. Lastly, I would like to thank my wife Judith A. Morgans for her help at the most opportune times.

Preface

In this work we have defined the Western Frontier from 1840 to 1865 as being on a line from the Western border of Iowa in the North to the Western border of Arkansas in the South. Although some of these locations went from being territories to being states, for the most part the area from Independence, Missouri, to Council Bluffs, Iowa, was the jumping off point for hundreds of thousands of Americans from the United States into the Western Territories. They headed for the Great Salt Lake Valley in the Utah territory, on the famed Santa Fe Trail, to the gold fields in California and later to the gold fields in Colorado. They could head to the lush fertile valleys of Oregon and Washington. The states of Arkansas, Missouri and Iowa were on the Western edge of the contiguous states of the United States for most of this time. South of Independence, Missouri, in Arkansas, you could travel westward into the Indian Nations of the area that would become known as Oklahoma.

As in the rest of America where there were humans held in bondage in the west there were also those who wished to escape that condition. It would have been impossible to detail all the slave escapes on the Western Frontier but we have tried in this book to give details on a sampling of those brave travels to freedom. In some cases there were only a few words in a slave runaway advertisement to tell of an escape and in others we had a full-blown narrative. We have tried to give details when possible on the conditions that led to the escape. In all cases, if possible, the bondsperson's own words were used to describe these escapes. However, many of the depictions of the slave treks to freedom attempted on the Western Frontier were written by white abolitionists or those attempting to catch the fugitive slaves and they often put themselves in the center of the drama.

I consulted slave advertisements in newspapers and newspaper articles of the time, including articles from Canadian newspapers about bondspersons who had successfully escaped to that country. Letters, reminiscences, books and narratives written by and about escaped bondspersons were also used. In the 1930s the WPA Federal Writers' Project interviewed over two thousand former slaves. This information was a gold mine about escapes and escape attempts of bondspersons. Applewood Books in cooperation with the Library of Congress produced these interviews in a format that recreated the actual size and layout of the original typed pages of the FWP interviews, including any marked-out words or notes on the sides of the interview pages. I liked using the Applewood Books best for this research.

Unfortunately, the Applewood Books only put approximately thirty-five interviews in these books of a particular state. They took the first names in the alphabet to put in the books—so you saw the interviews if the formers bondsperson's last name was Adams but not if it was Zee. The Library of Congress has a website called American Memory that has these interviews but I found it somewhat difficult to navigate the website without the last name of the former bondsperson. However, after much time, I was able to use the site to locate the interviews of bondspersons who had resided in the states on the Western Frontier at the time of their bondage. Also, some state historical societies added other interviews to the total and I was able to locate these. I would like to mention a book that I used for gathering these FWP interviews, *Bearing Witness: Memories of Arkansas Slavery Narratives from the 1930s WPA Collections*, edited by George E. Lankford.

Lankford pointed out in his book one major pitfall of these interviews. The former bondspersons were interviewed in the states in which they were currently residing during the 1930s—not the state or territory in which they had resided during their days as slaves. In Lankford's wonderful book he combed the other states' interviews for Arkansas slave interviews to include in his work. Just because the interview was done in Missouri, for instance, doesn't necessarily mean the interviewee was held in bondage in that state. Also, some of the interviews are done in such a manner that it is difficult to determine the state or territory where the former bondsperson was held as a slave.

The chapters are arranged by state but some of the escapes and treks to freedom occurred in multiple territories and states. I put them in the state or territory I thought would be most appropriate.

Chapter 1 is the story of the bondspersons' escapes from the Kansas Territory. Kansas was known as "Bleeding Kansas" at this time because of the brigades of pro-slavery and anti-slavery armies involved in a shooting war. The bondspersons had to negotiate this war-zone to find their paths to freedom. Also, there were organized criminals who tried to capture runaway slaves to sell them back into bondage. Accounts of the Underground Railroad in Kansas are discussed, including the sacking of Lawrence by U.S. marshals angered at that towns' Underground Railroad work.

Chapter 2 describes slavery and slave escapes in Missouri. The famous "Jerry Escape" of a Missouri bondsman who made his freedom trek to Syracuse, New York, then to Canada, and the abolitionist toe-hold in Marion County, Missouri, is discussed. The stories of other bondspersons and their journeys to freedom on the liberty line are also told. Escapes on the steamships on Missouri's water-highways is examined. The inspiring story of world-famous author William Wells Brown and his journey to freedom from slavery in St. Louis is recounted.

Chapter 3 finds the reader still in Missouri, with the report of John Anderson's legal battles to find freedom in Canada. This chapter tells the story of Henry Clay Bruce and his brother Blanche Bruce, who became a U.S. senator, and their trail to freedom in Kansas. It also discusses the "Little Dixie" area of Missouri and the Western boundary district of that state and these regions' impact on the importance of hemp-growing and its influence on slavery and slave escapes. Lastly, it discusses the chaotic conditions in Missouri brought about by the Civil War and the attempt by the state's bondspersons to find liberty during that time.

Chapter 4 describes the escape corridor out of the Mississippi River Valley and into the southeastern part of Iowa, the active escape route out of Central and Western Missouri through the Nebraska territory and into Western Iowa, and the story of the Underground Railroad lines across Iowa. John Brown's famous raid into Western Missouri and his travels through Kansas and into Iowa is also detailed.

In Chapter 5, slave escapes out of the state of Arkansas are discussed, as well as the importance of using steamboats to escape along the Western Frontier and the stirring escape story of Henry Bibb and his importance to the anti-slavery movement.

Chapter 6 discusses more of the freedom treks out of slave state Arkansas. Arkansas was next to the Indian Nations and this chapter discusses the desire of some of her bondspersons to escape to that territory. The interesting legal battle of slave Nelson Hacket and his escape to Canada and the frenzied conditions of the Civil War in Arkansas and the escape of her bondspersons are also discussed.

Chapter 7 tells the story of slave escapes on the Western Frontier. It discusses escapes from Arkansas and the Indian Nations into the little-known haven for bondspersons in Mexico, the slave escapes from the Native Americans of the Cherokee, Creek, Seminole, Choctaw and Chickasaw tribes, and also the Civil War and its impact on the Indians Nations.

In Chapter 8 the escapes of bondspersons in Kansas and Western Missouri and the work of abolitionists on the Western Frontier to keep slavery from expanding into new territories are discussed. The myths of the Underground Railroad are examined, as well as how racism after the Civil War helped shaped portrayals of the Underground Railroad.

1

Kansas

"Fight! fight hard!"
— Bondsman Napoleon Simpson's dying words after being fatally wounded while trying to gain his freedom

The Underground Railroad and freedom escapes on the Western Frontier often presented different challenges than escapes in other locations in the United States. For our purposes here we will define the Western Frontier as the states of Arkansas, Missouri and Iowa and the territories of Kansas, Nebraska and the Indian Nations (Oklahoma). The future states of Nebraska and Oklahoma were still only territories prior to the Civil War. Kansas would become a state just before the outbreak of the Civil War. These areas had only a rudimentary apparatus of a legal structure and many times the points of law were decided at the end of a firearm. The economic activity in these struggling new territories and Western Iowa was often minuscule and residents very often toiled to just feed their own families. In 1857, 1858 and 1860 the new territory of Kansas dealt with severe droughts which caused malnutrition, cholera and other diseases among her citizens. During the Panic of 1857 the fledgling territory of Nebraska had all its banks close except one and that was owned by a slave owner! The Western part of Iowa, a state since 1846, still had few roads, proper bridges or reliable postal service and she attracted little capital and was extremely "cash starved." Arkansas, although she had been a state since 1836, still had few settlers and little infrastructure. When the escaping fugitive bondsperson fled through these territories it was often hard to find the necessary food and water in these areas to sustain an escape.

Kansas, known during this period as "bleeding Kansas," had, since 1854, a shooting war between brigades of anti-slavery and pro-slavery armies, which made the escape of bondspersons even more treacherous. In Arkansas and Missouri, where slavery was the law of the land, severe penalties awaited any white citizen or person of color who aided any slave in their flight to freedom or attempted escape. The Kansas slave Constitution or Lecompton Constitution banned free Blacks from living in the state. Many slave owners were very suspicious of free Black persons and their ability to help their Black brethren in escaping. States that allowed slavery were often so paranoid about any effort to over throw their brutal system of human bondage that even the possession of abolitionist pamphlets could result in jail time.[1]

Additionally, in the slave state of Missouri it was illegal to even read the Declaration of Independence or the Bible to any slave lest they hear the word freedom. The territory of Oklahoma or the "Indian Nations" as it was known by many at that time in the United States and the state of Arkansas, offered a unique path to freedom via Mexico as well as through Canada. The Southwest corner of Iowa and the area along the Southern Iowa border with Missouri offered a portal to freedom to the bondsmen and women of slavery. The desire for freedom by bondspersons on the Western Frontier was just as strong as that of their eastern counterparts.

The path to freedom was often fraught with danger in the frequently lawless territories where justice was often administered by Judge Lynch. Because the new territories were just recently settled, even sympathetic white or Black residents of the area often could not give the escaping slaves an accurate description of the topography of the land they were in or ideas on climate or reliable places to find water or food. For instance, in many of these areas a bondsman escaping Arkansas in September and getting to a free state such as Illinois or Iowa in December might have no idea of what the harsh northern climates would bring. If the bondsman or woman decided to head south for freedom the shifting political climates of Texas and Mexico could be formidable obstacles to surmount.

If white citizens were caught aiding an escaping slave they could face jail time or civil lawsuits. The bondsperson, if caught, could face extreme beatings, disfigurements or even death. After attempting an escape and being captured, the returned slave was often branded on the face with an "R" for runaway. Ears or other features were lacerated or other attempts to disfigure were made to tell those looking at a bondsperson that they had attempted to run away. Hamstringing was the odious practice of cutting the bondsperson's hamstring so that any attempt to run would be futile and the slave would be easy to capture. This was usually a last resort for a repeat runaway.

When settlement was first officially authorized in 1854 in the Kansas territory, the federal government wanted the territory to eventually be a state that allowed slavery. The federal government appointed pro-slavery officials to the territory, such as Indian agents, postmasters and even United States marshals, to hold reign in the state to encourage pro-slavery settlers to vote in a constitution that would allow that loathsome institution. A state constitution, with the aid of Missouri border ruffians, people who came over from Missouri to vote in Kansas but actually resided in Missouri, allowed slavery in Kansas. What became known as the Lecompton Constitution in Kansas made any kind of aid to escaping slaves punishable with draconian measures. Also, in some cases United States marshals and local sheriffs considered abolitionists, and the work they were doing on the Underground Railroad, to be terrorists and warrants for their arrests were issued.

One of the most profound events that helped the advancement of the Underground Railroad along the Western Frontier was the passage of the law that became known as the Kansas-Nebraska Act of 1854. This act was the brainchild of United States Senator Stephen A. Douglas, the chairman of the Senate Committee on Territories. Many looked at this bill as another consolatory attempt at making concessions to the Southern slave-holding interests. Some historians have looked at this endeavor by Douglas as an attempt to cement the Democratic Party, which had been fractured by the question of slavery. Douglas desired the nomination for the presidency from the Democratic Party. After being president for two years, Franklin Pierce had managed to anger both the Northern abolitionists and the Southern slave-holding states. In fact, in 1856, Pierce, a sitting United States president, didn't even receive his own party's nomination for the presidency. Douglas, an extremely ambitious man, certainly saw this measure as a way to endear himself to the Southern wing of his party and saw that if he could hold onto the majority of the Northern vote the grand price would be his. However, in the end, all the maneuvering that the Kansas-Nebraska Act entailed backfired for the slavery proponents.

Slave interests interjected the principal of "popular sovereignty" into the Kansas-Nebraska Act of 1854. This would allow the settlers in Kansas and Nebraska to vote on whether they wanted to allow slavery in their territory or not. Douglas, with an eye to a map of the United States, reasoned that Kansas would be settled by people mostly from Missouri, a slave state, and that slavery would be voted into the territory. Nebraska would be settled mostly by residents of Iowa, a free state, and slavery would not be allowed in the territory. It was hoped that the Act would bring balance to the Senate of the United States between slave and free states and would be, hopefully, another compromise that would delay a civil war over the question of slavery.

The Act repealed the Missouri Compromise of 1820, which stated that slavery would not be allowed north of the southern border of Missouri. Many abolitionists had swallowed hard when the abrasive Fugitive Slave Act of 1850 was passed. They figured it was the law of the land and would have to be obeyed. When the Kansas-Nebraska Act of 1854 became law of the land and the Missouri Compromise of 1820 was, for all practical purposes, repealed, many abolitionists felt that the slavery powers in the United States were going to simply keep expanding their grasp on the new territories being opened up for settlement and slavery would coil her ugly grip and her influence on the United States forever. After the passage of this Act public opinion began to change all over America. The slave powers had thrown down the gauntlet and the abolitionists in the North had quickly picked it up. Noted historian Alan Nevins stated that, "What had been radical opinion in the North now became general opinion; Douglas had converted more men to intransigent freesoil doctrine in two months than Garrison and Phillips had converted to abolitionism in twenty years."[2]

In the East and Midwest abolitionists grew bolder in their talk. In Kansas the volatile situation exploded into a shooting war between those who wanted

This African American woman was believed to have been helped by the Underground Railroad in Wabaunsee County in the Kansas Territory. Unfortunately her name is not known. Wabaunsee County was one of the furthest points west on the frontier for a station on the Underground Railroad. Enoch and Luther Platt were members of the Beecher's Bible and Rifle Colony in that county and also were known helpers on the Underground Railroad. It is interesting to note that the young lady in this photograph displays a wedding band. This photograph had been passed down through the generations in the Platt family (Kansas State Historical Society).

slavery in the territory and those who didn't. The two sides even wore their own "colors": the anti-slavery settlers often wore blue flannel shirts to designate their allegiance to their specific cause while the pro-slavery forces often wore red shirts.[3] From Quindaro near the Missouri border to Wabaunsee in the western settled part of the territory various communities in the Kansas territory showed a willingness to help fleeing bondspersons.

Even though open warfare often raged around them, bondspersons in Kansas wanted out of slavery. Ann Clarke was a resourceful bondswoman who managed to escape from her two masters, Colonel Titus and George W. Clarke, both of whom were United States government employees. Ann managed to elude capture for about five or six weeks in the Topeka area. However, slave hunters found her and returned her to Lecompton, Kansas, for their reward. Lecompton was the center for the pro-slavery activity in Kansas. After her capture the slave hunters were drinking heavily and celebrating. The bounty hunters sent for slaver Clarke to come and pay their reward money. Ann was being watched by the women folk and she was on the lookout for another escape attempt. At this time Ann was about 40 or 45 years old. She saw another opening and made a dash for a ravine that was full of brush near the house where she was being held captive. After noticing that Ann had again escaped, the slave hunters went out hunting for her and almost came upon her hiding spot.

Ann waited for the morning and took stock of her whereabouts. She followed the ravine and came close to a road that ran southwest of Lecompton. She saw a man coming down the road with a book under his arm. She thought that since the man had a book he was probably an anti-slavery man. Her perception proved to be right. The man was a doctor who lived right next to Ann's owner. He agreed to hide her. The doctor then transferred Ann to John Armstrong. Armstrong kept her in Topeka for about six weeks. Armstrong made preparations in Topeka to take Ann north. He received money from various anti-slavery men in Topeka to defray his expenses—including money from Governor Charles Robinson.

John Armstrong took Ann up to Civil Bend in Iowa and gave her to well-known Underground Railroad conductor Doc Blanchard. It was a straight shot north of one hundred and twenty-five miles from Topeka, K.T. (Kansas Territory), to Civil Bend, Iowa. Armstrong was three weeks on the road to complete this journey. The length of time was due to the lack of roads and bridges in the territories at this time. Armstrong followed the track John Kagy (sometimes spelled Kagi), John Brown's right-hand man, took up north when he went to visit his father Abraham Kagy in Nebraska. Blanchard then forwarded Ann on to Chicago, where she lived for a number of years. Ann Clarke wrote to Armstrong several times from Chicago. She offered Armstrong a good deal of money, five hundred dollars, if he would retrieve Ann's daughter who was enslaved in Southern Missouri in Lawrence County. It doesn't appear as if Armstrong was able to do this task.

Armstrong explained how he took other bondswomen to freedom by going through Holton, Kansas, and then on to Iowa. He described how after these two escapes they apparently didn't escort the bondswomen north but sent them northbound to the Underground Railroad in Southwest Iowa. Armstrong stated that some of these bondswomen came from Missouri and some came from Kansas. He went on to say that a W.E. Bowker and a Mr. Plummer used to escort some "colored men" to freedom along this path.[4]

The before-mentioned Colonel Henry Titus owned other slaves. Titus was an obnoxious self-appointed Colonel in the pro-slavery army in Kansas. He had fashioned a fort out of his home in Kansas and dubbed it Fort Titus. On August 16, 1856, some four dozen anti-

Mrs. Elizabeth Ann Watrous Abbott. Mrs. James Abbott was the wife of one of the most prominent abolitionists and Underground Railroad stationmasters on the Kansas frontier. Like most pioneer wives Elizabeth received little credit for the work she did on the frontier Underground Railroad. Her husband James was often away and it was Elizabeth who frequently had to make sure the freedom seekers were forwarded on to the next stop of the Underground Railway. Many times Mrs. Abbott had to deal with the slave hunters and law officers who came looking for the fugitives and tried to intimidate her. Elizabeth and her husband decided, as did many UGRR conductors, that the less they knew about the runaways, such as their names or where they were from, the better off the runaways and stationmasters would be. If they didn't know the bondsperson's name and were asked by lawmen, "Have you seen a fugitive slave named Charles?" The Abbotts could honestly say no (Kansas State Historical Society).

slavery men attacked Fort Titus and its approximately three dozen defenders. One of these attackers was well-known Kansas Underground Railroad conductor John E. Stewart.[5] While the fort was under attack a cannonball went through a trunk that a bondswoman was sitting on. It went in one end of the trunk and through the other end. She was later able to escape and make it to freedom in Canada. She related her harrowing story to the Rev. John Todd, Underground Railroad conductor, while she was in Tabor, Iowa.[6] The anti-slavery men prevailed in the attack and captured Titus, four hundred muskets and $10,000. They freed Titus' other bondspersons and sent them on to freedom.

John E. Rastall of Topeka took a bondsman out of Kansas through Nebraska City. He went two thirds of the way through Iowa and delivered the bondsman to a Congregational minister in Oskaloosa, Iowa. A deputy United States marshal named Butcher became alarmed at the Underground Railroad activity in Topeka. He conducted some heavy-handed raids in November and December of 1857. Looking for runaways, he took a large group of men and knocked down the door of Topeka resident John Richie. At the Garvey household in Topeka a similar raid produced no results. The local newspaper, the *Topeka Tribune*, condemned Marshal Butcher's tactics.[7]

Mr. and Mrs. James Abbott had an Underground Railroad stationhouse south of Lawrence near Coal Creek in Douglas County, Kansas. Mr. Abbott instructed his wife to not inquire of the runaway slaves where they came from or where they were going. The less they knew about the escaping bondspersons the less information they could give slave bounty hunters who were sure to follow the escapees. One time, when Mr. Abbott was gone, a young bondsman about twenty-three years of age showed-up at Mrs. Abbott's door. Mrs. Abbott had a large swelling in her arm and was having difficulties doing housework. She found out that this young man had been a cook on a steamboat and was quite handy around the kitchen and house. The young former steamboat cook even gave Mrs. Abbott a recipe. However, soon a knock came upon the door and two slave hunters came wanting a meal. Mrs. Abbott shooed them away but the young man noticed that the slave hunters had a bloodhound with them and were obviously looking for him.

The young man did the only thing he could. The slave hunters went to the next house and they turned the dog loose in the woods. It would only be a matter of time before the bloodhound picked up the young bondsman's scent and tracked him down. The young bondsman took an axe and found the bloodhound in the woods and, not being the type who liked to harm living creatures, he missed the first time he swung, but the second time, trembling greatly, he did the bloodhound in. He then made his way to freedom.

Later Mr. and Mrs. Abbott moved to Vermont Street in Lawrence, Kansas Territory, and helped escaping bondspersons whenever they could. One day, two teenage boys came to their home wanting help in escaping from slavery. Mrs. Abbott stated, "they were real good looking mulattoes." They stayed in the house a couple of days and became very antsy at being cooped up. The teenagers wanted to go outside but Mrs. Abbott insisted it would be too dangerous if they were spotted. However, teenage rebellion won out and the two lingered outside in the warm sunshine one blue-skied Lawrence afternoon. Mrs. Abbott noted how the two desired their liberty and the free air they breathed in Lawrence. It was obvious the two would have to be moved and sent on down the "liberty line." They were moved to Joel Grover's barn that night and presumably advanced soon afterwards.[8]

Lawrence, Kansas Territory, became a stronghold of freedom escapes in this region. As happened with many such towns on the Underground Railroad, Missouri and Kansas slave owners "advised" their "human chattels" to avoid Lawrence or there would be dire consequences. One such slave had been warned to stay away from Lawrence by his "master." He later stated on his way to freedom, "when he started to come to Lawrence he didn't know if all de peoples in disha town war debbils as ole massa had said or not, but dis he did know if he could get dar safe old massa was fraid to come arter him, and if dey all should prove to be bad as ole massa had said he could lib wid dem bout as well as at home."[9] Lawrence, with its compelling activities on the Underground Railroad and the aid its people gave in helping escaping bondsmen find their freedom on this liberty trail, came to the particular attention of the pro-slavery authorities in Kansas and the supporters of David Rice Atchison.

David Rice Atchison, a former Missouri United States senator, was one of the most outspoken proponents of turning Kansas into a slave state. His primary reason for this was to keep slavery as a growing institution. He also wanted to keep Kansas from providing a harbor for escaping Missouri slaves. Atchison and others like him were providing a steady drumbeat of rhetoric and illegal activities to stop the escape of Missouri slaves into Kansas by any means available — be they legal or not.

However, a Missouri slave owner originally from Virginia wrote a very prophetic letter to the St. Louis *Intelligencer* dated January 22, 1856. Under the headline of "Letter from a Border Ruffian" the anonymous writer went on to say that he owned slaves as did both his father's and mother's sides of his family. He then declared that he would "defend my rights (to own slaves) with as much vigor and pertinacity as God and my powers will enable me to do." Interestingly, the man went on to say what many abolitionists and other Northern economists said about slavery. He declared he believed slavery depressed wages and kept down the value of land; it discouraged enterprise and energy, and it was a hindrance to the establishment of schools and internal improvements. In many Missouri newspapers and other periodicals in the south the residents of Kansas who didn't support slavery were described as nothing more than brutes and animals — so-called traitors to the "white race."

This "border ruffian," however, declared that he had been to Kansas and expected to shoot on site the abolitionist cowards and "nigger stealers." However, much to his surprise he found well-educated, industrious and sober people.

"Border Ruffian" went on to say that Atchison & Co. and their "barbarous assaults and stabs, *again*, upon the Constitution, upon the Bill of Rights, upon order, decency, morals, virtue and religion, upon law and justice, for the sake and intent of making *by force* Kansas a slave State ... [was] sowing to the wind they were likely to reap the whirlwind."[10] This slave-holding Missourian's prophecies proved to be most accurate.

The *Herald of Freedom*, the official newspaper of the New England Emigrant Aid Company who were bringing anti-slavery settlers into Kansas and who supported the efforts of fleeing bondspersons from Kansas and Missouri, was published in Lawrence, K.T. It reprinted an item from the *Frontier News* published in Westport, Missouri. This item read, "We every day see handbills offering rewards for runaway negroes, from Jackson (county Missouri) and neighboring counties. Where do they go to? There is an Underground Railroad leading out of western Missouri, and we would respectfully refer the owners of lost niggers to the conductors of these trains. Enquire of Dr. (Charles) Robinson, sole agent for the transportation of fugitive niggers."[11] Dr. Charles Robinson, a medical doctor, was the head of the New England Emigrant Aid Company and was later territorial governor and then first governor of the state of Kansas.

Sheriff Samuel Jones of Douglas County Kansas Territory, who was also an acting deputy United States marshal, led and allowed an army/posse of pro-slavery soldiers to attack and sack Lawrence, Kansas Territory, on May 21, 1856.[12] Also, United States Marshal Israel B. Donaldson and Deputy United States Marshal W.F. Fain threw the full weight of the United States government on the side of this highly illegal action. Former Missouri senator, David Rice Atchison, felt Lawrence was the center of the abolitionist and Underground Railroad movement and its destruction would end this activity. This would keep, in Atchison's eyes, the slaves of Missouri free from intervention. Atchison was allowed to make a speech to this posse/mob before it attacked Lawrence. Atchison said,

> Gentlemen, Officers & Soldiers!—(Yells) This is the most glorious day of my life! The U.S. Marshall has just given you his orders and has kindly invited me to address you. For this invitation, coming from no less than U.S. authority, I thank him most sincerely ... now allow me, in true border-ruffian style, to extend to you the right hand of fellowship. (Cheers) ... I greet you as border-ruffian brothers. (Repeated yells & waving of hats) ... today you will earn laurels that will ever show you to have been true sons of the noble South! ... Spring like your bloodhounds at home upon that d—d accursed abolition hole.... Yes, ruffians, draw your revolvers & bowie knives & cool them in the heart's blood of all those d—d dogs, that dare defend that d—d breathing hole of hell. (Yells.) Tear down their boasted Free State Hotel, and if those Hellish lying free-soilers have left no port holes in it, with your unerring canon make some. Yes, riddle it till it shall fall to the ground. Throw into the Kanzas (the Kansas River) their printing presses, & let's see if any more free speeches will be issued from them! Boys do the Marshall's full bidding!—Do the sheriff's entire command!—(Yells) ... so that whatever he commands will be right, and under the authority of the administration of the U.S.!—and for it you will be amply paid as U.S. troops, besides having an opportunity of benefiting your wardrobes from the private dwellings of those infernal nigger-stealers.(Cheers) Courage for a few hours & victory is ours, falter & all is lost!—Are you determined? Will every one of you swear to bathe your steel in the black blood of some of those black sons of—(cries yells of yes, yes) ... I know you will never fail, but will burn, sack & destroy, until every vistage of these Norther Abolitionists is wiped out. Men of the South & Missouri ... unless this days work shall annihilate from our western world these hellish Emigrant Aid paupers ... the resolves of the entire

South, and of the present Administration, that is, to carry the war into the heart of the country, (cheers) never to slacken or stop until every spark of free-state, free-speech, free niggers, or free in any shape is quenched out of Kansaz! (Long shouting and cheering).[13]

Atchison's speech was eerily correct as this mob/posse carried out its sacking of Lawrence. Clearly, Sheriff Jones was in charge of the some six hundred to eight hundred men in this posse/army.[14] Under banners from the state of Alabama and a group from South Carolina calling themselves the Palmetto Guards, came men not only from Missouri but from places throughout the South.[15] Also on hand were other luminaries in the Kansas pro-slavery movement with their men in tow. General William P. Richardson, with the territorial militia, and Dr. John H. Stringfellow, who rode with the infamous Kickapoo Rangers, attacked Lawrence. Warrants were produced and arrests were made in Lawrence, under Jones' direction, of men prominent in the Underground Railroad and abolitionist movement. The abolitionists of Lawrence took a non-violent approach and allowed these men to be arrested until a group agreed to give up their cannon but not their Sharps rifles. These Sharps rifles were synonymous with the abolitionist movement in Kansas and were sometimes referred to as "Beecher's Bibles." It was argued that the Sharps rifles were private property and couldn't be lawfully taken.

Jones, who had been shot at before on May 21 by abolitionists in Lawrence, was looking for a pretext to unleash this posse of men to begin a wholesale thievery and destruction of private property. When the Sharps rifles were not produced, bayonets were put on the rifles of the assembled posse. The Free State Hotel was often viewed as the headquarters of the abolitionists and the Underground Railroad of freeing runaway bondspersons in the area. It became the center of Sheriff Jones' ire as he gave the hotel staff just two hours to clean out the new furniture that had recently been fitted in their facility. The owners, the Eldridge brothers, quickly tried to comply with Jones' unlawful order.[16]

Cannons tried to bring the hotel down but its concrete walls stood and it took explosive barrels of gunpowder and a fire to gut the hotel. Next, the newspapers were sacked with editor George Washington Brown's *Herald of Freedom* newspaper, his printing presses, jobbers' office, papers, and thousand volume library destroyed. As predicted by letter writer "Border Ruffian," freedom of the press was being squelched by agents of the United States government. At the time, Brown was a prisoner in Lecompton, Kansas, stronghold of the pro-slavery partisans. He was being held by Federal troops and was charged with high treason for his anti-slavery stand.[17]

Dr. J.P. Root, who had been a prisoner of the pro-slavery forces and would later become lieutenant governor of the state of Kansas, happened to notice some of the bills charged to the United States marshal's account in the Lawrence sacking. Root states that quite an amount of whiskey at one dollar per gallon was charged, as was French brandy at eight dollars a gallon. The liquor bill charged to the United States government for this action was for three hundred and seventy dollars and eighty-six cents. Root also noted that each "Ruffian" engaged in the sacking of Lawrence received two dollars per day as pay in the service of the United States government.[18]

As night came about on the prairie things eventually got completely out of hand with stores being openly looted and Lawrence being sacked by the mob. But soon after the Atchison and Jones army left town plans were already being made to open the Underground Railroad and keep the abolitionist pressure on the pro-slavery forces in Kansas. This outrage didn't intimidate the abolitionists as Atchison and the slavery forces in Washington D.C.

and throughout the South had hoped, but only made them see the righteousness of their cause. The whirlwind would be let loose.

In 1855, in Atchison, K.T., the strong pro-slavery town named for David Rice Atchison, there resided a very brave Disciples of Christ preacher. His name was Pardee Butler and he not only preached fervent sermons that spoke out against the evils of slavery but he was also helping bondsmen and women escape slavery from nearby Missouri and sending them on their path to freedom. However, Butler's actions began to attract the attention of Atchison's pro-slavery minions and he came under strong suspicion. Butler wasn't arrested or brought to the attention of the local sheriff or federal authorities.

A group of pro-slavery men captured Butler and then sent him down the dangerous Missouri River to a sure death adrift on a raft. The pro-slavery men threw stones at Butler as his raft went down the river. The pro-slavery men attached a banner to the raft to let all know that Butler had helped to aid escaping slaves. The flag said, "Greeley to the rescue, I have a nigger"; "Eastern Aid Express"; and "agent to the Underground Railroad." The local newspaper the *Squatter Sovereign* warned that the same punishment awaited "all free-soilers, abolitionists and their emissaries." Fortunately, Butler managed to free himself from the raft and to the chagrin of the slavery proponents the reverend survived and continued his activities. Other abolitionists when found out in the area were often severely beaten.[19]

Several years later in Atchison, during the fall of 1859, a Kansas slave owner was going to take his bondswoman and her child to Missouri. The slaver was probably very concerned about the large percentage of Kansas slaves who were escaping from the Jayhawker territory. The slaver was in a hotel and apparently became distracted. A Mr. Bird took his bondswoman and her child and walked out of the hotel in broad daylight and hid her in Atchison until night time. The bondswoman and her child were taken by a circuitous route to Holton, Kansas. At times they had another white man pose as her "owner." The bondswoman and her child were next taken to a station in Nebraska and they eventually, it was believed, got safely through to Canada.[20]

Amos Lawrence was a wealthy merchant from New England who supported the abolitionist movement in Kansas. The anti-slavery town of Lawrence, Kansas, was named after him. David Rice Atchison once wrote Lawrence that if the wealthy merchant would use his considerable wealth to buy slaves in Kansas he would see the tremendous benefits that Atchison thought slavery provided. Instead, Atchison noted, that in the place of purchasing slaves Lawrence would use his considerable wealth to fund the abolitionists in Kansas and would thus, according to Atchison and others of his ilk, cause strife to the area.[21]

This was the attitude of most slave owners or supporters of slavery in Arkansas, Missouri and the Kansas Territory at this time. They felt their slaves were extremely contented with their lot in life and if the abolitionists and purveyors of the Underground Railroad would leave their human chattel alone and stop agitating for their freedom all would be peaceful and content in the slave-holding states and territories. Most of these slavers believed that on their own none of their slaves would want to leave them. However, many slaves, if given the chance, were only too happy to leave slavery.

The Underground Railroad in the territories was often hectic and, as with much of the Underground Railroad machinery in the United States, communication was sometimes almost nonexistent between stations down the line. Rumors and wild speculations were oftentimes rampant without any feedback from fellow stationmasters. Slave and bounty hunters were always on the lookout for a capture and reward and it was hard to know how many bondsmen and bondswomen were getting through this gauntlet to freedom in Canada or other places such as Chicago.

John E. Stewart was a stalwart Underground Railroad conductor from Kansas. However, after all his hard work in advancing the bondsmen and women he worried that there "was something wrong" in Nebraska and Iowa. Stewart had heard rumors that the runaways were being captured in those two areas and wanted to know in a letter if Thaddeus Hyatt, the President of the National Kansas Committee and a wealthy New York merchant could help. We don't have Hyatt's reply but in actuality there was very little anyone could do. With rewards and federal law on their side, slave and bounty hunters would always be tracking the runaway bondspersons.[22] However, more got through than were caught in the Nebraska territory and the state of Iowa on the Underground Railroad. This letter does point out the almost complete lack of communications between various Underground Railroad stations on the frontier.

Very often tactics used in Kansas greatly differed from those in the rest of the Underground Railroad in the United States. Because the territory was in a virtual war zone from 1854 to 1861 often times much more violence was condoned for Underground Railroad activities than in the rest of the United States. John E. Stewart is a good example of the extremely aggressive tactics used in Kansas. Stewart was a Methodist minister who at one time had preached in North Salem, New Hampshire. When the Kansas-Nebraska Act of 1854 was passed Stewart became so incensed about it that he headed for Kansas to fight the slavery forces in that state.[23] While in Kansas he became known as "the fighting preacher."

Stewart wouldn't wait in Kansas for runaways to appear on his farm. He would go into slave state Missouri and pose as a buyer of pigs, livestock or other agricultural products. He was always on the lookout for slaves who might wish to escape. When he saw any bondspersons he engaged them in a conversation and of course it always led to the question of "do any of you want to escape." If the answer was "yes" Stewart would hurriedly put the bondspersons into his lumber wagon and give them weapons if need be. He would grab the reigns to his wagon and off this freedom cart would go, as fast as he could coax his team — sometimes with revolvers cracking. Many brave bondspersons were only too willing to fight for their freedom and he had many of these as he called them, "hairbredth [sic] escapes."[24]

Stewart even refined his methods and got bolder. He would sometimes pose as a peddler and hide his wagon and team of horses in the woods. He would take his peddler's pack and go right up to the slave quarters pretending to sell some trinkets. Of course what Stewart was really offering was freedom to Canada. The bondsperson would be told where Stewart's wagon was located in the woods and that night the passage to Canada would begin if any were interested. Of course many in these slave quarters wanted their freedom. Other times Stewart would notice a slave plowing a field. Stewart would hide at the end of the field and tell the plow hand to fiddle with the horse's bridal or pretend to clear the plow blade while at the end of the row. This would give him time to explain the details of the planned escape. Usually another breakout would occur that night under the cover of darkness.[25]

In his letter to Thaddeus Hyatt, Stewart told of his liberation of 14 bondspersons including one unbroken family of which Stewart was very proud. In his letter Stewart told of the problems of the Underground Railway in Kansas. Many of the settlers in Kansas, such as Stewart, were very near the poverty line themselves. Stewart notes that the escaping slaves were in such a destitute condition that provisions of clothing and food would have to be provided for them by people hardly in a position of having enough provisions for themselves and their own families. He further comments that a trusted horse that he had used on many escapes had passed on and that he didn't know how he would replace the animal in the financial straits he found himself in at the present time.[26] It is obvious from Stewart's letter that he hopes the wealthy Hyatt will help him financially so he can carry on with his work of freeing slaves from bondage. Unfortunately, as we shall see, Stewart finds a less desirable way to finance his work on the Underground Railroad.

There were plenty of others in Kansas who were as radically abolitionist as John E. Stewart. John Brown, who later would attempt a slave revolt by attacking the federal arsenal at Harpers Ferry, Virginia, often escorted slaves out of Kansas for their ultimate freedom in Canada.

When John Brown and his sons first got to the Kansas Territory they often stayed in the cabin of Congregationalist minister the Rev. Samuel Adair. Adair had married Brown's half sister Florella and was a graduate of radical Oberlin College and its seminary. His wife Florella was also a graduate of that institution. As with most Oberlin graduates the Adairs became very active in anti-slavery and Underground Railroad activities. Adair's cabin became a center of goings-on around Osawatomie. Adair had a large cabin for the time and it was used as a grocery store and inn and there was also plenty of room for escaping bondspersons to bed down for the night or longer.[27] However, after a while Adair, a peaceful man, became alarmed at John Brown's and his sons' fascination with weapons and Brown's "war spirit." Adair wrote that he hoped Brown would use these weapons only in "strict self-defense or defense of the right of suffrage."[28]

Washington was a bondsman escaping around the Osawatomie area and he had two slave hunters and his "owner" on his trail. The Osawatomie Underground Railroad sympathizers became aware of Washington's plight. They confronted Washington's "master" and forced him to give Washington three hundred dollars. They also took from the slave hunters a silk hat, a horse, saddle and bridle that Washington could use on his trip north to freedom.[29] Because of actions like this the Reverend Adair would later say that there were few slaveholders who dared bring their slaves to live around the Osawatomie area when they were trying to establish Kansas as a slave state.[30]

However, in August of 1856 the strong activities of the anti-slavery men in Osawatomie attracted the attention of the slavery forces. Several hundred pro-slavery Missourians attacked the town on August 30 of that year. They killed one of John Brown's sons, Frederick. John Brown, with only a few dozen men, was not able to stop the onslaught and the town was sacked and burned. However, the town rebuilt and continued its activities on the Underground Railroad. On May 18, 1859, the town had recovered enough that they were able to organize the Republican Party in Kansas. Horace Greeley, the famed *New York Tribune* editor, spoke at this rally which was attended by an estimated five thousand people.

In the fall of 1856 John Brown his sons John Brown, Jr., Jason Brown and Owen Brown crossed the river in Topeka with a four-mule wagon and driver and a one-horse covered wagon. The mule wagon was full of firearms and ammunition the Browns were taking to Tabor, Iowa, for safe keeping. In the one-horse covered wagon was an escaping bondsman underneath a pile of hay. Also, the senior Brown lay in the horse wagon very sick. At Holton in the Kansas Territory the Browns saw a large troop of United States soldiers encamped on a stream.

The Browns thought they might have fallen into a trap. John Brown and his sons were some of the most wanted men in Kansas at this time. A few days after the sacking of

Lawrence by Sheriff Jones, David Atchison and their army, Brown and four of his sons and his son-in-law and two other men sought revenge. They murdered five pro-slavery men, most of them by hacking them to death with swords in what became known as the Pottawatomie Creek massacre. A few weeks after that, Brown and his small army of men defeated a contingent of pro-slavery Missourian men in what became known as the "Battle of Black Jack." The Browns were at the top of the list for all law enforcement and the United States Army at this time in Kansas for capture for their crimes.

His sons counseled staying away from the troopers but Old Man Brown and his son Owen, who always stayed at his father's side, took a bold step and drove one of the wagons and went right down to within two miles of the troopers' pickets and camped for the night. The soldiers never discovered that the most wanted man on the Western Frontier and his son were within a couple of miles of their guards. His other sons and the driver took the other wagon and went out of the way to avoid the U.S. troopers. They all finally met north of Holton and headed for Nebraska City to cross the Missouri River. They traversed the Mighty Missouri via a rope ferry and made it into Southwest Iowa and headed to Tabor.

When they made it into Iowa Brown felt it safe enough to let the escaping bondsman out from underneath the pile of hay. Once in Tabor, Old John Brown and son Owen stayed there so that the elder Brown could recover his health. Sons John Jr. and Jason headed some two hundred and eighty miles east for Iowa City, Iowa, to catch the railhead for the rest of their journey away from Kansas until they felt they could safely return. The bondsman found work in Tabor and later was transported via the Underground Railroad out of town to freedom.[31]

Brown and his sons would continue to bring bondsmen out of Kansas into Iowa on their way to freedom in Canada. Shortly before Brown's raid at Harpers Ferry he participated in one of the most controversial escapes on the Underground Railroad; this will be discussed in Chapter 4.

During the years of 1857 and 1858, disaster struck Kansas. A severe drought brought about crop failures and caused serious water shortages. Malnutrition and cholera and other diseases were often the results of severe droughts on the Western Frontier at this time. This calamity threatened to stem the flow of anti-slavery settlers into Kansas and it of course hurt the work of freeing slaves and forwarding them on to the Underground Railroad. Into this breech stepped Thaddeus Hyatt, a wealthy New York manufacturer and inventor, who was an ardent backer of abolitionist causes. Hyatt headed the National Kansas Committee, which sent food, clothing and other supplies to anti-slavery settlers in Kansas so as to keep the movement alive. Hyatt also spent time in Kansas surveying the situation himself. Hyatt became a financial life-line to many abolitionists and Blacks who wanted freedom in Kansas.[32]

Hyatt was a close friend of John Brown. When Brown or his sons were in New York City they made his Morton Street house their headquarters.[33] Brown, having been born in nearby Connecticut, often came back east to raise money or to hide out when things heated up in Kansas. After Brown's infamous raid on Harpers Ferry, Hyatt's name came up as a possible abettor to the raid in a United States Senate hearing. One of the members of this select committee was Mississippi Senator Jefferson Davis. Hyatt decided not to cooperate with the Senate committee and he was jailed in the Old Capitol Prison in Washington, D.C.[34]

Hyatt then went on to make a mockery out of his jail time. Hyatt had his jail cell decorated and furnished and then issued invitations to his society friends in New York City and to well-known politicians in Washington, D.C., to visit him — and visit him they did. Hyatt had checks printed-up with his jail cell as his address. While he was incarcerated, Hyatt had managed to arrange for large meetings in New York City for anti-slavery rallies at that city's Cooper Institute. Finally, the United States Senate, seeing that their jailing of Hyatt had backfired, freed him after three months. Hyatt wired friends that he had been "Kicked Out" of jail.[35]

In the latter part of the 1850s, things started to change in Kansas. Traffic on the Underground Railroad began to increase. Pro-slavery men like Sheriff Samuel Jones of Douglas County were replaced by men like Sheriff Sam Walker, an ardent anti-slavery man. Sam Tappan, wrote in veiled terms to Thomas Higginson in January of 1858 that the Underground Railroad was liberating many: "I am happy to inform you that a certain Rail Road has been and is in full blast."[36]

Sam Walker, who would later become sheriff of Douglas County, got his introduction into the dangers of being an abolitionist in Kansas even before he moved into the state. Sam Walker was leading a party of abolitionists sponsored by the Ohio Emigrant Aid Society into Kansas. The fastest and most economical way to get to Kansas at that time was by steamboat via the Missouri River. Walker and his party were traveling on the steamboat on the Missouri River and had gotten about half-way through the show-me state when pro-slavery men put them off the boat at Boonville, Missouri, because they were "damned Abolitionists." Walker had to purchase oxen and wagons and made the overland journey to Lawrence in the Kansas Territory on April 7, 1855.[37] Abolitionists heading to settle into the Kansas Territory via steamships began to be removed regularly from these boats by Missouri pro-slavery proponents. Although traveling via steamboat was the fastest and least expensive way into the Kansas Territory, these steamboats would have to be bypassed. An overland route into the state would be carved out in Iowa with Tabor, Iowa, being the last stop in the United States before these overland caravans would head into the territory of Kansas via the Nebraska territory.

Once in Kansas, the abolitionist women — not only the men — found they would need to be prepared to fight. Many of the women folk of the male abolitionists — the wives, daughters, and mothers — became experts at loading firearms and making cartridges. The abolitionist women also often fought alongside their men folk and a number of pro-slavery men lost their lives at the hands of a woman's firearm. One young female became an expert shot and won a large shooting match against many males on New Year's Day in 1858. When her brother was "arrested" by pro-slavery men and jailed in the slavery stronghold of Lecompton, she went to see her brother and broke him out of the jail. When they got about two miles away, the marshal and two other deputies overtook them. The young lady pulled out a pistol and told the marshal that if he detained them he was a dead man. The marshal, knowing her prowess with firearms, didn't challenge her and let her and her brother go.[38]

One day, the Reverend Cordley of Lawrence, K.T., had a visitor — a Mr. Monteith, who was a member of his church. Cordley had been born in Nottingham, England, and his family had immigrated to the United States and lived in Michigan where he had graduated from the University of Michigan. He then received his seminary degree from Andover Theological Seminary in Andover, Massachusetts. Cordley had ended up in Lawrence, K.T., when Kansas was in its volatile period before the Civil War. Monteith asked the Reverend if he would hide a former bondswoman named Lizzie. The Monteith family had been hiding Lizzie for several months and were afraid pro-slavery people might be onto them and thought Lizzie should be moved. When she was a slave Lizzie had been held in bondage in a Missouri border town before she made her way to freedom in Kansas. Cordley described Lizzie as being twenty-two years old, of slight build, and graceful in form and movement. Cordley stated that Lizzie never claimed to have been mistreated by her master, but was horrified of going back into the condition of slavery.

Not one to sit idly by, Lizzie took over the management of the Cordley household. The reverend noted that he had little money, but Lizzie managed to stretch every penny and made the most out of everything. A few months later it was thought best to transfer Lizzie back to the Monteith family lest anyone get suspicious.

Then one night Monteith and another figure came to Cordley's door. They were both so bundled up it was hard to see who they were. The other figure turned out to be Lizzie. Lizzie's master had found out where she was now living. He had gotten a United States marshal and a posse to track her down. Under the Fugitive Slave Law of 1850 it was the law of the land that all slaves must be returned to their masters. Lawrence was only about forty miles from the Missouri state line. Lizzie's master wanted to prove, and was willing to spend a large amount of money proving it, that a slave master could recover his "human property" in the stronghold of abolitionist Lawrence.

Things were really tense. A strategy to hide Lizzie was planned in case the United States marshal and his posse came to the Cordley door. They waited well into the night for a knock on their door. At half an hour past midnight Lizzie heard what was a large covered wagon turn into the Cordley place. Was it the U.S. marshal? It turned out it was Monteith and he was coming to begin Lizzie's journey to freedom. Monteith later said he was followed but no one approached his wagon.

Cordley heard that Lizzie headed north in Kansas and remained in the territory for a few months more. She finally made it to Canada where this wonderful young lady could find her ultimate freedom.[39] When William Quantrill and his Confederate guerrilla band sacked Lawrence, Kansas, during the Civil War in 1863, Cordley's name was on Quantrill's death list but the good reverend managed to escape Quantrill's wrath.

In March of 1859 there were five fugitives in Lawrence trying to make their way on the Underground Railroad. One was a Charlie Fisher who had been kidnapped twice before by bounty hunters. The other was a Bill Riley who escaped from the Platte City, Missouri, jail by burning out an iron bar from the logs in which it was fastened across the window. There was a young woman with her child who had been hiding out in Lawrence for some three months. She had probably gotten into town during the winter time and it was decided to wait until spring to move her and the child onward.

The fifth escapee was from Linn County, Kansas Territory, and had escaped from his master. It had taken him three or four nights to walk from Linn County, which was on the border with Missouri, and make it to Lawrence. He was a very bright young man and because he was by himself it was thought he could move on the Underground Railway right away alone. Ephraim Nute was the Lawrence resident who had hid the young man. It only took a quarter of an hour after the young Black man left for another Lawrence resident to ride to Nute's home to tell him slave hunters had tracked the young Black man to Lawrence and were on his trail. The slave hunters had put up for the night at a public house and the unfortunate young fugitive was hiding in the outhouse of the same hotel.

The young Black escapee was spotted in the morning by the slave hunters but he eluded them again. Nute went looking for the young man also and found him and hid him during the day. That night, the young Black man was taken by horseback via an infrequent route and was well on his way to freedom. The chief slave hunter was the nephew of the slaver who owned the bright young Black lad. He offered a huge reward in Lawrence of six hundred dollars (equal to about thirty thousand dollars in present-day money) for the return of the young man to Linn County or a reward of two hundred dollars (equal to about ten thousand dollars in present-day money) for information that would lead to his capture. There were no takers for this large amount of reward money.[40]

Charlie Fisher was taken to Leavenworth to the United States Commissioner's room. The United States Commissioner's office was a product of the Fugitive Slave Act of 1850 and was designed to make sure all escaping slaves were returned to their masters. A group of Kansas abolitionists stormed the United States Commissioners' office and freed Fisher. Dan Anthony, brother of Susan B. Anthony, was among the group that helped to free Fisher.[41] Fisher was then taken by a coach down to Lawrence dressed in female attire to the home of Unitarian minister Ephraim Nute. Fisher stayed at the Nute home for two days and then was moved from house to house for a couple of days. After a few days and nights in Lawrence he was to be moved out of town.[42] However, Dr. Doy reports seeing Fisher in the St. Joseph jail in Missouri and that Fisher was almost beaten to death by a slave trader in the jail. In all probability, Fisher was likely recaptured when he tried to make it north to Tabor. Apparently Fisher was owned by a slaver from Mississippi. Probably Fisher had been a barber on a steamboat when he jumped ship in either the Kansas City or St. Joseph area and came over to Lawrence. Fisher at one time had been a barber in Lawrence and had had a very profitable trade with a wife and child and now was sold down south, a broken man.[43]

After Fisher's escape from Leavenworth and with the actions of abolitionists who kept the slavers from pursuing him, a grand jury was empanelled. They returned indictments against these abolitionists for interference with official United States business. One night, these abolitionists broke into the courtroom and found the indictments and burned them. Judge John Pettit, whose courtroom had been invaded, was furious and vowed that those guilty of this crime would be severely punished. Dan Anthony pleaded with James Montgomery to come to the aid of the abolitionists.

Montgomery brought fifty tough long riders to Leavenworth in time for the next session of the court. Another one hundred local abolitionists also showed up for the court session. Montgomery had issued orders to shoot the judge and the United States marshal if any of these cases were brought to trial. Judge Pettit realized the danger he was in and dismissed all the charges and cases against the offending abolitionists.[44]

William Riley had broken out of the Platte City, Missouri, jail by burning out the bars of his jail window. Riley was in jail with a dozen other escapees who were with the Doy group. Riley had escaped from Lexington, Missouri, with his wife and had gone to Lawrence, K.T. They left Lawrence to head north but his wife was captured by slave hunters with bloodhounds. Riley thought they had probably taken his wife back to Lexington.

After being captured with the Doy party, Riley had broken out from Platte City jail and walked some ten miles to the Missouri River and crossed the river on floating cakes of ice. He would get to a sandbar and rest for a day or two and then make the rest of the journey across the river. He then walked the forty miles to Lawrence. Riley was going to be transported, it was thought, with two other bondspersons to another depot thirty miles to the north for his trip, hopefully ending in Canada.[45]

The Western Frontier, as elsewhere, was rife with rumors and at times wild speculation. The Underground Railroad had no shortage of these. It was rumored that when the anti-slavery settlers in Kansas had broken the back of the pro-slavery settlers large gangs of slaves in Texas and other points in the deep south would head for Kansas. This never proved to materialize.[46] However, many slave owners in Kansas saw the writing on the wall and began to remove their slaves from the Kansas territory. Thos. R. Bayne, himself a slave owner, wrote to the Kansas State Historical Society in 1895 when asked about slaveholders in Kansas. He said that one of the biggest slaveholders in the territory, James Skaggs, who owned twenty-seven humans, by 1860 saw the wisdom in taking them to Texas so they couldn't escape and find freedom. Skaggs, who had $10,000 in specie and was afraid of being robbed, armed his bondsmen as they moved south so he would not be held up.[47] Interestingly, Marcus Lindsay Freeman who was a bondsman owned by Thomas Bayne also told his story to the Kansas State Historical Society. Freeman wrote that James Skaggs was a "pretty rough old man." Freeman's sister was one of the bondswomen taken to Texas by Skaggs. Freeman wrote that Thomas Bayne, his white master, and he had grown up together and Bayne treated him well. Freeman wrote that Bayne allowed him to work in Kansas City and received two hundred dollars a year for Freeman's services. Freeman had a pass to move from Kansas City to Bayne's farm in Williamstown, Kansas, a distance of some fifty miles. At the beginning of the Civil War Freeman was working for the printing offices of Van Horn and A. Beal of the *Kansas City Journal*.[48]

South of Lawrence, near Mound City, Kansas Territory, was James Montgomery who was one of the leaders of the Underground Railroad; but, as seen in Leavenworth, his methods would come under intense scrutiny. After John Brown had been hanged for his attack on Harpers Ferry, James Montgomery, a resident of Mound City, K.T., got the financial backing of many of Brown's eastern abolitionist friends, including George L. Stearns. Montgomery would raid into Missouri and take slaves to be hidden in Kansas or to be sent on their way to freedom in Canada.[49] Montgomery would later write to Stearns that the "fugitives too, are as safe here as they would be in Canada. Two more have come to us since my last writing."[50] Montgomery also wrote to Stearns again and advised him, "We have several fugitives on hand, and more are expected. Some are from Missouri and some from Arkansas. When a keen, shrewd fellow comes to us, we send him back for more. As yet they have not been followed by anything like a force."[51]

With the financial support of Stearns and other eastern backers Montgomery was able to raise a small army of riders to help him on his raids into Missouri. Montgomery once boasted with some validity that the Fugitive Slave Law couldn't be enforced in Kansas. Montgomery's right hand-man was a C.R. Jennison.

Jennison also wrote to Stearns about a group who would entice slaves off of Missouri farms with the promise of gaining their freedom, only to sell them to other slavers. Sometimes they would simply kidnap free Blacks or Blacks who were searching for freedom on the Underground Railroad. Once the Blacks traveled with these men they would be sold on down the line to other slavers. One of the leaders of this group was a man by the name of Russ Hinds. Hinds was captured by Jennison and his men. Jennison held an impromptu court, with no legal standing, and found Hinds guilty of these crimes and then publicly hanged the man so others of his ilk would understand what would become of them if they tried this technique on other bondspersons.[52]

However, after a while, Montgomery and Jennison's raids into Missouri became pretty well self-sustaining with no need of financial assistance from anyone. It became hard to distinguish if the real intention of Montgomery and Jennison's raids into Missouri was to liberate bondspersons or to just plain "liberate" any Missouri property. Stolen horses from

Missouri were showing up in Iowa. Some witty people were saying that every good horse in Iowa had a pedigree of "out of Missouri by Jennison."

Montgomery, and especially Jennison's men, were beginning to be called "Jayhawkers" and were getting the reputation of being indiscriminate thieves and murderers. Their savagery would continue into the Civil War when their actions would often be called wartime atrocities.

The Underground Railroad in Lawrence became very concerned by the kidnappings of free Blacks and escaping fugitive Blacks in and around Lawrence. Jacob Herd was one of the leaders in these kidnappings. After the Black men and women had been kidnapped they would be taken into Missouri and sold—whether they be free or slave.

It was decided by the Lawrence Underground Railroad that Dr. John Doy, his son Charles and another young man named Clough on January 18, 1859, would escort a group of thirteen Blacks—some free and some fugitives—out of Lawrence to freedom in Iowa and eventually to Canada. Doy was to take the group to Holton, K.T. Doy, a medical doctor, had been born in Hull, England, and had immigrated to Canada and then made his way to Rochester, New York. Doy had come from Rochester with Dan Anthony to Kansas.

The Doy group was headed north some twelve miles from Lawrence when the dreaded Jacob Herd (sometimes known as Jake Hurd) and his gang overtook the Doy two-wagon caravan. Within Herd's gang was the pro-slavery man who would become postmaster of Lawrence. About five members of the Herd gang were from Kansas, and the rest from Western Missouri. Doy and his group were taken to Weston, Missouri, at gunpoint to be jailed. Dr. Doy and his group were threatened with being murdered and other vile oaths by Herd and his bunch of hooligans.[53]

It is interesting to note that when Doy was brought to breakfast the next morning all thirteen Black folks were sitting at a table. A place had been set for Doy at the "colored" breakfast table. Doy refused to eat with the Blacks at the table, stating he was not in "the habit of eating with colored people." The dining room manager told Doy, "a man that will steal a nigger is none too good to eat with niggers." The manager then told Doy that he would then get no breakfast if he refused to eat with the Blacks at their table. Doy still refused to eat with the Blacks and he got no breakfast that day. Dr. Doy was proud of the fact that he refused to eat with the "coloreds" that day and he even thought that his jailers gained more respect for him.[54] Many of the abolitionists who wanted to end slavery and helped out on the Underground Railroad were also racists and were unprepared to offer Blacks equal footing within white society.

Doy was then moved to the larger jail in Platte City, Missouri. Jake Herd was able to take possession of two of the unfortunate Blacks, Wilson Hays and Charles Smith. Both had been cooks at the Eldridge Hotel in Lawrence. Doy claims these two did not have free papers with them when they left Lawrence but were well known free-men in town. Doy said he learned Herd had sold them at Independence, Missouri, for one thousand dollars a piece.[55]

Doy and his supporters always maintained that of the eleven Black adults Doy had with him nine had free papers and the other two, Smith and Hays, were well-known free-men in Lawrence. However, Ephraim Nute, a minister who knew well the goings on of the Lawrence Underground Railroad, stated in a letter that "The party consisted of 13 col'd people (11 fugitives & 2 free by birth) with 3 of our citizens...."[56] Did Doy and his supporters maintain that his passengers were "free" Blacks in order to make it more of an "outrage" committed against Dr. Doy? If the wagon was full of "free" Blacks then what Jake Herd and his gang did was highly illegal. This was kidnapping at gunpoint pure and simple. However, if the passengers were in fact fugitives then Herd could claim he was taking them to their rightful owners — a tenuous point of law at best, but for a career criminal like Jake Herd probably the only legal point he could make.

A Missouri newspaper claimed to know the names of the rest of Doy's Black passengers and their owners. Supposedly all of them had at one time resided in Missouri and one in Kansas. However, the newspaper failed to mention William Riley, who had managed to break out of the Platte City jail and make it back to Lawrence, according to Ephraim Nute.[57] If one were to believe Nute's letter and the Missouri newspaper account then Doy's contention that his passengers were all "free" blacks falls on its face. In a paper read at the Kansas State Historical Society thirty years after this event James Abbott claims that all the Blacks with Doy were free persons. However, Abbott was highly partisan on this matter.[58]

On the other hand, many times slave authorities were more than willing to match-up any apprehended runaway with slave advertisements to clear-up a slave escape case: the slave owner got a slave — it might not be the one who ran away, but the slave owner was economically in the same place he was before the escape. The Missouri newspapers were running wild stories on the Doys, one of which even had the good Doctor and his son being hanged by a mob that had charged his jail cell. This did not happen.

Doy's case dragged on and he was threatened with death many times by the jailers and mobs that gathered outside his jail cell. He was charged with stealing slaves, and to his surprise he was granted a change of venue to the north in the St. Joseph, Missouri, jurisdiction. He was moved to St. Joseph and at his first trial the jury there came to a mistrial. Doy's son Charley was let go at that time; Clough had been released sometime before. Doy was accused of decoying a bondsman named Dick out of slavery in Missouri. Dick had once been the "property" of Weston, Missouri, Mayor Ben Wood.

At the second trial, which was also held in St. Joseph in June of 1859, Dick the supposed stolen slave was not allowed on the witness stand as it was not permissible for Blacks or mulattoes to testify against white persons in slave state Missouri. When Dick escaped from his master, Doy's defense team could prove the good doctor was nowhere near Weston to aid in Dick's escape. Newspapers all over Missouri were demanding a guilty verdict in this case. The slave powers in Missouri were very upset that Doy's first trial had ended in a mistrial. They wanted to make sure this didn't happen again. James R. Craig, who represented western Missouri in the Thirty-Sixth Congress, became a "volunteer" attorney for the prosecution. It was clear to Doy what Craig's true purpose was in becoming involved. Craig, using his prestige as a congressman, was to browbeat the jury into returning with a guilty verdict. Craig was seen illegally talking to the jurymen in a very animated way on many occasions.

The slave powers got their way and Doy was sentenced to five years in prison. He was kept in the jail in St. Joseph until the Missouri Supreme Court could hear his case and render a final decision. Doy's counsel had filed a bill of exceptions and asked for an appeal with the Missouri Supreme Court and this was granted. Doy felt after his conviction, and if the Missouri Supreme Court upheld his guilty verdict, that he would be taken to other Missouri jurisdictions in show trials and tried for the other slave runaways so that his final time in prison would be sixty years.[59]

The Underground Railway in Lawrence had been keeping abreast of the situation and attorneys had been provided for Doy. The territory legislature of Kansas had approved one thousand dollars for Doy's defense team of former Governor Wilson Shannon and A.C.

These are the 10 men who became known as the Immortal 10. These 10 men broke Dr. John Doy out of prison in St. Joseph, Missouri, where Doy had been tried and convicted of helping a bondsman escape from slavery. It is interesting to note that Dr. Doy is sitting in the picture. The reason could be because Doy had spent months being incarcerated and was having difficulty standing. The others identified in the picture were some of the leading names in the Kansas Underground Railroad. James B. Abbott was the leader of the Immortal 10 and is on the far left of the picture. Joseph Gardner is fourth from the left and the ubiquitous John E. Stewart is third from the right. Silas Soule is second from the right. Soule and his brother Brown were very active in helping the escaping bondspersons. One night they helped 13 bondspersons out of Missouri to the Grover barn in Lawrence. This baker's dozen was then forwarded out of Lawrence to the north and freedom (Kansas State Historical Society).

Davis, who would become the next Attorney General of Kansas. A local attorney from Platte City would also sit on the defense team. However, since it was unlikely that the Missouri Supreme Court would overthrow Doy's verdict, those in Lawrence knew they would have to act fast.

It was decided that ten men would go over to St. Joseph and boldly break Doy out of the Missouri jail before they took him to the state penitentiary in Jefferson City. Heading this group would be James B. Abbott, and of course John Stewart and Joseph Gardner. The group became known in Kansas as the "Immortal Ten." To gain entrance into the jail, three men would call on the jail at midnight. Two of the men would act as if they had apprehended the third, who they accused of being a horse thief. When asked if they had any paperwork the men admitted they had none and the jailer seamed perplexed by this. A true bureaucrat, the jailer needed paperwork to grease the wheels of the beauracy. He however, let the Lawrence men in and when he did a gun was pulled on the jailer.

Doy was ready to go. He had earlier seen the Lawrence men outside his jail cell on the street and he had even commented to the other prisoners that he was leaving that night. He had gotten all of his stuff and was ready to go. Doy, after six months of captivity, had a hard time walking and was carried from his jail cell. They made their way out of Missouri and into Kansas. Doy and the Immortal Ten were cheered on the way to Lawrence. Once they got to the city they were treated like heroes. Even the St. Joseph newspapers had made it to Lawrence one hour before Doy got there and told of his bold escape.[60]

Around Lawrence, Kansas Territory, appeared an odd young man who went by the name of Charles Hart. Hart had no apparent means of support and seemed allergic to work.[61] He had been born in Ohio and had come to Kansas with a group of buckeye settlers. Hart had even taught school in Stanton Township, K.T.,[62] but his penchant for thievery got his Ohio friends mad enough to run him off. At Lawrence he was lumped in with a group of pro-slavery loafers that hung around the river ferries mostly playing cards and drinking. Sometimes the loafers would be asked if they wanted to do some chores as day laborers, but Hart was always hard to find when the call went out.

Some did notice that these loafers, Hart in particular, looked long and hard at how much cash a traveler had when they dug into their pockets for money to pay the ferryman to transport their goods across the river. About this time there were some unexplained robberies of these travelers along the roadsides after they had crossed on the ferry. Tongues wagged in Lawrence that these loafers might be responsible for these crimes.

Charley Hart became good friends with the pro-slavery thug Jacob Herd. They were a study in dissimilarity. Herd was loud and aggressive — one had no doubt where Herd's sympathies lay. Hart, in contrast, was quiet and introspective, and he was also sneaky and treacherous.

Even after the Doy affair Lawrence was plagued by these kinds of kidnappings, with Herd and now Charlie Hart among those practicing this highly profitable endeavor. Although Lawrence was noted on the Western Frontier as one of the main stations on the Underground Railroad and as an abolitionist stronghold, the presence of these pro-slavery men like Herd and Hart were a definite thorn in the side of the freedom-loving residents of this town.

One day, a young Black man by the name of Ike Gains showed up in Lawrence. Gains had escaped from slavery in Platte City, Missouri, and had made it to Leavenworth, K.T. He then traveled south to make it to Lawrence. Gains' plan was to look up James Lane, one of the leaders in town of the Underground Railroad. Gains thought Lane could make sure he was put safely on the path to his eventual freedom in Canada.

Gains had reconnoitered his way in and out of Leavenworth, Kansas, which was not an easy task. He then had taken an old Native American trail through the Delaware Reserve to the ferry landing in Lawrence. Unfortunately, Gains ran into Jacob Herd's brother who turned him over to Charlie Hart and another pro-slavery thug. Hart and his group acted like they were conductors for the Underground Railroad and overpowered the unsuspecting Gains and then tied him up and put him on horseback and took him to Westport, Missouri, and then to Platte City.

Not content with the usual reward for a runaway, around one hundred dollars, Hart negotiated with the widow Gains in Platte City for a five hundred dollar reward (about twenty-five thousand dollars in present-day money), probably mixing in a few threats. This was a princely sum for the time for the return of a runaway slave. When the widow asked Gains why he had run away, Ike, with his spirit broken, said the man at the livery stable had talked him into it.[63] The widow Gains was, like the majority of slave owners at the time, unable to believe that their bondspersons would much prefer freedom over slavery and if given the opportunity would escape every time.

Charlie Hart was an alias used by William C. Quantrill when he was around Lawrence. Around those settlers who had known Quantrill in Ohio he was known by his given name of William Clarke Quantrill. During the Civil War Quantrill formed one of the most bloodthirsty guerrilla bands known in the history of warfare.

Quantrill's Confederate band had riding with him Bloody Bill Anderson, Archie Clements, Dave Pool, George Todd and many of the members of what would become the post–Civil War outlaw band of the James-Younger gang including Clel Miller, Frank James and Cole Younger. The infamous Jesse James never fought in the Civil War with Quantrill. Quantrill lost control of his men in 1863 and many of them followed Bloody Bill Anderson as did new recruit Jesse James.[64] Some would later say that the Devil also rode with Quantrill. Many of his Confederate guerrilla fighters such as Harrison Trow knew Quantrill in Missouri as Charles W. Quantrell.[65] When he was in Missouri Quantrill fabricated stories that he was born in Maryland, not Ohio, which was known as the great abolitionist state. He also stated that Kansas Jayhawkers had killed his older brother and that this was the reason for his great zeal for wanting to strike back at the abolitionists of Kansas.

William Quantrill as Charlie Hart was also masquerading in Lawrence as an abolitionist. He was good friends with Underground Railroad stalwart John Dean, who owned a local wagon repair shop, and with John Stewart among others. Quantrill was a master at playing both sides of the fence. He had convinced many in the abolitionist movement that he was in thick with Jake Herd and the other pro-slavery types and could provide good information as a spy for them.

Quantrill and Jake Herd threatened a young black man named Allen Pinks to betray his own people. Pinks, originally from Pittsburgh, Pennsylvania, became a barber and restaurant server in Lawrence. He would find escaping slaves trying to find their way on the Underground Railroad and bring them to Quantrill or Herd. Pinks would tell the unsuspecting bondsmen that these two would advance them on the line of freedom. Quantrill and Herd would, of course, take these unfortunate runaways back into Missouri and sell them into slavery. This would oftentimes prove to be more profitable than merely collecting reward money for the runaways.

The Underground Railroad apparatus in Lawrence became aware of Pinks' treachery and it was decided to have him killed. Quantrill offered to kidnap Pinks for the purpose of having him murdered. Some felt Quantrill agreed to kidnap Pinks to throw suspicion away from him and his pro-slavery work.

Quantrill had a man named Wilson ask Pinks to come to Wilson's house to work on Mrs. Wilson's hair under the pretense that she was too sick to do it herself. Pinks went there and then heard a ruckus and knew something was amiss. Quantrill and another man had rushed the house to kidnap Pinks. The barber escaped from the house but was still a marked man. John Dean then took matters into his own hands and he shot Pinks in the head but did not kill him.

John Brown had delivered a slave by the name of Neeley to a Kansas abolitionist by the name of Ezekiel Colman. Brown had obtained Neeley during one of his raids in Missouri. Neeley labored for Colman without any trouble until proslavery neighbors spotted him and they captured him and proceeded to march him to Missouri for the five hundred dollars reward. However, Neeley escaped from them and returned to the Colman farm. Neeley then went and hid in the stone foundation of an unfinished house of Judge Wakefield. As winter was coming and the house was not completed hay was put on top of the foundation to keep it dry during the winter. Jake Herd found out about this escape and brought along Quantrill and they attempted to capture Neeley. The bondsman fired upon Herd and Quantrill and a small firefight erupted between them and others on the Underground Railway. Quantrill and Herd set the hay on fire and flushed Neeley out. These two prevailed and took Neeley and proceeded to Missouri where they sold him back into slavery. However, when the Civil War broke out Neeley managed to join the Union Army. By coincidence he met his old friend Ezekiel Colman, who also was in the Union Army, when they both were fighting in Arkansas.[66]

Quantrill had at times stayed on the Delaware Native American Reserve north of Lawrence. They had fed and housed him on the Reserve for nothing when he didn't have the means to pay for his own keep. So of course Quantrill repaid the Delaware with his usual duplicitous thievery. He stole a young maiden's saddle and her ponies. She had confronted Quantrill in Lawrence about this. She told him there would be trouble if things weren't settled. When he didn't return the ponies a young Delaware named White Turkey came into Lawrence looking for him. White Turkey told the residents of this white man's thievery. Quantrill happened to be at the edge of a crowd when White Turkey was telling of his robbery. Quantrill said he didn't appreciate the "lies" about himself and he went for his revolver. However, White Turkey was faster on the draw and Quantrill meekly hol-

CITIZENS OF LAWRENCE!

☞ L. Arms, a Deputy U. S. Marshal, has come into your midst for the avowed purpose of NEGRO HUNTING, and is watching your houses, by his piratical minions, night and day, and will enter and search them for victims. KNOW YOUR RIGHTS, and STAND TO THEM. He has no right thus to INVADE your CASTLES. Do we live on the Guinea Coast, or in FREE America?

The Eldridge House is the head-quarters of the gang. — Mark them well.

This particular poster was warning the abolitionists of Lawrence, Kansas Territory, to be on the lookout for a United States deputy marshal who was attempting, legally it might be added, to hunt down runaway slaves. The abolitionists in Lawrence were told if they were hiding any runaways that even a U.S. marshal needed a search warrant and to not let them search their premises without one. The idea was of course to tell the U.S. marshal if they wanted to search your house that they would need a search warrant. If the U.S. marshal went and got the warrant in the meantime, the abolitionists would try and move the runaway to another location. This poster was a very brave and brazen proclamation by the Underground Railroad in Lawrence that they were not going to follow the law when it came to helping runaway bondspersons (Kansas State Historical Society).

stered his weapon and managed to slink away. When Sheriff Walker tried to arrest Quantrill for horse stealing he was hidden by staunch abolitionists John Dean and John Stewart.[67]

Quantrill on occasion went into "business" with John Stewart, the most ardent Underground Railroad conductor in Kansas. As stated before, Stewart's financial condition was usually bleak. His farm south of Lawrence on the Wakarusa River contained a stockade that some called a fort. However, since he spent so much time on abolitionist activities the farm produced very little income. Stewart felt that stealing cattle and horses from pro-slavery owners in Missouri and Kansas wasn't illegal but was a proper way of striking a blow to the coffers of the pro-slavery element and aiding his own financial situation. Many in the abolitionist movement around Lawrence and even the anti-slavery newspapers such as the *Lawrence Tribune* merely winked at Steward's proclivity to engage in thievery because of his "burning zeal in behalf of the Free State cause and the freedom of the colored race."[68]

Stewart acted as a "fence" on occasion for Quantrill when the latter stole cattle and horses from pro-slavery farms in Missouri and especially in Atchison and Leavenworth Counties in Kansas. Stewart sold the stolen livestock to people south of Lawrence who didn't ask a lot of questions, although on occasion Stewart was known to accompany Quantrill on his livestock raids. Quantrill and Stewart made out pretty good on these larcenous transactions. On one occasion Stewart and Quantrill almost got caught at their game.

Quantrill and another man named Sinclair had stolen some cattle from the Salt Creek Valley in Kansas. Quantrill drove the cattle through Lawrence on the way south to Stewart's farm. Unbeknownst to him the owners of the cattle were close on his trail and contacted Douglas County Sheriff Sam Walker to help them recover the cattle. Walker had seen Quantrill driving the cattle though town and had a pretty good idea where he was taking them.

Walker went to Stewart's place and sure enough the cattle were there. Two of the cattle were slaughtered when Walker got there. Stewart concocted the story that some men had driven the cattle to his place for safe keeping and Stewart had bought the two cattle that were slaughtered. Walker saw right through his story but figured he could get the cattle off the property without a fight and return them to the rightful owners so he pretended to buy the preachers tale. All the while Quantrill was playing cards with some of his cohorts, never saying a word and letting Stewart twist in the wind.[69]

At another time Quantrill went to Sheriff Walker with an incredible tale. The *Lawrence Tribune* recounted the tale. Quantrill told Walker he had seen two Missourians around Lawrence looking for escaped slaves. Quantrill claimed that two leaders in Lawrence's Underground Railroad (the great deceiver never named the two men) told the slavers they knew where the escaping slaves were hiding and took them down by the Kaw River. When the abolitionists got the two slavers down by the river the slavers were murdered. Quantrill claimed the abolitionists had tied the two Missourians together with cords and to prove his story was true he could take the Sheriff to where the slavers' horses were located.

Sure enough, Quantrill took the Sheriff to a dense area overgrown with brush where there were two horses that obviously had been unattended for several days. The Sheriff advertised the horses in the newspaper but had no takers. In about twelve days two bodies tied together with rope were found in the river in close-by Eudora, Kansas. Sheriff Walker in no way believed Quantrill's story. He surmised that Quantrill and possibly a confederate had come across the two men and robbed them and then killed them. The Sheriff believed that Quantrill had tied their bodies together and dumped them in the river. Undoubtedly, Quantrill knew that the story of slavers being killed by abolitionists in Lawrence would play well to the locals and concocted the story to throw suspicions away from himself. With no other evidence coming forward the Sheriff was never able to charge Quantrill with murder.

When John Stewart provided an alibi for Quantrill and the stolen cattle it didn't take Quantrill long to repay Stewart with duplicity. Stewart had been busy providing a station on the Underground Railroad for escaping bondsmen and had a number of them at his "fort." Slave owners from Missouri came to Lawrence looking for their runaways. It didn't take them long to find "friends" in Jake Herd, Quantrill, Jake McGee, Tom McGee, "Cuckold Tom" McGee, Esau Sager and Henry McLaughlin. Quantrill told the slavers that he thought they could find their runaways at John Stewart's fort, waiting to be transported north on the Underground Railway.

The Missouri slavers, Herd, Quantrill and the rest of the "posse" went to John Stewart's place to secure the runaways. Quantrill stayed in the background so Stewart wouldn't see him. No sense in ruining any future "business" deals with the abolitionist.

The slave hunters demanded the return of their slaves but Stewart refused and returned a volley of fire. Although outnumbered, Stewart had armed the escaping bondsmen and they were only too willing to fight for their freedom. A firefight ensued between the slave posse and Stewart and the bondsmen in his fort. The slave posse managed to recapture one of the escapees but the withering fire of the Black men wanting their freedom and Stewart proved to be too much for the slave posse. The slavers went back to Missouri, tails between their legs, without the rest of the escaping bondsmen. It is believed that these bondsmen managed to make their way to freedom on the Underground Railroad.[70]

At one point, the Missouri slavers had had enough of John Stewart's activities of stealing their slaves and then putting them on the Underground Railroad. A large price was put on Stewart's head. The bounty of course became too big a prize for Quantrill to ignore. He began to try and maneuver Stewart into going on raids with him in Missouri for the purpose of murdering him for the reward money. However, Stewart knew at hand what Quantrill was up to and refused to have any more to do with him.[71]

Quantrill was keeping Judge Samuel Riggs busy. Riggs issued warrants for Quantrill (Hart) for horse stealing, the attempted kidnapping of Pinks, and for the burning of Judge Wakefield's house. Riggs also issued a warrant for Quantrill for breaking and entering the powder room of a wholesale dry goods store.[72]

Quantrill's greatest treachery against the Underground Railroad was about to begin in what was known as the "Morgan Walker Raid." It was an extremely bizarre event filled with Quantrill's usual penance for duplicitous behavior and outright murder.

A young Quaker named Charles Ball from Ohio and then later Springdale, Iowa, moved from Iowa to Kansas. He resided in Pardee, Kansas, named after the fiery preacher Pardee Butler. In this town Ball started to attend Butler's church and became a disciple of Butler and his ideas concerning the Underground Railroad and freedom for the slaves in Missouri. Ball started to go on raids into Missouri with John Dean.[73] It was through Dean that Ball unfortunately met up with William Quantrill.

Chalkley T. Lipsey was a Quaker born in Ohio and he, along with his family, made his way to Iowa. Lipsey's sister lived near Pardee, Kansas, and he went to visit her there and ended up teaching school in town and joining the Reverend Pardee's church. Lipsey went on a gold expedition to the Pike's Peak country in Colorado but it proved to be a failure. He was forced to walk back to Pardee almost dying of hunger on the way. He then went on a buffalo hunt shortly before he got caught up in the Morgan Walker raid. Edwin S. Morrison was a Quaker carpenter from New York who ended up in Springdale. Morrison and his cousin Albert Southwick, also a carpenter, went to Kansas with Albert Negus and his wife Martha. Martha was a sister to Charles Ball.[74]

While still in Springdale Ball, Morrison, Lipsey, Southwick, along with others, were in a secret lodge that had been organized to send slaves forward to their freedom on the Underground Railroad. During the winter of 1857-58 John Brown had left Lawrence, Kansas, and had moved through Tabor, Iowa, to Springdale, where he established his winter quarters. Old Brown directed his men to hold lyceums in Springdale to discuss events in Kansas and on the national scene concerning slavery. Brown's men John Kagy, Richard Realf and John Cook debated these questions in Brown's lyceum with much passion and eloquence.[75]

In Springdale, Ball, Morrison, Lipsey and Southwick became so fired up by Brown's lyceums that they couldn't wait to get into Kansas. They wanted to join the fight against slavery and try and free as many slaves as possible.

Once in Pardee, Kansas, Ball, Morrison and Southwick began to plan how they would help lead slaves in Missouri to freedom on the Underground Railroad. On one such raid the men went into Missouri and secured, along with Dean, who also was from Iowa, and possibly Stewart, ten to twelve bondsmen and took them directly to Springdale, Iowa. They bypassed one of the normal Underground Railroad routes from Kansas. This route went out of Kansas into Southeast Nebraska and then through Tabor, Iowa, to Lewis, Iowa, and then to Grinnell, Iowa, and then on to Springdale. It is believed some of these bondsmen stayed in Iowa while others went on to Canada.

Three former slaves, William Thompson, his brother John, and a friend, John Martin, from the Cherokee Nation in Oklahoma showed up in Pardee. They had escaped to Canada previously but now wanted to get back to the "Cherokee Nation" to free relatives and then make their way back to Canada.

Charley Ball, Albert Southwick, Chalkley Lipsey and Edwin Morrison proceeded south to Lawrence with the two Thompson brothers and Martin. It was planned to bring out not only the Thompson and Martin relatives but as many others as possible. While in Lawrence they had trouble procuring other abolitionists to go south with them into the Indian Nations because it was November and many felt it was foolhardy to start out at this time of the year. The group managed to get Dean to go, as well as a man using an alias of "Mr. Baker." Also, the ubiquitous Quantrill volunteered to go.

Quantrill traveled south to Osawatomie first. He was well known in the town and had gone on raids out of there with Kansas Jayhawkers such as Charles Jennison to Cass and Bates counties in Missouri. However, some in Osawatomie didn't trust Quantrill; some thought he was an out and out traitor to the cause.

It is interesting to ponder if Quantrill ever raided one of the farms owned by Cole Younger's father. Henry Younger, Cole's father, was one of the richest men in Cass County Missouri and was a slave owner. He and his son Cole often complained that Kansas Jayhawkers often raided his inviting farms and livery stables. The Youngers had the largest livery stable on the Western frontier due to the fact that the elder Younger had hundreds of contracts with the United States government to haul the U.S. mail. The Youngers often protested the raiding of their property by Kansas "Jayhawkers." Later, during the Civil War, Cole Younger, an officer in the regular and irregular Confederate Army looked up to Quantrill, who was at times Younger's commanding officer. Cole Younger would have been mortified to learn that Quantrill had raided with Jayhawkers in Cass County, Missouri.

Later, after the Civil War ended, Cole Younger would gain infamy as one of the leaders in the notorious James-Younger outlaw gang. Younger's career as an outlaw would end during his famous raid on Northfield, Minnesota, with Jesse and Frank James, his brothers Jim and Bob, Clell Miller, Samuel Wells, aka Charlie Pitts, and William Stiles, aka Bill Chadwell.

John Dean and the others outfitted themselves in a wagon and acted as if they were headed west going on a buffalo hunt and reached Osawatomie several days after Quantrill. Dean was a loud, arrogant man who probably thought this ruse would fool everyone in the territory as to what were their real intentions. The men tried to raise money for the long journey and were told it was foolish to start out at this time of the year on this type of mission.

It was soon realized by everyone that the mission to Oklahoma at this time of the year and with no money was not practical.[76] However, Quantrill had another plan. He wanted them all to go on a raid to the rich Missouri farm of Morgan Walker and steal his slaves and send them on to freedom. Of course Quantrill's real plan was to sell the Thompson brothers and Martin back into slavery in Missouri and betray the others in his group to Morgan Walker.

William and John Thompson and John Martin had traveled thousands of miles by themselves and on the Underground Railroad. After a while, travelers on the Underground Railroad would develop a sixth sense about people. They quickly had to ascertain if people could be trusted or not on the route of the Underground Railroad. Not everyone who claimed to be part of the abolitionist movement or the Underground Railroad had the bondsmen's best interests at heart. The Thompsons and Martin thought there was something odd about William Quantrill, something that wasn't true. They just didn't like the guy and thought he was deceiving them and they refused to have anything more to do with him. Quantrill, seeing his potential profits go out the window, tried to sweet talk them even more into joining the raid but the three were adamant. The Thompson brothers and Martin were told of all the cattle, horses and cash that could be taken from the Morgan Walker farm and what a nice nest egg this would make for them when they went to Canada or back to the Indian Nations to retrieve their relatives. However, the trio of bondsmen wanted nothing more to do with any project that Quantrill was involved in.

A Captain Snyder, who had ridden with Quantrill into Missouri on Jayhawking raids and distrusted him immensely tried to talk Dean and the others out of having anything to do with him. But the blustery Dean was too blind to see Quantrill's shortcomings. Morrison, Ball and Lipsey were too eager to enter the fight, and they joined Quantrill. However, Baker, and Southwick took heed of the Thompsons, Martin and Snyder and left the group.

The band headed off to Missouri carrying only knifes and revolvers. It was thought long guns would have been too suspicious. Morrison left his Sharps rifle, the known weapon of choice of the abolitionists, with Snyder fearing that would be a dead give away to the Missourians about their true intentions. The story Quantrill and the others had dreamed up for the reason they were in Missouri was that the group was looking for work around Lafayette County, Missouri. The Missouri Pacific railroad track bed was being graded around that area.[77]

Quantrill led them to Morgan Walker's place near Blue Springs, Missouri. It contained over two thousand acres of prime land, and over one hundred head of horses and mules. Walker also had enslaved thirty human beings on his farm.

The Springdale Quakers and Quantrill camped near Walker's place for several days. It is believed that Dean was bringing a wagon for use on the raid. The boys met secretly with some of Walker's slaves to discuss with them about going back to Kansas and escaping on the Underground Railroad. Many seamed eager to join the Quakers for the escape.

Unbeknownst to Ball, Morrison, Lipsey or Dean, Quantrill met with one of Morgan Walker's sons to discuss the plot and how to give the boys up to a murderous trap. Quantrill told Andrew Walker that some abolitionists from Kansas were coming to steal his slaves and to rob him. Andrew Walker procured the services of four neighbors armed with double-barreled shotguns to lie in wait for the Quakers. Morgan Walker was in Independence, Missouri, on business.

Morgan Walker arrived at his home only ten minutes before Quantrill arrived with the Quakers. When advised of the situation, Walker wanted to have everyone killed including Quantrill but his son and wife pleaded to spare the scoundrel.

Quantrill, Charles Ball and Chalkley Lipsey went into the Walker home while Edwin Morrison stood guard on the porch. It was December and dusk was falling on the landscape outside. John Dean was in the escape wagon. While inside Ball informed Walker that their purpose was to take his slaves into Kansas with the intention of escaping bondage. Ball also informed Walker that they would steal his horses and take whatever money was in the house.

Walker asked Ball if he had talked with the slaves about escaping and Ball affirmed that he had. Walker told Ball that if any objected to going to Kansas they should be allowed to stay on the farm. Walker also stated that since they were taking his slaves they should leave him his horses and money.

Quantrill put an end to the charade and told Ball and Lipsey to go out and gather up the slaves. Quantrill told Ball that he would stay inside the house and "take care of the old folks."[78]

When Ball and Lipsey stepped outside, the December night had grown dark and it was starting to sleet and rain. They were met with blasts from the shotguns. Morrison was killed outright and Lipsey was wounded in the groin.[79]

Dean was wounded in the foot and took off in the wagon, leaving the Quakers with no means of escape. Dean headed back to Lawrence, afraid that Missouri authorities would arrest him for his part in the Walker raid or possibly afraid that Quantrill would assassinate him. Dean proceeded to Sheriff Sam Walker's jail in Lawrence and admitted to the attempted murder of Allen Pinks. He thought jail in Kansas would be preferable to what awaited him for any aftermath of the Morgan Walker situation and if he were to stand trial in Missouri.

The diminutive Lipsey cried out in pain and Ball found him. Ball then carried the seriously wounded man into the woods. Walker and his heavily armed band didn't follow the two. The next day Western Missouri was in an uproar over the attempted freeing of Morgan Walker's thirty slaves. A mob wanted to hang Quantrill. His hope of being treated like a conquering hero was temporarily put on hold. He was arrested and put in the Independence, Missouri, jail with the rabble outside wanting to string him up. Quantrill retold the lie that he was born in Maryland and Jayhawkers had killed his older brother and he was seeking vengeance on those who had killed his brother. Supposedly, Ball and the rest of the Quakers were part of the Jawhawking crew who had killed his brother. In reality Quantrill was born in Ohio and he had no older brother but this yarn stuck for many years in certain quarters. Andrew Walker rescued Quantrill from jail after a day.

Ball and Lipsey had stolen a horse and were trying to make their way back to Kansas. They had found a hog and butchered it as best they could under the circumstances. They were found hiding some three days after the firefight on the edges of the Walker place. A bondsman hunting for the missing hog found them and reported their location to his master.[80] Word got out to Morgan Walker and he, Quantrill and three others went to the location.

Walker had a large gun, perhaps a Hawkins, probably used for hunting buffalo. Ball had seen the Walker group ride up and made a run for it. Walker fired his massive gun at Ball, hitting him in the back of the head and slaying him instantly. The rest of the group pumped lead into the wounded and prostrate Lipsey, killing him.[81]

The planning of this "raid" leaves one to wonder where everyone's common sense had gone. Quantrill probably couldn't believe his luck at finding such gullible men. Dean should have seen through this inane plot and warned the others. It would have been almost impossible to pull off this raid with only the few men that were in this group. To roundup one hundred head of horses and mules and thirty bondsmen with only three men was foolhardy. The mules alone would have taken everybody's attention to move them anywhere. If the plot was on the level Quantrill would have had to stay in the house to guard the Walker family and keep them from interfering. Dean would have had to stay with the wagon. This left only these three, Ball, Lipsey and Morrison, to round up one hundred head of horses and mules and then alert and move the thirty some bondspersons, all the while being on the lookout so no one saw them or fired upon them. If fired upon all three of them would have had to fire back and who would have looked out for the livestock?

Suppose they got off the farm with the bondspersons and with the livestock and some of the bondspersons could help with the livestock and handle weapons. Did they think such a large group of some thirty-five people, a wagon and one hundred head of livestock could move the twenty miles to the Kansas line in the dead of the night and attract no attention with slave patrols all over the area? When they originally went to Missouri they concocted an elaborate ruse that they were looking for work. At that time there were only five of them — what story would they tell to explain away thirty-five people and one hundred head of livestock? As soon as the group left the farm the Walkers would have alerted everyone in the area and they would have had the right to follow the Quakers to Kansas and even Iowa, if necessary, and have everyone arrested.

Suppose they got over into Kansas safely — now what? If they stole the two thousand dollars from Morgan Walker this was a lot of money for this time. However, it might not take such a large group of people that far. Remember, in Lawrence no one wanted to take three bondsmen going south to Oklahoma in November because they knew it was not practical. How would taking over thirty people to Iowa and then Canada in the dead of winter be practical even with two thousand dollars in your pocket? In January of 1857 on several occasions temperatures in Southwest Iowa were reported at minus twenty degrees below zero.[82] The Quakers from Iowa and Dean must have had some idea of the conditions there. I don't believe there was anyway this raid would have been successful.

Some later accounts of this tragedy put fellow Quaker Albert Southwick with Dean in the wagon. This makes no sense as Dean didn't need any help at the wagon. If Southwick was at the Walker raid he would have been needed in the yard with Ball and the others to round-up the livestock or look out for potential attackers. Southwick never really says he was there and makes some nonsensical statements about the raid later. Southwick was not there. Andrew Walker thought Lipsey was Southwick and this is the cause of the confusion. Perhaps Quantrill had gotten them confused and it was later determined that it was Lipsey who was killed. Southwick later joined the Union Army during the Civil War. His fellow Quakers were killed at Morgan Walker's farm. If he had been there he also would have been killed!

Kansas was pretty well through with Quantrill at this point. Word of the Morgan Walker raid and the brutal killings of the Quakers were heard in horror back in Lawrence. However, the Civil War was just around the corner and Quantrill wasn't yet through with the town on the Kansas River.

In 1858, 1859 and 1860 the flood gates began to open on the Underground Railroad in Western Missouri. Bondspersons began making their way across the Missouri border to freedom in Kansas, often with Lawrence as their destination. John Bowles, a leader of the Lawrence Underground Railroad, said in a letter to F.B. Sanborn "In the last four years I personally know ... the fact of nearly three hundred fugitives having passed through and received assistance from abolitionists here in Lawrence. Thus you see we have been continually strained to meet the heavy demands that were almost daily made upon us to carry on this ... *gradual emancipation.*"[83] During Christmas time in 1858, twenty-four fugitives arrived in Lawrence, straining the resources of the UGRR community. Five or six of the escaping bondspersons had the means to continue on by themselves but the other eighteen or nineteen had to be held back until one hundred and fifty dollars could be raised to forward them on the Underground Railroad to the north.[84]

Very often the Underground Railroad in Lawrence or Topeka didn't escort the escaping bondspersons to the next "station." Instead, they sometimes gave them directions usually through Oskaloosa and Holton, K.T., and some cash to try to make it at least to Tabor or Civil Bend, Iowa, where they could continue on their journey to Canada. This was especially true of young strong males who looked as if they could take care of themselves. However, women, especially if they had children, were more apt to be provided an escort On the Western Frontier it took cash to travel these distances and, if possible, this was provided to those escaping bondage. On the frontier, as in many places, the great equalizer was money. If you had money you could go places, if you didn't you were stuck. However, a number of bondspersons made it through Kansas with little help. Many were able to accumulate cash on their own and were sometimes leery of any contact with white people.

As one may expect in a wild place like Kansas even political rivals had to work together to make the freedom of runaways possible. James Redpath, a newspaper editor in northeast Kansas, despised the mercurial James Lane. However, even Redpath had to admit that Lane once helped a fugitive slave escape in Nebraska.[85]

Even in the life and death struggle for freedom on the Kansas plains good-natured humor could occur. A group of Free-State young men made their way by steamboat from Leavenworth, K.T., to Elwood, K.T., in Doniphan County in the extreme northeast corner of the territory. About a dozen free-state boys made their way to Troy, the seat of government for Doniphan County. While in Troy, they went to the local eatery and demanded pies. When the usual round pies were produced the leader of the group, Nelson Abbey, proclaimed that Free-State men didn't eat round pies but only square pies. Only square pies would do for the Free-State men. After a while, a dozen square pies were produced. The Free-State boys whooped and hollered. This story was told all over the Kansas Territory. From then on Free-State men and Black Republicans would show their allegiance to the cause by only eating square pies.[86]

Napoleon Simpson was a black man who had been enslaved his whole life. He had lived around the Jackson County area in Western Missouri. Simpson was an excellent worker.

He had a wife and children. When his master sold him for one thousand and five hundred dollars (around seventy-five thousand dollars in present-day money) to a slaver that was going to take him south, Simpson knew he would have to make his move.

He escaped from slavery in the fall of 1859. His strategy was to go over into Kansas then on to Iowa where he thought he would be safe. His plan was to later come back in the spring of 1860 and get his wife and children. He made his way to Kansas and was directed to the home of Joseph Gardner who had a station on the Underground Railroad. Gardner pointed Simpson north to Iowa and he made it there safely. It is unknown if Simpson went any further North than Iowa such as Chicago or Canada.

According to his plan Simpson came back to Kansas in May of 1860. He was going to slip over into Jackson County, Missouri, and get his wife and children who he longed to see again. Simpson once again hooked up with Joseph Gardner. It was decided that the redoubtable John Stewart would take Simpson over into enemy territory in Jackson County to recover his family.

In a covered wagon Stewart took Simpson to his old place of enslavement in the middle of the night. Simpson crept up to the door of his wife's shanty only to discover in horror that she was too sick to travel. Simpson had to think fast and he decided to go back to the Gardners' station house and come back in a couple of weeks to see if his wife had improved. Simpson knew he couldn't stay in Missouri and be captured, for then all hope would be ruined.

It was a dejected Simpson and Stewart who made their way back to Kansas and the Gardner's homestead. It was decided that Simpson could help him until it was time to go retrieve his wife in a couple of weeks, hoping she would be recovered from her sickness. There was another bondsman on the Gardner place helping him build a fence. Perhaps this was the bondsman that Gardner mentions in a letter to George Stearns. In escaping, this bondsman knocked down a watchman on a steamer on "the big muddy." He made good his escape but was captured again by four young men on the Kansas side. The young men were attempting to tie the bondsman up but he succeeded in pitching one of their number over the Kansas river bridge some sixty feet below and he made his escape. The bondsman then headed for the Gardners' place.[87]

The two men worked on the fence, but this did not go unnoticed by pro-slavery men. Gardner was well watched in the area as he had a five hundred dollar bounty on his head by the Sheriff in Buchanan County, Missouri, for his part in helping abolitionist Dr. John Doy escape from jail in that county.

The Gardner log cabin was a stout structure one and a half stories high. On June 9 dogs began to bark. Mr. Gardner and his wife were asleep in a trundle bed along with two children and one of the bondsmen was asleep on a pallet on the first floor. On the second floor slept four more Gardner children and another of the bondsmen. Two men with cocked revolvers were banging on the door and it was obvious what they wanted. They demanded Gardner open the door, which he did. The Underground Railroad stationmasters in Kansas were not a timid lot. Gardner, opening the door, immediately knew what was going on and he quickly put the muzzle of his Navy colt on the breast of one of the slavers at the door and fired. The man staggered away. The door was quickly closed only to open slightly so Gardner could fire his revolver. The ruffians were firing back.

The firefight continued with the slave hunters arming themselves with shotguns. Most of the windows were shot out. Meanwhile, Napoleon Simpson had taken up his Sharps rifle and began firing at the slavers. He went outside the house to track the bounty hunters

This was the log cabin where Napoleon Simpson and Joseph Gardner had their shootout with slave hunters. Unfortunately Simpson was killed. The previous year Simpson had escaped from slavery and was coming back to get his wife in Missouri. When she was too ill to travel he waited for her to recover at the Gardner cabin in Kansas. Slave hunters found out he was located at the Gardner cabin and a shootout occurred. These crude log cabins, like Gardner's, were the type of housing in which many Kansas Underground Railroad stations resided. Many in the Kansas UGRR were new arrivals to the territory and struggled to feed their own families but tried to provide aid to the escaping bondspersons (Kansas State Historical Society).

down. He saw one of the attackers and fired at him. Simpson was reloading when another of the slavers, hiding by the well, fired a double-barreled shotgun at him, hitting him in the side.[88]

Simpson managed to make it back inside the house, gasping for air. He was obviously in death's throes. According to a newspaper article in the Lawrence *Republican* on June 14, 1860, Mr. Gardner leaned down to ask Napoleon Simpson, already dying in a pool of his own blood, if there was anything he could do for him. Simpson replied, "Fight! fight hard!"

2

Missouri: Freedom Escapes

> "I am here as a piece of property. I am a slave according to the laws of the United States.... No one can read, Mr. Chairman, the declaration of the American independence ... without being struck with the marked inconsistency of the theory of the people and their acts."
> — *William Wells Brown, former Missouri slave, public lecturer and author, delivering a speech at the Town Hall in Manchester, England, August 1, 1854.*[1]

On August 10, 1821, Missouri was admitted as the twenty-fourth state to the Union, but not after some controversy. This controversy, of course, centered on the question of slavery. The United States already had an equal balance of free and slave states. Missouri, which as a territory had allowed slavery, wanted to be admitted as a slave state. Many abolitionists wanted this institution to die out but if slave states kept being admitted to the Union then how could this question be resolved? Hence the Missouri Compromise of 1820. In the land that comprised the Louisiana Purchase no slavery would be allowed above what would be the southern border of Missouri. A large region in northern Massachusetts would be carved out and the state of Maine was born. One Free State, one Slave State and the balance of power was kept in the United States Senate.

Even from its inception most slaves in Missouri were used for agricultural purposes. Some were used in mining — especially lead mining — and later, as the state matured, some in factories. Missouri became a very important terminus for the steamboat trade and Blacks both free and slave were used readily for that business. Most slave owners in Missouri had few slaves — only two or three at each farm. Until hemp farming and its back-breaking labor came along, mostly in the 1850s, Missouri oftentimes seemed to be a state in search of a reason to have slavery.

As America made its way west, slave planters and farmers were often toiling on Eastern soil that was greatly depleted. They could make their way to Missouri almost the whole way by steamboats, which were the most inexpensive and fastest way to travel at the time. These slave planters and farmers sold their land and paid off their debts and took what was left over and with their slaves made it out west to Missouri and its pristine prairies. Once in Missouri many found out that their slaves were worth more if they sold them to the Deep South rather than used them for farm chores.

With thousands of Southerners and their slaves passing through Missouri on their way to the gold fields in California, along the Santa Fe Trail, the farm fields of Oregon or to the

Great Salt Lake region, Missouri always had a lively slave trade going on in the state. Many of these travelers and farmers found that the slave prices in Missouri were profitable and too good to pass up and they sold their slaves in the state. Platte City, Lexington, Columbia, Marshall, St. Joseph and of course St. Louis had a vigorous trade in human beings. St. Louis was one of the largest cities in America that allowed slavery yet she had only around four thousand bondspersons in the whole county by 1860, mostly working as domestics. Yet the city had over thirty slave traders. The only way they could stay in business was with a large traffic of slaves being sold south to untold misery.[2] Although Missouri didn't have a large number of slaves in the state, so many bondspersons passing through the state always provided for opportunities for escape.

Former bondswoman Harriet Casey said, "De traders would come through and buy up slaves in groups like stock. On de way south dey would have regular stopping places like pens and coops for de slaves to stay in; at each of these stoppin' places some of de slaves would be sold. My uncle's father was his master and de master sold my uncle who was his own son." Harriet went on to add that "Dey would whip with a cat-o-nine tails and den mop de sores with salt water...."[3]

In the jails of Platte City and St. Joseph, Missouri, Dr. John Doy described a very brisk trade in Blacks being sent or taken south for sale. Groups of slaves for sale, runaway slaves and Free Blacks would be chained together and taken out of the jails in the middle of the night and sent to points in the Deep South for sale. If an escaping slave was rounded up in these sweeps and the slave trader thought they could get away with not returning the runaway to his rightful master, the runaway was sold down south. Runaway slaves were worth a lot more to a slave trader if they could sell them for their full value rather than turn them in for the reward bounty which would be a lot less. Doy and bondsman Allen Pinks reported that if a Black man or woman was found to be a free person their papers were simply torn up by these slave traders and they were then sold down south. Doy also said that Blacks had told him they had seen white persons in these groups to be sold south. One bondsman who was put in such a gang had uttered to his "master," "I hope to meet you at the bar of a just God, before you are sent to hell." The slave trader deemed the bondsman's attitude to be "unchristian."[4] It mattered little to these slave traders if the Black bondsperson was free or was a fugitive slave trying to escape bondage or had been legitimately sold to the slave trader. The fact that Doy said they left in the middle of the night would indicate that many were escaping bondspersons who had been caught in the dragnet of the slave patrollers. They left in the middle of the night so their rightful "owners" would not see them.

The census of 1840 put the number of Missouri slaves at 57,891, the census of 1850 at 87,422 and the census of 1860 at 114,931.[5] By 1860 around 70 percent of the slaves in Missouri resided in counties along the Missouri River and on its western border where much of the hemp in the state was grown. In eastern Missouri by 1860 some counties were actually showing a reduction in the number of slaves. In the border counties in western Missouri during the decade of the 1850s there was actually a close to 50 percent increase in the number of bondspersons in that region.[6]

This, of course, proved to be a very interesting situation. As Kansas grew more pronounced in her desire to become a free state and as her abolitionists became bolder and bolder, the area along Missouri's most western border where many bondspersons resided made a perfect situation for escapes.

Missouri was like most slave states with the white power structure of the state believing that all slaves in the state were perfectly contented with their condition and had no desire to escape. Although there was ample evidence to the contrary, the slave owners felt that if any slave did escape it was due to the fact that some white abolitionist had enticed them to do so. These slave owners completely overlooked the fact that for the most part slaves lived in conditions that were substandard. Many were not given enough to eat or were not given proper medical attention. Many did not have proper housing or clothing. Many children were torn away from their parents and husbands from their wives. However, almost all slave owners were in complete denial that their bondspersons wanted out of slavery and that bondspersons were more than willing and able to change their status by escaping if given the opportunity.

As stated before, most of Missouri's bondspersons were engaged in agriculture on small farms. As many of these small farms had considerable amounts of down time farmers were always of a notion to try and lease their slaves out to mining, factory, larger farms or other endeavors for cash payments to the slave owner. Sometimes lease agreements were drawn up for six months or a year or another specified time. Often the party leasing the bondspersons cared little about their welfare and would often almost work them literally to death. This would often be a cause for an escape scenario.

Charles Baker related a story that his mother Jane Baker, a slave in Missouri, had told about conditions during that time. Baker reported that the worst side of slavery was when a slave was farmed out or sublet to another man for so many months at so much money. Baker said that the slaves were treated "like animals."[7]

Betty Abernathy told how her master hired out his slaves to a neighboring farmer. One time he hired out her two brothers and they were treated so badly they decided to escape. After they had escaped their master became so enraged that he came to her mother's cabin and tied a rope around her neck and tied the other end to the rafters. When she wouldn't talk — when she would not give up her own children — he beat her to within an inch of her life. After that Betty and her mother were treated very badly and beaten often. Fortunately, this was during the Civil War and a neighbor helped them escape with twelve other bondspersons. They went to Cape Girardeau, Missouri, where Union soldiers were stationed and could protect them. Had this happened before the war they would have had to endure these merciless beatings with no end in sight.[8]

The specter of being sold often led many bondspersons to seek freedom. Alexander Hamilton was a bondsman from St. Louis. Hamilton believed God made all men to be free and equal. He had seen a lot of terror while a slave. He had seen a lot of bondspersons beaten and treated badly — husbands sold away from their wives, children sold from their mothers and sent where they would never see each other again. He had seen a man cut the fingers off his left hand with an axe to prevent himself from being sold down south. Another man, when told he was going to be sold, had shot himself and died. A mother whose children were the biological offspring of her "master" had drowned herself when told she had been sold. Hamilton had seen her body taken from the water.

Hamilton, although he had not been told he was being sold, figured it would be his time soon. He escaped to London, Ontario. He came north and only had one dollar and fifty cents to his name when he reached Canada. He found work right away and soon accumulated enough money to own three houses and several lots in Ontario. Hamilton became a British citizen and noted many more bondspersons were coming into Canada and out of slavery.[9]

When the Fugitive Slave Law of 1850 was passed many whites in the North were not sure how this act would impact them. However, a slave escape in Missouri would change many northerners' attitude on the subject of this slave law. The Fugitive Slave Act was part of a package of laws that became known as the Compromise of 1850. The Compromise of 1850 allowed California to enter the Union as a free state. It barred slaves from being sold in the huge Washington, D.C., slave market. However, the Compromise of 1850 did not ban slavery from the capital city. Other aspects of this act cleared up some territorial matters arising in Texas and from the Mexican War.

The Fugitive Slave Act of 1850 allowed commissioners to be set up who would oversee matters concerning fugitive slaves.[10] Tremendous pressure was put on law enforcement individuals such as marshals and their deputies to actively pursue any fugitive slave even if the marshals resided in a northern free state. If it was decided these individuals did not pursue fugitive slaves actively enough the marshal or their deputies could receive fines of up to one thousand dollars, a very large amount of money for the time. Also, if these marshals or deputies captured a slave and that slave escaped from their custody they could also be fined for this event. These commissioners could compel all bystanders, or *posse comitatus* of the proper county, even if they resided in a free northern state, to help in the apprehension of any or all fugitive slaves—no matter if the individuals were abolitionists or opposed to slavery.[11] Henry Ward Beecher, noted abolitionist, spoke for many of those who held his position when asked if he would ever help in "negro catching" as required by law. Beecher replied, "...I would see my arm wither in its socket.... Before I'd lift one finger.... Towards sending a slave back to bondage."[12]

When an alleged fugitive slave was brought before these commissioners the proceedings took on the air of a kangaroo court. If the alleged fugitive was in fact a free Black person in a free northern state their right of *habeas corpus* was suspended as was that of any alleged fugitive. Even if the free Black citizen had "free papers" and witnesses to back up their testimony that they were a free person and not a slave they could not be heard. They had no standing in the court. Under no circumstances was any testimony of the alleged fugitive allowed to be heard. This of course led to the kidnappings of free Blacks and other miscarriages of justice.

Another highly unusual aspect of these "court proceedings" involving fugitive slaves was the method by which the commissioners were paid: they received no salaries, but were paid when they heard cases. When they judged that a Black person was in fact a fugitive slave and should be returned to their "master" the commissioner received ten dollars in payment for their services. However, if the commissioner judged that the Black person was not a fugitive slave they only received five dollars. In its first full year of operation in 1851 these commissioners in northern jurisdictions sent 82 percent of Blacks brought before them back into slavery.[13]

No court of law could overturn a decision made by these commissioners. It was reasoned that the commissioners were not judges and they were not appointed by the president, they received no fixed salary and as such were not considered part of the regular judiciary. The Supreme Court of the United States never ruled on the fact that the commissioners had a pecuniary interest in the outcome of the hearings, which violated the due process clause of the Fifth Amendment. Also, the United States Supreme Court never decided on the matter that the commissioners' rulings could not be overturned by any other courts.[14] The U.S. Supreme Court refused to hear any of these types of cases brought before them.

The Southern slave holders' viewpoint was that slaves were mere chattel and as such they had no rights or standing in the courts. To Southern slave holders all Black persons were slaves and it was up to them to "prove" they were free. Of course, in these proceedings the accused had no chance to prove he was a free person. The Fugitive Slave Act of 1850 furthermore took the position that once a slave always a slave. It didn't matter how long ago a slave had escaped or where they went — they were always the property of their "masters."

This aspect very often had ugly and brutal overtones. A man by the name of Harris had resided in St. Louis County in Missouri. He and his wife escaped bondage to the Chicago area and were living in peace. Their "masters" found them and filed papers with the commissioners. Harris was required to go to Springfield, Illinois, to a hearing before the commissioner at that location. The commissioner ruled that Harris and his wife and their two children were fugitive slaves. Harris and his wife had two different "masters" and thus the family was split up. Harris and his family were required to go back to St. Louis County, Missouri, and live in bondage, Harris with his "master" and his wife and two children with a different "master."[15]

The Fugitive Slave Act, as one might expect, took special aim at abolitionists and those who would help out on the Underground Railroad. It specifically mentions that those that would aid, willingly obstruct, hinder, "or shall rescue, or attempt to rescue, such fugitive" will receive stiff fines and imprisonment for such actions. Those that aided in the escape of any fugitive slave would also be liable for civil damages.[16]

William Henry (sometimes also known as McHenry) lived in bondage in Marion County, Missouri. Hannibal lies on the eastern edge of that county. Sometime in the late 1840s Jerry, as he became more commonly known, escaped slavery from the McReynolds farm in Marion County. Jerry managed to make his way north. Prior to the passage of the Fugitive Slave Act of 1850 many times Black escapees like Jerry could head for a northern city, blend in, and have little to worry about concerning being recaptured.

Jerry managed to make it all the way to Syracuse, New York. He set up trade as a cooper and lived there for a considerable amount of time and became well-known and well respected in that city. However, an agent of McReynolds made his way to the empire state. Jerry was arrested in Syracuse.[17] McReynolds' agent filed papers with the commissioner, Joseph F. Sabine, in Syracuse on September 30, 1851, to have Jerry arrested as a fugitive slave and taken back to Missouri to serve out the rest of his life in bondage. Deputy United States Marshal Harry Allen was to serve the warrant issued by Commissioner Sabine the next day on October 1, 1851.[18]

Allen made up a lie to tell Jerry. Henry was a very athletic and powerful man and Allen feared that if he told Jerry he was to be arrested under the provisions of the Fugitive Slave Act with the possibility of being returned to slavery Henry would overpower Allen and his deputies. So Allen told Jerry he was wanted on a state matter of theft. Jerry was puzzled by the marshal's false charges but quietly complied with him thinking he could get things straightened out. However, when Allen saw he had Jerry in custody he manacled him and told him the real charges against him. Allen and his deputies proceeded with Henry to Sabine's offices for a hearing.

The citizens of Syracuse were aghast. Seeing a well-known Black citizen of the town shackled and paraded in the streets of the city like a slave shocked the residents of Syracuse. This might have been a common occurrence in St. Louis, Missouri, in the 1850s but it certainly wasn't in Syracuse, New York. Word spread quickly about Syracuse and church bells were rung to call people to this alarming situation. Allen took Henry to Sabine's office and a crowd began to gather.

However, "Jerry" Henry had luck on his side. On October 1, 1851, two events were going on in Syracuse, New York: the Onandaga County Fair and, more importantly, the annual Liberty Party Convention. The Liberty Party had as its main plank in its platform the end of slavery in the United States. Although not a major party, by 1851 it was still capable of having several thousand members show up at its convention. It had many important and wealthy backers like Gerrit Smith. Smith was a scion to a huge real estate fortune and he financially backed many abolitionist projects.

Syracuse was full of both Black and white abolitionists on that October 1. Among the Black abolitionists were the Rev. Samuel Ringgold Ward and the Rev. Jermain Loguen. Other abolitionists in town were the Rev. Samuel J. May and Martin Stowell. Stowell would later become involved in abolitionist activities in the territories of Kansas and Nebraska.

The abolitionist crowd outside the commissioner's office became bolder. As the meeting was about to adjourn the Black and white abolitionists attacked the building and Jerry managed to escape. Henry eluded the police and Allen and his deputies. He was chased to one of the bridges over the Erie Canal and was recaptured by the Syracuse city police. He was then taken to the police justice offices.[19]

The Liberty Party delegates and other interested parties convened to plan their strategy. As evening came upon Syracuse a crowd of an estimated two thousand five hundred people surrounded the police station. Battering rams were used to break down the doors. A burly ironworker, J.M. Clappe, was the first to breach the door to the police station. Black and white rescuers stormed the jail and overwhelmed the officers in the building. Jerry was located and rescued from the lockup, placed in a carriage and driven away.[20]

William "Jerry" Henry was carefully taken out of Syracuse and sent north. He finally made his way to Kingston, Ontario, in Canada and finally to his ultimate freedom. He would never again be a slave in Missouri or anywhere else.[21]

Deputy Allen and his subordinates couldn't lay their hands on Jerry Henry anymore. Canada would not allow United States law enforcement officers to enter the country to search for fugitive slaves or to extradite slaves. Henry Bibb, a former fugitive slave and then an owner and editor of a Canadian newspaper stated, "Slaveholders are frequently seen and heard, howling on their track up to the Detroit River's edge but dare not venture over lest the British lion should lay his paw upon their guilty heads."[22] The Rev. Samuel J. May wrote Jerry was "treated as if he were the worst of felons; and learnt that it was only because he had assumed to be what God made him to be, a man, and not a slave."

The Rev. Samuel Ringgold Ward, the Rev. Jermain Loguen, and J.M. Clappe were all advised to go to Canada to escape any retribution for their part in what would become known as the "Jerry rescue." Unfortunately, William "Jerry" Henry only lived for two more years after he reached freedom in Canada.[23]

The United States government was deeply embarrassed by this incident. Powerful Southern slavers howled and demanded justice be done regarding this matter. The United States district attorney tried to build a case of treason against Gerrit Smith and the Rev. Samuel J. May and six other defendants but lacked the proof to do so. Finally, a federal grand jury indicted 26 individuals with being "engaged with the Syracuse riots." Samuel J. May said that 12 of the defendants were Black and all but three fled to Canada probably because they were in fact fugitive bondsmen. Four of the indicted whites also left the country for Canada.

Finally, on January 21, 1852, Enoch Reed's trial was the first to go to a jury and he was found guilty. However, the second defendant was acquitted and on two other defendants the jury was divided. The remaining nine cases were dropped.[24]

Enoch Reed appealed his case but died while the appeal was going forth. In retaliation for these indictments and as an attack on the Fugitive Slave Act, Smith and the others were able to get a grand jury in Onondaga County to indict Deputy Marshal Henry W. Allen for the kidnapping of William Henry. Gerrit Smith, as special counsel, was even allowed to prosecute the case for the state.

Basically, Smith put the Fugitive Slave Act of 1850 on trial. Judge R.P. Marvin rejected Smith's arguments. Marvin ruled that a United States marshal could not be arrested under New York law for enforcing a federal law. The jury agreed and Allen was found not guilty.[25]

Every year after this event the abolitionists of Syracuse and New York held a celebration of "Jerry's rescue." Gerrit Smith presided over all of these events; however, in 1859 he had second thoughts. Smith was very despondent in a letter to event organizer John Thomas. In this letter Smith stated that the rescue of "Jerry was a great and glorious event." However, Smith had become very downcast because slavery hadn't been outlawed by this time. He noted that after the "Jerry rescue" the enthusiasm for the repeal of slavery was high but to him now, in 1859, slavery seemed stronger than ever. Smith thought they should not celebrate the event anymore lest they sully Jerry's memory by not ending slavery.[26]

Less than two months after this letter was written by Gerrit Smith, John Brown would attack the Federal Arsenal at Harpers Ferry, Virginia. His purpose was to start a slave insurrection. The raid would not be successful. It was found out that Gerrit Smith, a friend of Brown's, and one of his financial backers knew of the raid beforehand. Some in the Federal government wanted to indict Smith on a variety of charges. Smith became known as one of Brown's "secret six," but no official charges were ever brought against him.

The *Chicago Tribune* had information from one of John Brown's sons that indeed Gerrit knew of these plans and was a financial backer of Brown. Smith sued the *Tribune* but they countersued. The situation became too much for Smith and he had a complete mental breakdown and on November 7, 1859, Smith, one of the richest men in the United States, was checked into the Utica, New York, asylum for the insane. Smith did make a complete recovery after almost two months in the asylum.[27]

The William Henry affair certainly didn't end the use of the Fugitive Slave Act to return Missouri slaves to their "masters." In 1852 Joshua Glover escaped slavery in Missouri and headed for Wisconsin. He landed in Racine, Wisconsin, and resided there, becoming a well-respected citizen of that state. In March of 1854 Glover's "owner," a Benjamin S. Garland of St. Louis, Missouri, tracked Glover down in Racine. Garland, along with a deputy United States marshal, broke into Glover's home and after a violent fight managed to arrest him. Glover was taken to the county jail in Milwaukee and incarcerated at that location. A mob from Milwaukee surrounded the jail when it was learned a fugitive Missouri slave was being held in their city. The courthouse bell was rung to alert the citizens of Milwaukee of the injustice being done. In the afternoon a steamboat of about 100 men, including Sheriff Morris of Racine, came to Milwaukee. They rushed the jail and freed Glover.[28]

Glover was put into a carriage and eventually made his way to Canada and freedom. However, the litigation from this freedom escape dragged on for several years. Morris had a warrant for the arrest of slaver Garland and four other men for the assault and battery of Joshua Glover. Garland was arrested and jailed but District Court Judge Miller ordered

Garland released. Miller further ruled that Garland was legally aiding the marshal in his duties of capturing a fugitive and had not broken any law.[29]

Another man, Sherman M. Booth, was charged by a slave commissioner with assisting Glover in his escape. This case had jurisdictional disputes between state and federal courts. Booth was eventually fined $1,000, which financially ruined him. He was also imprisoned. Booth's lawyers put the Fugitive Slave Law on trial but to no avail. Supreme Court Chief Justice Roger B. Taney ruled, as he always did, on the side of the slavery interests and said the law was completely constitutional. On the eve of the Civil War President James Buchanan directed that a pardon be issued to Booth.

Missouri, as most slave states did, passed laws against disseminating any abolitionist literature or speaking to slaves about escaping. In 1837 Missouri passed a law making it illegal that "...any person should ... utter by writing, speaking or printing any facts ... tending directly to excite any slave or slaves ... to rebellion, sedition, mutiny, insurrection or murder." The first offense was punishable by a fine of $1,000 and up to two years in prison. The second offense was a 20-year sentence in the state prison and the third offense was a life sentence in prison.[30]

In Marion County two young men, Williams and Garrett, had settled in Philadelphia, Missouri—the home campus of Marion College. They were members of the American Colonization Society. This society wanted to buy slaves from their masters and send them to Liberia in Africa. A mob of slave proponents caught up with the two young men and thinking they were abolitionists told them they could leave the state or they would be hanged immediately from the nearest tree. Needless to say, the two young reformers choose to leave the state. Those in favor of slavery were not ones to make fine distinctions between abolitionists and those who wished for African colonization. All these slavers knew was that both groups wanted to end slavery in America and the slavers' way of life.

Abolitionists in Marion County in the northeastern corner of Missouri were able to gain somewhat of a toehold in a slave state for a short period of time. Named after Francis Marion, the famed "Swamp Fox" from South Carolina in the Revolutionary War, Marion County had as its eastern border the Mississippi River. The county seat was at Palmyra and, of course, Hannibal on the Mississippi River would become its most famous town. However, it was in little Philadelphia, Missouri, in the western part of Marion County, that for a short period of time there was agitation for the cause of freedom.

Tiny Marion College's first president and co-founder was Dr. David Nelson, a well-respected scholar and composer of religious music. Although he came from Kentucky he let everyone know he was for the emancipation of all slaves. The principal fund-raiser and another co-founder of the college was William Muldrow. Later, Dr. Ezra Ely invested $100,000 in the school and opened a preparatory school in what became known as East Ely and West Ely. The college became affiliated with the Presbyterian Church. By 1837 the college had an enrollment of 116 scholars and had seven professors.[31]

Around the school abolitionist pamphlets were disseminated as were those of the American Colonization Society. It was not known for certain if any of the faculty or students of Marion actually participated in any bondspersons escaping from Marion County but the rumors were flying. Later, one of the former professors at Marion College would come into the county to try and help bondsmen escape. It was also believed that Arthur Tappan, the famed New York abolitionist who championed and helped finance the Underground Railroad and the Liberty Party in the United States, had given the college $2,000. It is known for sure that much of the money for the financing of the college came from New

York.³² Muldrow was an extremely effective fund-raiser back east in New York and Pennsylvania, for the college, and for another project of his—the raising of a city called Marion City that lay north of Hannibal on the Mississippi River. It was said Muldrow would eloquently tell these eastern backers "of the need of funds to reclaim the wild wicked west...."³³

As Dr. Nelson began to speak out more and more about the need to emancipate the slaves in Missouri, tensions arose. Then, at a revival, Nelson chided those who had run Williams and Garret out of Missouri. Nelson was attacked and then William Muldrow defended him and stabbed Bosley, one of the attacking slavers. Muldrow was taken to the St. Charles jail. Bosley lived and Muldrow was tried but was acquitted of any wrongdoing.³⁴

Things were coming to a head in Marion County. A group of slavers confronted Dr. David Nelson at his home and told him he would have to leave the state or there would be violence. Nelson left Marion County and moved to Quincy, Illinois, where he became president of another college with abolitionist beliefs. It is believed that while at Quincy, Nelson encouraged faculty and students to help Marion County and other Missouri slaves to escape. A Dr. Potts took over Marion College and a change was felt. The faculty put out a statement that it was "unchristian" to not support slavery. The faculty forbade its students to talk sedition to slaves, circulate anti-slavery literature, hold antislavery meetings or discuss slavery matters.

To make matters even worse for the small college, Dr. Ely had lost all his money on the college venture. Muldrow's fund-raising dried up when the college changed it focus away from ending slavery. By 1844 Marion College had closed its doors. It is hard to tell what, if any, influence little Marion College had in its clarion call to freedom in Northeast Missouri, but what is known is that the county seemed to attract its share of escaping bondspersons and out-of-state abolitionists.

It is interesting that the slavers in Marion County ran Dr. Nelson out of the state. This was what was usually done in all slave states. If anyone hinted ever so slightly at any abolitionist tendencies they were immediately run out of the state if they were lucky or many times they endured physical punishment such as being tarred and feathered or even, on occasion, murdered. However, the slavers of Marion County allowed William Muldrow to stay in Marion County even though Muldrow had physically attacked a slaver and stabbed him. It is quite possible that they viewed Dr. Nelson as an outsider and Muldrow as one of their own. In Marion County Muldrow was somewhat of a legend. F.A. Sampson described him as "one of the most remarkable men to live in Missouri...." Muldrow had first developed ways that the farmers could break the thick sod in Marion County and successfully till the soil. By the late 1830s almost all the land in the county was being farmed, while in counties adjacent to Marion County the Federal government still owned one third to one half of the land in the counties because the sod could not be broken and because there were other difficulties in farming. Muldrow had discovered salt wells and drilled for salt successfully in the county for this much-needed item.³⁵

One of Muldrow's major projects was the development of Marion City, a planned metropolis that he hoped would become the biggest city in the west. Marion City had a great steamboat landing and much of the supplies for the county came into the area from Marion City. It was built on swamp land, but Muldrow noted that Chicago was also built on swamp land as were other cities. However, Marion City was chronically under water and the streets were a muddy mess with few settlers. Across the pond the great writer Charles Dickens was writing a book, *Life & Adventures of Martin Chuzzlewit*. The book was serialized, as were many of Dickens' books, and sales were not good. So he decided to switch the location of the action to America where he could satirize the people of this country much to the amusement of the people of the British Isles. Dickens was on a lecture tour in America when he heard of Muldrow's project and he satirized Marion City as "Eden" in Chapter 23 of the book. After Marion City collapsed Muldrow did head out to California.[36]

In Mark Twain's *The Gilded Age*, some have speculated that Twain's character Colonel Sellers was based on William Muldrow. However, Twain scholar Minnie Brashear doesn't believe this was the case. Interestingly, Twain did write about an abolitionist being hanged in Marion City in a story titled "A Scrap of History." The abolitionist had helped a slave escape from Palmyra to Illinois. Then others in the area started to follow the one they called "the martyr." The story seemed to involve itself more with the motivations of following a martyr rather than abolitionism and the Underground Railroad.[37]

Richard Eells, who taught at Dr. David Nelson's college in Quincy, Illinois, conducted a bondsman from Marion County, Missouri, to the next Underground Railroad station in Adams County, Illinois. It was unclear if Eells came into Marion County to get the bondsman or if the bondsman found Eells in Illinois. Eells and the Missouri escapee were caught and brought before the Adams County magistrate which happened to be Stephen A. Douglas of the Lincoln-Douglas debate fame. Eells was fined $400 by the state of Illinois.[38] Eells who was also a member of the Liberty Party, would not give up his activity of freeing slaves. He then went next door to Marion County and found a bondsman from Lewis

This is a very rare illustration of Missouri abolitionist William Muldrow. It came from the book *History of Marion County, Missouri, 1884* by R. I. Holcombe. Muldrow was an extraordinary individual. He was an abolitionist in a slave state who openly expressed his opposition to that institution and even stabbed a slave owner to defend another abolitionist. Muldrow was acquitted of the stabbing. When incidents occurred like this in most slave states the abolitionist would be jailed for a long period or hanged on the spot. Even for speaking out against slavery some abolitionists in slave states were tarred and feathered, run out of the state or even murdered. However, Muldrow was considered an agricultural genius. He had helped many farmers in the northeastern part of Missouri conquer the prairies and turn their farms into profitable enterprises. This is probably why the slavers left him alone. Muldrow continued to live most of his life in Missouri (used by permission, State Historical Society of Missouri, Columbia).

County, Missouri, who wanted to escape. The escape took place. Missouri authorities asked that Eells be extradited back to Missouri from Illinois for the Lewis County freedom escape. However, Governor Ford of Illinois refused to extradite Eells on the grounds there was not enough evidence he was involved.[39]

Alanson Work had been a professor at Marion College and had moved to Quincy, Illinois, to teach at Dr. David Nelson's new college there. In July of 1841 Work brought two of his students with him — George Thompson and James Burr — to Marion County to help entice slaves from four different farms to escape.[40]

During this time Missouri was also experiencing a number of slave kidnappings. These were white persons who would take a bondsperson from their owner and sell them to another slave owner. Many times these bondspersons would be kidnapped and taken to the large slave markets in New Orleans. These kidnappers would oftentimes tell the slaves they would take them to Canada for their ultimate freedom in order to entice them away. Along with these kidnappings and other abolitionist activities, slave owners in Marion County and other northeast Missouri counties had warned their bondspersons to be on the lookout for kidnappers. Emma Knight was a former bondswoman in the neighboring county of Monroe and she said in her Federal Writer's Project slave interview that her mistress told her if any bondsperson would run away then someone would "kill them" after they had made their escape. She said the bondspersons in the area were always scared when someone "strange" came along.[41]

When Work, Thompson and Burr approached these bondspersons they were unfamiliar with them and they thought they might be kidnappers. The bondsmen notified their owners of this suspicious activity and Work, Thompson and Burr were arrested. This unfortunate trio were tried and sentenced to twelve years in prison. This trial showed how the sometimes tortured justice system in a slave state worked when Black people were involved. Since the testimony of a Black person couldn't be used in a court of law against any white person the state's case against Work, Thompson and Burr would fall apart without these bondsmen's testimony. The court got around this by having white persons testify what the bondsmen had told them. Clearly this was hearsay testimony and in many courts this type of testimony would not have been permitted.

Work, Thompson and Burr were pardoned before they served their complete terms. John Clemens, Mark Twain's father, served on the original jury that convicted this abolitionist trio.[42]

However, as William "Jerry" Henry showed, the bondspersons of Marion County did not need any help from white abolitionists in escaping from Missouri. In 1859 a free Black man was jailed in Palmyra for trying to get bondspersons to run away from bondage. Two bondsmen belonging to Captain Silas Clinton of Marion County left their captivity on two horses in the middle of the night. One rode a sorrel mare and the other a dark-colored horse. It was not sure if they headed across the Mississippi into Illinois or if they went straight north into Iowa.[43] A large escape of bondspersons occurred in Palmyra when eleven bondspersons eluded capture and made it to freedom.[44]

Four bondsmen from Marion County were chased into Henry County, Iowa, by slave hunters. The bondsmen proved to be too wily for the slave hunters and the slavers lost the trail of the Marion County men. It was believed that the quartet made it to Canada and to their ultimate freedom. Because of its location so close to Illinois and Iowa, Marion County had a history of slaves escaping in the night, never to be seen again.[45]

One of the local newspapers in Marion County, the *Palmyra Weekly Whig*, often lamented about the large number of slave escapes from northeast Missouri in the last half of the decade of the 1850s. If a good rowboat could be secured the bondsperson could make it across the Mississippi River. Slave patrols along the Mississippi made sure all small vessels such as skiffs, rowboats and such were locked up at night so any escaping bondsperson could not use them for fleeing from Missouri to freedom across the river. The owners of such vessels would be fined if such crafts were not locked-up.

If it wasn't possible to make it across the Mississippi by small water craft then the bondspersons could walk north or ride north on a horse and they could find themselves on the border of free state Iowa. There is a peninsula formed on the southern border of the Hawkeye state with the Mississippi forming the right arm of this land mass and the much smaller Des Moines River forming the left arm. The Des Moines River has a number of spots in it that were easily forded by a horse and that could even be forded by foot if necessary. It is not certain how Isaac McDaniel, a free Black man, orchestrated the escape of his bonded wife and five other bondspersons in the fall of 1856, but they managed to avoid being discovered and made their way out of the county.[46]

When Missouri slaves escaped into Iowa slave owners would advertise not only in Missouri newspapers but also in Iowa newspapers. In May of 1846, seven months before Iowa was admitted as a state, Lucy made her escape from Waterloo in Clark County, Missouri. She was described in the slave advertisement in the *Keokuk* (Iowa) *Argus* as being about 36 years old and very stout and heavy made. The ad said "It is believed that she will be conducted to the territory of Iowa in the direction of Keosauqua or beyond that place to a settlement of free negroes, that was set free by Meirs living in Tully, Lewis County, Missouri some years ago." It was also noted that the slaver would pay "a liberal reward and pay all reasonable expenses."[47]

Because of the frequent escapes of bondspersons in Marion County and abolitionist activities the slavers doubled their efforts to have a vigilant slave patrol in the county even up until when the Civil War was going on. The slave patrollers would make sure all the bondspersons in the county were accounted for and would look for any who may be attempting to escape. They were also on the lookout for any suspicious whites who may be abolitionists. William Black, a bondsman who spent most of his life in Marion County or the surrounding area, said in his FWP interview, "Durin de war we could not leave de master's house to go to de neighbors without a pass. If we didn't have a pass de paddyrollers would get us and kill us or take us away." Black also told of an incident in his sisters' life that she told many years after slavery times. At age thirteen his sister was sold to a mean man. At Christmastime the master was extremely drunk, and probably trying to sexually assault his sister, and he hit at his sister. She related, "I ducked and run 'round de house so fast I burnt de grass 'round dat house and I know dere ain't no grass growing dere yet!"[48]

One escape in northeast Missouri electrified the region as it involved a gunfight. In August of 1854 in Monroe County, located next to Marion County, three bondspersons made their escape to freedom. The trio included two males and one female. They were obviously headed for Iowa on fleet horses and well armed. They proceeded north from Monroe County and made it through Shelby County but were spotted in Knox County, Missouri, about forty miles from the Iowa border. A firefight ensued with the Black men dismounting from their horses and firing at their pursuers. The slave posse managed to capture the Black woman and wound one of the Black men. However, the two Black men managed to escape and hopefully got away permanently.[49]

Promoters of Missouri settlements along the Missouri River which were more to the interior of the state used to proclaim that few of their slaves escaped as compared to those settlements along the Mississippi River. They encouraged slave owners who wished to move to Missouri to settle along the Missouri Valley and they would suffer fewer losses of their "chattel." They claimed that slaves along the Mississippi were too close to freedom with only the waters of the Mississippi to keep a slave at home while those in the interior had to navigate many miles and were less likely to try and escape. Even Orion Clemens, older brother of Sam Clemens (whose nom de plume was Mark Twain), wrote a chamber of commerce-like promotional piece telling slave owners to settle in Hannibal where their property would be secure from runaways. Clemens incorrectly wrote that slaves were safer along the Mississippi and that ten slaves escaped from the Missouri River Valley to every one slave from the Mississippi River Valley. However, in 1860, after spending time in Keokuk and Muscatine, Iowa, Clemens changed his politics to Republican and became an anti-slavery man. Following the lead of his mentor in St. Louis, Judge Edward Bates, Clemens stumped all over northern Missouri for Abraham Lincoln. Many thought he was a dreaded abolitionist. He was rewarded after Lincoln's successful election by becoming the Secretary of the Nevada Territory. In 1861 his younger brother Sam accompanied him out to that territory.[50]

Missouri was a major terminus for many steamship lines. With two major rivers—the Mississippi on its eastern boundary, and the Missouri slicing through it mid-section—the steamboat trade in Missouri was a huge business. These steamboat lines in the Show-me state hired both free and slave labor. Naturally, because of the nature of the business, steamboats provided excellent opportunities for escape.

Laws passed in Missouri were similar to those in other slave states. The steamship companies were liable for fines and remuneration to the slave owner if any bondsperson escaped using the steamship company for a means of transporting the bondspersons to freedom. Steamboat lines were to use "due diligence" to keep any slave from escaping. They were to keep slaves from booking passage, stowing away or finding employment on the steamboats to facilitate their escapes.

Free Blacks helped many of the enslaved in assisting them to escape. They often knew which steamship captains would hire slave labor without the proper paperwork. The job of fireman, the man who stoked the boiler on the steamship, was especially hard to fill. The fireman had to work in very hot, uncomfortable, and dangerous conditions and the boilers were prone to explode in which case the firemen were sure to be killed. To fill this position sometimes steamship captains would hire someone without the proper papers—someone they knew was probably a runaway slave. Slaves could legally work on the steamships with the proper lease forms from their "masters." Terms would be set out in the lease form usually prohibiting the slave from working in any free state. An amount would be agreed upon to pay the "master" and the steamship would be required to feed and clothe the slave for a specific period of time, and length of service to the steamship line would be agreed upon. This was the standard procedure for these kinds of leases for slave labor. The slave of course would be paid nothing for their labor. If they were part of the wait staff they might receive tips, which they could keep. There was a going market for forged lease papers for slaves. For about twenty-five dollars, a bondsperson, if they had the money, could purchase forged papers in St. Louis or other riverboat towns allowing them to work on the steamship and hopefully make a successful escape. If a slave had the money, papers could sometimes be secured in Black-operated boardinghouses along the river that catered to the Black steamboat men. These places became the center of the Black boatmen's off-the-boat social life. In St. Louis such a boardinghouse was run by Peter Charlesville and his wife Leah. Sometimes runaway slaves at such boardinghouses could possibly find someone who could procure forged free papers or forged passes that allowed a slave to work on a steamboat bound for a free state.[51] Also, undoubtedly these Black boardinghouses would at times hide fleeing bondspersons on their way to freedom in the north or Canada.

Some bondspersons who were almost white were known to escape on the steamships by posing as "free white workmen" or as passengers. The steamboat of course would provide the fastest means of transportation for getting away from any slave posse or slave hunters.

A reward of one hundred dollars was offered for the return of Henry, who had run away from the steamship the *St. Paul*. He had made his escape in the fall of 1847. His St. Louis master advertised him as a runaway.[52] Septo, a fifty year old male, escaped on the steamboat *Diana* in the spring of 1840. Unfortunately, he was captured in Arkansas in Phillips County on the Mississippi River. He was jailed and an advertisement was issued by the Sheriff of Phillips County for his St. Louis master to come and get him and pay the cost of his incarceration.[53]

It might seem odd that a bondsperson wishing to escape slavery would take a steamship that was heading south. However, many times those wishing to escape slavery took whatever opportunity was presented to them. A bondsperson could head south and then try to catch a boat heading north. Sometimes the slave patrols were less suspicious of Blacks trying to find employment or boarding on steamships that were headed south. Once in Memphis or New Orleans or any such terminus a steamship could be boarded heading north. In the case of Septo it is not clear if he had illegally managed to obtain work on the steamship or if he had merely stowed away and was caught by the captain of the *Diane*. Perhaps Septo was trying to visit a spouse, relative or a friend who had been shipped to Arkansas or Louisiana before he was caught. Many times bondspersons did not clearly understand the opportunities for freedom to the north or perhaps they just didn't want to move to the north. In these cases they would often use steamboats to escape and they would live and work on them for as long as they could. There are instances where bondspersons worked illegally on steamboats for years without making a serious attempt for permanent freedom in the northern states or Canada.

John Hatfield was a free Black man who worked as a barber on steamship lines on the Ohio River and the Mississippi River. He traveled through Missouri waters on many occasions. Because John was a Black man, even though he was free, he was often treated like a slave. Many of the steamboat ports he traveled greatly restricted the slave boat workers and free Blacks from leaving their boats when they docked. Once while docking in New Orleans he visited a friend in the Crescent City. He knew when the steamship was to leave and his plan was to simply go on board minutes before the boat left. However, the steamship was delayed in leaving by a day. John got to the boat a day early and was arrested, having committed no crime except being a Black man. He had iron handcuffs put on him and he was taken to jail. The conditions in the jail were terrible. John was even charged an excessive rate for the meager amount of food he was given in the jail. Fortunately, since he had a job and had saved a lot of money he was able to pay for his room and board in the jail and managed to get out.

Even though he was a Free Black man, because of conditions like this John decided to make his way to Canada where he could be really free — not just in name only. He decided to go to Canada by means of the steamship. He made his way to Cincinnati via the boats and then overland to Amherstburg in Canada. This was a town with about 500 Black citizens in it and they were prospering finely. One thing John Hatfield was very proud of was the fact that as a free Black man he had helped liberate many bondspersons. In Cincinnati he saw a situation where thirteen Blacks were holed-up in a cellar by slave-hunters. John watched the man guarding them and he carefully escorted two out at a time until all were free of the slave-hunters. John managed to take them to Michigan but the bondspersons were all captured again. However, a freedom-loving judge let them all go and they made their way to Canada.

On another occasion slave hunters were closing in on a young woman and she was smuggled into John's house. He dressed her in the clothes of a young man who boarded at John's house. John and the young lady, dressed in men's clothing, and who John addressed as "Jim," left his house amidst the slave hunters who were in the area looking for the young lady. She made her way to Canada and freedom. While living in Canada John was able to open up his house to as many as fifteen fugitives at one time. He helped as many as 27 runaways get started in their new life in Canada. John Hatfield stated that he had as many friends as ever a man had in the United States, both Black and white, but because of the oppressive laws there were against him he was forced to take residence up in Canada.[54]

Bondsman Abraham was hired out by his master to work on the steamship *Rozetta* bound for New Orleans in the fall of 1841. Abraham and his master lived in Hannibal, Missouri. His position was to be a fireman on the ship. While the steamer was taking on wood at the Flower Island in Arkansas, Abraham walked away from slavery. However, he did not get far and was captured near Osceola in Mississippi County in Arkansas. He was jailed and the sheriff ran an advertisement for Abraham's master to come and get him and pay for his jail costs. It is interesting to note that in the advertisement for Abraham they misspelled the name of the town he was from and said it was Hamilton in Marion County, Missouri, instead of Hannibal.[55]

A young bondswoman was found to have boarded the steamship the *Aubrey* at St. Joseph, Missouri, in 1855. The watchman for the river ship brought her on board. It was not sure if she went on board on her own will to escape slavery or if there might have been some sort of a romantic relationship. The watchman brought her on board without the knowledge of the ship's Captain. The official statement given said the watchman had "decoyed" her on board, which would indicate he was going to sell her downriver at some point. However, the watchman might have concocted this story in order to save the young lady from any retribution from her master. It is not known what the watchman's real motives were in this affair. Those in power in slave states were reluctant to admit that any "slave" would ever want to escape from their masters. When the young lady was discovered the boat was near Boonville, Missouri. She was put off in that city and jailed and her master was telegraphed about her whereabouts. The watchman was fired immediately. The steamship line was fined $450 which they paid without complaint. The slave master gave the steamship line a full release against any claims against them for this matter. The rather hefty fine was probably due to the fact that St. Joseph was involved in the affair. Because St. Joseph was so close to the situation in Kansas the judiciary in the state of Missouri was very cognizant of the potential for an escape into that territory.[56]

It may do well to look at the life of William Wells Brown who escaped bondage via a steamboat from Missouri. Brown's life experiences were in some cases somewhat similar to many who escaped bondage. However, after Brown freed himself from oppression he went on to do some amazing things and set the literary world on its ear.

Brown was born in Lexington, Kentucky, in 1814 and was given the name William. His mother was named Elizabeth and she and William were close all his life. William's father was George Higgins, a relative to his master. His master, who was a physician, moved his farming operation to about 40 miles north of St. Charles, Missouri. On the farm mainly tobacco and hemp were grown. The physician had about 40 slaves of which 25 were field hands. William worked inside the house and his mother was a field hand. Even at an early age William determined that he should not be a slave all his life and he hoped to take himself, his mother and his half brothers and sisters out of bondage.[57]

Brown's master moved his operation again, this time to nearby St. Louis. On his farm the master hired a man from New England to be his overseer. Brown noted that in his experience New Englanders made the cruelest overseers. As was the custom in Missouri, Brown was hired out by his master to another man, an extremely cruel master, a drunkard who treated his dozen slaves very badly. After five months Brown could take it no more and plotted his escape. He took off for the woods and stayed away for as long as he could. Finally one day he heard bloodhounds and they treed him. He was taken to jail and then back to the master who had leased him. Brown was severely beaten with a whip and then taken to a smoke house. While he was in the smoke house tobacco stems were set on fire, causing the smoke house to be filled with thick dense smoke. Brown was severely coughing and sneezing. He was then immediately put to work in the fields.[58]

Fortunately for William this leased master, being the drunken sot he was, failed in business and Brown was leased to go to work on a steamboat line. Brown loved the work as did many others in his condition. He stated at the time it was the most pleasant work he had ever done. The freedom of moving up and down the river meeting new people was a great stimulus to Brown and his creative mind. The steamship he was on moved between St. Louis and Galena, Illinois. However, his lease ran out and he was rented to another cruel master in St. Louis who owned a large hotel with a large staff of slaves. This master was a northerner and one of the cruelest slave owners William had ever seen. This master once beat a girl so badly that even the hotel guests asked him to quit beating the girl as her screams and sobbing made them uncomfortable.

Brown was mercifully removed from another slave hellhole and was sent to work for Elijah P. Lovejoy, the kindest master Brown ever had. Lovejoy was editor of the *St. Louis Times* and what little "book learning" Brown received at this time came from Lovejoy,[59] although it was illegal to teach any slave to read and write at this time in Missouri.

When he was working for Lovejoy a group of young thugs attacked Brown when he went to exchange type at another newspaper. Brown was injured and lost his position at the *St. Louis Times*. Lovejoy went on to become a martyr for the abolitionist cause. A free Black man named Francis McIntosh was a steward on the steamboat *Flora*. Two policemen came on board the ship and tried to arrest two drunken crewmen. McIntosh interfered with these arrests and the crewmen got away. McIntosh was arrested and marched to jail. When they got close to the jail McIntosh stabbed both policemen, killing one and seriously wounding the other. A mob captured McIntosh and he was burned to death in the middle of St. Louis. Lovejoy condemned this action. A mob came and destroyed his press in St. Louis. Lovejoy moved to nearby Alton, Illinois, which was north of St. Louis on the other side of the Mississippi. Mobs attacked him in Alton on three different occasions. On the final attack he was shot and killed while trying to defend his press and building on November 7, 1837.[60]

After he recovered from this attack, Brown was once again leased to a steamship as a waiter. The ship was named the *Enterprise*. The ship often plied the upper Mississippi in Free states but Brown did not escape as he wanted to find the right situation that would allow him to free himself, his mother and his half sister and brothers. Brown would tell of how his mother had left the work fields to nurse him only to be whipped for doing her motherly duties.

Brown was then hired out to a slave trader who took enslaved humans from St. Louis down the Mississippi to New Orleans. This was a dreadful job for him as he had to watch to make sure all were secured with chains. If they were not, many times some became so distraught by their circumstance and felt there was no more hope in their lives that they would try and jump overboard to get relief from their horrible condition by committing suicide. Brown had to ready his poor fellow bondspersons for market. He had to pluck out all gray hairs and to blacken hair to make them look younger so as to bring more at the various slave pens. They stopped at Natchez, Mississippi, and other places and sold slaves on the way down to New Orleans. Brown found the whole situation sickening. When they got back to St. Louis he tried to get out of his lease but his master said no and the entire nauseous process was repeated down to New Orleans and back to St. Louis. After a year was up Brown was out of this slave lease and he concluded this was the longest year of his life. To be part of this sickening chain of human misery was too much to bear.

Brown had met with his sister who was being sold to Natchez and she told him to try and make an escape on his own. He would never see his sister again. Brown decided to escape and take his mother with him. He was sent to St. Louis to find employment. He rescued his mother from her master and they headed to the Mississippi River. Brown found an unattended skiff and managed to make it across the river. With only the North Star to guide them and completely unfamiliar with Illinois, Brown and his mother managed to push on to the great white north. However, as so often happened to escaping bondspersons, their provisions ran out. Even though they didn't trust any whites they had to stop at a farm house and ask for something to eat. Fortunately, they were well fed and the farmer and his wife even gave them provisions.

The Browns traveled on but they were soon captured by three men. Brown found out he had a two hundred dollar reward for his person. After the men had captured Brown and his mother they held a prayer service with the bible and Brown bitterly noted they were heading back to the land of whips and chains and the bible.

When they got back to St. Louis he and his mother were separated and Brown would never see her again. Brown's master chastised him and said he told him to go to St. Louis to find work not to go clear to Canada! Brown was sold to another master and his old master fortunately didn't tell him that he had tried to escape. This made the new master less suspicious and more willing to let Brown work again on the steamboats and his plan to finally escape slavery might finally be realized. Brown's old master didn't tell the new master that he had tried to escape not out of any kindness, but so he could fetch a higher dollar. Slaves who tried to escape were known as runners and this dropped their asking price. Slave owners and slave trader were constantly cheating each other.

William Wells Brown was sometimes very bitter towards the Christian religion. He saw the cooperation that organized white Christian religion provided to the slave owner to make slavery possible. He had seen masters who went to the same church as their slaves and then beat their bondspersons unmercifully for a trifling offense. Brown commented on a female slave who was being sold at a slave market and repeated the words the auctioneer used, "How much for this woman. She is a good cook, good washer, good obedient servant. She has got religion."

Brown commented that in Missouri, as in other slave states, the religious teaching consisted of teaching the slave that he or she must never strike a white man; that God made him or her a slave; and that, when whipped, he or she must not find fault-for the bible says, "He that knoweth his master's will and doeth it not, shall be beaten with many stripes." Brown noted that such slave owners find such religion "very profitable to them."[61]

Brown's new master had him work as a domestic and the master's wife took particular interest in him. She wanted to see him get married — probably to keep him from trying to escape. Brown feigned interest. His master's wife even purchased the young lady in whom Brown had supposedly shown interest. He needed to get back on a steamboat to flee from bondage. He had to act like he was perfectly contented with his life.

The master owned a steamship, the *Chester*, and he loaded up his family and Brown and his other servants and went on a trip up and down the Mississippi. The master asked Brown if he had ever been in a free state. Brown answered that he had but he didn't like it. Finally, the *Chester* docked in Cincinnati. Brown knew it was now or never. He walked off the ship, never to look back. He hid in the woods and vowed he would never ask for help from anyone, white or Black. He would not take any chances of being turned in to the authorities. He traveled by night and hid during the day. On his fourth day of escaping he ran out of provisions. He found some corn and was able to go on. He had no idea where he was at. His only navigational tool was the North Star.

Then the weather turned against him in a most inhumane way. Freezing rain began to pelt his body in a most merciless manner. He traveled for two more days. His malnourished body fell prey to a deep cold in his lungs and his feet were frostbitten. Like so many before him he would have to make a decision that could mean everlasting freedom or everlasting slavery. But who could he trust? Brown knew he was going to have to seek shelter and get some food in his body or he could easily perish in the elements. He found out later he was near Dayton, Ohio. He watched as several persons passed by him on the road. Finally, he saw a man who was leading a white horse. Brown knew this could be his last chance. He approached the man and asked him for help.

The man told him he was in pro-slavery territory. The man said he would go get a wagon and take Brown to safety. The man left. Was this a trap? Was the man going to get the local authorities and have him arrested as a fugitive slave? He waited for a couple of hours, his heart pounding. Should he just run away from what could be a trap? Finally the man, true to his word, came with a covered wagon that would hide this transaction. Brown would learn this man's name was Wells Brown.

Wells Brown took William Brown into his home for about two weeks. Wells and his wife, both Quakers, fed and clothed Brown and got him back on his feet. He was treated with the most kindness. The Quaker asked Brown what he was going to call himself and he said William would need more than one name now that he was a free man. William said he would let the Quaker name him. Wells Brown said he would be honored if William took his name. William said he would take the Quaker's name Wells Brown and add his own first name William. From now on he would be known as William Wells Brown.[62]

The Quakers gave William some food to eat on his way to Cleveland and he went on his way to find the city on Lake Erie. He ran out of food on the way but found some sympathetic folks who fed him. He made it to Cleveland in three days. William Wells Brown found work quickly at a hotel the Mansion House as a waiter.

Brown then found work on a steamship that plied Lake Erie. He found that he could help other slaves escape bondage into Canada. He usually tried to take four or five fugitives with him from Cleveland to Canada. He immersed himself in the anti-slavery campaign, subscribing to anti-slavery newspapers and reading all he could on the subject. While living in Cleveland Brown met and wooed Elizabeth Schooner with whom he married and they started a family. After two years of residing in Cleveland, William Brown decided to move his family to Buffalo, New York. Buffalo was a terminus for the steamship lines and it was far easier for a worker in the steamship trade to find work there than in Cleveland. Also, at this time Buffalo had a larger Black population than Cleveland, which, after the navigational season on Lake Erie, made it easier to locate work there.⁶³

Brown continued his work on the Underground Railroad in Buffalo. He participated in the capture of Bacon Tate, a slave trader from Nashville, Tennessee. Tate had trailed a Black man named Stanford to Saint Catherines, Ontario, Canada. He kidnapped the man and his family, bound and gagged them, and brought them back to the United States with plans to return them to slavery in Tennessee. Brown and a group of about fifty other Blacks from Buffalo found out about this and captured Tate and the Stanfords. A melee involving 60 whites occurred over this incident but the Stanfords were taken back to Canada safe and sound.⁶⁴

Brown's house became a station on the Underground Railroad for Blacks in Buffalo. He continued to escort fugitives into Canada via the steamships. In 1842, during one navigational season on Lake Erie from May to December, William Wells Brown transported 69 fugitives to freedom. In 1843 Brown visited a village in Canada named Malden in which he counted that there were 17 people whom he had helped escape.⁶⁵

In 1843 Brown left the steamship trade and became a lecturer for the New York Anti-Slavery Society. In May of 1847 he was hired by the Massachusetts Anti-Slavery Society. Some of his assignments were before tough crowds. In 1848 at an anti-slavery meeting in Cape Cod, Massachusetts, Brown was heckled by some hooligans yelling, "Pass out that nigger."⁶⁶

In 1847 his famous book *Narrative of William W. Brown, a Fugitive Slave, Written by Himself* was published. The book sold well and established Brown as a major literary figure. In 1849, Brown traveled to Paris for a Peace Conference where he met the literary great Victor Hugo, who befriended him. Brown then moved to England, where he was treated as an important author and lecturer. In England he published his famous novel *Clotel; or, The President's Daughter: A Narrative of Slave Life in America*. This novel dealt with slave Sally Hemmings and her relationship with President Thomas Jefferson.⁶⁷

Former bondsman William Wells Brown. This illustration was found in his last book, *My Southern Home, or The South and Its People*, published in 1880. Brown escaped from slavery in Missouri to become one of the most eloquent speakers in the north against this horrible institution. Known as William when he was a slave, a Quaker man who helped him escape said he would be honored if William took his name of Wells Brown. From then on he became known as William Wells Brown. William also helped many bondspersons escape from slavery when he lived in Cleveland and Buffalo. Forced to leave the United States because of the Fugitive Slave Act of 1850 he sailed for Europe. Brown's autobiography told of the evils of slavery and he followed this book with other literary works. He became a worldwide literary phenomenon and was friends with many of the greats in the literary world of that time including Victor Hugo. After the Civil War concluded Brown practiced medicine in the Boston area (used by permission, State Historical Society of Missouri, Columbia).

While in England several benefactors purchased Brown's freedom, making it possible for him to return to the United States, which he did in 1854. Once he returned to the states he continued writing and lecturing. He published plays, travel books and three books on Black history. Brown passed away in 1884, his place firmly established in American history.

For the most part the Christian clergy in slave states were of little help in alleviating the suffering of the American slave or in helping them to escape bondage. One large factor in this was the fact that many of the clergy owned slaves. Some Christian clergy were afraid to speak out against slavery for fear of offending some of their minister brethren who owned slaves.

In 1851 the American and Foreign Anti-Slavery Society estimated that 16,346 ministers of the Methodist, Presbyterian, Baptist and Episcopal faith owned slaves. In the northern Free states a few bold members of the clergy and laypersons formed the backbone of the abolitionist movement in the Congregational, Unitarian, Methodist and Quaker religions.

However, most northern clergy were as timid as the southern clergy about alienating their parishioners with the cause of abolition or about providing ways slaves could escape bondage or helping them escape bondage. In a letter of August 1851, Lewis Tappan, a wealthy abolitionist who financed many of the causes' programs, wrote to the *British and Foreign Anti-Slavery Reporter* that the American clergy of the north acted "as if they were indifferent or hostile to the cause of freedom.... Their ecclesiastical connections with southern ministers, their deference to political men in high office ... their unwillingness to offend rich parishioners in trade with the south or associated in political parties with southern men, are the reasons why many are silent, equivocal or opposed to the cause of abolition."[68]

The American Bible Society was aghast when abolitionists suggested bibles be sent to slaves in the American South. Lewis Tappan called the organization a "pro-slavery institution." Even in the north ministers such as Thomas Wentworth Higginson in Newburyport, Massachusetts, lost their pulpits for speaking out against slavery and supporting the abolitionist cause. Samuel J. May, the Unitarian minister who was involved in the "Jerry Rescue," stated that of the some 30,000 Christian ministers in the United States "not one in a hundred" openly condemned slavery or "lifted a finger" to protect a fugitive slave.[69]

Dr. John Doy reported that when he was in the Platte county jail in Platte City, Missouri, a young bondsman was brought into the lock-up to be sold in one of the gangs going to the deep south. He said his master and father were the same person and he was a preacher. He said the preacher had had sex with the young man's mother and he was the result of this union. He said the preacher's wife was relentless in criticizing the minister for this sexual liaison years ago. The preacher got tired of his wife's accusations and sold off the young man's mother and then sold his own son to a hellhole life of 15-hour work days on the plantations of the deep south.[70]

In 1858 Galusha Anderson was called to be the minister to the Second Baptist Church in St. Louis and he did much evangelizing throughout the city to both the white and Black laity. After the Civil War the Reverend gained fame as an important theologian. Anderson was an abolitionist and as such was asked to leave his church. However, he stayed on and did what he could to advance the cause. During the Civil War, when the Rebel Army was near St. Louis, Anderson learned that his name was on their death list.

In 1859 a group of eastern ministers were visiting St. Louis having previously been in New Orleans and were crooning over the hospitality they had been shown in the Crescent

City. The next day the Reverend Anderson said he would show them the sights of his city. They first went to the Mercantile Library with its art treasures and tasteful rooms and beautifully bound books. Then Anderson said he would take the group to the slave and auction pens to see other side of southern cities.

First, Anderson took them to Lynch's slave pen, which was only a few doors down from his church. The slaves who were to be sold were in a jail-like structure with a bare earthen floor. No beds, just three wooden benches. Both men and women were in the same room with no privacy. One woman begged the group to buy her before she was sold down south to New Orleans. This solemn group then went to the slave pen at 5th and Myrtle streets.

At this slave pen and auction house the specialty was children aged five years to 16 years old. This slave pen was larger than Lynch's but again both boys and girls were mixed together with no privacy. Screams of parents forced away from their children were heard. Anderson noted that this slave pen did a brisk business. One beautiful mulatto girl of 16 was being auctioned off with the notation that she had the blood of a United States senator running through her veins. Anderson said these repulsive and heart-breaking scenes were repeated at every auction. Some of the eastern Christian clergymen in his group were almost to the point of being physically ill. Seeing little five year old children being torn away from their mothers' side and then made to stand alone sobbing with little food and then auctioned off like livestock was unbearable. It would be hard to imagine that the entire group of ministers didn't go back east as hardened abolitionists.

Three years after this event in 1862 a Black drayman who had been around St. Louis forever was seen chuckling and talking to himself. He was full of merriment this day. His employer asked him what was the cause of this outburst. The drayman, who could hardly contain himself, said, "Strange tings happen des day!"

The slave pen at 5th and Myrtle had been overtaken by the Union Army and turned into a prison for Confederates and secessionists. His boss asked the drayman what strange things. The drayman answered, "You kno's dat slave-pen, corner of 5th and Myrtle?" "Yes" "Well de col'ed folks used to carry in tings fo der chillen to eat. Dis mawnin, boss I seed white folks carring in tings for der folks to eat. Ha! Ha! Strange things happen des days."[71]

In the fall of 1851 George Bell, a former bondsman from Fulton, Missouri, arrived safe and sound in Canada. This fact was announced in the Canadian newspaper the *Voice of the Fugitive*. This particular newspaper always called out the bondsperson's former "keeper" and told them not to worry anymore as their "property" was safe and sound and now in Canada. *Voice* editor Henry Bibb, himself a former bondsman, proudly announced that "We are happy to inform our friends that we are having fresh arrivals ... everyday."[72]

Two months earlier Bibb had announced that he had several bondsmen arrive from Louisiana, Kentucky and Missouri. He said these men came from "the land of whips and chains, to the land where colored men are free."[73]

Slaver owners were very paranoid about slave uprisings and the work of abolitionists. In September of 1855 the slave holders in the area around Columbia, Missouri, held a meeting. There was a rumor going around that a certain slave in Howard County was supplying other slaves with poison. It proved to be untrue. They were also concerned that certain peddlers coming through the area were abolitionists. A large worry at the meeting was that a free Black man named Squire and a bondsman named Jeff were aiding and abetting and providing a harbor for runaway bondspersons.[74]

Another grand scheme pointing to the paranoia of the slave holder was reported by

Hattie Mathews and Charlie Richardson. Hattie said her mother's slave owner was afraid his slaves were plotting against him so he installed a polly parrot to spy on the slaves and repeat any untold escape or other plots against the master. Charlie Richardson, also a slave in Missouri, reported that his master had a parrot to spy on his slaves and try to uncover any escape or insurrection plots. Richardson's master was so afraid he would not let any bondsperson feed the parrot lest they try to poison it. Also, the parrot wouldn't accept any food from any Black person.[75]

Sometimes this slave owner paranoia masked real problems such as the kidnapping and reselling of slaves. Sometimes bondspersons were kidnapped and the slave owner was very quick to blame the "evil" abolitionists. This was the case when Letitia, who was 16 or 17 years old, had just given birth. She left her baby and didn't take any of her clothes when she went missing. Her master thought this was the work of a vile abolitionist. However, I believe common sense would say if the young lady left her baby and didn't take any of her spare clothes that she was probably kidnapped to be sold elsewhere.[76]

Many times newspaper slave advertisements in Missouri proclaimed that abolitionists had "decoyed" their bondspersons away from the slave owner. However, very few of these incidents actually occurred. It was declared illegal to decoy or carry away any slave from the state of Missouri. The offender would receive five years of imprisonment. The inspectors of the State Penitentiary reported in 1854 that there were only seven inmates incarcerated for this crime. In 1858 there were six and in 1860 ten inmates were such prisoners. All had been convicted of "attempts" so it is not known how many actually succeeded in this "crime." It was not possible to tell how many of these prisoners actually were abolitionists and how many were just thieves trying to make a quick buck.[77]

George Bollinger remembered that as a youth he was to be sold but his "master" was talked out of it. However, the "master" set his sights on Bollinger's father. His father had made baskets at night and sold them when he could and had accumulated a handsome amount of money. When he heard he was to be sold to a far away place he got his money and took off, never to be seen again by the "master" or Bollinger's family. They heard he went to Indiana; however, nobody knew for sure if he survived after the Civil War.[78]

Benjamin Miller had a good business built up as a slave in St. Louis. He was in the boot and shoemaker trade and his partner was a free Black man. Miller's "master" received a tidy sum for the time of $120 per year for his labor. Miller could have been making $220 per year as a free man. On top of all this he was buying his freedom from his master and had paid him $380 and only owed $280 for his freedom. However, as often happened in cases like this, Miller received the information that his master was going sell him after he had paid for his freedom. A slave or free Black man had no rights in a slave state such as Missouri and Miller would not have been in a position to sue his dishonest "master" in the courts.

Miller took off and made his way to Canada and settled around the London, Ontario, area. When he got to the great white north he continued his trade as a boot and shoemaker. He had accumulated almost $1,800 in property while in Canada. He had managed to make it north with his wife and children. He had eight children who were still living in Canada. He had lost 10 children. He had buried three children in St. Louis while living there and the rest had been lost while living in Canada.

Miller also served as a minister of the gospel to his people without pay while in Ontario. He noted that he had traveled all over the area and those who had escaped slavery were

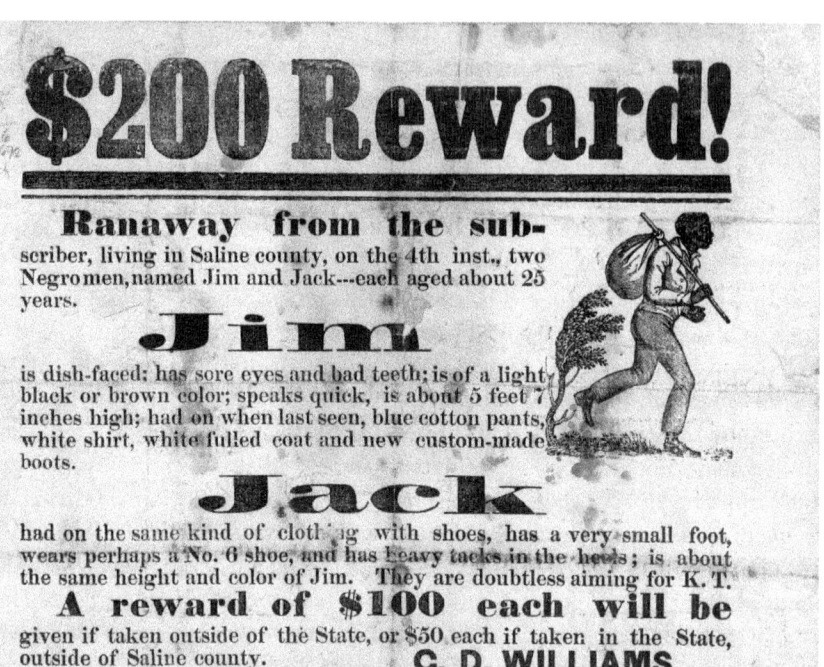

This is a runaway slave poster for two Saline County, Missouri, bondsmen, Jim and Jack, who escaped. It was thought they both were trying to make it to the Kansas Territory in June of 1860. Saline County is roughly in the center of the state in the area known as "Little Dixie." The format of the advertisement was fairly common. There would be a picture of a Black man with his possessions on a stick. The ad would state what the bondsperson was last wearing when they escaped and give a general description of their physical appearance. The bounty was common for the time — $50 if captured in the state of Missouri and $100 if captured outside the state such as in the Kansas Territory. (In today's currency the rewards would have been in the area of $2,500 if captured in the state of Missouri and $5,000 if captured in Kansas.) If the escapees had been from a western county in Missouri the reward would more than likely have been $200 if captured in the K.T. (Kansas State Historical Society).

prospering in Canada and he knew of no one who had to go on welfare. Miller noted the obstacles that the former bondspersons had to overcome once in Canada. One of the biggest was to learn to read and write as adults and gain the basic knowledge one would have learned in school while a child. The other was by the time the bondspersons made it to Canada they had no money at all. However, he noted that the Blacks had made the transition from bondspersons to free persons who contributed to society.[79]

On a Saturday night in June in 1848 three bondspersons two— males and one female— escaped from Columbia, Missouri. They rode away on three fine horses. Several people from town and from the countryside joined in the search for the freedom-seeking trio. For some reason the search centered on Samuel C. Grubbs' place and one of the trio was found there on Sunday night. The female freedom seeker, separated from her two other comrades, became frightened and rode back to her home place and was captured. Woodford, one of the trio, was not captured in this raid and hopefully made his way to freedom. The mob that searched for this trio became convinced that Grubbs, a white man, had decoyed them off their home places. Although there was no evidence to support this claim, Grubbs was arrested. In slave states many were unwilling to admit that their bondspersons would want to escape for freedom unless enticed by a white person. It is not known if Grubbs was ever tried or convicted of any crime.[80]

In the summer of 1839 Jordon escaped bondage from the George Gallaher place in Johnson County, Missouri. Jordon was described in a runaway slave advertisement as being 5'11", well made, about 25 years old and smart and sensible. He took with him a flint lock rifle. What is interesting about this advertisement is that it was placed in the St. Louis *Argus* newspaper and offered a liberal reward. Johnson County is on the western edge of Missouri while St. Louis is on the eastern edge of the state some 220 miles away. That Gallaher was sure that Jordon would be heading east was a fairly safe bet. To the west, some 60 miles away, was Kansas—not yet organized into a territory and thinly settled only by squatters. To head that way would have been probable death from starvation. To go north would have been a long trek to Iowa which had been recently organized but was also only thinly settled. The only logical direction Jordon would have headed would have been to the east. If Jordon had attempted this escape some 15 years later he would have mostly surely headed west instead of east for freedom.[81]

In September of 1851 Allen tried to escape from his place of enslavement in Waverly, Lafayette County, Missouri. Allen was described as being 6'1" and being well dressed. He was unfortunately captured about 80 miles away in Boone County, Missouri, still approximately 130 miles away from the free state of Illinois. Again Allen was heading east. If he had attempted this escape several years later there is a good chance he would have headed west to Kansas as that border would be only 90 miles away.[82]

Even the rich and famous in Missouri were not immune to having their bondspersons escape. Thomas Hart Benton, the United States senator, who dominated Missouri politics for over 30 years, owned slaves. He had inherited many slaves and was one of the few senators that brought slaves with him to Washington, D.C. Benton admitted that he had two bondspersons escape from him. However, he would only acknowledge that the two had been taken from him by abolitionists. He did say he made no attempt to try and recapture them. Benton went onto say that he had "liberated a third who would not go with them."[83] Like most Missouri slave-holders Benton was incapable of understanding that his bondspersons would want to flee from being owned by him. He was in complete denial and could only comprehend that the two had been spirited off by some "evil" abolitionists.

Benton had an interesting career and was an example of how difficult it was for any politician or leader in a slave state such as Missouri to show any restraint or moderation towards slavery. Benton was first elected a United States senator in Missouri in 1820. He was elected for five terms—the first Senator in United States history to ever accomplish this feat. Born in North Carolina to a family of distinction, Benton moved to Tennessee.[84] He served as an aide to Andrew Jackson in the War of 1812 but when Jackson insulted Benton's brother a melee ensued and Benton shot and wounded Jackson. Thereafter he and his brother set up shop in Missouri. A crack shot, Benton was involved in a duel with Charles Lucas on Bloody Island and killed him.[85] There is a quote attributed to Thomas Hart Benton, which goes, "I never quarrel, sir, but I do fight, sir, and when I fight, sir, a funeral follows, sir."

Benton favored the western expansion of the United States but always chafed at how often the subject of slavery impeded the growth of the western part of the United States. About Texas, Benton thought that slavery should not be introduced into areas where it had not been before. He said on the floor of the United States Senate, "...I shall not engage in schemes for the extension into regions where it (slavery) was never known — into the valley of the Rio del Norte, for example, and along a river of two thousand miles in extent, where a slave's face was never seen."[86]

When the Kansas-Nebraska Bill was being discussed, Benton called it "A bungling attempt to smuggle slavery into the territory, up to the Canada line and out to the Rocky Mountains." This was a dramatic comment for a slave state politician to make on the subject of slavery. Most slave state politicians were in lock-step on the subject of always expanding slavery and never abolishing it no matter how outrageous the circumstances. Benton went on to say, when asked why he did not vote sectionally with other slave state United States senators, "I am also a Southern man, but vote nationally on national questions."[87]

Benton was also alarmed at the rhetoric of the slave state congressmen and how it gravitated towards the possible break-up of the Union. This position was often articulated by John C. Calhoun of South Carolina and his nullifiers. Benton began to break with the slave state senators and congressmen who wanted to pass legislation that would ban abolitionist literature from being sent in the United States mail. They also wanted legislation that would not allow petitions that sought to ban slavery to be recognized by legislative bodies. This was done in the Missouri Legislature in 1845 by a vote of 64 to 0 when such a petition was presented to this elective body.[88]

Benton's large ego and sarcasm made him a target of the slavocracy that sought to rule the United States at the time. Another "sin" of Benton in the eyes of the slavers was to deliver an impressive eulogy for John Quincy Adams. Adams was considered the leading abolitionist in the country at that time and had been an esteemed colleague of Benton's. However to slave state congressmen Adams' long-standing fight against slavery made him a non-person in their eyes.[89]

In 1849 Benton stated that he was "against the institution of slavery." Benton's last important act as a United States senator was to oppose the Fugitive Slave Act of 1850.[90] The slavery interests in Missouri and throughout the nation were at this time planted firmly against him. In the United States Senate a Mississippi senator had said Benton was "shielded by his own established cowardice." This Mississippian, when he continued his verbal attacks on Benton, pulled a gun on the Missouri senator when Benton, who was unarmed, went after the Mississippi senator. Other senators broke up this hostility on the floor of the United States Senate.[91]

At this time the state legislatures elected United States senators. Even though Benton was a Democrat and the Missouri legislature was dominated by Democrats Benton was defeated for his sixth term in the election to the United States Senate in 1850. This was an ominous signal to any slave state senator, congressman or legislator not to ever speak out in any way against slavery. If Thomas Hart Benton could be defeated then the slavocracy of the south could have anyone defeated.

Benton ran for congress and served two years in the House of Representatives from 1853 to 1855. However, he lost his bid for reelection when he voted against the Kansas-Nebraska Act of 1854, which expanded slavery into new territories. He ran to be the governor of Missouri in 1856 but was defeated by a large margin by Trusten Polk. Ironically, Polk only served as governor for less than two months when he became the United States senator from Missouri. Polk was ousted from the United States Senate for disloyalty to the Union in 1862. Dying of cancer in 1857, Benton was trying to finish his monumental 16 volume work *Abridgement of the Debates in Congress* when the Dred Scott Supreme Court

Thomas Hart Benton was a powerful United States senator from Missouri. However, when he expressed reservations about slavery and thought the country might be better without the institution he ran afoul of the powerful slave-state senatorial block. Some historians feel that these slave state senators made sure Benton was defeated in the election of 1850 in Missouri. The slave states voted in lockstep to produce laws that made slaves' lives unbearable and escape very difficult. Two future United States presidents, Theodore Roosevelt and John F. Kennedy, wrote about Thomas Hart Benton and his courageous stand. Benton had put the interests of the United States above the interests of his own state thus costing him his political career (used by permission, State Historical Society of Missouri, Columbia).

decision was handed down. He found the decision to be deplorable on common sense and judicial grounds. He turned away from his *Abridgement* project and wrote "with incredible speed" a scholarly book of 130 pages plus a 62 page appendix on the subject of the Dred Scott decision. One biographer described this Dred Scott book of Benton's to be "one of the most meticulous, thoroughly documented, and closely reasoned pieces of historical research ever done on a single subject of constitutional law."[92]

Thomas Hart Benton died in 1858. His memory has been kept alive in many ways—some traditional, others less conventional. His son-in-law John C. Frémont ran unsuccessfully as the presidential candidate for the Republican Party in 1856, the first *major* political party to run on a platform opposed to slavery. His namesake and great-nephew, painter Thomas Hart Benton, born in Neosho, Missouri, was one of the leaders of the regionalist art movement in the United States and gained fame world-wide for his murals and other art work. President Theodore Roosevelt wrote a biography of Senator Benton in 1886. In 1955 President John F. Kennedy wrote of Senator Benton in his Pulitzer Prize–winning book *Profiles in Courage*. Other biographies and magazine articles have also been written about Senator Benton. But perhaps without realizing it thousands of people throughout the world pay homage to Senator Thomas Hart Benton everyday. Benton fought to have Arkansas admitted as a state. In appreciation a county was named after him in Arkansas. The county was named Benton County and the county seat was also named for Thomas Hart Benton and called Bentonville.[93] Ninety-two years after Benton's death Sam Walton opened up Walton's 5 & 10 in Bentonville, Arkansas. As they say, the rest is history. Walton's companies Wal-Mart and Sam's Club, using Bentonville as world-wide headquarters, have become the world's largest employers and largest publicly-held corporation by revenue. Every year thousands of corporation and business leaders throughout the United States and throughout the world make the trek to Bentonville, the town named after a Missouri senator who tried to stop the spread of American slavery at the cost of his own political career.

Many bondspersons escaping from Missouri found Chicago to be a friendly destination city. Going across the Mississippi River and heading to Quincy, Galesburg, or other friendly stations or just freelancing the bondsperson would often wind up in the Windy City. Going north through Iowa and crossing the Mississippi in the Hawkeye state the bondsperson could find their way to Chicago. Also, leaving western Missouri the bondsperson could go to Kansas and make their way to Lawrence or Topeka and then up to Nebraska City in the Nebraska territory and cross the Missouri River. They could proceed onto Tabor, Iowa, Lewis, Grinnell and then cross the Mississippi at Davenport and then the bondsperson could make their way to Chicago.

All along the way the bondsperson, no matter what route they were taking, had to be on the lookout for those who would turn them in for a reward. Once in Chicago there were a number of Black abolitionists who could conceal them and forward them on to Canada. Also, white abolitionists could help. One such Underground Railroad conductor, Philo Carpenter, helped to forward over 200 bondspersons onto Canadian bound vessels. Many of these bondspersons were from Missouri.[94]

Arthur Atkins, whose sisters and father were involved in the Underground Railroad, described in a letter an incident involving a fugitive slave in Chicago dated June 3, 1851. He wrote to his mother, "There is a good deal of excitement here on act. Of a Fugitive Slave being claimed by its masters & the Chicago folks sure to feel inclined to turn out enmasse to rescue I do not think they will get away with him but they may."[95]

Henry and his wife Fanny escaped for freedom from Boone County, Missouri, late in June of 1851. Henry was described as being 26 years of age, 5'10", and 145 pounds. His wife was 22 years old. It is interesting to notice the difference in the rewards offered for each. For Henry, if taken anywhere in the state, the reward was $50. For Fanny, if taken not more than 20 miles from her residence, the reward would be only $10. If Fanny was taken 20 miles from home then the reward was $50. If either was taken out of state as law required then the reward was $100.[96]

Not all bondsperson escapes were for permanent freedom. Sometimes bondspersons would run off to blow off steam. Rachael Goings stated in her Federal Writer's Project interview that she got along with her Missouri "master" okay. However, her mother Cynthy called the master "Damn-O." She hated him for taking her from Arkansas and leaving her twins and their father down there. According to Rachael her mother's father was a full-blooded Cherokee and this caused Cynthy to be "always mad and [have] a mean look in her eye." Rachael continued that, "When she (Cynthy) got her Indian up de white folks let her alone. She usta run off to de woods till she git over it. One time she tuk me and went to de woods an' it was nigh a month fore dey found her — and I wuz nigh dead."[97]

Madison Frederick Ross stated in his FWP interview "My granfathuh was mos'ly Indian an he usta go out into the woods an stay for days at a time. Ole Mastuh always called him Old Yeller Abe — But this one time he ran away — crossed the river ovah heah an' went up to Canada. He usta write tuh Ole Mastuh an' he'd read the lettuhs tuh us." Ross went on to say that during the Civil War he joined the Union Army and played in the band. He served in Arkansas and was mustered out in St. Louis in 1866.[98]

Delicia Patterson said she didn't get along with her master's wife but did with her master. One time she ran off when the mistress criticized her and the master tapped her on the shoulder with a fly swatter. She ran off and hid out in the woods. When hungry she went to the slave cabins and was fed. Master sent people after her and told her he wouldn't bother her again. She came back after two weeks and they left her alone.

At age 15 Delicia was put on the auction block. Judge Miller had a reputation in the county as being the meanest slave-owner in the area. When Miller began bidding for Delicia she said from the auction platform, "Old Judge Miller don't you bid for me, 'cause if you do, I will not live on your plantation, I will take a knife and cut my own throat from ear to ear before I would be owned by you." Judge Miller backed off from the bidding. Delicia's father tried to get his master to buy Delicia. His master said he would not buy her because she was "A sassy niggah."[99]

Esther Easter's master took her from Tennessee to Westport, Missouri, near Kansas City "long before they started fighting about slavery." Her master and his wife used to whip Esther all the time as they did their other slaves. Ester told her master, "you better put me in your pocket (sell me), Master Jim else I'se going to run away. He don't pay no mind, and I don't try to run away 'cause of the whips."

Esther saw what they did to runaways that were caught and as she said, "They wasn't no fooling about it." She continued, "A runaway slave from the Jenkin's plantation was brought back, and there was a public whipping, so's the slaves could see what happens when they tries to get away."

"The runaway was chained to the whipping post, and I was full of misery when I see the lash cutting deep into that boy's skin. He swell up like a dead horse, but he gets over it, only he was never no count for work no more."

When the Civil War started Esther, like many other Missouri slaves, was sent down south to Texas as too many bondspersons were escaping out of Missouri or were being liberated by the Union Army. Of the trip to Texas Esther said it was "wild most of the way." She said they crossed a "big river that's all brown and red looking." This was of course the Red River. When they got to Texas Esther was sold in Bonham, Texas, to another master and she stayed there until the end of the war.[100]

3

Missouri: Hemp and "Little Dixie" Empires

> When Charles Richardson was a child slave in Missouri he said his life was, "no games, no play, only work, [after work we] mostly go to bed. We kids did early. But I wake up lots of times and hear my Ma and Pappy praying for freedom. They do many times."[1]

Unfortunately for the Richardson family the congress and courts in the United States were doing little to help answer their prayers. The Fugitive Slave Act of 1850 greatly inhibited any bondsperson's chances of ever acquiring freedom. When the Kansas-Nebraska Act of 1854 was passed which tried to expand slavery into these territories many in northern free states felt action had to be taken to restrict the grip of the slavocracy in the United States. Since the federal government and the federal judiciary would do nothing to ease slavery's draconian grasp on the United States and her laws, individual states tried their hand at releasing the slavers' influence on her laws.

Vermont was the first to pass a so-called personal liberty law in 1850 in reaction to the restrictive measures of the Fugitive Slave Act of 1850. When the Kansas-Nebraska Act of 1854 was passed many in the north saw these measures as a blatant attempt by slave states to expand slavery and to make sure it was enforced throughout both the north and the south by restricting bondspersons' ability to escape. Between 1855 and 1859 the states of Connecticut, Rhode Island, Massachusetts, Michigan, Maine, Ohio, and Wisconsin passed personal liberty laws which restricted the enforceability of the Fugitive Slave Act of 1850 and the kidnapping of Free Blacks.

These laws offered three provisions: the first was that any alleged fugitive slave had the right to legal counsel. The second was that any Black person arrested and held as a fugitive slave had the right to the writ of habeas corpus and trial by jury and that the kidnapping of free Blacks was punishable by fine and imprisonment. In the third there were also provisions that state jails would not hold any persons accused of being fugitive slaves.[2] It should be noted that none of the free states that bordered Missouri had passed these personal liberty laws. Except for the city of Chicago the rest of Illinois was consistent in supporting the Fugitive Slave Laws.[3]

The courts of the United States during this time gave little hope to families like the Richardsons. The Supreme Court would hear few cases that dealt with the slavery issue and when they did it was a disaster for the bondspersons and abolitionists. The famous Dred Scott case in Missouri was probably the best example of this apathy of the courts in the United States to the plight of the bondspersons.

Dred Scott was a Missouri slave who petitioned the St. Louis Circuit Court for his freedom. This was based upon the fact that he had lived with his master, a doctor in the United States Army, for a time in the free sates of Illinois and Wisconsin. The foundation for his petition was that since he had resided in states where slavery was illegal he must be considered a free man. At this time Missouri had a statute that stated any person Black or white who was wrongfully held as a slave could petition the courts for their freedom. This famous court case was financially supported to some extent by abolitionists but it must be also noted that Dred Scott himself poured a rather substantial amount of money into the legal fees of this case, which was difficult for a slave; he was a lot more than just a pawn in this case as he has been sometimes portrayed.[4]

This case went on a 10 year legal odyssey through state and federal courts. Scott and his wife's ownership changed hands and at times it was unclear who owned them. Finally the case made it all the way to the Supreme Court of the United States—*Dred Scott v. Sandford*. Two days after James Buchanan was sworn in as president of the United States the Supreme Court met to a packed courtroom of journalists and spectators on March 6, 1856. Scott was not in the courtroom but was still a hired-out slave in St. Louis. John F.A. Sanford, whose named had been misspelled on the Supreme Court document, was Scott's "owner" and was languishing away in an insane asylum.

The Chief Justice Roger B. Taney was very much interested in maintaining slave owners' rights over their chattel property. In a seven to two decision Scott's request to be made a free man was denied. But the decision went far beyond that matter. It ruled that no Black man or woman could be a citizen of the United States or a citizen of any state free or slave. Also, the Dred Scott ruling stated that congress did not have the power to exclude slavery in the territories. The decision was a bombshell.[5] Free Blacks, enslaved Blacks, and abolitionists were appalled by the decision.

The famed Dred Scott of Missouri. Scott sued to have his freedom. He had once lived in a free state and sought to win his freedom because of this fact. Many have depicted Scott as a mere pawn in this suit but he was more active in his own case than some historians have portrayed. He also gave hundreds of dollars, an incredible amount of money for a slave, to help pay for his legal fees. While the suit was dragging on Scott's daughters escaped from slavery. The Supreme Court decision in the Dred Scott case was so derisive that abolitionists kept on doing their work and bondspersons kept escaping. The decision stated that no person descended from black Africans could ever be a citizen of the United States. Scott became a celebrity around the St. Louis area when his trial was going on to both white and Black individuals who wanted to shake his hand. He was finally freed by his master but died soon after (used by permission, State Historical Society of Missouri, Columbia).

When a reporter for *Frank Leslie's Illustrated* found Dred Scott in St. Louis in 1857 Scott had been working unsupervised for two or three years uncertain of who owned him and his wife due to some sloppy paperwork in an estate case. His two daughters were not willing to wait to find out who "owned" them and they had escaped Missouri to find their freedom on the liberty line. Dred said he didn't know where his daughters were located but was probably trying to protect their freedom by not disclosing their whereabouts. Dred Scott had become a celebrity around St. Louis with both whites and Blacks wishing to meet him and wanting to shake his hand. Scott remarked, and the Leslie reporter agreed with him, that if permitted he could go on a speaking tour of the north and earn thousands of dollars.[6] Taylor Blow, who was one of Scott's earliest masters, freed Dred Scott, his wife, and daughters soon after.[7] His case had been resolved.

There were two court cases of international importance that related to escape attempts by bondsmen on the western frontier. One of these cases involved Nelson Hackett of Arkansas and will be discussed in Chapter Six of this book. The other case involved John Anderson.[8]

Anderson had been a bondsman in Saline County, Missouri, of a Colonel McDaniel in the central part of the state. Anderson, who had been recently sold to McDaniel, had to leave his wife and children after he was sold. When he asked for a pass to go visit his wife McDaniel told him to find a new "wife" from the bondswomen who lived on his farm. Anderson decided to escape and later come back to get his wife and child and step-children. Anderson had escaped Saline County in the fall of 1853 and was making his way east in Missouri. He stopped by his father-in-law Lewis Tomlin's place while on the run. His father-in-law was a free Black man who earned his living as a barber in Fayette, Missouri. Tomlin offered Anderson a pistol for protection along with food and shelter. Ironically, Anderson declined the pistol stating he had a long dirk that he could use for defense. After leaving his father-in-law's, back on the run, Anderson was spotted by Seneca T.P. Digges who farmed and was a slave-holder. Digges saw Anderson in one of his fields with some of his other slaves. Digges gave chase to Anderson for some two miles when Anderson ducked into a wooded area. When Digges got close to Anderson and attempted to detain him, Anderson stabbed Digges twice, inflicting severe wounds to his person. Later Digges would die of these wounds.[9]

Lewis Tomlin, who had provided aide and comfort to his son-in-law, was in a very precarious position as a free Black man. Retribution was quick against Tomlin when white authorities found out the help he had provided for Anderson. Tomlin was whipped with five lashes and his license to operate as a barber was revoked and he was ordered to leave the state of Missouri.[10]

After Anderson had stabbed Digges he made his way across Missouri surviving mostly on nuts, raw corn and potatoes and an occasional chicken. Anderson managed to find a boat on the Mississippi River and crossed on it into Illinois. He managed to hook up with some abolitionists and made it to Chicago. From Chicago he managed to cross over into Windsor, Ontario.[11]

Anderson lived in Canada for many years changing his name and occupation and location on several occasions. A slave hunter tried to lure Anderson across the border into Detroit but he didn't take the bait. In 1860 Anderson made a huge mistake and told another man of the murder he had committed. He had a falling out with this man and the man turned him into authorities. Missouri sought to have Anderson extradited back to Howard County for murder. Anderson was arrested, charged with murder and jailed and then bought before Chief Justice Robinson on the Court of Queen's Bench.[12]

There was tremendous sentiment in Canada not to extradite Anderson over to the Americans. A mass meeting was held in Toronto in support of Anderson. The Crown's

Chief Justice Robinson knew if he were returned to Missouri Anderson would face either an impromptu trial and execution or a summary lynching. It was noted by some that in Canada, anyone who protected himself against enslavement acted in self-defense.[13]

The battle raged on for John Anderson. The Canadian anti-slavery movement was joined by its counterparts in London with the desire to keep him in Canada and not set a precedent for turning over a fugitive American slave no matter what they had been charged with in the United States. The trial dragged on until early in 1861 and with the United States splintering into the United States and Confederate States no one wanted to turn Anderson over to Missouri authorities. Finally the Canadian bench decided on a technicality to set Anderson free. They felt what he had committed was manslaughter, not murder, and since only murder was an extraditable offense he was let go a free man. Anderson later left Canada for England afraid Missouri authorities might again try to catch him. From England he set sail for Africa. In January of 1863 Anderson was in Liberia.[14]

Plenty of other Missouri bondspersons wanted to gain their freedom. Former Governor Meredith Miles Marmaduke had five "valuable runaway" bondsmen escape from his place near Arrow Rock in Saline County in 1856. Arrow Rock was the starting point of the famous Santa Fe Trial and by 1860 half of its population of 1,000 was Black. Marmaduke was searching for these bondsmen some 50 miles away from Arrow Rock around Huntsville, Missouri, but did not find them.[15]

Charles was a blacksmith who wanted his freedom. As a skilled laborer he was able to accumulate enough money when he made his escape in the spring of 1854 to possibly buy a forged pass of some kind. He was described as being about 26 years old, six feet tall and about 180 pounds. He also had a number of nice clothes with him which would also aid in his escape and make it possible for him to board a steamboat or train with the proper pass. The normal reward of $25 if captured in the county, $50 if caught in the state of Missouri and $100 if apprehended out of state was offered as a bounty.[16] Davenport's Tom was described as "about six feet high, 27 or 28 years old, weighing about 175 pounds" and had fled his bondage in the summer of 1857. Tom had broken his leg at one time making him slightly lame. He had a "pleasant countenance."[17] It is not known if Davenport's Tom or Charles the blacksmith were successful in their attempts to make it to permanent freedom.

Late in 1859 James Gray escaped slavery from New Madrid, Missouri, with two other men and made his way to Illinois. While in Sandoval Township in Marion County, which is located in extreme southern Illinois, Gray was captured by three men whose intention was to resell him back into slavery. However, their deed was found out and Gray was jailed in Union County, Illinois.[18]

A man by the name of Root wanted to see Gray set free. Root went clear up to northern Illinois to get an Illinois Supreme Court Justice Canton to issue a writ of habeas corpus for Gray. A jailor started north with Gray from Union County to Ottawa, Illinois, but was accosted by Gray's New Madrid master on the way. The master also had a writ issued by the United States Commissioner in Springfield. This writ would have Gray appear in the Illinois Capital to have the Commissioner earn his $10 and declare Gray a runaway slave. With a little judicial maneuvering a United States marshal deputized the jailor who was able to hold Gray under both writs and proceed to Ottawa.

Jim Gray was to be tried in Ottawa — a city with abolitionists who wished to see him freed. At his trial, which was not going his way, abolitionists made it possible for Gray to escape. He was taken away by carriage and made his way to Canada. Eight of the Ottawa abolitionists were charged with crimes. Four of them were tried in Chicago and given small fines and short jail time. These four were treated like heroes in the Windy City and banquets were given in their honor.[19]

There was a large reward for Charles Wesley Welch if he was captured outside the state of Missouri. Welch, who had lived in Boone County, Missouri, had escaped in late spring of 1857. The normal reward of $25 was offered if taken in the county and $50 if captured in the state of Missouri. However, $200, a very large reward, was offered if Welch was captured out of the state. It is not known if Welch was ever captured and returned to slavery.[20]

William Brown lived in Fauquier County in Virginia with his master. His wife and three children lived on another plantation with another master. Brown's master was not doing well financially and decided to move to Missouri with his slaves. Brown's wife's master offered to buy William so he and his family could be kept together but his master said "no"—he could get more money for William in Missouri. So the Brown family was permanently broken up by a slaver.

Brown and his fellow bondspersons and his master went by steamship to Missouri. When they got close to Cincinnati Brown's master put all his other slaves on a boat on the Kentucky side of the river. This was often done by slave-owners to keep their chattel from attempting to escape into Cincinnati and its vigorous Underground Railroad network.

However, Brown was allowed to stay on the steamship that was docked in Cincinnati to care for his master's five horses. The master trusted Brown as he had always been responsible. The master warned Brown not to go off the boat as there were people who would kidnap him and take him to New Orleans to be sold to a cotton plantation. But Brown realized this was a chance to leave his vile owner.

He looked around for his bag of possessions and realized that his master had hidden them from him to keep him from leaving the steamer. He left the ship sans his bag and went into the strange city. He hoped to find a Quaker or abolitionists who would help him secure his freedom in Canada. He found two men who would help him and they forwarded him on to freedom in the north.

Brown settled in Chatham, Ontario. This was one of the larger Black enclaves in Canada. Brown terribly missed his wife and three children. He made it to Canada in about 1853 and when Benjamin Drew interviewed him he hadn't seen or heard from his family for three years. He was trying to contact them but had not been able to do so.[21]

Alfred Edgar was a slave hunter who worked out of St. Louis and specialized in slave escapes that used the steamboats. He was summoned to help in the flight of three bondspersons from the area of Lafayette County, Missouri. Edgar came into Lexington, the county seat town of Lafayette County, in 1853. A slave holder had noticed that one of his male house servants and a bondswoman named Ann, who was pregnant, had escaped. It was also noted that another free Black man had left the area the same time as these two. This trio had left the region when the steamship *El Paso* had left port in Lexington. Edgar, the slave hunter, never found the two men. However, Ann had been located in a jail in St. Louis. The jailer never advertised her as was required by law and she had languished in the prison for five months. Her child had been born but died while she was incarcerated. Ann was in bad shape and was bloated from her prison time. She had been once described as "a lively fine girl." Ironically, this was one time when being "captured" by a slave hunter might have actually saved a bondswoman's life. Had Ann remained in jail under these horrible conditions she might have died. Edgar took possession of Ann and was able to sell her—but only at a huge discount because of the deterioration of her health because of her incarceration.[22]

Although Lafayette County was only a short distance, about 50 miles, from Kansas, most slave escapes prior to 1854, such as the one involving Ann, found the bondsperson usually trying to head east to find their freedom. After the Kansas Territory was opened in 1854 many of these freedom escapes were taken west out of Western Missouri to the Kansas Territory although the steamboats heading east were always an inviting escape route.

Richard Bruner was a bondsman in the central part of Missouri in Saline County. As a boy he carried water to the field hands. When he was big enough to work in the fields he hoed tobacco. He remembered being whipped once. He was made to hug a tree and then was beaten with a whip.

Richard said his master let his slaves join whatever church they wanted — the Baptist or Methodist. Mr. Bruner noted that the Blacks went to the white people's church in that part of Missouri and they all sat on the mourner's benches at the camp meetings together. Richard noted that when it was feared the bondspersons were getting "obstreperous" the master would blow a horn that would bring the neighbors to help quell any trouble.

Bruner apparently got along well with his "master's" children. He noted the two older boys joined the Confederate Army and Richard remarked, "De was mighty good boys, I liked dem fine." After the Civil War his "master's" daughter taught him to write his name.

However, like many bondsmen Bruner chafed under the idea of being a slave. Before the Civil War he made his getaway to Kansas. He traveled some 125 miles to freedom. After the Civil War started Bruner joined the 18th Colored Infantry Regiment under Captain Lucas in July of 1864. Bruner showed he was a leader of men and obtained the rank of sergeant and he was mustered out of the service in February of 1866. He spent parts of three years in a federal uniform. When the war was over Bruner came back to Nelson, Missouri, and owned a small slaughterhouse. He was also a preacher of the gospel.[23]

Mr. Bruner proved to be an adept entrepreneur as he owned several pieces of property in the county.[24] The importance of these interviews of former slaves can be understood in the case of Richard Bruner. At the time of the interview he was 97 years old — the oldest person in the county. Within a year Mr. Bruner would pass away. Without the Federal Writer's Project of the WPA all of this important information about Mr. Bruner's life may have been lost.[25]

It may be of interest to note that Mr. Bruner passed on his entrepreneurial abilities to his son Owen. Owen owned and operated a very successful barbeque restaurant in central Missouri for many years. When Owen retired and sold out his business he marketed separately his famous barbeque sauce to the Marshall Packing Company.[26]

A large group of 11 freedom seekers left Marion County from six different farms of enslavement. They made their escape on a Saturday evening and made it across the Mississippi River to Quincy, Illinois. Before Sunday morning was up they had made it to Menden. They were obviously trying to make it to Chicago. The slave-holders were convinced the escapees had help from abolitionists, although there was absolutely no evidence of this. The slavers all believed the slave-holder propaganda of the time that their bondspersons were perfectly content with their life as slaves and thought the abolitionists were luring them off their farms. The slavers just couldn't conceive that anyone would want to leave the paradise they had built on their farms. This was the self-delusional thinking process of the slave-holders of the time. It was hoped these bondspersons made their way to freedom.[27]

Another escape attempt into Illinois didn't prove to be as fortunate. Hiram had sought his freedom and run away. Hiram made it to the Naples, Illinois, area where he was spotted by three slave hunters. They wanted to arrest Hiram for the incredibly large reward of

$1,000. Hiram's motivation was not known; however, he wasn't going to be taken back to a life of slavery. He attacked the three men and Hiram was shot and killed.[28]

A free Black woman, Mary Meachum, used her home in St. Louis as a meeting place for a group of bondspersons trying to escape in May of 1855. An assembly of freedom seekers, after meeting in the Meachum home, got on a skiff and tried to cross the Mississippi River but they were met by a hostile party of slave owners and police on the Illinois side of the river. Some accounts say shots were fired and two men effectively managed to escape. Runaway advertisements were run in newspapers to find them but no record exists as to whether they were successful or not in their escape. A woman named Esther was captured with her two children. Esther was sold down to New Orleans but it is not known if she was allowed to keep her children. Mary Meachum and a man named Isaac were arrested and accused of abetting the escape. Fortunately, Mary was acquitted and Isaac was never tried. In 2001 the National Park Service, to pay tribute to Mary Meachum and other free Blacks like her who helped in the escape of Black bondspersons, dedicated the Mary Meachum Freedom Crossing. This was Missouri's first site in the National Park Service's Network to Freedom program.[29]

Henry Allen, a free Black man living in northeast Missouri during the summer of 1853, aided bondspersons trying to find freedom on the liberty line. Unfortunately he was finally caught while helping the bondspersons of a Mrs. O'Conner to escape. It was not known how many freedom seekers Henry had helped besides those on the O'Connor farm. Authorities in Palmyra were questioning him about his activities and excessive punishment would, in all probability, be handed out to Henry Allen.[30]

As has been stated before, not all escapes were to the north. A husband and wife team left Greenville, Missouri, in January of 1840 and headed south to Arkansas and it was believed they ended up in the Batesville area. The husband, Henry, was about 35 years old and about six feet tall. His wife Maria was 25 years old and said to be very petite. It is not known why they headed to the Batesville area — possibly children or relatives had been sold to this locality. It was believed they were hiding in the Black or Current River swamp areas. It is not known what the outcome of this escape was.[31]

Unfortunately, because of the horrible conditions many bondspersons were forced to live in, suicide sometimes seemed to be the only way out. A young man from near Glasgow, Missouri, attempted a freedom escape in the fall of 1853. He was captured and then jailed and facing a severe whipping for this offense. While in the jail the young man hanged himself.[32]

A bondswoman ran away from her master in the fall of 1854. After a few days on the run she was found hanging from a tree near a house. It is not known if she was about to be captured and she hanged herself rather than go back to a life of slavery or if she became frustrated over her lack of progress in running away. Either way it way another tragedy brought on by the institution of slavery.[33]

Christopher Hamilton's slave family came from Virginia to Missouri and he was sent to the lead mines in that state. The owners of these mines often liked to use slave labor because they could make the slaves do dangerous work that free workers would not do. To pay off the debts of their owners, various member of Hamilton's family were sold. He ended up in St. Louis where he was raised. He went to Sunday School and regular school — in violation of state laws — and learned to read and write. However, Christopher was learning too fast and he was pulled from the schools.

Hamilton married and he described his master as a good man. However, when his master remarried his new wife proved to be a terror. The new mistress took an instant dislike to Christopher's wife. She wanted to whip her and sell her down the river to New Orleans. The Hamiltons decided not to wait to see if their master granted his new wife her wish of selling Christopher's wife. The Hamiltons took off for Canada with only $16 in their pocket. Fortunately, they made it to the great white north. Broke, they found Christopher's brother who helped them find work in London, Ontario. The Hamiltons settled in and made a good life for themselves in London.[34]

Apparently, by 1857 maps began appearing in Cooper County in central Missouri telling bondspersons routes they might take to freedom. They were called "Blair's Emancipation Maps" or sometimes they were labeled more crudely by the slavers as "Republican's free nigger maps." It was said in the newspapers that ten of thousands of these maps had been circulated. However, much of this may be attributed to the slaver's paranoia and it is certain that fewer than that appeared. The slavocracy, of course, wished to destroy the up and coming Republican Party with its platform of emancipation. The newspapers which backed the slavery interests stated that whoever was responsible for these maps would be prosecuted to the full extent of the law.[35]

Lewis escaped from Columbia, Boone County, Missouri, and headed south during the summer into Arkansas and not north to freedom in Canada. Lewis was owned by Moses Payne and Jesse Perkins. Payne owned land in Arkansas and had plantations in that state. Was Lewis trying to join a loved one who had been sold or transferred down to the Razorback state? He was captured and jailed by the Sheriff of Desha County. Payne was a brilliant entrepreneur who owned businesses and many slaves in Missouri and Arkansas. However, it was obvious he had some misgivings about the institution of slavery. More about Moses Payne will be discussed later in this chapter.[36]

Jonathan W. Shooks harbored an escaped bondswoman from a man in his own neighborhood. Shooks apparently harbored the woman for over 18 months. Shooks or someone acting on his behalf had also spread the rumor that the bondswoman had taken off for Kentucky. The slaveholder took this information to be true and went to the bluegrass state to find his runaway bondswoman when all the time she was hidden in his own neighborhood! Unfortunately the bondswoman was returned to her master and Shooks was arrested.[37]

As stated before, it was sometimes difficult to determine if a bondsperson had escaped on the liberty line or was "decoyed" off their farm by someone posing as an abolitionist only to try and sell the bondsperson at a different location. Apparently Moss, described as a Canadian Frenchman, "decoyed" five bondspersons from Boonville, Missouri, and was later arrested. Moss was sentenced to five years in the state penitentiary for this crime.[38]

Isaac Riley and his wife came from Perry County in Missouri. However, they reported no cruel treatment and said that the Blacks and whites got along well in that area. Isaac also said that the break up of families was not often done in that county. However, many of the boys in Perry County, when they got to be a certain age, were taken 20 miles away to work. The Rileys were also concerned that their master might die soon and what would happen to their family? The bottom line was they didn't want to see their child grow up to be a slave. After a camp meeting one day Mrs. Riley and her husband decided to leave for Canada. They crossed over at Windsor but at first had a hard time in the French region of Potico. Sometimes, Isaac crossed back over into Michigan where he could work for higher wages. His employer even offered to build Isaac a house in Michigan but Riley said he never felt safe or free in Michigan.

The Rev. William King was a slaveholding minister from Louisiana who felt that slave-holding was a sin. He brought his 14 bondspersons to Canada and set them free. The Reverend King, along with others, formed an Elgin Association in an area called Buxton to purchase farms and offer low cost loans to the newly arrived bondspersons. Isaac Riley helped survey the land that Mr. King and the association had purchased. Mr. Riley was able to purchase 100 acres and did very well as a farmer. Their children, instead of being slaves, went to school and learned Latin, Greek and music as well as the other traditional studies for children of the time. Isaac and his wife said in the United States they were in darkness and now here in Canada they were in the light.[39]

Harriet Casey lived a hard life as a slave near Farmington, Missouri. She saw many abuses of bondsmen. Harriet reported that in Farmington, as in most slave areas, they had a "nigger-breaker" who would take so-called "unruly" bondspersons and break their spirit. Harriet's brother escaped slavery along with five other bondsmen and managed to maintain his freedom. Her brother never came back to slavery. In her interview in the 1930s Harriet said her brother went out west and eventually died in Honolulu, Hawaii.[40]

Henry Clay Bruce was born a slave in Virginia in 1836 and moved to central Missouri with his family in 1844. Bruce's oftentimes blunt and sometimes uncompromising viewpoint of slavery has been seen by some as controversial. However, Bruce does offer a unique view of slavery by someone who was an unwilling participant.

While in Missouri Bruce was a laborer hired out frequently yearly to different "masters." In 1847 his master, a man named Perkinson, became disgusted with Missouri and moved back to Virginia but kept his slaves in Missouri and rented them out. While a slave, Bruce was a laborer, tobacco worker, rail splitter and eventually a farm hand supervisor. At this time he learned to read but not to write. This would cause him trouble at a very inopportune time in his life.

It was Bruce's opinion that some intelligent slave masters treated their slaves with respect and worked them at a reasonable pace. Bruce was of the opinion that these slave owners got more production out of their slaves and had less slave escapes. Bruce noted that when some young bondspersons had disobeyed rules that this type of slave master would take the matter before the young bondspersons' own parents and let them deliver any punishment.[41]

The cruel masters created a malaise in their bondsperson because they would oftentimes be punished even when trying to do the right thing. Bruce noted one time he was near Brunswick, Missouri, in 1857, when he spotted some cattle that had knocked over a fence and were eating up a field of green corn. When he suggested they go and fix the fence and shoo out the cattle the bondsman, whose master owned the land and cattle, said, " It's massa's corn and massa's cattle and I don't care how much they destroy; he won't thank me for driving them out, and I will not do it."[42]

Bruce told of slave runaways who would head up north on the freedom line. However, he said there were runaways, especially in the more southern climates, who would run away in the spring only to return in the late fall when the weather got cold. He said some bondspersons would want to get away from mean masters and they would run away and stay on the loose for as long as they could. When they were finally captured the runaways would give a false name and place of enslavement. This way they would take their chances of being sold elsewhere and hope their new master and conditions would be better.

As a young man Bruce had come into contact with two runaways. Once when he was looking for a calf he came upon a runaway. The runaway told him where the calf was located.

Bruce never told his master about this encounter and hoped the runaway found freedom. Another time he noted the desperate nature of the runaway and was somewhat frightened of him. Bruce was driving a team with a wagon full of meal and the runaway took a half a bag of meal to supply himself with food on his journey. When Bruce got home he reported this incident, as he would be held responsible for the missing meal.[43]

Bruce told of another interesting incident in which a bondsman was promised his freedom if he could defeat his master in a fist fight. A bondsman named Armsted was told to "shut-up" by his master, a Mr. W. Both men were known as tough hombres and had bully personalities. Words were spoken and Mr. W. said if Armsted could defeat him in a fist fight he would give him his freedom and if not, Mr. W. would whip Armsted 29 times. Bruce said it was the "prettiest fist and skull fight" he had ever seen. It lasted for one half hour. Finally, Armsted said enough. Mr. W. only whipped his challenger six times because of the brilliant fight he had put up. As often happens after a fight like this the two men, even though one was a slave and the other his master, became fast friends until the war was over.[44]

Bruce, like many bondsmen as they grew older, made it be known they would not allow themselves to be whipped. Bruce was splitting rails with another man but the other man was not working most of the time. Unbeknownst to Bruce the master was watching both men for some time and saw what was going on. The master and a subordinate came upon them and began whipping the man who was not working. Bruce didn't know what was going on and thought he might be next for a whipping. He made up his mind to take off running and make a get-a-way before allowing himself to be whipped. However, he did not receive any punishment.[45]

Another whipping had dire consequences on a slave owner in 1855. A bondsman by the name of Bluford in Saline County, Missouri, worked for a large hemp grower. Bluford was going to be whipped by an overseer for some alleged offense. Bluford overpowered the overseer and severely whipped him. The master called for Bluford to receive his punishment but Bluford turned the tables on the master and whipped him.

The bondsman then took off and left Saline County and crossed the Missouri River into Howard County. Bluford hid in a wheat field. The area had been alerted to Bluford's escape and the owner of the wheat field jumped a fence at almost the exact spot Bluford was hiding.

The slave owner tried to capture Bluford but the bondsman had armed himself with a large knife and cut the slaver's abdomen deeply, almost to the spine. The slaver died soon after.

Bluford was on the run again but he had an advantage over many bondspersons who attempted to escape: he could read and he especially liked to look at maps and topography. Bluford understood that if he followed the Grand River near Brunswick, Missouri, to its head waters near Winterset, Iowa, it would take him to freedom. Winterset also had people there who would hide a runaway bondsman with no questions asked. Bluford, a very resourceful man, managed eventually to make it into Des Moines, Iowa, where he lived until the start of the Civil War. He joined the Union Army and found himself in Leavenworth, Kansas, at the close of the war. While in Leavenworth he saw Bruce one day and filled him in on the details of his escape.[46]

Bruce lived in Missouri well after the start of the Civil War. Slaves in Missouri during the Civil War were many times in no-man's-land. The Emancipation Proclamation only freed slaves in areas not controlled by the Union Army. Missouri was controlled by the

Union Army so many times its slaves were not free. However, as a practical matter many Union commanders freed slaves as contrabands of war and some slave owners were realistic enough to see that the institution was over and treated their bondspersons as hired hands. This is what happened to Henry, as his master paid him a salary. However, Henry wanted to marry a young lady on a neighboring farm and her master did not like Bruce. This master felt that since Bruce knew how to read this would have a negative affect on his other slaves and he forbid Henry to see his wife-to-be. Henry strapped on two colt revolvers and he and his wife escaped to Kansas on the train. On March 30, 1864, Henry and his bride were married in Leavenworth, Kansas.[47]

Henry remained in Kansas after the war and became a bricklayer and owned several businesses. For some time Bruce served as the doorkeeper for the state senate in Kansas. In 1881 Henry Bruce's brother Blanche secured a job for him in the post office in Washington, D.C. Henry wrote his autobiography in 1895. Blanche was also a slave in Missouri, although there is some confusion about this. Some say Blanche's biological father and his master, Pettis Perkinson, educated him and freed him. However, his half-brother Henry in his autobiography states he defended his half-brother when a slave owner attempted to strike Blanche—which would indicate Blanche was treated as a slave. We do know that Perkinson had left his slaves in Missouri while he lived in Virginia. Apparently, at the start of the Civil War Blanche felt it necessary to escape from Missouri and he found freedom in Kansas. During reconstruction Blanche became a wealthy landowner in the Mississippi delta area. He held several public offices including sheriff of Bolivar County in Mississippi. Blanche Bruce became the first Black American to serve a full term as a United States senator, from 1875 to 1881, representing the state of Mississippi. On February 14, 1879, Bruce presided over the United States Senate becoming the only former slave to do so. In 1881 President Garfield appointed Blanche Bruce to be the Register of the Treasury, making Bruce the first Black person whose signature was represented on United States currency.[48]

Blanche Bruce was a slave and lived in Missouri. After the Civil War, Bruce became a rich plantation owner in Mississippi and then a United States senator from that state. Bruce is the only ex-slave ever to preside over the United States Senate. He was later appointed as Register of the Treasury and became the first Black person whose signature was represented on U.S. currency. His brother Henry Clay Bruce wrote the book *The New Man: Twenty-Nine Years a Slave, Twenty-Nine Years a Free Man,* which offers insight into slavery and slave escapes in Missouri before the Civil War (used by permission, State Historical Society of Missouri, Columbia).

In the fall of 1856 in Callaway County and in Boone County, Missouri, two bondsmen with different owners living in two different counties apparently planned simultaneous escapes so they could flee slavery at the same time. They both left on a Saturday night probably hoping they might not be missed until Monday morning. George, from Calloway County, was described as 21 years old, five feet eight or ten inches tall and 170 pounds. He also had a good set of clothes on and a new coat. Sandy, from Boone County, was described as a bright mulatto about 21 years old with a stout build, round face, heavy and bushy head of hair and one front tooth missing. The usual rewards were offered: $25 if captured in the counties they were from, $50 if apprehended in the state of Missouri and $100 if taken outside the state of Missouri. It is hoped they made their way to freedom.[49]

Five bondsmen from Marion County were not so lucky when they tried to find their freedom during the fall of 1857. They were soon captured and returned to their master, a doctor.[50] However, two whole families managed to escape from Hannibal in 1857. Running away could be a very dangerous business as many times slave hunters, if they thought the bondspersons were going to get away, would just as soon shoot them dead as to let them escape.[51]

The building of the iron railroad started in Missouri in 1851. Many of these early rail lines were short runs which would offer the escaping bondsperson very little chance of getting very far in their bid for freedom. By the end of the decade the railroads were fairly common in Missouri. However, newspapers and court papers of the time list very few escape attempts made by the railroad.[52] The *Hannibal Whig Messenger* on September 20, 1855, reported that two bondsmen with forged passes escaped from inland Missouri to St. Louis on the railroad. The two apparently were never apprehended. The slave owner sued the Pacific Railway for the value of the bondsmen for allowing the two to escape on their transportation line.[53]

Perhaps the reason the steamboats offered many more opportunities for escape was twofold. The routes of the steamships stretched clear across the nation so great distances could be traveled by the escaping bondsperson. Also, the crews of the steamboats had many Blacks — both free and slave — so the sight of a Black person on a steamboat was not unusual. The crews of the railroad were made up mostly of white persons.

During the early part of the decade of the 1850s came a convergence of events that had a profound effect on the Underground Railroad on the western frontier. Up until that time most of the slaves in Missouri were located near the counties along the Mississippi River. However, slave owners became concerned by the number of slave escapes into Illinois and Iowa from the nearby counties in Missouri. Many slave owners began to move their bondspersons to the interior of the state along the Missouri River and along its western border. Slave owners in Missouri had been assured that the Territory of Kansas would be brought into the Union as a slave state, thus protecting Missouri's western backdoor. The interior counties of Missouri along the Missouri River became known as the "Little Dixie" region of Missouri because of their large percentage of Black to white populations. Missouri's large increase of slaves from the 1850s total of 87,000 to 115,000 in 1860 was due to the increased use of bondspersons in western Missouri and "Little Dixie" during that decade.

The area called "Little Dixie" in Missouri was a 12 to 17 county region. Six of the counties in this region — Boone, Callaway, Chariton, Clay, Howard and Lafayette — had slave populations of 25 percent of the white population. In the case of Lafayette County the ratio of whites to Black slaves was 50 percent white to 50 percent Black. Statewide, most counties in Missouri had slave populations less than 10 percent. In only one other county, New Madrid, a cotton growing county in the southeast portion of the state, was the Black population as high as 25 percent.

The second thing that affected the Underground Railroad on the western frontier was the superb soil condition in this region of western Missouri for the growing of hemp. Many of the new settlers in this region came from Kentucky, the number one hemp growing state in the union. In the 1830s Kentucky grew three fourths of the hemp used in the United States.[54] Missouri in the 1850s and 1860s would soon challenge Kentucky for her supremacy in the growing of hemp.

The uses for hemp were not only for consumption here in the United States but also worldwide. However, its use in the United States was considerable. Hemp rope was used to tie huge bales of cotton, farmers and ranchers had many uses for it, it was used for bagging, and naval use was considerable for canvas and on sailing ships. In 1853 drought in Kentucky caused the hemp crop to dry up and the demand for Missouri hemp increased tremendously.

The growing of hemp was extremely hard work and many agreed it was almost impossible to hire free labor to do the work. During this time mostly slave labor was used on the hemp crop. It was usually soil along the river bottoms that made the best hemp growing land. The hemp seeds were planted in April and May and then in August the really hard work appeared. By then the hemp stalks had grown to be eight feet tall and had to be cut with a sickle-like tool. The stalks would be spread out over the ground to cure in the sun.

The tough fibers of the hemp plant were the desired portion; the rest of the plant would be rotted away. This could be done naturally by dew rotting but this produced a lesser quality than water rotting. Water rotting produces a higher quality of hemp products but requires heated tanks of water and more labor. After the rotting was done the hemp was separated from the wood by a hemp brake. The hemp brake required extremely hard work and only the strongest bondsmen with particularly extended stamina could last and be productive in this operation. The whole process of hemp production was long and tedious. Sometimes the slave masters in the hemp regions actually gave bonuses to the bondsmen who broke large amounts of hemp.[55] Usually, 100 pounds of hemp was the required amount to be broken in one day. Bonuses were usually paid for every pound over this 100-pound mark. Sometimes, 200 or 300 pounds of hemp could be broken by the best workmen. The bonus was usually one penny for each pound broken. Sometimes a bondsman could make one dollar a day or more on this bonus system and that would be as much as a free white laborer could make; however, the work was much harder.

A good-sized hemp farm would have around 20 or 30 slave workers. This was fewer slaves than the several hundred slaves that would be found on a good-sized cotton plantation in the deep south. However, these hemp farms could be very profitable.

Missouri was the sixth-largest tobacco growing state in the Union. Most of the tobacco was grown in the western part of the state, increasing the need for slaves in that area, and was very labor intensive.

The third and last thing that affected the Underground Railroad on the western frontier was the creation of the Kansas Territory in 1854, which had a large number of abolitionists who were only too willing to help escaping bondspersons. Even if the bondspersons were not to use the white abolitionists, the mere fact that this area was becoming dotted with farms allowed the escapees a place to find water and food. The open prairie could be very hostile to the bondspersons attempting to escape. The filling in of stations in the Nebraska Territory and southwest Iowa were also an aid to escapees. The important town of Tabor, Iowa, was founded in 1852, thus completing the arc out of western Missouri and the beginning of the 300-mile trek across the Hawkeye state. By the late 1850s to the end of the Civil War this journey out of Western Missouri produced thousands of escapes through Kansas, Nebraska and Iowa.

It is interesting to note that abolitionists in Kansas remarked in newspapers early during its territorial days that if Missouri men tried to come over and vote in any Kansas elections after the one on November 30, 1854, there would be consequences. During this election droves of Missouri slaveholders and paid supporters came over the border into Kansas and illegally voted in a slave constitution. Abolitionists warned that if this occurred again the Underground Railroad in Kansas would start carrying off Missouri slaves. A shot across the bow of Missouri slaveholders was fired. They were warned that their western border was in danger of becoming a sieve that bondspersons could escape through.[56]

However, Missourians saw many from the east and midwest spill-over into Kansas and with the paranoia of the time they thought every one of them to be dyed-in-the-wool abolitionists. A newspaper in Richmond, Missouri, remarked in February of 1855, "On yesterday a train of about forty abolition vagabonds and negro stealers passed through our town enrout [sic] for Kansas Territory. May the devil get them before they arrive at their journey's end."[57]

A reward of $800 was offered for four freedom seekers who escaped from St. Joseph in the fall of 1855. The two owners of these bondsmen thought they were headed north to Iowa and thence on to Chicago. Because the escapes of bondspersons in western Missouri were becoming so frequent sometimes the rewards were upped to $200 per escapee from the normal $100 per escapee if found in another state[58] ($200 would be about $10,000 in present-day money). Also, in western Missouri the number of escapees running away at the same time grew to larger numbers especially just prior to the start of the Civil War in 1859–1860. It wasn't unusual to see ten or a dozen bondspersons successfully escape at the same time—especially from western Missouri.

Western Missouri had been put on notice that slave escapes were to become a problem as early as 1850. At that time, 30 bondspersons made an escape armed with knives, clubs and three guns. However, a heavily armed slave posse put an end to this large escape attempt.[59]

When it became obvious that Kansas was going to become a haven for runaway slaves, paranoia set in among the western Missouri slaveholders. Two bondsmen escaped from Harrisonville, Missouri, in Cass County during the summer of 1855. Accusations were made that a white minister (W.H. Wiley) and others had aided the freedom seekers in their escape. It was said that Wiley and others were accused of being abolitionists who were aiding in the escape of other bondspersons. The attitude of the slave-holder was that their bondspersons were contented with being slaves and if they attempted to escape it would only be through the efforts of white abolitionists who would entice them.

Wiley protested that he was a southern man and had never preached any abolitionist rhetoric and was completely innocent. A mob of slave-holders and sympathizers "arrested" Wiley. Wiley certainly feared for his life and didn't know if he would be hanged by the mob or not. Passions were running high. It is not known of the outcome of the Wiley case. *The New York Times* ran an article about this matter under the title of *Mob Law In Western Missouri*.[60]

Prior to the settlement in Kansas slave escapes to the west were kept to a minimum due to the fear of being attacked by tribesmen of Native Americans. In fact, some slaves in western Missouri prior to 1854 were allowed to arm themselves by law when in this region due to fears of attacks by Native Americans.

Escaping and being caught, as we have seen before, very often proved to be a death sentence. In 1848 a Missouri bondsman escaped from slavery but was captured and incarcerated in the Clay County jail in Liberty located in western Missouri. A presumably white criminal in jail for theft beat the bondsman to death.[61]

Isaac Berry, Sr. was a masterful violin player. Born in 1832 he lived in Garrard County, Kentucky. When his master died Isaac was willed to his daughter, Mrs. James Pratt, who lived in Missouri. There must have been some tension between Mrs. Pratt and her husband about Isaac. Mrs. Pratt gave Isaac permission to escape. Isaac took off and headed north to Michigan. Berry said he followed the railroad tracks to the north. Mrs. Pratt's husband was furious that Isaac had run away. He offered a huge reward of $500 for Isaac, *dead or alive*. The amount of the reward plus the notation of dead or alive denotes there was probably some trouble in the Pratt household about Isaac.

Isaac Berry, Sr. managed to get as far as Ypsilanti, Michigan. While there he came under the care of George McCoy, a Black man who had escaped from Louisville, Kentucky. McCoy had built a successful cigar business in the state of Michigan and had wagons moving about the area. The cigar business was the perfect cover for moving escaping bondspersons. Berry got into one of the wagons loaded with cigars heading for Detroit and crossed over into Canada. It took Isaac Berry, Sr. three weeks to go from Missouri to freedom in Canada.[62]

In western Missouri, as in the rest of Missouri, any kind of white or Black resistance to the slavery norm was quickly stamped out. In Parkville, Missouri, now a suburb of Kansas City, two white men, George Park and W.J. Patterson, started a free-soil newspaper which was published for a short time. The free-soilers wanted to ban slavery from any of the new territories, such as next-door Kansas.

The newspaper was called the *Industrial Luminary*. A mob of some 200 men attacked the newspaper office. The presses of the newspaper were paraded through town and then thrown into the Missouri River. Park was not at the newspaper office that day but the mob kidnapped Patterson and threatened to tar and feather him. The slavers relented but ordered Patterson and Park to leave the town in three weeks. Patterson was also told by the mob that if he or Park went to Kansas then they would be followed and hanged. They were called traitors and others were warned that the same thing would be done to them if they didn't support the slavery cause.[63]

The sometime barbarity of slave owners and the lack of any oversight in their oftentimes cruel treatment of slaves was exemplified in the treatment of an old bondsman in 1860. A man from Virginia noted that slave owner James Hicklin, from Lexington, Missouri, was extremely cruel to his slaves. The bondsman in question was a very elderly gentleman and was forced to wear a 20 pound ball at the end of a five foot chain. The elderly man had to work dragging the ball and chain. The shackle had rubbed his leg raw from the ankle to the shin. The sores on the poor man's leg emitted a most foul odor.

The man from Virginia apparently facilitated the escape of the bondsman. He took him to a blacksmith, Robert McFarland, in Lexington who was in sympathy with the antislavery cause. The blacksmith cut the shackle and ball and chain from the man's leg. The bondsman, it was believed, took off by walking upstream along the Missouri River, the common way from Lexington to the Kansas border. McFarland threw the ball and chain into a nearby well so he would not be implicated in the bondsman's escape. After the Civil War McFarland's wife Olive operated a school for African American children in the basement of their home in Lexington. McFarland retrieved the shackle after he moved to Kansas in the 1870s and donated it to the Kansas State Historical Society.[64]

A Native American by the name of Jo Park lived about ten miles from Westport in western Missouri. Park owned many slaves. Two bondsmen took two horses and found refuge in Kansas. Westport is only a short distance from the Kansas border. The two bondsmen quickly found work in the harvest fields of Kansas close to the Missouri border. They felt they were safe amongst the abolitionists there. Park procured warrants for the two bondsmen and found them in Kansas. However, when he tried to have the bondsmen arrested they resisted and the abolitionists told Park they would have him arrested for kidnapping. Park went back to Missouri without his bondsmen or horses.[65]

The exodus of the bondspersons continued from Missouri in 1860 to 1861 as the warclouds began to gather. Most of the bondspersons left unaided on their journey to the north. However, from Kansas came James Montgomery and Charles Jennison and others with bands of men who escorted the bondspersons across the state line and secreted them away in Kansas or forwarded them along the Underground Railroad through Kansas, Nebraska, Iowa, Illinois, and Indiana and on to Michigan and Canada.

In November of 1860 the nation elected Abraham Lincoln president. Lincoln only garnered 10 percent of the vote in Missouri. Kansas City real estate broker E. Fraser proudly wrote to Iowa abolitionist John Todd that 180 Kansas City, Missouri, residents had voted for Lincoln. Western Missouri was Lincoln's worst area. Some of the Lincoln voters in Kansas City had to go to the polls locked arm-in-arm. They asked for Lincoln ballots and made sure they were deposited in the ballot boxes instead of the wastebasket. Stephen Douglas and John Bell received the most votes for president in Missouri and they were both Union men.[66] The state's citizens were overwhelmingly in favor of staying in the Union. However, both United States senators from Missouri and the new governor, Claibourne Jackson, were pro-slavery men. Jackson (as governor, and as such, head of the state militia) in particular would plunge Missouri into a nightmare of conventional and guerrilla warfare. Possibly a more skillful and not such a pro-slavery ideologue might have rescued the state from this dreadful situation.

When Jackson came into office, with the question of Civil War looming over the state, he engaged in political double-speak. Jackson didn't recommend secession but said Missouri should stand by the states that had seceded. He refused to call up men for the Union Army and made other provocative moves. Pro-slavery men seized a small federal arsenal in Liberty, Missouri, and distributed the arms among secessionist men in the state. Jackson then stated that the state militia would resist any invading force—meaning the Union Army. A young Samuel Clemens, later to be better known by his nom de plume Mark Twain, and two other steamboat captains refused to help the Union Army by piloting federal troopships up the Missouri River.[67]

Many slave owners in the state believed the strong pro-slavery rhetoric of the governor and others. However, some slave owners began to panic in Missouri and planned to send their slaves further south to Texas or elsewhere where they would be "safe" from the Unionists. Slave auctions, for the most part, came to an end in the state; there was not enough demand for any more slaves at this time. Many owners were just trying to hold onto what slaves they had and were not interested in adding any new bondspersons. The Union Army took control of St. Louis and then captured the state capital in Jefferson City. A defiant Governor Jackson fled from the state capital along with the accoutrements of state government and the legislature and assorted bureaucrats also followed.

Ellaine Wright was a 20-year-old bondswoman in Missouri at the start of the Civil War. She had known plenty of sorrow in her life. Even though Ellaine was 97 years old at the time of her FWP interview she could remember that traumatic moment when she was four years old and her mother was sold away from her to another state. She could remember in her mind's eye holding onto her mother and both of them sobbing. Her mother told her "Ellaine, honey mama's gwan way off and ain't never goin to see her baby again."[68]

Ellaine was a bondswoman near Springfield, Missouri. The Union Army under Nathaniel Lyon and the Confederate Army under Ben McCulloch were about to clash at Wilson's Creek, 12 miles from Springfield on August 10, 1861. This was the first major clash in the western theater of the Civil War. The Federals had won the day on the battlefield. However, the Union lost their leader Lyon. The Federals went back into Springfield to regroup but the Confederates stayed in Southwest Missouri. Although this was a somewhat limited victory for the Confederates many slave owners like Ellaine's were nervous about the future of slavery in Missouri. Ellaine and the rest of the slaves at her farm were sent southward soon after the Battle at Wilson's Creek.[69]

The situation in Missouri became chaotic as the Union Army swept across the state. Many slaves went into the Union lines for protection and their freedom. Some were taken in but others were turned back. Company "E" of the First Iowa Infantry regiment welcomed a runaway bondsman named Mason Johnson. Johnson had no formal papers and was a fugitive slave but had been a veteran of the Mexican War where he had been a valet to Henry Clay's son. "Old Mace," as he became known, was a godsend to the raw recruits of Company E. Mace knew the ways of the Army and he gave these recruits the benefit of his wisdom. Mace became their cook and, as Private E.F. Ware said, "from this time we lived high." Old Mace knew where the milk cows were and the boys of Company E always had fresh milk and fresh eggs. In southern Missouri and northern Arkansas the razorbacks ran free and were a tasty bit of pork when the boys ran a bayonet through them and Mace fixed them on the camp fire. The Company E men had their wives and girlfriends send them goodies which Mace could improve on.

He also acted as their nurse. He popped their blisters on their weary feet with a needle. When Private Ware came down with a horrible case of dysentery he thought he might have typhoid fever. The Union doctor confirmed he didn't have typhoid and prescribed some medicine for Ware's dysentery. Ware didn't trust the doctor's medicine so Mace fixed up a batch of blackberry roots and cleaned and cut them up. Mace made a bitter astringent decoction for Ware, and within 12 hours he was cured. Another time, Ware's shoes became impossible and with no socks to speak of he was in a bad situation. Mace had seen this before and he told them to melt a bar of soap in his shoes and this would make them wearable. Ware did this and said, "They [his shoes] felt delicious. I skated around in them."

At one time, Mace proved his mettle and the men of Company E made him an honorary corporal. Later Ware would write "I shall never forget 'Old Mace'; he is the only black idol I ever had."

As often happens in the fog of war, Mace became separated from the men in Company E. Later, one of the men of E saw Mase in a Union Army Black artillery unit that was located in Arkansas. Mace pointed to his corporal's chevrons and proudly proclaimed that these were real this time.[70]

Marilda Perry told about the muddled conditions in Missouri at this time during the Civil War. She said her father got tired of the whippings he received as a slave and he ran off to join the Union Army to try and help free his family.[71]

Marilda told an amazing story. Her master, a very wealthy and cruel man, showed her where he had hidden his money. He told her if she told anyone he would cut her throat.

Her master, a rebel sympathizer, took off when the Union soldiers came into his area and occupied it. A rogue detachment of Union soldiers came by her plantation and, figuring a wealthy plantation owner lived there, threatened Marilda if she didn't tell them where his loot was located. The Union soldiers threatened to cut her throat if she didn't tell them the location of the money. Marilda would not give up the site of the cash and valuables and the rogue Union detachment left empty-handed.

Another slave on the plantation asked Marilda why she just didn't give the Federals the money as both her master and the Federal soldiers had threatened to cut her throat if she didn't do what they wanted. Marilda answered that she knew the Union soldiers were just "foolin'" with her so she didn't tell them the location but she knew her master would in no uncertain terms cut her throat if she gave up the location of the money.[72]

Many arrogant slave owners thought their bondspersons would never escape under any circumstance. However, when the bedlam of war descended over Missouri many bondspersons took advantage of the situation. The Rev. Galusha Anderson, the erstwhile Baptist minister from St. Louis, was invited to an elegant dinner by a slave owner who had been born in Mississippi and was now an officer at a St. Louis bank. This slave owner wanted to show Anderson the "beauty" of African slavery and all its benefits.

The slave owner had two slaves, one of whom was named Wash, a man of great energy who performed many duties around the home with utmost proficiency. Wash was also one of the best judges of horseflesh in Missouri and the slave owner never bought or sold a horse without first getting Wash's opinion. The slaver owner bragged that Wash had been with him a long time and would never think of running away. The other slave was a female bondswoman named Mammy. She was the cook and had raised the slave owners' children in a most loving way. He was convinced there was no way she would ever consent to leave their wonderful household. Once the Civil War began and the chaos began these two wasted no time in leaving the slave holder's home.

Anderson couldn't help but notice that Wash's name appeared in the newspaper as the first bondsman to escape in St. Louis after the start of the Civil War. Two weeks after that Mammy also escaped in the middle of the night from the arrogant banker. Anderson reported that scenes like this were being repeated in Missouri by the hundreds.[73]

Many people in Missouri were elated when into this wartime mix the Federal government made a move that would have a profound reaction as to the direction of the Civil War. In early July of 1861 all the territories and states, including Missouri, that were west of the Mississippi River and east of the Rocky Mountains, including New Mexico, would be formed into the Western Department.[74]

John C. Frémont was put in command of this department. Many Missourians took heart that the pathfinder of the west could restore Missouri from the chaos that was enveloping her, including the never-ending question of slavery. But Frémont proved a disappointment. When Lyon needed more troops in southwest Missouri at Wilson's Creek, Frémont thought the main attack was to come in the southeastern corner of the state at New Madrid. He sent a flotilla of steamboats and 5,000 men to no avail.[75] They called him "fuss and feathers."

In the fall of 1861 Frémont declared martial law in the state—an extremely unpopular move.[76] Frémont had also manumitted two St. Louis slaves and issued their manumission papers over his signature as a major-general. Was the war to be about the freeing of the slaves? Of course at this time, early in the war, some Union officers had told their commanders that their men would likely desert if this became a war about freeing the slaves.

This was brought to the attention of President Lincoln and he was not happy. Lincoln pointed out that Frémont was transcending his authority. Lincoln gave Frémont the opportunity to change the order but he refused. Frémont wrote to Lincoln that he preferred that Lincoln himself should modify the proclamation. Lincoln publicly set aside the provision in the proclamation that freed the St. Louis slaves.[77]

Lincoln wrote to Senator O. H. Browning, a friend and senator from his home state of Illinois, about the Frémont situation of freeing these slaves. He wrote that freeing slaves was a "political" matter not a "military" matter. However, Lincoln said Frémont had every right to take slaves away from their owners if their labor was needed in the Union cause. He also left the door open for a future possible emancipation of all slaves. Lincoln also wrote of his real concern of Frémont's action. He said that a whole company of Union volunteers in Kentucky had thrown down their arms and left after hearing that Frémont had freed these two slaves. Lincoln knew there were other Union companies that felt the same way — that this was not to be a war of freeing the slaves but of holding the Union together.[78]

John C. Frémont was a hero to many in the Republican Party. Many rejoiced when he was put in charge of the military department with responsibility over the state of Missouri in 1861. They thought he would bring order to the chaos that had enveloped the state. However, his military blunders cost him support in the state and in the White House. When Frémont emancipated two slaves in Missouri on his own signature a howl went up amongst the slavers in the state. Lincoln became miffed that Frémont had overstepped his authority. This was early in the Civil War and Lincoln knew if the war became about emancipating the slaves he would have trouble holding the Union Army together. Frémont was sacked. As the war dragged on and the Union Army saw the poor conditions slaves were forced to live in and the ramifications of bondage they understood the importance of ending slavery. It is interesting to speculate whether if Frémont had been successful as a military commander he could have forced the White House' hand on the slavery issue and caused emancipation of the slaves to be the priority of the war at an earlier date (State Historical Society of Iowa, Des Moines).

It was a very ticklish situation. Since Missouri had never officially seceded slavery was a local issue to be decided by those in the state of Missouri. However, Frémont blundered again. The Rebel Army moved from southwestern Missouri to the important river town of Lexington in the western central portion of Missouri. Once again Frémont failed to reinforce his troops there and the Confederates were successful. Frémont was fired for these mistakes plus a lack of financial accountability. Frémont had many loyal friends and they were very upset and threatened to leave the army. Many of his followers believed in the total emancipation of the slave population. However, Frémont rose to the occasion and told them to be loyal to the Union and not to him.[79] It is interesting to speculate whether, if Frémont had been successful in prosecuting the war on the western frontier in Missouri, he could have put pressure on Lincoln to free the slaves at an earlier time. However, as it was, Frémont was just another Union general unable to defeat the rebel army and without a good grasp on how to do it.

But that didn't stop the bondspersons in Missouri from taking matters into their own hands. Many of them wanted their freedom now and they were not willing to wait for the politicians to sort things out. Bondsman Gus Smith reported that there were a lot of runaway freedom seekers in those days.[80]

The state of Missouri was still in the business of tracking and capturing runaways, even with the presence of the Union Army in the state. On May 9, 1862, the acting sheriff of Clay County Missouri had lodged in his jail four escaped bondspersons who had made it to Kansas but were captured in that state. They were a male named Jacob, age 27, who had been kicked by a horse and still showed signs of that accident; a female named Mandy, aged 22; and a small girl named Milley, about three years old. Another male named Robert, about age 35, was also with this group. What is interesting is that these bondspersons were from Buchanan County of which St. Joseph is the county seat. Buchanan County is north of Clay County, Missouri, and it is somewhat a mystery as to why these bondspersons were brought back to a different county than the one in which they resided. Possibly the actions of the Civil War made it impossible to return them to their proper owner or county.[81]

Later that month the acting sheriff in Clay County at the county seat town of Liberty had incarcerated two male bondsmen. These two had escaped from central Missouri in Cooper County and were headed west but apparently were captured around Clay County. One was named Charley, aged 23, and the other was a young man aged 17 who didn't give his name. It is probable they were trying to escape into Kansas. The usual exhortation for these public notices was give in the *Liberty Tribune* newspaper: their masters had to prove ownership of the bondsmen and pay for their incarceration and any other expenses before they would be released to the master. Otherwise, these bondsmen would be sold at the courthouse at a public action.[82]

James Lane was given a command of Kansas troops and he invaded Missouri. He had his usual sidekick Charles Jennison with him. Instead of attacking the Confederate Armies, Lane made war on the civilians of Missouri. One of the first towns to feel Lane's wrath was Osceola, Missouri. This was a prosperous river town that in population was close to Jefferson City and Springfield. Its bank was full of cash from the flourishing merchants in town. Lane overwhelmed the small detachment of Rebels guarding the town and then cleaned out its bank and other stores and then burnt the town to the ground. His troops were drinking freely. His actions greatly angered the Unionists in Missouri and many Union Army officials felt Lane's exploits helped the recruitment of Confederates in the state.[83]

However, despite Lane's looting and murderous intent towards the white citizens of

Missouri, the bondspersons in Missouri always found that the Kansas troops welcomed them to their lines. Many Union units would send the bondspersons back to their masters, but not the Kansas boys. In the autumn of 1861, with slaves streaming into their lines in Western Missouri, Lane sent many of these bondspersons to their freedom in Kansas. There was a labor shortage in the state and they were sent to help with the fall harvest of crops.[84]

Unbeknownst to some slave masters in Missouri they had traitors in their own households that helped to liberate their slaves. U.S. Hall, a nine year old boy in Missouri when the Civil War began, stated that very often the sympathies of the children of slave-owners were defiantly on the side of the bondspersons. Hall reported he learned to read and write at age six. He stated he could "remember of taking delight in writing pass after pass supposedly for Negroes from their masters."[85]

On Monday, February 10, 1862, three regiments of federal infantry, including 2,500 men with a baggage train of 130 wagons, passed through Boonville, Missouri, on the way to St. Louis. Several bondsmen joined this caravan with the idea of making their escape from bondage. Federal soldiers shielded the freedom seekers from their masters and the officers of the regiments made no effort to send the bondsmen back to their masters.

This action was brought to the attention of Major General Henry Halleck at Union headquarters in St. Louis. Halleck had taken over the Missouri command when Frémont was sacked. One of the first things Halleck did was to issue General Order #3, which barred fugitive slaves from Union lines. After this incident in Boonville Halleck vowed he would arrest every officer who violated this order. Halleck bragged that he had jailed a colonel who had violated this order.[86] Many Union officers were afraid to allow fugitive slaves to be in their lines after Halleck's Order #3. A Union Colonel Guitar in command in the Fulton, Missouri, area allowed 12 fugitive slaves who were working as army teamsters to be seized by their masters.[87]

Halleck was basically a paper pusher and under his command nothing really happened in the field and the Confederates were a force in much of Missouri. But things would change when General Samuel Curtis, a former Iowa congressman, was given a field command and he chased the regular Confederate Army out of Missouri into Arkansas.

James Lane, not out of any concern for the bondspersons of Missouri, but looking pragmatically at the situation, decided it was in the best interest of the Union to start recruiting Blacks into the Federal Army. Lane and his men started recruiting Black men into the Union Army in the summer of 1862. Lane certainly was one of the first if not the first to do so. Lane started his recruiting efforts without any clear instruction from the Lincoln Administration. At times some like Secretary of War Stanton questioned whether Lane had the authority to raise these units. Whenever he was questioned about the recruiting of Black units Lane just ignored such questions and kept up his recruiting efforts. These units would have white officers.[88] However, some point to a report that Charles Jennison in November of 1861 had a whole company of Black soldiers when he moved into Jackson County, Missouri. What is also interesting about this report is that the Black company was led by a Black officer.[89]

Many of the slave owners in Missouri couldn't see that a new day was coming and they became even more oppressive than ever. Mary Bell told about her father, Spottwood Rice, during the Civil War. Rice was a bondsman whose master was a man named Lewis. Lewis was a very cruel and shortsighted man.

He grew tobacco and used Rice as a foreman of his operation. Lewis acknowledged that Rice knew more about growing and processing tobacco than anyone else in the area.

Rice also directed the work efforts of the other slaves on Lewis's farm. However, Lewis freely whipped and beat his bondspersons, including Rice. Rice escaped, but as the slave patrollers closed in to capture him he went to a slave trader he knew and begged him to buy him to get him away from Lewis.

The slave trader wanted to buy Rice because he knew how valuable he would be to another tobacco grower. However, Lewis refused to sell Rice, saying Rice was invaluable to his operation. Rice had learned how to read and he told the other Lewis slaves that after the war was over freedom would be theirs. This angered Lewis and eventually the slave trader had to bring Rice back to him.

Lewis sat down with Rice when he came back and told him he knew the war would eventually free all of his slaves. He told Rice that if he would stay with him when the war was over he would build him a new house and would give him plenty of money for his family. However, Rice knew Lewis was a liar and could not be trusted. Rice stayed with Lewis for six more months and then took off again. When Rice escaped this time he brought with him 11 of Lewis' best slaves and they went and joined the Union Army in Kansas City, Missouri. Lewis knew this would ruin him. He went to the Union Army commander and demanded Rice and the rest of his bondsmen be returned to him. The Union commander told Lewis that the men were now United States soldiers and not slaves anymore and that Lewis had no claim on them. Mary Bell also reported that her brother was killed as a Union soldier during the Civil War.[90]

More and more bondsmen were joining the United States Army in Missouri. Louis Hamilton's father joined the Union forces and then after the war came back and purchased a farm.[91] James Monroe Abbott also reported that when the Civil War came a lot of the bondsmen went and joined and fought for the "government."[92]

These bondsmen were quickly tested in battle conditions on the western frontier in what many believe were the first combat conditions for Black soldiers during the Civil War. In October of 1862 five companies of the First Kansas Colored Volunteer Infantry marched into Bates County, Missouri. Three days later they were engaged in a firefight with Confederate forces ending up with eight dead and 11 wounded men. This engagement became known as the Battle of Island Mound.[93] These Black units would see much more combat on the western frontier.

As the war dragged on there arose a situation very dangerous to the bondspersons still in slavery. As the Rebel Army was driven out of Missouri, Confederate guerrillas moved in — often to conduct illegal and brutal warfare mainly on civilians and the Black population of Missouri. The Confederate guerrillas, sometimes known as bushwhackers, were completely ruthless and were led by William Quantrill, Bloody Bill Anderson, George Todd and others. Bloody Bill Anderson liked to scalp his victims and carried their scalps on his bridle. These guerrillas usually wore the blue uniforms of the Union Army — this way, they could often ride around Missouri unmolested and sneak up on their unsuspecting victims with greater ease. These guerrillas often financed their battle units by kidnapping escaping or free bondspersons and reselling them or turning them in for rewards or bounties.

Dave Harper had a unique experience regarding the bushwhackers. When Bloody Bill Anderson and his men were camped in Calloway County, Harper's mistress collected the mail for Anderson and his men. She would send Harper to give the mail to Anderson and his band. Later Harper escaped his condition of bondage and joined the Union Home Guard and served for six months. The main objective of Harper's military unit was to keep Bloody Bill and his men from tearing-up the railroad tracks in Eastern Missouri![94]

One of the great outrages of the Civil War on the western frontier was Quantrill's murderous raid on Lawrence, Kansas. Riding into Kansas, Quantrill had a list of Union men to be murdered. He also kidnapped civilians to guide him to Lawrence and then shot them when they were of no use to him. Quantrill had 450 men as he road into Lawrence before five o'clock in the morning on August 21, 1863.

Every male they saw they shot and killed. They indiscriminately fired into windows and doorways, killing who knows how many children and women. They came upon an encampment of 22 men of the Fourteenth Kansas and they literally trampled 17 of their members to death. Quantrill and his men found a camp of new Black recruits and also tried to trample them but these Black troopers proved to be too quick and they all escaped certain death.

Quantrill's men then headed down Massachusetts Street, Lawrence's main street, firing and killing everything in their way. Jim Lane was at the top of their kill list but they were unable to find him. Lane had been in his house but a Black man had told Quantrill that Lane was not in town and Quantrill tarried getting to Lane's house. This gave Lane time to slip out of his home clad only in a nightshirt into a nearby cornfield. The other bushwhackers then set about to murder, burn and plunder Lawrence. The men especially shot and killed any white males or Black folk they encountered. It was estimated that in this town of 3,000, 150 lay dead and 30 others were wounded. A hundred homes were burned and the stench of burning flesh was oppressive in town.[95]

The bushwhackers left when they thought a detachment of Union soldiers was coming. Lane and others in town tried to follow the bushwhackers but they had too big of a lead and Quantrill and his men got away.[96]

As more Black soldiers moved into combat roles the likelihood they would be involved in atrocities increased as racist Confederate commanders refused to treat them as combatant soldiers. Jo Shelby, probably the best Confederate field commander west of the Mississippi, disgraced himself by stripping captured Black Union soldiers and whipping them severely. He also let Quantrill and his men torture Black soldiers who were captured at Roseville, Arkansas.[97]

At the Battle of Poison Springs Confederate General John Marmaduke, who would later become governor of Missouri, allowed his men to commit atrocities on Black troopers. The First Kansas Colored Infantry was on a foraging mission when Marmaduke's cavalry surprised them. The First Kansas, which was made-up of a lot of former escaped Missouri bondsmen, fought off two charges but the Rebels' overwhelming numbers overran their positions. When some of the First Kansas troops attempted to surrender they were shot down. After the battle, Marmaduke's men scalped and brutalized wounded members of the First Kansas Colored Infantry before killing them.[98]

The Fort Pillow affair was one of the most brutal in the war. Black union troops were massacred at Fort Pillow in Tennessee by the men of Confederate Major General Nathan Bedford Forrest's command after they had surrendered. This became a rallying cry for the Union Army. When Union commander Thomas Ewing was confronted with an overwhelming Confederate force at Pilot Knob in Missouri he stood defiant. He had a number of Black troops with his small, outnumbered garrison. When the Confederates spread out to show Ewing their overwhelming, superior numbers the Rebels sent demands for surrender under a flag of truce. He sent the flag of truce and surrender terms back with an insolent message. After some time the Rebels again sent a flag of truce with surrender terms. Ewing sent them back with the message that if they sent another flag of truce he would fire on it. Ewing noted that this was the dishonorable tactic used by Forrest to get the Union command to surrender and then the massacre began. Ewing noted "They shall play no such game on me."[99] Lincoln tried to get the Confederate government to treat Black Union soldiers the same as white Union soldiers but the government in Richmond refused all such offers.

Despite these atrocities Black soldiers were filling their quotas in the Union Army. Charles Gabriel Anderson was a slave when the Civil War broke out. He managed to escape slavery in 1864 and then joined the Union Army. He was wounded in battle and was sent to a hospital in Madison, Wisconsin, where he recuperated. He said the hospital was full of wounded Union soldiers. As Charles got better he began to act as a nurse to the other wounded soldiers. When he was completely healed he was asked by the doctors in the hospital to stay on and help with the wounded, which he did. Charles stayed in the Army for two years and six months and eventually made his way back to St. Louis. His brother Jim did not fare as well. Jim had joined the Union Army in 1863 with a different regiment than Charles. Jim died while in the Union Army.[100]

Joe Higgerson escaped from slavery and went to Boonville, Missouri, on November 23, 1863, to join the Union Army. He became a member of the 25th Corps 2nd Division under General Whitsell. Mr. Higgerson fought in the last battle of the Civil War at the Battle of Palmetto Ranch in Texas, 36 miles from the Gulf of Mexico. Ironically, this battle took place a week after Abraham Lincoln was buried.[101]

A lot of Missouri's wealth was tied up in the value of her slaves and the state was hemorrhaging slaves. From 1860 Missouri, according to the Federal Census, had 114,931 slaves. By 1863 that number had dropped to 73,811. That was a difference of 41,120 bondspersons. Many of these bondspersons had enlisted in the Federal Army; others had escaped on the Underground Railroad to free states. The politicians in Missouri were concerned that her bondsmen were escaping to free states and enlisting in the Federal Army and thus Missouri would get no credit for these enlistments. These Missouri politicians at their "Charcoal" convention demanded that General Schofield allow them to recruit "colored men" belonging to disloyal slave owners and have these men be credited on the quota list of Missouri troops.[102]

One of the most unusual cases of bringing Missouri bondspersons out of slavery into a free state was done by the bondspersons' master! Moses U. Payne was a businessman at this time based out of Rocheport, Boonville, and Columbia, Missouri. He had an extensive business empire that spread out over many states. He would by present-day standards most certainly be a multi-billionaire. He had part ownership in many of the mercantile businesses in these three towns. He owned a cotton yarn spinning factory, he acted as a banker to many in central Missouri as well as to many large cotton planters in Alabama, Mississippi and Louisiana. He had a seat on the cotton exchange in New Orleans and was a commission broker of cotton and sugar to ports in Europe. He had extensive holdings in mules, wagons and other livestock.

Payne also owned slaves. He became a member of the Rocheport Colonization Society which had as its goal the sending of slaves back to Africa. However, it is believed that no slaves were actually purchased by this group for this purpose.[103]

On the eve of the Civil War in 1860 Payne owned 60,000 acres in Missouri, Arkansas, Nebraska and Iowa. Despite his large fortune he became a Methodist minister. As he saw the headwinds of the Civil War develop Payne started to divest himself of his property below the Mason-Dixon line and reinvest it in land in the north.[104]

Once the Civil War broke out Payne cooperated with the Union Army officials. In

October of 1864 Payne was issued a permit by the military commander at Fort Leavenworth to conduct a train of 25 ox wagons loaded with corn. He did a lot of long distance hauling for the military. Payne was never required, as were some large land and slave owners in Missouri, to post a bond to guarantee their loyalty to the Union.[105]

Payne was starting to move his operations into Iowa. In 1863 he asked the provost marshal in Missouri on February 26, 1863, for permission to drive a large herd of sheep into Iowa and allow three herders to go with the sheep. The permit was granted on June 27, 1863.[106]

As the Civil War ground on Payne brought his bondspersons from Louisiana, Arkansas and Missouri to the southwest Iowa town of Hamburg and set up a large base of operations. He might have brought as many as 200 to 300 former slaves to this part of the country. He gave them their freedom. He built new houses for them and schools for their children to attend and provided a way for their children to get to school.[107]

Moses Payne became a great benefactor to many colleges far and wide. He gave a huge endowment to one of the first African American Methodist colleges in the country, Paine College in Augusta, Georgia. He also gave money to female colleges and to the rock-ribbed abolitionists at Tabor College in Tabor, Iowa.[108]

The last hurrah for the Confederacy and slavery in Missouri occurred with General Sterling Price's raid of 1864. Price came up from Arkansas with 12,000 men wanting to attack St. Louis and capture all its stores. On the way to St. Louis Price passed through Pilot Knob. Many Blacks who had escaped slavery and found freedom were concerned with Price's movements. They knew Price and his Confederates would capture them and force them back into slavery.

Robert Bryant described his attempt to get away from Price's men. He said the Union soldiers had given his father a wagon and he loaded up Robert and his family to try and make it from Pilot Knob to St. Louis to keep out of the way of Price's Rebels.

Bryant described how the Confederates caught up with the family and their wagon and chased them into the woods. This must have been very frightening for Robert's brother, whom he described as "deaf and dumb." Robert said he hid in the woods for three days by himself as the family had gotten separated. Finally, a Black woman found him and took him with her. She was on the run from Price's men also. For about three weeks they had to hide, trying to avoid Price's men and the bushwhackers who had moved into the area. They would stay in the woods when it was not safe and then go to people's houses for food. Finally, young Robert met up with his family. He and his brother talked in signs again. However, they still had to stay on the run as it was not safe to show themselves. After a few more days the danger had passed and they were able to put their lives back together again as free persons.[109]

Price veered away from St. Louis as it was too heavily fortified. He went across Missouri, fighting skirmishes all along the way with the Federal Army. Finally at the Battle of Westport, Price's 8,500 men met the combined Union forces of 22,000 and were defeated in the largest Civil War battle west of the Mississippi River. Price retreated back into Arkansas with only 6,000 men.

The slave economy of Missouri was collapsing. Most every male was in the Union or Confederate Armies or had left the state. Pearce Buffington, a mill operator near Claysville, Missouri, was sued for using fugitive slaves at his mill. However, the suit was dismissed.[110]

Finally, on January 11, 1865, Missouri governor Thomas C. Fletcher issued an Emancipation Proclamation freeing all slaves in Missouri. Some masters did not tell their bondspersons this news right away but most found out fairly soon. The long nightmare of slavery was over in Missouri.[111]

After the war was over Peter Corn, a former bondsman, met his ex-master on the road. His master was named Jim and he could hardly walk. Peter remembered back to a severe beating Jim had inflicted upon him when Peter was just a boy. Peter said, "I was ridin' my horse and thought about getting' down and whippin' him but when I looked at him I thought I might as well be whippin' a year old child. I let him go." Peter said later Jim got sick and couldn't take care of himself and family members refused to take him in. Jim was taken to the poor folks home where apparently no one but Peter saw him. Peter said he thought of revenge but God would say to him, "No, don't do dat. He will pay for dat." When Jim died in the poor house asylum Peter noted that "he sure did pay for it."[112]

4

Iowa-Nebraska

> "It was mighty slow traveling ... our masters had people looking all over for us. We would ride all night, and then maybe, we would have to stay several days in one house to keep from being caught ... there came along a gang of slave hunters ... (Stevens, one of Captain Brown's men said) Gentlemen you look as if you are looking for someone. (the slave hunters answered) Aye, yes! ... (Stevens) opened the door long enough to grab a double-barreled gun.... You want to see your slaves does you? Well, just look up them barrels and see if you can find them ... they (the slave hunters) ran away as fast as they could."
>
> *Samuel Harper's account of an encounter with slave hunters on the way to freedom in Canada. Harper was one of the bondspersons who gained freedom on John Brown's last famous raid into Missouri.[1]*

Iowa was the first state that did not allow slavery that was carved out of the area of the Louisiana Purchase. When Iowa entered the Union in 1846 her long southern border with slave state Missouri caused concern among some in the Hawkeye state. Since there were no natural impediments on its southern border such as rivers, mountains or escarpment many feared a mass exodus across Iowa's southern boundary with Missouri of slaves into the Hawkeye state. In its early years Iowa's congressional delegation often voted along with those in the slave states, fearing an easing of slave laws would inundate the state with Black bondspersons. Iowa passed laws that required any Black person or mulatto living in the state to post a $500 bond.[2] This was a large sum of money for any person, white or Black. The purpose of this law was to discourage Blacks from moving into the state. Someone said Blacks in Iowa were not very free; they were just "north of slavery." However, as the decade of the 1850s came these attitudes began to change in some of the Iowa residents.

Missouri's northern counties contained very few slaves and as such the traffic of bondspersons seeking independence across Iowa's southern border at times could be brisk but never produced large numbers of freedom escapes. However, in Iowa's southeastern corner the number of bondspersons seeking freedom was significant. Missouri's northeastern river counties had a substantial number of bondspersons residing in them, desirous of obtaining their freedom. Even when Iowa was a territory the southeastern portion of the state provided a haven from slavery for Missouri's bondspersons.

By the middle of the 1850s the western portion of the state became very active in the fight against slavery. Tabor and Civil Bend in southwest Iowa became two very important stations on the Underground Railroad. They also fought to keep slavery out of the territories of Kansas and Nebraska.

One of the most unusual freedom escapes into Iowa occurred when Charlotta Gordon MacHenry Pyles navigated a large group of freedom seekers into the Hawkeye state. Growing up in Kentucky as a slave Charlotta Gordon was an intelligent and attractive and exotic looking young woman. She was tall and majestic and had beautiful black hair. Her heritage included Seminole, Black and German. Charlotta attracted the attention of Harry MacHenry Pyles, a free Black man living around Bardstown, Kentucky. Harry had been granted his freedom by his master who was also his biological father. Harry was taught the trade of harness maker and repairer of shoes. He had his own shop and by all accounts had built up a sizeable business in the area. He and Charlotta became husband and wife and had 11 children together; Charlotta also had another daughter from a previous union, making a total of 12.

Charlotta's master died and left her to his daughter, a Miss Frances Gordon. His daughter vowed to give Charlotta and her children their freedom. This was done in 1853. However, as was often the norm in cases like this, one of Miss Gordon's brothers objected this granting of freedom to Charlotta and her family. Miss Gordon's brothers wanted to keep Charlotta and her family in the chains of slavery. He kidnapped one of Charlotta's grown sons and sold him to a slave trader in Mississippi.[3]

Out of fear that her brothers would kidnap the rest of Charlotta and Harry's family Miss Gordon had the family jailed until a court could rule them her property that she could dispose of as she saw fit. Her brothers took Miss Gordon to court to have her ruled as mentally unfit to take care of her own business. The courts ruled in favor of Frances Gordon and she kept her word and freed the Pyles family. It was felt it would be better if the Pyles family would head north to keep them from being kidnapped by Miss Gordon's brothers or others.[4]

Charlotta and Harry took their remaining 11 children and five grandchildren from her two married daughters. Miss Frances Gordon also traveled with the Pyles as well as an abolitionist white minister from Ohio. It was felt that when going through the slave states of Kentucky and Missouri white escorts would be necessary to keep the Pyle, family from being kidnapped—a huge problem at the time. The two fathers of Charlotta's grandchildren were still held in slavery and had to be left behind.[5]

Before this group headed north on their journey Charlotta, known far and wide in Kentucky as a great cook, fixed prepared meats, gingerbread, cakes and food of every description to feed this large group on their perilous expedition. Supplies were taken to cook corn pones and coffee on the trip and also venison and other game would be hunted and dressed on the mission to eat. The Pyles family plus the two extra passengers set out for Louisville, Kentucky, in a prairie schooner drawn by six fine horses with four horses in the back to relieve the lead team. They made it to Louisville and then left that city on a side-wheeled steamboat and made it to St. Louis. While in St. Louis it was decided to travel overland to their final destination of Minnesota. One wonders if the group wanted to get as far away from the slave states as possible. They hired a white man named Stone to guide them for $100 to the northlands.[6]

It was a tiresome journey. Often bears and wolves would make their presence known and food would have to be thrown out so as to keep these predators from bothering the wagon at night. They were stopped many times in Missouri by whites and slave patrols who wanted to see what this large group was up to. Stone blackmailed the group and demanded another $50 to continue as guide. He said if the money wasn't forthcoming he would tell the authorities that the Pyles family were fugitives and there were many slave traders in Missouri who would be more than willing to sell the group down the river with or without the proper papers.

Finally they made it across the Des Moines River into Iowa. Winter was setting in and the group decided to settle in Keokuk. Harry Pyles started to build a brick house for the group on Johnson Street. The oldest boy, Barney, who had driven the wagon all the way, got a job as an overland freighter hauling cargo from Keokuk to Des Moines. However, it was becoming more difficult to feed all the mouths in the group.[7]

Charlotta devised a bold plan to get all of her family back together again. She would buy the freedom of her two sons-in-law. She found out they could be purchased for $1,500 apiece. Charlotta secured letters of recommendation and with these started for the lecture circuits in the East. She went and spoke in Philadelphia at Independence Hall about the evils of slavery. There had been very few female bondswomen who had gone on the lecture circuit and Charlotta proved to be equal to the task. She was treated well by the Quakers in that part of the country.

Her lectures went over well and she met William Lloyd Garrison, Harriet Beecher Stowe, Lucretia Mott, and Susan B. Anthony. They admired Charlotta and her story of the wickedness of slavery. She traveled thousands of miles and within six months she had earned the $3,000 to purchase her sons-in-law. This was done and they were reunited with their families. Unfortunately, Benjamin, Charlotta's son who had been kidnapped, heard that the sons-in-law had been bought and he naturally wanted his freedom purchased. Charlotta reasoned that the sons-in-law had families to support and that they needed their freedom to provide for their families. Benjamin was single and it was felt he should try and gain his own freedom. Later Charlotta tried to locate Benjamin by running advertisements in newspapers but sadly the Pyles family lost track of him.

Charlotta and her family busied themselves in Keokuk with providing bondspersons with a stopping place on their way to freedom. The Pyles' place in Keokuk, Iowa, became a gateway to freedom for the long trip to Canada for many bondspersons in Missouri, Kentucky and elsewhere. Since many bondspersons didn't trust white people the Pyles furnished a way station on the Underground Railroad to help instruct the bondspersons on how this liberty line could provide them freedom in Canada.[8]

Besides Keokuk in southeastern Iowa there were other spots that provided a gateway to self-emancipation for the bondsperson seeking freedom through the northeastern corridor of Missouri. Croton, Denmark and Salem in Iowa were all tested portals for the freedom seekers. The Quaker and Congregational influences were very strong in these areas. J.H.B. Armstrong was an abolitionist from Ohio who operated a mill near Croton. Croton was just over the Missouri line in Iowa and Armstrong navigated runaways to either Salem, a Quaker settlement, or Denmark, a Congregational stronghold.

Denmark, Iowa, became a stronghold for abolitionist and Underground Railroad activities when the Rev. Asa Turner filled the pulpit in the Congregational Church in town. Later, Dartmouth-educated Dr. George Shedd joined the community. Also, Deacon Theron Trowbridge was very active in helping bondspersons seek freedom. One Sunday morning Trowbridge had a number of escapees in his house. So as to not arouse suspicions he attended church as usual but he told his son to prepare some poisoned biscuits and feed them to the slave-hunters' bloodhounds. When slave-hunters approached the Trowbridge house with their bloodhounds the dogs ate the poisoned biscuits. It was said that the slave-hunters were reluctant to use bloodhounds near Denmark again.⁹

A young bondswoman appeared at Trowbridge's house one day very distraught. She had escaped from Kahoka, Missouri, in Clark County and had been forced to leave her baby in Kahoka. Trowbridge is supposed to have said, "Any mother is entitled to keep her baby." The Deacon strapped on his gun and left for Missouri. Two days later he returned the child to its excited mother.¹⁰

Denmark's activities didn't go unnoticed by others who felt that those who were abolitionists or workers on the Underground Railroad were doing the work of the devil. The Fort Madison (Iowa) *Plain Dealer* edition of May 27, 1857, said that Denmark was a disgrace to the county and the state of Iowa. The newspaper went on to say "Denmark has the name of being a rendezvous of men who occasionally engage in *negro-stealing*, at the same time professing the religion of the gospel. Men ... have been hanged — have received their just deserts — for engaging in practices of which respectable citizens of Denmark have been accused." When the Civil War started in 1862 the *Plain Dealer* objected to Denmark promoting the equality of the races by the socializing of Blacks with whites when it sarcastically objected to "an intelligent *colored* gentleman, late of Virginia, but now sojourning in Denmark, who was introduced to the multitude of white ladies and gentlemen by Parson Turner."¹¹

Many of the escaping bondsmen didn't trust whites and were very apprehensive about them. One such bondsman found himself in southeastern Iowa and was armed with a club and knife. He would permit no one to come close to him and let everyone know he would use his weapons. The abolitionist folks pleaded that they would help him, but to no avail. They finally left food where the bondsman could get it and he ate it heartily and then left the area to gain his freedom. Things didn't always go well in Denmark or elsewhere in the southeastern part of Iowa. One unfortunate fugitive was captured on his way to Denmark. Two brothers named Berry who were farmers in the area turned the fugitives in and received a reward of $200 for this capture. Although many in the area didn't help in the escape of fugitive bondspersons the sentiment in this region was that to turn the fugitives in was wrong. The locals noted that after this episode

Asa Turner was a Congregational minister in Denmark, Iowa. Denmark, along with the Quaker community of Salem, was an important portal out of slave state Missouri into the southeastern corner of free state Iowa. Turner was one of the stationmasters on the Underground Railroad in Denmark. These communities were located in the southeastern part of the state and became important corridors out of the Mississippi River Valley in Missouri. There were low points on the Des Moines River forming part of the southern boundary of the state of Iowa that could be easily forded by a horse or sometimes even walked across. After making it out of slave state Missouri, then across the Des Moines River, the bondspersons could easily make it to Denmark or Salem. From these points the freedom seekers would be put on a path to the east for their permanent freedom (State Historical Society of Iowa, Des Moines).

the Berry brothers' farms didn't prosper and local citizens shunned them. Eventually the Berry brothers sold out and left the area.

Usually from Salem or Denmark the bondspersons were taken down the road to Burlington, Iowa, for the crossing of the Mississippi River. Because slave hunters often patrolled this road, armed men from Denmark would escort the bondspersons in order to get them across the river. If armed men were not available sometimes the escapees, especially if they were coming from the Quaker community of Salem, were garbed as Quakers. Also, wagons were used with produce piled on top of the bondspersons to disguise the true nature of the load to get them across the Mississippi ferry.[12] From Burlington many of these escaping bondspersons would head for Galesburg, a major Illinois Underground Railway station. From Galesburg many would proceed on to Chicago.

Salem and New Garden, Iowa, were settlements in which persons of the Quaker faith dominated the Underground Railroad movement. The hotel in Salem was, at least on one occasion, used as a hide-out for a fugitive slave. Salem was close to the Missouri border and was surrounded by numerous wooded streams that provided many hiding places for the freedom seekers. This little town was full of people in plain grey clothes and broad-brimmed hats that provided the bondspersons with a hiding place from the slave hunters.

Wagons filled with human cargo would leave the town beneath grain sacks filled with bran. The usually quiet Quaker folk seamed to have an awful lot of business that required midnight drives to unknown mills or markets. The children of Salem were trained to not answer any questions posed to them by unknown strangers lest they be slave hunters. The children were to have no eyes or ears concerning this solemn business. The adults in town sometimes talked in a vague language and were very guarded during certain discussions.

The Quakers in Salem even had a split in their group concerning this business of the Underground Railroad. Some thought they were too bold in their help of the bondspersons; others thought they were not bold enough. Aaron Street, Jr., Thomas Frazier, Elwood Osborn, Henderson Lewelling, Marmaduke Jay, James Comer, Eli Jessup, Nathan Hammer and Jonathan Cook all split off from the main branch of the Quakers in town and formed their own "Abolition Friends" to provide more aid to the escaping slaves.[13]

However, Salem is probably best known for its part in the escape of the bondspersons of Ruel Daggs. Ruel Daggs owned 16 slaves and farmed in Clark County in the extreme northeast county in Missouri. Daggs found, as did many of the slave-holders in northeast Missouri, that it was hard to keep his bondspersons on his farm as it was so close to freedom in Iowa. He decided to sell off some or all of his chattel property. This, of course, caused a panic among his bondspersons.

It is believed that bondsman John Walker, age 22, headed north to Iowa and found a safe haven in Salem in 1848. The residents there heard Walker's story and the impending sale of his fellow bondspersons and encouraged Walker to go back to Missouri and retrieve them. Two months later Walker went back to the Daggs farm and rescued his wife Mary and seven others. The other seven were Sam Fulcher, age 40 to 45, and his wife Dorcus; a female named Julia, age 18; another young female, Martha, age 10; a small boy named William and two other small children whose names and ages were not known, one of them being an infant.

The first night, this group headed to northern Clark County in Missouri and went to the dwelling of Dick Leggens and a free Black man named Sam Webster. Leggens' place was very isolated in dense woods just south of the Des Moines River. It was raining extremely hard and the group had to stay an extra day and night but the rain also probably delayed their pursuers. Leggens was an eccentric who had sold off his slaves and apparently Daggs' bondspersons knew they could trust him and Sam Webster.

Leggens helped the group build a raft and instructed them on the best place to cross the river. The group managed to get to the other side of the river near Farmington, Iowa. They proceeded to Salem but were captured by two slave hunters.[14]

As the slave hunters were leading the party of nine away, a dozen residents of Salem led by Elihu Frasier, Thomas Clarkson Frasier, and William Johnson surrounded the slave hunters and demanded that they go to Salem to stand before justice of the peace Nelson Gibbs. The slave hunters reluctantly agreed. As the group moved towards Salem a crowd of between 50 and 100 followed the troupe of freedom seekers. As one might expect escape opportunities arose and all but Sam Fulcher and his son were left as they made it to Salem. Once in Salem the normal office of justice of the peace Gibbs at the Henderson Lewelling house proved to be too small to accommodate the large crowd. The crowd retired to the Anti-Slavery Friends Meeting House two blocks away.[15]

Once there Gibbs asked the Missouri slave hunters if they had written authority from Daggs to act as his agent. The slave hunters replied no. The slave catchers also admitted they didn't know what the fugitive slaves of Daggs looked like and they were just going by general descriptions of them. Gibbs pronounced that the slavers had no right to detain the Fulchers and he could do nothing but dismiss the proceedings. It is not known how well versed Gibbs was in the law but Gibbs was acting in accordance with the Fugitive Slave Act of 1793 which was the law of the land at that time. These slave hunters, having no proof that they were acting on behalf of Daggs and having no written proof that they were his representatives, could not be considered his agents under the Fugitive Slave Act of 1793, Chapter 7, 1 Statute 302. Thus, Gibbs had no other course than to dismiss the proceedings. This point of law as far as slave owners were concerned would be cleared up in the Fugitive Slave Act of 1850.[16]

After the dismissal Paul Way rode up on a sorrel mare with another horse in tow and Sam Fulcher and his son mounted the second horse and rode off. The slave hunters, seeing they had been completely bamboozled, left town extremely agitated. However, this incident didn't end there.

The slave hunting Missourians returned to Salem with a mob estimated between 60 and 300 men. They set up road blocks around the town and began, as they said, to search every "nigger-stealing house" in Salem. They found none of the fugitives but "arrested" eight or nine residents of Salem and held them overnight in the hotel in the town. The sheriff of Henry County, hearing of the disturbance in Salem, rushed to the town to keep things from getting out of hand. When he reached Salem the sheriff was able to arrive at an understanding with the slave hunting mob from Missouri. If the mob released its "prisoners" they would appear in federal court in Burlington, Iowa, to answer charges. This was done. However, four of Daggs' bondspersons were returned to him — probably for the reward money. They were Dorcas Fulcher, who almost certainly became separated from her husband and the rest of her family, the 18-year-old Julia and two of the young children.[17]

Daggs brought an action in trover against Elihu Frazier et al. for $10,000 in 1849. A trover is a legal remedy that allows for the replacement in monetary damages of the wrongful taking of property — in this case Daggs' slaves. Its unique feature is that it allows for the *value* of the property to be awarded, not the actual property. From Daggs' standpoint this seems reasonable since most of his property was long gone and probably on its way to Canada.

However, the federal court in Iowa did not allow this action and Daggs' attorney withdrew it. Through different legal proceedings the suit was continued from court term to court term. Finally in 1850 a suit was filed against Frazier et al. by Daggs to recover the value of the slaves under the Fugitive Slave Act of 1793 and this suit was finally brought to trial. It appears as if the federal district court records pertaining to the *Ruel Daggs v. Elihu Frazier*, et al. proceedings have been lost and the only record of this trial was put into a pamphlet prepared by George Frazee.

Unlike most fugitive slave cases of this type the defendants did not challenge the constitutionality of the Fugitive Slave Act of 1793. Rather, they argued that the Blacks captured were in fact not the fugitive slaves of Ruel Daggs. This was an interesting ploy because of course five of the bondspersons had gotten away and no positive identification of them could be made by the slave hunters. Since the slave hunters had never seen the fugitive bondspersons before they captured them near Salem they could not for sure say that these were in fact Ruel Daggs' escaped slaves. Daggs never provided paperwork that these two slave hunters were in fact acting on his behalf as required by the Fugitive Slave Act of 1793. Sam Fulcher and his son had been released by the justice of the peace so that Frazier and the other Underground Railroad workers had not in fact aided any "fugitives" to escape in the eyes of the law.

Frazier's defense attorney argued that there was little or no substantial evidence in this case to find the defendants responsible for any loss by Daggs. However, the federal jury in Burlington saw the case differently. The judge told the jury to put aside any feelings they might have about slavery and make a judgment. They found that Frazier and four others had helped the slaves escape and Daggs was awarded $2,900 for the loss of his human "property."[18] Some historians and legal scholars feel this may have been one of the last fugitive slave cases tried under the old Fugitive Slave Act of 1793.

Even with this hefty judgment against them the residents of Salem continued to aid escaping bondspersons. Iowa's racist United States senator, Augustus Caesar Dodge, applauded the ruling in Burlington. Dodge had no use for the Underground Railroad or abolitionists. Dodge, like many of his time, felt that since the United States constitution sanctioned slavery then the abolitionists who opposed it were trying to tear down the most holy of United States' documents. Dodge liked to cite the case of *Daggs v. Frazier* as an example of how the citizens of the Hawkeye state were against the workings of those who wished to abolish slavery.[19] However, by the middle of the 1850s, Dodge and his kind were having a hard time getting elected to office in Iowa. Men like James W. Grimes, who became governor and then United States senator from Iowa, had views more in line with the abolitionists of the Hawkeye state.

Some of the abolitionists in southeastern Iowa wanted to try and find a political solution to stop the expansion of slavery in the United States. They started a branch of the Free Soil Party in that area. One of these men was Dr. Curtis Shed. When an opponent of the Free Soil Party tried to ridicule the group and said that the whole state convention of the Free Soil Party in Iowa was organized and engineered by only a dozen men, Shed replied, "Oh, that is a lie, there were only a half a dozen of us."[20]

There were other communities in southeastern Iowa who helped in various degrees in the operation of advancing bondspersons seeking freedom farther north or in Canada. We might mention some of them. Northeast out of Salem was Mount Pleasant, Iowa. Three and a half miles from Mount Pleasant was the home of Professor L.L. Howe. Howe was a graduate of Ohio University in Athens and he had run an academy in Lancaster, Ohio. Two of his better-known pupils were William T. and John Sherman. William T. Sherman became a very controversial but effective general for the Union Army in the Civil War. John Sherman became a well-known United States senator and presidential candidate whose Sherman Anti-Trust Act leveled the playing field for American business.

Howe established a "station" on the Underground Railroad and helped many by providing food and shelter, teams of horses to advance the bondspersons, and generous amounts of money to bondspersons to help them complete their journey. Howe became editor and then owner of the only Free Soil newspaper published west of the Mississippi, the *Iowa Freeman*. Because of his abolitionist sentiments Howe's life and property were in constant peril. His property on occasion was destroyed by pro-slavery men and once in Mount Pleasant he was beaten to the point that many thought he would lose his life. Howe recovered from this beating and continued with the abolitionist cause.[21]

Newport, Iowa, was a point that supported the escape of bondspersons to the north. Some of its residents subscribed to the most radical abolitionist newspaper of the time, *The Voice of the Fugitive*. This newspaper was published and edited in Canada by a former fugitive slave named Henry Bibb. Bibb was a remarkable editor as he would tell of successful bondspersons who had made it to Canada and he loved to mock and thumb his nose at the slave-owners. When some of the abolitionists in Newport began subscribing to this journal the local postmaster said he would burn the next copy of this newspaper he saw coming through his office![22]

Quick thinking was always a necessity for bondspersons and the "conductors" on the Underground Railroad. Henry Morgan was one of the "conductors" in Jefferson County, Iowa. Morgan was escorting a group of fugitives across the Skunk River. Just before he got to the ferry their slave owner rode up to Morgan's wagon and was getting ready to take a look at his cargo when Morgan said, "We've got smallpox in there." This dampened the slave owner's interest in looking and he and his troop of slave hunters wheeled and were seen no more.[23]

Cincinnati, in southern Iowa, also proved to be a portal for escaping bondspersons from Missouri. J.H.B. Armstrong had moved there from Croton. Sometimes free Blacks from Missouri grew tried of the harassment of slave patrols every time they tried to move about. They grew tired of the potential of being kidnapped and sold down south to slavery. One such free Black man with the historically interesting name of Davy Crockett from Missouri sought permanent freedom by escaping via the Underground Railroad in Cincinnati, Iowa. He made his way to Armstrong's house and was directed to freedom in Canada.[24]

At Cincinnati Armstrong helped two bondsmen, John and Archie, escape slavery from Missouri. What made this escape a little out of the ordinary is that Armstrong received a letter from John and Archie when they were safe and sound in Canada. It was unusual for "conductors" to ever hear from their "passengers" once they were sent along the way to freedom in Canada.[25]

Also in southern Iowa is the county of Davis. Near the Missouri border businessman H.B. Wagers often made frequent commercial trips into Missouri. He also made sure slaves knew where his place was in Iowa. He received knocks on his door occasionally to find escaping Missouri bondspersons. Wagers would forward them north on to Ottumwa, Iowa.

One day a bondsman and his wife and three children appeared at his door. They were spirited away in the attic and no sooner had they found their hiding place than a sheriff and a slave posse came to their door. The sheriff crudely asked had they seen any "niggers" pass. The Wagers said "no" and to throw off suspicions they invited the sheriff and his posse in for breakfast. The Wagers then mentioned that these fugitives must have taken the road a half-mile farther east. The sheriff and his posse replied that they didn't have time for breakfast and galloped off to check out this phantom hunch.[26]

George Gaston was the founder of Tabor, Iowa, one of the leading abolitionist towns on the Western Frontier. Gaston and most of the residents of Tabor had ties to Oberlin College in Ohio. Some had called Oberlin one of the leading forces in the abolitionist movement in the United States before the Civil War. Gaston wanted the town of Tabor to be abolitionist and deeply involved in the Underground Railroad and almost all of the town was. John Brown stayed at his house on many occasions and the Gastons housed runaways often. Once while dining with John Brown, Gaston heard a knock on the door and it was a slave hunter. Brown had brought with him two runaways who were also at the dining room table with Brown and the Gastons and their children. The slaver talked for a while and finally asked Gaston if he knew the location of the two runaway slaves. George Gaston answered, "If I did I shouldn't tell you." The slave hunter left empty handed (courtesy Todd House Museum and the Tabor Historical Society, Tabor, Iowa).

Pioneers from Oberlin College in Oberlin, Ohio, George and Maria Gaston, Sam Adams and Darius Mathews had settled in Civil Bend, Iowa, in 1848. They joined Civil Bend residents Lester and Elvira Platt, also an Oberlin graduate, and tough-as-nails Doc Blanchard. Later, in 1850, this group was joined by the Rev. John Todd, Martha Todd and two children and others from Oberlin.[27] This group would form the nucleus of the Tabor and Civil Bend Underground Railroad. Two years later George Gaston and his family, along with the Rev. John Todd and his family, Darius Matthews, and Samuel Adams and his family, and others would move and found the town of Tabor in Iowa. Tabor would become a linchpin in the route of bondspersons escaping from Central and Western Missouri going through Kansas, Nebraska and then into Iowa. As mentioned before, by the mid–1850s the "Little Dixie" and Western sections of Missouri contained some of the highest concentrations of bondspersons on the western frontier. Cecil Turton wrote and researched under the direction of Underground Railroad pioneer writer and researcher Wilbur Siebert. Turton wrote that, "One could fill a book with the instances of aid afforded to fugitives at Tabor."[28]

Civil Bend and Tabor worked in concert with each other to advance escaping fugitives on their way to freedom. Civil Bend was the first point across the dangerous Missouri River crossing coming from the territories of Kansas and Nebraska into Iowa. The Platts had a shingle business and used that as a cover to advance runaways. Dr. Blanchard was bringing an escaping mulatto slave into Civil Bend and asked the Platts to take him to Tabor. The Platts were taking two loads of shingles in two different wagons to Tabor. They put the escapee in Mrs. Platt's wagon on a bed of straw covered by a canvas sheet. When they were in friendly territory the traveler to freedom would sit on top of the wagon watching in every direction. When they weren't sure of his safety he would go into his hiding position. Once they made it to Tabor the fugitive was advanced on down the line.[29]

Dr. Ira Blanchard sometimes used a wagon with a false bottom to bring bondspersons wanting freedom from Kansas to Civil Bend. On one occasion he was coming up from Topeka with three freedom seekers when he made it into Nebraska City, Nebraska Territory. There were a sizeable number of residents in that town that supported slavery. Once they got to Nebraska City John Kagy (sometimes spelled Kagi) took over the operation. Kagy's sister was Barbara Mayhew who, along with her husband Allen, had a cabin known as a place that was friendly to escaping fugitives. Kagy's father Abraham also had a place several miles outside of Nebraska City that gave refuge to those wishing to find freedom. Kagy was one of John Brown's most trusted men. Kagy was an extremely talented young man who had hitched his wagon to Brown's trouble star. Kagy often served as a newspaper correspondent in Kansas when the slavery and anti-slavery forces fought against each other and the eyes of the nation were on the Kansas Territory. Kagy wrote for many newspapers back east about the advancement of slavery in Kansas. These newspapers were the *New York Tribune, Cleveland Leader, Chicago Tribune, New York Evening Post, National Era of Washington D.C.* and the *Kansas Tribune*.[30]

While in Nebraska City the wagon was stopped but its true contents were not fully recognized. Kagy must have decided that the normal ferry crossing at Nebraska City was too dangerous to traverse. They went north of Nebraska City to the Missouri River crossing at Wyoming. However, the ferryman refused to take Kagy's wagon across the river because of treacherous ice flows. Kagy then told the ferryman to make a choice: either his pistol or the ice blocks. The ferryman, seeing the resolution in Kagy's eyes, felt that the ice flows would be better a probability. The ferryman, Kagy and the three bondsmen made it across the river. However, the ferryman's concern over the blocks of ice in the river proved to be real as he had to avoid them and ended up a half a mile from the proper landing site. Kagy then took the group to Doc Blanchard's place in Civil Bend. After some rest the group headed for Tabor and then were sent on the way to Canada.[31]

The Kansas-Nebraska Act of 1854 allowed for slavery in the Nebraska Territory. Several of its residents took advantage of this law and owned slaves. As a matter of fact, Nebraska didn't outlaw slavery in the territory until shortly before the Civil War. One of the leading newspapers in the Nebraska Territory, the *Nebraska City News*, was boastful of the fact that the territory had not outlawed slavery. On November 20, 1858, the newspaper's headline read: "Slavery Not Abolished in Nebraska." The article then goes on to say, "slavery still here. The niggers coming.... The clanking of the chains of slavery may be heard upon her (Nebraska) great plains ... the people will do as they are a mind to and will have niggers where it pays and when it suits their convenience." The *Nebraska City News*, on December 24, 1859, said, "indefinitely postpone the nigger bill. Poor Sambo!" *Nebraska City News*, November 10, 1860, on the election of Abraham Lincoln had to say "This event (the election of Lincoln) as much as it is to be deplored and lamented.... Fanaticism and radicalism have triumphed...."[32]

Steven Friel Nuckolls, better known as S.F. Nuckolls, was the first man to bring slaves into the Nebraska Territory.[33] Nuckolls was an incredible business entrepreneur in the Nebraska Territory and was the founder of Nebraska City. He owned several large general mercantile stores in the area. Nuckolls owned the only banking institution in the territory that didn't fail in the panic of 1857. He owned a railroad and several other businesses in the area. As the territorial representative for this area he voted not to abolish slavery and to exclude free Blacks from the territory.[34]

Nuckolls also owned five enslaved humans including two females, one of whom was named Eliza. Eliza's path crossed with John Williamson.

John Williamson was of mixed heritage from Arkansas and was part Black and part Cherokee. Williamson somehow made his way to southwest Iowa from Arkansas. He fell in with the Oberlin College colony in Tabor and Civil Bend, Iowa. One resident of Tabor, Iowa, stated that he cut a striking figure and John Todd said he was very shrewd and wise beyond his years. In the census of 1860 Williamson listed himself as being a "free mulatto." It is not known if Williamson was actually free but he certainly was safe in Tabor or Civil Bend. Williamson was a very enterprising young man who bought eggs and butter and other commodities, mostly from the farmers on the Iowa side of the river, and then sold them to the numerous travelers heading west. He also sold his commodities to the merchants in Nebraska City, the largest population center in the area. In addition he sold jewelry and other items.

In this way Williamson had a perfect cover for bringing runaways from the Nebraska side of the river to the Iowa side for escape on the Underground Railroad. These runaways, who had mostly had come from Missouri, Oklahoma or Arkansas or other slave states, had then journeyed up through Kansas and then to Nebraska. A Black man from Kentucky named Thomas Reid (sometimes spelled Reed) threw in his lot with Williamson. It has been theorized that Williamson had helped Reid in an escape in the area — possibly when Reid's master was on the way from Kentucky to the West. In 1860 Williamson was living in Council Bluffs, Iowa, with Reid and another Black man. The other Black man was possibly a fugitive using an alias and it is also probable that Williamson might have obtained forged papers for the man, allowing him to pose as a "free man."[35]

In early December of 1858 Williamson used a skiff to cross the Missouri River and brought Eliza and another female slave from Nebraska City to Civil Bend. Doc Blanchard then took them from Civil Bend and traveled the 20 miles to Tabor at daybreak.[36]

The Rev. John Todd and George Gaston and the rest of the Tabor Underground Railroad brain trust decided it was unsafe to move the young ladies during the daytime and determined to wait until night. However, when the early December nightfall came it was on a moonless, cloudy and misty Iowa night. A wagon was procured for the trip but the driver couldn't see his horses, much less the road. Deacon Origen Cummings then took a lantern to guide the wagon loaded with Eliza and her fellow bondswoman.

Unlike slave owners hundreds of miles away in Missouri or other slave states Nuckolls was very familiar with the work of Civil Bend and Tabor and knew exactly where to look for his fugitive slaves. He had a brother who was a merchant in nearby Glenwood, Iowa, and two brothers-in-law who sold goods in Sidney, Iowa. He sent messengers to both places and had them post lookouts on the bridges across the Nishnabotna River and Silver Creek, likely spots for the Underground Railroad train to cross. Fortunately Cummings, with his lantern and wagon with the young ladies, had already crossed Silver Creek before a member of Nuckolls' slave posse could reach the crucial bridge.[37]

Nuckolls offered a $200 reward for the return of the two young ladies. The *Nebraska City News* was sure the two had been "enticed away ... by some vile, white-livered Abolitionist."[38]

Nuckolls searched all over southwest Iowa with a large slave posse and did not find the young females. He became convinced that his slaves were still in the Civil Bend area. He had 75 men search the houses in Civil Bend without the authority of search warrants.[39]

Reuben Williams lived in Civil Bend and he vehemently protested the illegal searches of his house and those others in Civil Bend. Nuckolls rode up and hit Williams with a blunt instrument and disabled him and produced deafness in Williams from which never recovered.[40] The Nuckolls mob descended upon other houses in Civil Bend, including that of James W. Smith.[41]

Henry Garner, a young Black man who lived in the Civil Bend area, was attacked by Nuckolls and 14 of his thugs. They choked and then stripped him of his clothing and then tied him to a tree where he was beaten to within an inch of his life. Reports stated that Garner had cuts, bruises and lacerations of a most critical nature from his neck to his waist. Joseph Garner, Jr., Henry's brother, was set upon and then choked and hanged by his neck.[42]

A messenger was sent out from Civil Bend for authorities to come and arrest Nuckolls and end his terrorist actions. Authorities set the trial date to be for the next day and Nuckolls was allowed to return to Nebraska City. However, two of his men were kept in Iowa to make sure the Nebraska City businessman would show up for the trial.[43]

Word was then sent out from Civil Bend to Tabor for a company of men to come and make sure the trial was a fair one and that Nuckolls would not bring more armed men into Civil Bend. Because Tabor had periodically received threats from slave state men that the town would be raided and sacked the State of Iowa had equipped Tabor and allowed it to form its own militia unit. Every able-bodied man in Tabor was issued a musket or rifle and 12 cartridges. On a snowy, blustery, cold December day the company of armed Tabor men headed down to Civil Bend. However, blocks of ice in the Missouri River made it too dangerous to cross and the defendants stayed in Nebraska City.[44]

The *Des Moines Valley Whig* newspaper fully supported the Tabor people. They wrote, "We trust that the people of Tabor will be prepared for the attack of the drunken band of filibusters from Omaha (this paper mistakenly thought Nuckolls and the young woman held in bondage were from Omaha) and give them a warm reception."[45]

Eliza and her friend were forwarded onto the Underground Railroad system in Iowa and then to Chicago. Eliza felt she could be safe in the burgeoning Black community of the Windy City. However, Nuckolls chased her to the city on Lake Michigan. Obviously Nuckolls had expended a lot of time and money to find the young lady. With an accomplice Nuckolls saw Eliza walking down Clark and Van Buren streets in Chicago. He came in a carriage and tried to force her into it. Eliza cried out and some citizens passing by heard her pleas and came to her rescue. When police came to investigate this attempted kidnapping Nuckolls produced arrest warrants for Eliza that had been issued in the Nebraska Territory.

By this time a large throng of Black Chicago citizens and white abolitionists had surrounded Nuckolls, Eliza and the police. Her fellow African Americans spirited Eliza off from the scene. Nuckolls heard the mob yell, "Hang the Slaver Man! Throw him in the lake!" The police told Nuckolls they couldn't guarantee his safety and told him to go back to Nebraska. More police arrived and they broke up the crowd and took the slaver to a safe area.[46]

Eliza felt that Chicago was not safe for her anymore because of the Fugitive Slave Laws. So she left Chicago for Canada and settled there.[47]

In all probability Eliza and her friend were sexual slaves of Nuckolls. Many wealthy slave-owning men during this time would buy attractive young slave women, many times light-skinned mulattoes. These unfortunate young ladies would be dressed in the latest fashions, fed well and housed in acceptable accommodations and used as unwilling mistresses. Nuckolls was a close friend of the publisher and editors of the *Nebraska City News* and they supported his slave-holding ways. They wrote in the *Fremont Herald* that the young ladies were well fed and clothed and that they had been promised their freedom and some property and that they should feel fortunate that Nuckolls had been their benefactor.[48]

Later, the *Nebraska City News* wrote a vitriolic piece on this matter and said, "A number of white and very black Republicans-degenerated into full blooded negroes resist. They take her from an officer of the government, and sent her kiting to Canada, to finish her existence in a house of ill-fame, it is to be hoped as respectable as the one in which she was found in Chicago. The Republican journals, if we may except our contemporary in this city, unanimously rejoice over the escape of Eliza. They think it very fine; they deem it a very excellent thing for a nigger to be run off from a home of luxury and plenty to end a miserable existence in a low and dirty brothel. Such is practical northern Republicanism as exemplified in the Eliza case."

Previously they had penned in the same edition, "she was in a free-love and freedom loving brothel in the very Black Republican city of Chicago.... Abolitionists thought she would do better if she were to put on city airs and emigrate to the free and independent city of the lakes. And she left."[49]

There seems to be no truth to these accusations of prostitution by Eliza or the other young brave girl who escaped with her. Canada was very strict in keeping her new arrivals on the straight and narrow. There was absolutely no evidence that Eliza was engaged in anything but an honest living in Chicago. It is doubtful so many would have come to her aid if she had been doing what the *Nebraska City News* so cowardly and without fact accused her of doing so. Unfortunately, it seems as if Nuckolls and the editor of the newspaper could only see Eliza and her friend in sexual terms so they made bitter and unfounded charges of prostitution on her part. Later, two male slaves of Nuckolls escaped and he made no effort to find them. It is believed John Williamson also helped to free them.[50]

Reuben Williams, who had been struck by Nuckolls and suffered a permanent injury, sued him. Williams was awarded an $8,000 judgment. He built a new barn with the settlement from the suit. Nuckolls moved to Colorado and prospered as a mine owner. After a while, Nuckolls came back to visit friends in Nebraska City. John Todd couldn't help but notice that when Nuckolls was back in the area Reuben Williams' barn burnt to the ground. Todd's obvious thought was that Nuckolls or friends of his had committed the arson.[51]

Henry Garner, after he had taken a beating at the hands of the Nuckolls thugs, took advantage of a new law passed in Iowa in 1857. The law stated that Blacks had the same standing in the Iowa courts and could testify against white citizens. Henry Garner, Green Garner and Thomas Reid all testified against Nuckolls and his drunken men.

Because of its racial nature, this case brought out all the bigots in the area and there were many threatening shouts aimed at the Garner brothers and Reid and their attorneys. The racist bullies made many statements that they would not allow the trial to proceed. However, Sears, the presiding judge in the case, took control of his courtroom and told the racists he would not allow them to disrupt the proceedings. Sears made a superb address to the courtroom about the majesty of the law and that everyone, regardless of the color of their skin, was entitled to their day in court. The trial proceeded without any interruptions.[52]

Another interesting escape occurred in Civil Bend and Tabor from slaves who had originated from Nebraska City. Alexander Majors, whose huge freighting operation of Russell, Majors and Waddell dominated the frontier, was a slave holder who had six humans in bondage. Majors had moved his freighting operation, where he had at one time over 5,000 employees, from Missouri to Nebraska City, N.T. Before he would move to Nebraska City he made the city fathers promise they would allow no saloons or liquor stores in town.[53]

Majors' slaves included two females in their 40s, a young woman in her 20s, a girl and boy of 14 and another boy of 12.[54] These bondspersons had obviously heard of the opportunities for liberty and crossed the river to the two southwestern Iowa towns that were their gateway to freedom. Majors was away a lot from home for business reasons and this probably made the escape of his bondspersons easier. The business mogul offered a huge reward of $1,000 for the return of these escapees.[55] No one ever collected on the reward and it is hoped that this group made it to Canada and their ultimate freedom.

In 1860 Alexander Majors, along with his partners, formed the Central Overland California and Pikes Peak Express Company. It became better known as the legendary Pony Express, moving mail from St. Joseph, Missouri, to Sacramento, California.

Oftentimes those involved with freedom seekers would use their occupation to help advance bondspersons down the line to liberty. A Congregational minister in Atchison, Kansas, who had graduated from Oberlin College, knew the Rev. John Todd in Tabor and advanced a young Black woman. Todd planned to take the young lady to a meeting of Congregational ministers in Council Bluffs, Iowa, and hand her off to one of the ministers there, George Hitchcock. Hitchcock was the stationmaster at Lewis, Iowa, one of the points east of Tabor on the Underground Railroad. However, for some reason Hitchcock was not able to make the meeting. When Todd got back home he had to change plans and he decided to dress the young lady as much as possible as Mrs. Todd.

Todd took off with the veiled and heavily-wrapped young lady and rode off across the Iowa prairie in a carriage. To the casual observer it looked as if the minister and his wife were taking a casual trip across the rolling hills of Southwestern Iowa. When Todd got to Lewis he gave the young Black lady to Hitchcock and she was advanced to her freedom.[56]

Two young woodcutters found their way into Tabor by a very circuitous route. They came from the Lexington, Missouri, area. Possibly, they were woodcutters who had helped to supply the enormous amount of firewood used by the steamboat trade along the Missouri River. It is also likely that they even used the steamboats for part of their escape. These two young men made their way through Kansas and then into Nebraska. Unfortunately they were recaptured in the Nebraska Territory. They were bound and crossed the Missouri River and cut

The Rev. John Todd, a Congregational minister from Tabor, Iowa. This photograph suggests how John Todd would have looked about the time he was doing his work on the Underground Railroad. Todd and Gaston also wanted to start a college in Tabor, Iowa, like Oberlin that espoused the idea of equality for the races and genders. Todd graduated from Oberlin College Seminary and felt equality was an important message. He once wrote to his cousin who was neutral about the abolitionist movement that "...I don't think any man in the world can justify the war of the American Revolution & at the same time condemn the slaves for rising to obtain their liberties. 'All men are created equal.' Is that rhetorical flourish? Or is it sober truth? If so, then the African has right to pursue *his*...." Tabor became an important link with the Kansas Underground Railroad movement. Once in Tabor the bondspersons were sure to be advanced to their freedom. Because there were so many slave and bounty hunters in the area usually the people of Tabor would escort the bondspersons to their next stopping point so as to not risk a capture (courtesy Todd House Museum and Tabor Historical Society, Tabor, Iowa).

across southwest Iowa. The slave hunters made their way into Missouri as quickly as possible with these men. They were jailed in a small town just over the border in Linden, Missouri.[57]

When the two woodcutters were caught the slave hunters asked them where they were going and they replied to "Tabor." The slavers replied that all that the abolitionists in Tabor were interested in doing was selling the slaves down the river to New Orleans.[58] On a cold December's night, while the slave hunters drank themselves into a stupor, the two young woodcutters were busy. They had been supplied with a pan of coals to keep themselves warm. They used the coals to burn a hole in the floor of the jail. The jail was built up off the ground, allowing them to escape.

With no maps or direction the two headed towards the Missouri River bottoms and knew if they followed them north they could make their way into Iowa and then eventually to Tabor. They apparently saw right through the slave hunters' "advice" to stay away from Tabor and they knew this little village was their key to finding freedom. Then, a white-out snow storm occurred. During these snow storms it is impossible to see your hand in front of your face. The two became separated. One of the woodcutters made it safely into Tabor and stayed at the house of George Gaston. The people of Tabor wanted to forward the young man on his way on the Underground Railroad but he refused to go until his partner could go with him. The young woodcutter set about to earn his keep and cut wood in Tabor. He also undoubtedly earned extra money to help on his way to freedom.[59] After some time the two woodcutters were reunited in Tabor and made it on their way to freedom.

However, soon after the two bondsmen left Tabor the town was visited by well-armed slave hunters. They banged loudly on George Gaston's door, swearing oaths and wanting their fugitive slaves. The men of Tabor, despite being pious Christians, felt they had every right to defend themselves and their friend George Gaston. The Tabor men grabbed their rifles and told the slave hunters they were badly outnumbered and that the slavers had better leave town. The bounty hunters left but swore they would come back to Tabor — only this time armed with search warrants.[60] The slave bounty hunters never came back.

Tabor was not only active in the Underground Railroad system but also served as a warehouse and recruiting point for the Kansas National Committee and other such organizations. The town was often full of clothing, food, ammunition, rifles, and even cannons meant for the settlers who were fighting to keep slavery out of Kansas. The Rev. John Todd even stored in his basements over 200 Sharps rifles that John Brown would use on his raid on the Federal arsenal at Harpers Ferry, Virginia.[61] Also, thousands of abolitionist settlers came through Tabor bound for the Kansas Territory to keep the territory out of the hands of the slave interests.

After the fugitive bondspersons left Tabor they were escorted to the next station on the way. The town of Lewis in Cass country was a frequent destination. Congregational minister George Hitchcock's impressive two-story house, made of native sandstone, must have given the escapees a feeling of safety. As routes had to be changed often so as to throw off the chase of the slave hunters the bondspersons were sometime taken to Quincy in Adams County. At Quincy the Rev. Isaac Burns, a Methodist minister who had been run out of Missouri for his anti-slavery views, helped the escapees. Also helping at the station in Quincy were Daniel and Martha Richey.[62]

Another route was to go straight out of Tabor to the area of Red Oak and Frankfort. Sometimes bondspersons were also run up from Amity, Iowa, to Red Oak. Amity was a village only three miles from the Missouri border. In this town was a college and the townspeople there were very much anti-slavery in sentiment. In the election of 1860 of the 71 votes cast in Amity Township 69 were for Abraham Lincoln.

Frankfort is a community that no longer exists but at one time before the Civil War it had 17 buildings to its credit. It lay just outside of Red Oak, the present seat of Montgomery County. The Rev. William W. Merritt was the head of the Underground Railroad movement in the area. The sheriff of Montgomery County, L.G. Clark, was like many law men in the north. The Fugitive Slave Act of 1850 stated that he must pursue with vigor any fugitive slave or he could face imprisonment or be fined himself. Obviously, Sheriff Clark was in sympathy with those who wanted to see the slaves on their way to freedom.

One day, the Rev. William Merritt was in a store in Frankfort talking with an acquaintance when Sheriff L.G. Clark came in and loudly accused Merritt of harboring "niggers" and warned Merritt against committing any criminal acts in the county. When Merritt went out to the hitching rack to retrieve his horse the sheriff came up to Merritt and in low tones warned the minister that he had been ordered to search his premises by a United States marshal. The sheriff said he and a posse would be out at Merritt's place at nine o'clock that night. Obviously, the sheriff's loud proclamation in the store to Merritt about not committing any "criminal act" was for the benefit of the Unites States marshal.

Merritt wasn't too concerned about the raid because he had no fugitive slaves at his place at the present time. However, when he got to his home he found in his living room the Rev. John Todd reading the bible. Todd had brought with him two adult males, three adult women and three child bondspersons. Merritt fixed the large group a hearty breakfast and then told Todd that law officers were on their trail!

Merritt immediately loaded up his cargo of eight humans in a covered wagon and took them north into Cass County, Iowa, and made the hand-off. The good reverend made it back to his home place. After he had gotten home, true to his word Sheriff Clark and his posse came to the Reverend Merritt's place. They made a thorough search of his home and out-buildings, but of course found no one. Again, probably for the benefit of the U.S. marshal, Sheriff Clark loudly proclaimed after the search came up empty that he would give out of his own pocket two dollars "to catch anyone running niggers through his county."[63]

From these points the bondspersons were moved eastward into central and eastern Iowa. Through a series of places and towns such as Stuart, Winterset and the Quaker Divide near Earlham the bondspersons made their way. Sometimes they were escorted by the locals, but at other times they had to fend for themselves. Another trail went south of Des Moines and included coming from southwest Iowa to Winterset, Indianola, Knoxville, Pella and Oskaloosa and then farther east across the Mississippi River.

Once near the Quaker Divide two sisters arrived from western Missouri. Their master was also their biological father and they had run away when they heard he was going to sell them down south. They made it to a Quaker family named Cook close to Summit Grove, now Stuart, Iowa.

They rested at the Cook house for a while but one Monday afternoon they spotted their master/father coming to get them. Their master and a slave posse came to the Cook's house and demanded entrance to look around for his chattel property. Cook tried to stall them, demanding to see a search warrant.

However, Cook's wife appeared and told her husband to allow the men in and let them look around. This was done and the slave posse looked high and low but found no fugitive slaves. Once the posse was gone Anna Cook revealed that she had hidden the girls between two feather mattresses and then made the bed.[64]

Eastward, the bondspersons were taken to the Jordan House in west Des Moines or to Mitchellville, Lynnville, Sully or Newton. At Mitchellville, Thomas Mitchell, founder of the town, used his knowledge of the wool trade to communicate with J.B. Grinnell on the coming of fugitives into the town of Grinnell. Mitchell once wrote, "Dear Grinnell: Uncle Tom says if the roads are not too bad you can look for those fleeces of wool by to-morrow. Send them on to test the market and price, and no back charges. Yours, 'Hub.'"[65]

Newton, Iowa, lay between Mitchellville and Grinnell. Joseph Arnold and Matthew Sparks were two of the men who kept the tracks greased in that area. One day they spotted coming down the road three Black men who had come from the Cherokee Nation to seek freedom. The three men had the names Arnold and Sparks written on a soiled piece of paper. These three men were forwarded on to the next stop.

In the years just prior to the Civil War the escapes began to change. Instead of one or two bondspersons escaping at a time it was obvious that whole families and extended family members began to escape. Large groups of sometimes 10 liberty seekers or a dozen or more began to show up at a time on the freedom trail. Near Newton on August 13, 1860, a group of 15 bondspersons escaping from Missouri via Kansas and Tabor showed up in central Iowa. They filled two wagons and were escorted by a dozen men. That same day another party of 19 fugitive bondspersons passed by Newton on the freedom trail to Canada.[66]

Among those escorting the first group of freedom seekers that camped near Newton was Barclay Coppoc who himself, ironically, was a fugitive from justice. Although a frail young man who suffered from consumption, Coppoc was one of John Brown's men who attacked Harpers Ferry in October of 1859. He managed to escape capture by Robert E. Lee and his United States soldiers. He fled to Canada and then came back to his home in Springdale, Iowa. The governor of Virginia asked Governor Kirkwood of Iowa to extradite Coppoc for the crimes at Harpers Ferry. Kirkwood refused on technical reasons. The governor of Virginia corrected his original mistakes on his extradition papers and again requested from Kirkwood to extradite Coppoc. After these corrections Kirkwood issued a warrant for Coppoc but was unable to find him. Coppoc apparently then left for Kansas. He then joined up with a group of men and led a troop of fugitive bondspersons from Missouri through Iowa — all this while Coppoc was himself a fugitive from justice. In 1861 Coppoc joined the Union Army's Third Kansas Infantry, which was led by Colonel James Montgomery. A first lieutenant, Coppoc was killed when the train he was riding in fell from a 40-foot-high trestle into the Platte River. The trestle's supports had been burnt away by Confederate soldiers.[67]

From Newton the next stop on the liberty line through Iowa was Grinnell. Josiah Bushnell Grinnell was the founder of the town and its biggest promoter. Grinnell, full of boundless enthusiasm, was also a big promoter of himself. He liked to claim that when Horace Greeley uttered his famous statement, "Go West, young man, go West," Greeley was talking to him, although others also made this claim. Grinnell also liked to boast that he was the "president" of the Underground Railroad in Iowa, which was more narcissistic than true. Grinnell's skills at self-promotion came in handy when he became a United States congressman during the Civil War. Although a Congregational minister, Grinnell became one of the biggest wool merchants in the state of Iowa. His large barn for wool was a good, warm hiding place for fugitive bondspersons.

Ironically, when Grinnell first came out west to settle he first stopped in Marion County,

Missouri, at the site of Marion College where his wife had inherited 640 acres of land. His wife's wealthy family had also contributed funds to Marion College when it espoused the abolitionist cause to help increase the value of their lands in the county. Grinnell noted the influence of slavery and how it had snuffed out the promise of this progressive college.[68]

A railroad man, Henry Farnam, advised Grinnell to settle in Iowa, a free state, and to stay away from the slave state Missouri as there were more opportunities in free states. Grinnell wanted to found a town with the help of his wife's money that would promote his anti-slavery views. Grinnell conferred with Grenville Dodge, at that time a railroad surveyor, about where the best location would be for a town. Dodge proposed the site where Grinnell now stands.[69] Dodge would later be the chief engineer to build the transcontinental railroad.

Into Grinnell came a couple of crackerjack helpers on the Underground Railroad. Leonard F. Parker, an Oberlin College graduate, came into town to be an educator. He became a leader at Grinnell College teaching Greek, Latin and history. He also taught at the University of Iowa. Parker had an interesting knowledge of the Underground Railroad on the western frontier. In 1856 he had first gone to Lawrence, Kansas, and met many of the abolitionist leaders there when the town was in turmoil over the question of slavery and the liberation of bondspersons who came into town. Parker also knew John Brown and John Todd and the work done in Tabor, Iowa. Parker noted that most of the escaping slaves who came into the town didn't come from the south into Grinnell, but instead came from the west from Tabor and what was known as the John Brown route into Grinnell.[70]

Amos Bixby was also an ardent anti-slavery man in Grinnell. Bixby would later settle in Boulder, Colorado, and become a well-known newspaper owner and editor in that part of the country. In a letter to Parker, Bixby told of a young, 16-year-old female who had escaped from Missouri through eastern Kansas and came to Grinnell via the Tabor route. The girl's name was Fannie Overton. Since the Bixbys already had a Fannie in their family they renamed her Frances.

Bixby was able to keep the girl in his house for three months. Grinnell was different from Salem or Denmark in southeastern Iowa or Tabor or Civil Bend in southwestern Iowa in that slave hunters didn't often make it that far north and into the interior of Iowa, so Bixby felt safe harboring her for that long. What made this young lady remarkable was her capacity to learn. When she came to the Bixby home she could not read or write and did not even know her alphabet. However, Bixby noted that this girl was like a sponge for knowledge and literally soaked up everything and read everything she could get her hands on. The church in Grinnell had a contest for all the youngsters of high school age to memorize the most bible scriptures. Young Frances Overton won that prize even though three months prior she could not read or write! The white parents in the town of Grinnell were very much outraged over Amos Bixby's young Black protégée winning this much-coveted award.

Young Frances had come to the Bixby household about the time of the escape of Eliza, the Nuckolls' female bondswoman. Nuckolls sent slave hunters to scour the state of Iowa to find her. When the slave hunters got south of Grinnell someone informed them of the fugitive slave girl living at the Bixby household. Bixby felt it necessary to send the young girl out of town to a Quaker settlement for safe keeping. She did not go back to the Bixbys and it is not certain what happened to her. Bixby had heard later that her life did not turn out well but he wasn't certain of the accuracy of that report. Bixby did relate to Parker that the poor girl had been raped by her master's sons in a most disgusting manner.[71]

From Grinnell the runaways were often directed to Iowa City, West Branch or Springdale. Springdale was a very active Quaker town. For much of the decade of the 1850s the railroad tracks into Iowa ended in the Iowa City area. When in this locality John Brown and his sons liked to stay in Springdale. The Quakers would protect his identity and Springdale was close enough to the railhead in Iowa City so that if they needed to go east it was a fast exit. Often, fugitives would stay in Springdale until enough money had been collected to move them farther east.[72]

The situation in eastern Iowa as far as the Underground Railroad was concerned was much different than in the sparsely settled western part of the state or in the Territories of Kansas and Nebraska. Eastern Iowa was much like the Underground Railroad in Ohio or Pennsylvania. The area had been settled for some time and the farms were close together. Orchards had been in existence for years, wells had been dug. If need be, like William Wells Brown did in Ohio you could duck into a barn and find ears of corn there in storage. In the newly settled territories or in western Iowa wells were farther apart, orchards were years from bearing fruit, and there was little surplus in the barns. In eastern Iowa the farms were well established and there were railroads, reliable steamship travel, a telegraph system and the mail service was regular and on time. These all could be used to the advantage of the weary fugitive traveler. However, because this area was more populous, this also presented problems and often the traveler would have to hole-up somewhere for several days until safe situations presented themselves.

From Springdale, West Liberty or Iowa City and stations near these points the escaping bondspersons would be advanced to positions that would allow them to cross the Mississippi River. Then they would go into Illinois and hopefully cities to the east like Chicago or Cleveland or to the ultimate point of safety in Canada. Clinton, Davenport and Low Moor would be used as crossing points for the large river that provided Iowa with her eastern boundary.

Mr. Tatum was taking a load of runaways in a wagon from Springdale to Mechanicsville, 18 miles away, when the wagon became stuck in quicksand at Gray's Ford on the Cedar River. Tatum went to the nearest house and got help. The helper made the obvious suggestion of unloading the wagon to make it lighter and Tatum strenuously objected. The helper seemed to understand why Tatum didn't want to unload the wagon for fear his cargo would be recognized as fugitives. The men found a fence rail and managed to raise the wagon to higher ground and the journey was successfully continued.[73]

Just six miles south of the important station at Springdale was West Liberty, which was on the tracks of the Chicago, Rock Island and Pacific Railroad. Sometimes escaping bondspersons were put on the rail line at West Liberty for transportation across the Mississippi River at Davenport and then on to Illinois to Lake Michigan and freedom in Canada.[74]

As stated before, the mail service in eastern Iowa in the late 1850s was good enough that letters could be sent to advancing stations telling of new arrivals. G. W. Weston in Low Moor, Iowa, wanted to tell C.B. Campbell in Clinton, Iowa of new arrivals. Weston sent this note:

Low Moor, May 6, 1859

Mr. C.B.C.

Dear Sir — By to-morrow evening's mail, you will receive two volumes of the 'Irrepressible Conflict,' bound in *Black*. After perusal, please forward, and oblige.

G.W.W.[75]

One of the most controversial Underground Railroad passages on the western frontier was by John Brown shortly before he attacked the federal arsenal at Harpers Ferry in Virginia and electrified the nation. In December of 1858 John Brown was in southeastern Kansas with James Montgomery where they were renewing a guerrilla war against pro-slavery forces in Kansas and Missouri.

Earlier, from 1855 until late 1857, George W.S. Lucas, a Black man who had been with Brown and his men in that area of Kansas, made a remarkable statement. In an interview with Underground Railroad pioneer Wilbur H. Siebert, Lucas stated that Brown and his men had liberated 560 slaves in Humboldt in Allen County to the rich valley of the Neosho River to Oswego in Labette County on the border to the "Indian Nations." Lucas later went to Ohio where he helped on the liberty line.[76]

Montgomery invited Brown to come on an expedition with some 100 of his men against Fort Scott, Kansas, where a free-state man, Benjamin Rice, was being held captive. Brown chafed when another man was in charge of a military operation. Brown wanted to burn Fort Scott to the ground but Montgomery was opposed to such unnecessary violence. The raid went fairly well and Rice was liberated. The only bloodshed occurred when a pro-slavery man who had been the ex–deputy marshal fired a shotgun at John Kagy and Kagy's heavy overcoat saved him from severe injury. Then Montgomery's men killed the pro-slavery man with a shot to the forehead. Jennison led the plundering of the pro-slavery man's store.[77]

Brown was spoiling for some kind of action when he took his own men and rode away from Fort Scott. Brown had hoped that God "would provide him a basis of action." It didn't take long for Brown's prayer to be answered.

John Brown was one of the most controversial figures of this era. Although he had a place near Osawatomie, Kansas Territory, because there were murder warrants out for Brown he often stayed in Tabor and Springdale, Iowa. Whenever Brown came to Iowa either to get away from Kansas when things got too "hot" there for him or to go back east to raise funds, he would bring bondspersons to Tabor. The slavers in Kansas were terrified of Brown because of his uncompromising violent ways. He and his sons had hacked to death five slave owners on Pottawatomie Creek in the K.T. Other incidents in Kansas had made the name of John Brown the most feared in the territory to slave owners. Was John Brown a "martyr" or just a cold blooded killer? The many biographies about him paint him in different lights (State Historical Society of Iowa, Des Moines).

Brown's men were at a fortified position near the Missouri border when Jim Daniels, a slave who was selling brooms, drifted across the Missouri-Kansas boundary. He came in contact with George Gill, one of Brown's men, and told him his story. Not only was he to be sold but his wife and babies belonged to an estate and they were to be put up for sale at an administrator's auction. Very often in situations like these each family member would be purchased by a different slave owner and the family unit would be horrendously broken up forever. Babies would literally be torn from their mother's arms.[78]

It didn't take Gill long to report to John Brown. It was now Brown's intention to "carry the war into Africa." On the night of December 20-21, 1858, Brown led a party of 10 men, including Jenison, Kagy and Gill, to the home of Harvey G. Hicklin (or Hicklan) in Missouri. He was Daniel's temporary master. Another of Brown's men, Aaron Stevens, would take eight men to liberate a couple of other slaves that Daniels said wanted their freedom.

At midnight Brown and his men entered the home of Hicklin revolvers drawn and told him of their mission. In and around Hicklin's house was the property of the Lawrence estate — the actual owner of Jim Daniels and his family. Brown intended to take some of the property of the Lawrence estate for the maintaining of the Daniel's family on the way north. This proved to be a very difficult matter. Brown told Gill to keep the men from plundering the farm. Gill reported that this proved to be a very difficult task. Watches and other property were taken. Hicklin reported that Brown and his men "ransacked (his) house in search of money." Brown's men took horses, oxen, wagons, saddles and provisions. They also took bedding and clothing for the four members of the Daniels family.

Next, Brown and his men headed to the farm of John Larue. From the Larue farm five bondspersons were liberated. As had been done at the Hicklin place all the property that was available and portable was looted and in addition two white men, Larue and a Dr. Ervin, were taken as hostages.

However, the Stevens raid didn't go as well. The raiders entered David Cruise's house and he naturally thought he was being robbed as this action took place in the middle of the night. Stevens claimed that Cruise was going for a gun and Stevens shot him dead. The Stevens brigands then looted the dead man's property of anything portable they could carry off. They also took one bondswoman from him and also robbed livestock from a neighbor of Cruise.

The next morning the two groups of raiders met up and counted that they had 11 bondspersons between them and wagonloads of loot. They headed for Osawatomie, Kansas, some 35 miles to the north. Brown delayed his trip north and headed back towards Fort Scott to see if an armed force from Missouri would try and invade Kansas and capture Brown and his men and return the bondspersons to slavery. Being on the run didn't stop Brown from giving a newspaper interview. William Hutchison, the Kansas correspondent for a New York newspaper, was a recipient of such an interview. However, no such invasion from Missouri came to pass and on January 11, 1859, Brown had reached the bondspersons and his men in Osawatomie.[79]

The two white hostages were let go. One of the women gave birth to a male child whom she named "John Brown." Now there were 12 escaping former bondspersons. Heading for J.B. Abbott's house in Lawrence, only Brown, Anderson and Gill were left as Kagy had pressed forward to scout and the other men had headed home. By the time they got to Lawrence, Gill's feet were frozen and Brown's fingers, nose and ears were also frozen. The group rested in Lawrence.[80] At this point Jeremiah G. Anderson told his brother he was still with Brown and would not be writing much as he had to tend to his "railroad duties."[81]

As described by bondsman Samuel Harper the trip to Topeka was slow-going. By this time all the newspapers in Missouri had naturally condemned Brown's raid but even some anti-slavery newspapers in Kansas were concerned by this action. The *Herald of Freedom*, a Free State newspaper published in Lawrence, damned the raid. The governor of Kansas was outraged by Brown's incursion. Free State settler George Crawford visited with Brown and severely criticized him, saying Brown could ride off but proslavery fighters in Kansas and Missouri would strike a "retaliatory blow" at settlers like Crawford. Even James Montgomery renounced the violence he had committed in Kansas and he also renounced Brown's violence. Montgomery gave himself up to authorities.[82]

The Brown group made their way to Holton, Kansas, in late January of 1859 when a terrible plains snow storm blew up. Gill had dropped out and Stevens had rejoined Brown and William F. Creitz. Brown and the whites took refuge in the Holton Hotel while the former bondspersons were in the wagons. According to Creitz, whose brother and he had owned one of the first grocery stores in Holton, those in the wagons were "provided with the necessary comforts of life ... they suffered little inconveniences from the elemental strife that was raging furiously all night."[83] What is interesting about this is Creitz, a local from Holton, only knew Stevens by his alias Col. or Captain Whipple. Stevens used this alias because he escaped from prison in Fort Leavenworth, Kansas, for a mutiny and resisting authority in Taos, New Mexico, when he was in the United States Army. However, he had told one of the bondspersons, Samuel Harper, his true identity. Harper knew Stevens by his proper name.

Word got out to the slave hunters that Brown's group was in Holton and of course both the state and federal government were interested in arresting Brown for his "crimes." Federal troops at Fort Leavenworth were summoned to go and capture the former bondspersons and Brown.

The next day the ex-bondspersons and the Brown group headed for the next stop at Spring Creek (or Straight Creek) at Fuller's cabin. However, the creek had flooded and was too high to ford. The slave hunters thought they had Brown trapped.

Brown armed the Black men in his group like Samuel Harper, and with some white reinforcements he prepared to do battle. The slave posse, now numbering about 80 men, dug in across the swollen creek. Others counseled Brown to go around the dug-in posse but Brown said no and with only about 20 men he proceeded to cross the dangerous swollen creek — wagons and all.

So feared was the name of John Brown in Kansas by this time that when the slave posse saw the much smaller band of Brown's men crossing the creek they began to run.[84] Because the slave posse put their spurs to their horses and ran this "battle" is sometimes called the "Battle of the Spurs."

Brown and his men, including the bondsmen, pursued the slavers and captured a few of them. Brown "liberated" some of the slave hunters' horses and let the bondsmen ride while the slavers had to walk some 20 miles in ankle-deep mud. Brown then let the slavers go but their desire to hunt down fugitive slaves was greatly dampened by then.[85]

The group drove north and at Sabetha, Kansas, they waited a day for Pony Creek to freeze over. The frozen creek could stand the weight of a man but not a wagon and team so they had to break down the wagons to individual pieces and push them across; they then laid poles across with rails and brushes and boards on them, and over this bridge they led the horses. A Native American named Tessaun let the group stay in his double log cabin on the Sac and Fox Reservation for a night.[86]

At Nebraska City the Brown group crossed the Missouri River into Iowa. Editor Morton of the *Nebraska City News* was not glad to see Brown or his bondspersons come through his city. He wrote, "John Brown, Captain John Brown, Old John Brown of Osawatomie, the 'Old John Brown' Gerrit Smith said had done more for the freedom of Kansas than the whole Republican party, passed through the city Friday evening at the head of a herd of stolen niggers taken from Southern Missouri, accompanied by a gang of horse thieves of the most desperate character. They had a large number of stolen horses in their possession-two of which were taken and now held by the deputy sheriff of this county."[87]

The Brown group headed towards Civil Bend across the Missouri River in Iowa. A crew

Samuel Harper and his wife. Harper and his wife were bondspersons in Missouri with Jim Daniels. They let Daniels know they also wanted to escape bondage and were rescued by the John Brown party. When the group got outside of Holton, K.T., Brown had to arm Harper and some of the other male escaping bondsmen. Samuel and his wife made it safely to Canada, where they prospered (Kansas State Historical Society).

of 50 United States marshals had gotten to Civil Bend before Brown and had thoroughly searched Doc Blanchard's house for Brown or any of the bondspersons. Fortunately Brown managed to elude this large posse and head to Tabor where he knew he and his entourage would be treated as royalty as they usually were.

Brown had been in and out of Tabor in the last three years— even living in the town for a spell. At one time Brown's sick son and wounded son-in-law spent lengthy periods of time recuperating in Tabor. Brown had found a soldier of fortune in New York City by the name of Hugh Forbes, and brought him to Tabor to train an army he was to take into Kansas and possibly elsewhere. The Forbes adventure proved to be a flop but Brown had always felt a special kinship with these Oberlin people.

Usually, when in Tabor Brown and the bondspersons he had with him would stay in the Jonas Jones or George Gaston house. This time Brown would stay in the Gaston house with his sons who had joined him. The Gaston house wasn't large enough to accommodate all 12 bondspersons so the schoolhouse was fixed up for them complete with a cooking stove.

However, Brown detected coolness amongst the normally affable Tabor people. The people had heard of the violence Brown and his men had committed — the killings and the robberies. Tabor was still close enough to the frontier to take horse thievery as a very serious matter and Brown was a master of that craft. That Sunday Brown gave the Reverend Todd a note that read: "John Brown respectfully requests the church at Tabor to offer public thanksgiving to Almighty God in behalf of himself, & company: & of their rescued captives, in particular for his gracious preservation of their lives, & health; & his signal deliverance of all out of the hand of the wicked, hitherto. 'Oh give thanks unto the Lord; for he is good: for his mercy endureth forever.'"[88]

The Reverend Todd refused to read the note because of Brown's violence until a meeting could be held on Monday to discuss the matter. At the appointed time for the meeting Brown arose to tell his "side" of the story. However, as John Brown began to speak a Dr. Brown, a slave-owner medical specialist from St. Joseph, Missouri, who came to Tabor periodically, sat in the audience. John Brown refused to speak anymore. He recognized Dr. Brown in the audience and probably feared that anything he might say would be used by the doctor in a trial against him.

John Brown left the meeting. The people in Tabor had a long discussion in which Dr. Brown participated. After the lengthy discussion the people of Tabor condemned John Brown for his use of violence in freeing the bondspersons and for the robberies committed. They issued a resolution: "Resolved, That while we sympathize with the oppressed, & will do all that we conscientiously can to help them in their efforts for freedom, nevertheless, we have no Sympathy with those who go to Slave States, to entice away slaves, & take property or life when necessary to attain that end."[89]

Maria Gaston, whose house John Brown and his men were staying in, was an insightful writer and had this account of Brown leaving the meeting and Tabor: "Captain Brown was sick at this time also, and not finding the same sympathy as formally, it almost broke his heart. He thought we had sadly lost principal, not realizing that he was in a school with very different teachers from ours. I shall never forget his disappointment and anguish accompanied by many tears, when his men returned from a meeting expressing disapproval of his course. He said he must trust the Lord alone and not rely on earthly friends. The blow was crushing. He had expected so much, it was hard to be blamed. At other times he was welcomed and had received all he asked for, and he could not understand why we should not take this advanced step with him."[90]

John Brown left Tabor after his men and his party of freepersons had rested and had been fed and given provisions. The path and stops they made were on what was called the Jim Lane Trail. Brown had been advised not to take this well-known trail as the United States marshals, slave bounty hunters, or United States Cavalry could be looking for him and the reward for Brown and his former bondspersons was growing larger. However, old Brown, in true fashion, never was one to run from a fight and he kept on this well-known path. The Brown group headed in a direction that would take them to Des Moines. Less than two years previous the state capitol of Iowa had been moved from Iowa City to Des Moines. It took 10 teams of oxen to move all the accoutrements of the state government to Des Moines.

Once in Des Moines the editor of the *Register*, John Teesdale, paid for the ferry to get the Brown party across the Des Moines River. Neither Brown nor his men had any money to pay the ferryman. This is further proof that Brown's men had divided the loot taken in Missouri and left Old Man Brown with little to take the bondspersons north. A month later Brown would write an explanation of his invasion of Missouri to Teasdale and the reasons for his thievery. As he explained, "we had no means of moving the rescued captives without taking a portion of their lawful acquired earnings." Of course there is no proof Brown ever gave any of the freepersons any portion of their "lawful acquired earnings." Also, by the time Brown had reached Lawrence, Kansas, apparently all the stolen goods had been divided among his men and they had taken their share and left. This left the freepersons with nothing of their "lawful earnings." Villard states that "Brown recruited his finances while near Lawrence and his wagons when he drove away, were creaking with the weight of provisions contributed by Major Abbott and Mr. Grover."[91] However, I don't think Brown ever took any of the Missouri loot for himself. I believe his men callously let John Brown go north with this large group knowing he would have to beg and borrow his way to Canada. I think Brown tried to cover up his men's thievery because he felt this was a strong motivation for riding with him. His men could loot the slave owners' property for their own financial gain.

Maria Gaston was another of the pioneer wives who was very active on the Underground Railroad. She was a wonderful writer of events including John Brown's visit to Tabor when Brown was rejected. Unfortunately not many of Maria's writings have been found to this date. She and husband George had been missionaries to the Pawnee tribe in Nebraska when they discovered this fertile region of Iowa. Maria and George gave away much of their wealth to those in need on the Underground Railway and elsewhere (courtesy Todd House Museum and Tabor Historical Society, Tabor, Iowa).

The Brown caravan came into Grinnell in late February. The town pulled out all the stops and gave Brown a rousing reception. Grinnell showed Brown his parlor, which he called his "liberty room" because of all the escaping bondspersons who had sat in it. Brown couldn't resist writing a note to Tabor about his great reception in Grinnell.

The Brown procession moved on to Iowa City and then on February 25 to Springdale. At Iowa City while Brown and Kagy were eating in a restaurant two men with a rope in their hands with which to hang Brown appeared, wanting to find that "damned nigger-thief of Kansas." The restaurant manager sent the men away. After they ate Brown and Kagy were spirited away. At West Liberty, William Penn Clarke made arrangement with the railroad to place a boxcar at his disposal. Brown and the freepersons rode in the boxcar while John Kagy and Clarke traveled in a passenger car.[92]

The rail train chugged through eastern Iowa until they got to Davenport where the U.S. marshal had formed a posse. The Marshal went through the passenger car but could see no fugitives so he let it go onto Chicago. When the train got to Chicago the freemen were unloaded in secrecy so as to not implicate the rail line in any "misdeed." Since the boxcar had been procured under somewhat false pretenses Clarke and the others didn't want the rail lines to be held liable in a court of law for the theft of these bondspersons. Allan Pinkerton, of the famed Pinkerton Detective Agency, took charge of the freepersons and sent them to Detroit on March 10, 1859. Two days later under John Brown's direction they crossed the international border with Canada and freedom was finally at hand for the former bondspersons.[93] Seven months later John Brown and 21 men would attack the Federal Arsenal in Harpers Ferry, Virginia. Brown's intent was to create and arm Black men for a massive slave uprising in the Southern slave states. His plan failed but it energized the abolitionist movement in the United States and Brown became a martyr to the cause of slave emancipation when he was hanged on December 2, 1859, for this crime. The men who were mentioned here and joined Brown for his raid into Harpers Ferry met violent deaths. John Kagy was killed during the raid on Harpers Ferry. Aaron Stevens was severely wounded four times during the Harpers Ferry raid. His wounds were around his head and neck. He was tried for his part in the raid and hanged March 16, 1860. Jeremiah Anderson was the grandson of a slaveholder but was a strong anti-slavery man and a loyal soldier in Brown's Army. Anderson was killed at Harpers Ferry. Before Brown was led to the scaffold for his hanging he said, "I, John Brown, am quite certain that the crimes of this guilty land will never be purged away but with blood."

John Williamson was probably the foremost Black worker on the Underground Railroad in Iowa. He had helped the female and male Nuckolls slaves escape and undoubtedly many others. He had access to a skiff that crossed the Missouri River and a business that gave him a reason to cross the mighty river on a daily basis. This was a major asset in bringing bondspersons from the Nebraska side to the Iowa side of the Missouri River. In 1860 Williamson, Henry Garner and his sister Maria were on their way north to Omaha. Jacob Herd, the career criminal from Kansas, had been observed hanging around the Civil Bend area for several weeks. He was obviously watching the activities of the Garners and Williamson and any Black runaway he could observe in the region. Aided by two other thugs, N.B. Beck and Joe Wildey, this criminal trio overpowered Williamson and the Garners. Henry Garner was struck savagely in the cheek bone, breaking it.[94]

Herd took Williamson and the Garners down into Missouri with the intent of selling them. Doc Blanchard and George Gaston got wind of the kidnappings and rushed down into Missouri to aid their comrades. Some have speculated that the kidnapping of Williamson was a payback for his helping the Nuckolls' slave girls escape. Nuckolls had paid back Reuben Williams for having sued him by burning down his barn. It is obvious Herd had been watching the Williamson group for a time as he knew their whereabouts and when the best time to attack them. He waited until Williamson and his group was far enough away from Tabor or Civil Bend to be vulnerable to an assault.

Williamson managed to get away in Missouri from Herd. But he was recaptured and detained in Rockport, Missouri. Williamson protested he was a free Black man to the sheriff of Atchison County, Missouri. He was allowed to write to friends in Council Bluffs, Iowa. They sent $75 down to post bond for him. Then the city marshal from Council Bluffs, Iowa, and sheriff from Pottawattamie County in Iowa did an extraordinary thing. They personally came down to Rockport to make sure Williamson got back to Iowa safe and sound.[95]

The Garners were not so lucky and were taken to a hellhole of a slave pen in St. Louis and sold by Herd and his outlaw band. Blanchard and Gaston were hot on their trail. Gaston had to go back to Tabor for business but agreed to finance Blanchard on this quest. Blanchard miraculously found the Garners in the slave pen and forcefully told the slaver of this miscarriage of justice. Usually such cases were ignored but the slaver put Blanchard to the test. The warden of the slave pen brought the Garner brother and sister out. Henry Garner had received no medical attention for his broken cheek bone and in particular was in a downcast mood and never looked up. However, his sister Maria looked up and saw her beloved friend Doc Blanchard and she screamed out in joy, "Oh! Dr. Blanchard! Where did you come from?"[96]

The slave warden knew at that moment that Blanchard's story was true. Authorities were called and the Garners were released. Jake Herd and his gang were found and then arrested around St. Louis.

The Garners and Doc Blanchard headed back to Iowa on the steamship *Warsaw*. Unfortunately Jake Herd and his gang were also put on the same steamship accompanied by law officers who were supposed to take the Herd gang back to Iowa to stand trial. At various steamboat landings when passengers and cargo were loaded and unloaded it would be known that Blanchard and the Garners were on board as well as Herd and his gang. Herd would proclaim that he would be hanged if taken back to Iowa. Crowds began to gather and they treated Herd like he was a hero.

When the steamship landed in St. Joseph, Missouri, the crowd became so out of control they threatened to take Herd off the boat and "free" him and his gang. A group of gold miners headed for Colorado stepped in and aided Blanchard and the lawmen and kept Herd on the boat. After the steamship left St. Joseph it headed to Hamburg, Iowa. Hamburg was just over the Iowa line but the steamboat landing was actually in Missouri.

The St. Louis law officers got cold feet and said they were only going to hand over Herd and his outlaws to Iowa authorities at the Iowa line. They were not going to take Herd into Iowa to stand trial.[97]

After this a real spectacle occurred. A mob of some 50 pro-slavery people followed the law officers, Blanchard, the Garners and the Herd gang demanding Herd and his men be turned loose. At one point Blanchard had to draw his gun to keep the crowd at bay. The law officers and the Herd gang at one point were all chained together. The St. Louis policemen had had enough and took Herd and his men back to St. Joseph. While in St. Joseph it was discovered that there were four warrants out for Herd's arrest and to save face the lawmen kept him there.[98]

The other two outlaws were taken into Council Bluffs, Iowa, to stand trial. However, they escaped before they could be brought to justice.[99] The fact that these two escaped from their day in court also feeds into the theory that the Nuckolls faction had something to do with the kidnappings and possibly wanted to aid the outlaws by freeing them. It is believed Herd's illegal activities caught up with him and he was hanged for horse thievery a year or two after these kidnappings.[100] Maria and Henry Garner finally made it home to Civil Bend as did Doc Blanchard. They were able to continue with their work on the freedom trail during the Civil War.

The Nebraska Territory provided a very important link in the freedom corridor from central and western Missouri through the Kansas Territory and then into Nebraska and on to the Hawkeye state. Also, bondspersons from the Native American lands in what is now called Oklahoma and some from Arkansas came seeking liberty through the Nebraska Territory.

Brownsville, Nebraska, was a town named after slave owner Richard Brown. It was also the first settlement in the territory to receive telegraph service in August of 1860.[101] However, if you wanted to make a successful journey to freedom it was a village to steer clear of at all costs. Three armed bondsmen were seeking their freedom south of Brownsville in the autumn of 1857. A four-man slave posse spotted the liberty seekers by some willows south of town. A gun battle ensued. One of the slave posse was killed and one of the bondsmen was severely wounded.

The two bondsmen managed to take the horses of the slave posse and they acquired more firearms and managed to make it into Iowa. However, another gun battle erupted between the bondsmen and other slave bounty hunters wounding one of the freedom seekers and unfortunately both were captured. They were taken back to a life of slavery.

The first bondsman who was severely wounded was taken to the hotel in Brownsville, N.T., and his arm, gravely mangled by the gunshot, was amputated. Pro-slavery men wanted to take this bondsman back to Missouri where they were going to torture him for having killed a white man. However, cooler heads, including Richard Brown the slave owner, prevailed and the freedom seeker stood trial. Incredibly, considering the racist times, the wounded bondsman was found not guilty of any crime![102]

Falls City, in the Nebraska Territory, was founded by controversial Kansas abolitionist James Lane. Lane thought the falls on the Big Nemaha River had potential economic value; however, some years later the river changed channels and the falls disappeared. The town was supportive of the efforts of the fugitive freedom seekers. The editor of the local newspaper *Broad Axe*, Sewall Jamison, often aided in these escapes. Just south of the town was a village of Sauk Native Americans. One time Jamison found some white men wanting to purchase a fugitive bondsman who apparently had been captured by the Sauks. Jamison managed to take control of the situation and took the bondsman and advanced him on the Underground Railroad to freedom. Jamison's paper also did something that was rarely done by abolitionist newspapers: it told of an escape by bondspersons. In the *Broad Axe* he proudly proclaimed in August of 1860 an escape on the freedom line: "A cargo of six or more fugitive slaves passed through Salem (N.T.) escorted by thirty or forty whites."[103]

A certain amount of rivalry occurred between the pro-slavery newspaper in Nebraska City and the abolitionist *Broad Axe* in Falls City. The *Nebraska City News* accused the residents of Falls City of being from the notorious gang-infested Five Points region of New

York City. The Bellevue, N.T., *Gazette*'s editor, Henry Burt, was called by the *Nebraska City News* one of the most uncompromising Black Republicans in the western world.[104]

Although some of the important leaders in the notable frontier town of Nebraska City were pro-slavery there were a number of people in town who were willing to help freedom seekers traverse the dangerous crossing of the Missouri River. Allen Mayhew and his wife Barbara's cabin was a stop for the liberty line. Barbara was the sister to John Kagy, one of John Brown's top men who would die at Harpers Ferry. Abraham Kagy, the father of Barbara and John, had an 80 acre place at Camp Creek and it was a well-known place to the Underground Railroad in the area. When James Lane brought his first band of 1,200 anti-slavery settlers into the Kansas Territory; after leaving Tabor they came to the Abraham Kagy farm.[105]

Later in life Edward Mayhew, son of Allen and Barbara, remembered as a boy of two different occasions when bondspersons sought shelter in their cabin. The first was a Black woman who stayed one night. Another time Barbara's brother John Kagy brought 14 bondspersons to the cabin on their way to freedom. Breakfast was served for this large group. The slave hunters came but could not find any of the slaves. Kagy was upstairs in the house and fully armed. The slave hunters apparently didn't want any part of an armed Kagy so they did not search anymore and they left in a bad mood. They went into town and accused Kagy of having a stolen horse. The horse was confiscated and the slave hunters sold the horse and divided the spoils.[106]

Carstens N. Karsten, who came from Germany and became a prominent business man in the city, remembers taking bondspersons from the Mayhew cabin to the Missouri River crossing at Wyoming, north of Nebraska City. They would have been taken to Civil Bend in Iowa across the river. Calvin Chapman, who later became the major coal dealer in Nebraska City, related that as a boy of 16 he drove a wagon belonging to his brother. The wagon would be loaded with Black freedom seekers and the Missouri River crossing was also made at Wyoming. They were taken to a little Iowa hamlet with the descriptive name of Lickskillet. From Lickskillet they were forwarded on to Tabor.[107]

As stated before, bounty and slave hunters were thick on this part of the liberty line. Nebraska City, being the largest commercial town in the region, was often used as headquarters for these people. Fortunately, many of the freedom seekers made it through this gauntlet; however, some were not so lucky. One such group of slave hunters working out of Nebraska City caught 11 bondspersons seeking freedom in Iowa and returned them to bondage. Originally, the 11 had been helped by a free Black man, but once they were in Iowa their luck ran out.[108]

The Lockwood family, near Nemaha City, N.T., would take fugitives from Falls City to Nebraska City to cross the Missouri River into Iowa. There was an empty house in Nemaha City that was used to hide any freedom seekers that came their way.[109]

As mentioned before in the late 1850s and as the eve of the Civil War approached larger groups of bondsperson appeared to be seeking freedom. As a small girl Alice Lockwood Minick saw her parents and others in the area help move bondspersons on the liberty line. Once she saw a vegetable cave full of a large number of fugitive slaves seeking freedom. Her recollection confirms that of another small female child in Tabor who remembered seeing a large group of freedom seekers in her brothers' bedroom. The next day she noted they were all gone—forwarded on the freedom line to Canada.[110]

5

Arkansas: Liberty Via Steamboats

> "His shirt am rough and his back am tough,
> Do, pray, Mr. Paddleroller, give 'im 'nough."
> — Harry (Jim) Johnson, former bondsman

When King Cotton began to wear out the soils of Georgia, Alabama and Mississippi cotton growers began looking for even more land on which to plant cotton and the Arkansas delta looked like the real deal. Of course, slave labor was a fact of life in Arkansas and slavery became a fixture in that state.

When Arkansas was a territory before 1836 the question of slavery began to become the main topic of the national conversation. Arkansas was somewhat different than Missouri in that she was, for all practical purposes, completely surrounded by states and territories that employed slave labor.

The Ozark and Quachita Mountains made much of the land not fit for cotton plantations but for small agricultural units and the type of slavery seen in Missouri with small farms and few slaves at each agricultural location. During this time much of Arkansas' agricultural lands lay along small, narrow river valleys isolated from each other. Covered with tremendous amounts of forested areas, slaves had to clear much of the land that would later be used for farming. In his autobiography English journalist Henry Morton Stanley, who later traveled to Africa and uttered the famous line "Dr. Livingston I presume," wrote of working along with Arkansas Black slave laborers in clearing the tall pine trees in that state.[1] However, even after clearing the tall pines off the land it would take years before the soil could produce cotton or other staples such as wheat and corn. Even by 1860, 24 years after she had become a state, almost one third of Arkansas was still owned by the Federal government and only about 20 percent of its land was listed as improved.[2] There were very few roads or bridges in the state, making even normal commerce difficult and of course making the attempt to escape slavery a demanding proposition. The rivers in the state such as the Mississippi, White and Arkansas became even more important travel-ways in the absence of good surface roads. In the delta area of Arkansas and in some southern counties of the state there were considerable plantations growing cotton on a large scale.

The rugged mountain terrain and heavily forested areas made escaping slavery in those regions very complicated. Because of this the numbers of free whites and enslaved people of color were not huge in Arkansas. By 1860 the free population of Arkansas was 324,335 and its enslaved population was 111,115.[3] This population base was barely enough to consider it over the minimum to define it as a frontier area by the United States government.

When it became a state Arkansas had slavery written into its constitution with many of its slave laws modeled after Missouri's codes; plus, she added other slave laws to her state regulations. Arkansas was also concerned, when she was admitted to the union in 1836, that her legislature would at some point abolish slavery. To counter the legislature's ability to abolish slavery it gave itself no power to pass laws to emancipate slaves—slaves could only be emancipated by the consent of their owners.[4] However, her codes were considered less harsh than those of some of the original colonies such as Virginia. Arkansas established slave patrols and these patrols administered whippings and beatings for any minor infraction. They were effective in terrorizing the bondsmen and women in their state. When a patrol was established by a circuit court it had to be on duty at least 12 hours a month. These patrols were not only on the lookout for anyone deemed an escapee or bondsperson traveling about without a proper pass, but were also charged with examining slave quarters. The patrollers wanted to make sure all who were living in these lodgings were genuine residents of such quarters and that the actual inhabitants were not harboring any bondspersons trying to escape slavery. These patrols also looked for any other place where bondspersons hiding or making an escape attempt might congregate. Excessive whippings were commonplace for any Black person caught day or night by slave patrols when the bondsmen or women didn't have passes or permission to be off their residence. When her bondsman asked her for a pass one sadistic female Arkansas slave owner wrote on a piece of paper. Harry "Jim" Johnson reported that the woman did not write a pass but rather wrote these words, "His shirt am rough and his back am tough, Do pray, Mr. Paddleroller, give 'im 'nough." The bondsman, thinking he had a legitimate pass, was stopped by the slave patrol. Johnson accounted that when the patrollers saw the note they nearly beat the bondsman to death.[5] Another sadistic slaver thought it would be a funny "joke" to write on a pass for his illiterate Arkansas bondsman, "Whip Arthur Boone's [ass] and pass him out. When he comes back, whip his [ass] again and pass him back." The patrollers stopped Boone and read the note and made him pull his pants down and administered the unjust and unnecessary humiliation.[6] The Black population in Arkansas lived in fear of these barbaric patrols and their cruel and excessive whippings.[7] These patrols no doubt helped to curtail some escapes.

Even with the existence of the slave patrols in Arkansas this did not preclude, when an escape was made by a bondsperson, the slave owner hiring or offering rewards to slave or bounty hunters. Sometimes before rewards were offered or bounty hunters hired the slave owner would try to track down the runaway with bloodhounds and neighbors were asked to help in these searches.

Occasionally, the tremendous forested areas in Arkansas provided cover for bondsmen to escape the brutality of the slave system. At times the bondsmen didn't get very far in their escapes before the bloodhounds would be set on them. On one aborted escape the bondsman was found then whipped. He had a coach whip wrapped around his arms and the rest of his body. The whip had cut gashes as if he had been cut by a knife with blood gushing out. Salt was poured on the wound to stop the bleeding and it was thought salt would also stop infection or "poison" as it was called then but of course it caused indescribable pain. Soot was sometimes used to stop the bleeding but it left black marks. The salt left white marks and the soot left black marks which were always looked at by buyers of human flesh as a sign that the bondsman or bondswoman had tried to escape and was punished or that he or she was a troublemaker.[8]

Sometimes, the bloodhounds or tracking dogs could be vicious when finding runaways and many had been trained to be extremely violent. At times the dogs were known to completely tear the bondsmen's clothes off. Supposedly this would keep them from trying to escape again. Bondspersons reported seeing escaping slaves killed by hounds.[9]

Most of the slave laws passed in states like Arkansas were to keep the slaves from running away or from participating in an insurrection or from preventing striking out against the slave system by committing arson or other acts of physical protest that endangered the white population. Emboldened by the Supreme Court's Dred Scott decision in March of 1857, which stated that free or enslaved Black persons were not and could never be citizens of the United States, the Arkansas legislature felt that the slaves in their state were perfectly content with their treatment and lot in life and would only try to escape when provoked by some outside influence like free Blacks. The pro-slavery element in Arkansas was always fearful that free Blacks in the state played a large part in the escapes of enslaved Blacks. Also free Blacks in the state gave enslaved Blacks something to aspire to to change their life's situation. The Arkansas legislature passed the Expulsion Act of 1859, which stated all free blacks who did not leave the state within a year would be reverted back to being in the condition of slavery. This caused a migration of free blacks out of the state and left fewer than 144 free blacks in the state by 1860.[10]

As mentioned before, the great steamboats that plied the major riverways sometimes offered possibilities for escape in Arkansas. Arkansas, as well as other states along the Mississippi River, were fearful that free Blacks working on the steamboats might offer ways to escape for the enslaved Blacks when the steamships would dock at various ports. Arkansas put restrictions on free Blacks working on steamboats coming from other states from moving about once their boats had docked at Arkansas ports.[11]

Because of her location Arkansas became a transfer point for others making escapes from slavery from other slave states. Bondspersons escaping Tennessee, Louisiana, Mississippi and other deep south slave states often made their way through Arkansas seeking freedom. As the cotton plantations of the deep south of Alabama and Mississippi and the sugar plantations of Louisiana began to grow, the need to expand slave labor gangs soon followed. More and more bondspersons wanted out of this intolerable situation. They made their way to the Mississippi River or to the wilds of the frontier of America and this caused Arkansas to be a crossroads area.

Black Solomon, a 22-year-old clever bondsman from Columbia in Murray County in Tennessee, was determined to seek his freedom. Using several aliases, including "Jim," Solomon made his escape but was recaptured and imprisoned on July 28, 1841, in the Pulaski County jail in Arkansas. Not deterred, Solomon, described as stout and about 5'8", escaped this jail two weeks later but was again recaptured. This time he was sold to John Walters of Jefferson County, Arkansas. Walters reported that the creative Solomon had escaped from him in Arkansas in December of 1841. Newspapers reported in March of 1842 that Solomon was still at large. This was the last time this bondsman was mentioned and one can only hope he made good his escape from slavery for good at this time.[12]

Well-known Underground Railroad conductor, the Rev. Calvin Fairbank, helped to free Little Rock bondsman William Minnis. It was an elaborate escape — much more than the usual seen in Arkansas.

The determined Fairbank went to Arkansas in May of 1843 especially to help Minnis escape.[13] Minnis was originally from Jessamine County some 15 miles from Lexington, Kentucky. Fairbank had heard that Minnis' master had willed that he be set free upon his death. When the master died his son, an heir to the estate, simply ignored his father's wishes. Even the executor of the will simply disregarded its content as far as freeing the servants of the deceased. Minnis had been sold by the heir to a slave trader named Pullum. Pullum then sold Minnis to a slave owner in Little Rock, Arkansas.[14] This unfortunately happened many times in the slave south and since bondsmen had no standing in the courts it was a simple matter for heirs or the executor of the estate to ignore the requests of masters who wished to reward faithful bondsmen. Many slaves worked diligently and faithfully with the hope that they had been told their hard work would be rewarded with their freedom. However, the heirs only had to ignore this request with no fear of reprisals.

One famous case of this was told by Harriet Jacobs, whose pen name was Linda Brent, in her book *Incident in the Life of a Slave Girl*. Jacobs changed the names of all the participants in the book. Jacobs relates that her grandmother, whom everyone, Black and white, knew, was well respected by everyone in the area. Her grandmother was a gifted baker who, after she had worked a full day for her master, made biscuits and other goods and sold them to everyone, white and Black, in her neighborhood. She was well esteemed by everyone and accumulated sums of money to buy her children. Everyone knew the story in that region about her master wishing to set her free after his death.

When her master died, Jacobs' grandmother and everyone expected her to be set free. However, his heirs refused and they even "borrowed" money from her that she had set aside to buy her own children out of slavery and never repaid the money. Her new owners had mismanaged their inherited money and they were forced to sell Jacobs' grandmother. Knowing that her grandmother's reputation was better than her master's they wanted to sell her at a private auction. However, her grandmother refused this and wanted to be sold in public so that the neighbors, both white and Black, would know what dastardly fools had "owned" her. When she was put on the public auction block none of the white buyers would bid on her and there were cries of "shame, shame" from the crowd. Everyone knew this great woman had been promised her freedom and her new owners were held in low regard because of their actions. A sister of her old master bid $50 for Jacobs' grandmother and then set her free. Unfortunately for William Minnis stories of fair and equitable treatment for Blacks, free or slave, was rare during this time period in the antebellum south.

The Underground Railroad community in Cincinnati, Ohio, had Minnis' situation brought to its attention by Kentucky friends of his, Dennis Seals, Nancy Straus and Father Feral of Lexington. Fairbank was called upon for this work and $250 was raised for his journey and mission to Arkansas. Fairbank was somewhat apprehensive about going to the "natural state" as at that time she had a reputation of being a wild and lawless place.[15] Fairbank left Cincinnati for Little Rock by steamboat. Once there he checked into a hotel in the capital city of Arkansas. Fairbank noted that being from the north he was viewed somewhat suspiciously. It took him almost a month to find out Minnis' location in the city. Any white man inquiring about a specific Black person would be looked upon with great reservations—especially if that white person was from Ohio, the great abolitionist state. Imagine his great surprise when Fairbank found out that Minnis had been hired out by his master to work in the very same hotel where Fairbank was staying! Minnis was contacted and was anxious to escape as he had spent one year as a bell man in the hotel. Minnis was very happy to learn that his friends had thought enough of him to devise this elaborate scheme to free him.[16]

Fairbank and Minnis designed an intricate ruse. Minnis was a light-skinned mulatto. Two "experts" were brought in to lighten his skin even more and to change his hairstyle and add a mustache and a beard. These two white residents of Arkansas were only too willing to help this escapee even though the penalties were extreme. After this was all done it was noticed that Minnis had an uncanny resemblance to a "Mr. Young," a well known figure in that region. Hopefully this would aid in his escape. Since Minnis was only 18 years old it would be necessary to make him look older to pass him off as an up and coming planter. The Mr. Young to whom Minnis bore some resemblance had long, black hair so this was added to his appearance by a French-Creole barber who had agreed to help in the escape. His skin was lightened by a teacher in the area who painted portraits. The disguise was complete — now, to see if it worked.

Minnis, who had observed white gentlemen in the hotel, proved to be an apt student and performed an impressive impression of an up and coming planter. With the proper cloths on Fairbank and Minnis headed for a steamboat bound for Vicksburg, Mississippi. Minnis also added to his disguise a cane with a gold handle.

Fairbank records that Minnis' white master Brennan was also on this steamship going about some business. Fairbank reported that Minnis' act was so good that Brennan and he exchanged greetings without the master thinking a thing about it. Brennan fortunately left the boat the next day. Minnis had nailed the accent of a southern white planter and he was going by the name of John Crawford.[17]

When the steamer got to Memphis, Tennessee, Fairbank met the slave selling Pullum and they talked at length. Pullum was the slave trader that had sold Minnis and the former slave couldn't resist the opportunity to walk by the flesh peddler several times in his new costume and as a free man. Pullum even mentioned to Fairbank that he remembered selling a William Minnis to a Little Rock man. Fairbank and Minnis finally made it to Cincinnati. It was deemed that even Ohio was too dangerous for Minnis to stay so the young man left and made his way to Canada. In 1851 Fairbank reports that he saw William in Toronto and that Minnis left for California in 1852. During the Civil War Minnis was pleased to join the Union Army to "shoulder arms" for the great cause.[18]

Unfortunately, the remainder of Fairbank's life was filled with much grief. He would spend 17 years of his life in Kentucky prisons where he received an incredible number of whippings and lashings because of his work helping slaves escape.[19] Earlier in his life Fairbank would travel into the south to tell enslaved Blacks about escape routes to Canada. It is hard to tell how effective this work by Fairbank and others was in helping subsequent escapes. The famed Levi Coffin also traveled about the south buying free-labor cotton and telling of the benefits of ending slave labor.[20]

Fairbank became a licensed and ordained Methodist minister. He had enormous zeal for the Christian religion; however, he was somewhat lacking in formal education as were many ministers at this time. He recognized his education wasn't thought to be enough to matriculate into Oberlin College so he entered its "preparatory school" in 1844. At this school they gave the student the basic skills so they could properly handle college course material in the future. While in Oberlin Fairbank drank in its considerable anti-slavery attitude. Oberlin also "majored" many collegians in the art of Underground Railroad conducting and Fairbank was an apt student.

Fairbank began escorting bondsmen out of the south to freedom. He delivered many of them to Levi Coffin who often went by the sobriquet of "President of the Underground Railroad." In 1844 he helped Lewis Hayden to escape from slavery. Hayden was a waiter in a restaurant in Kentucky, put there by his master. Fairbank asked Hayden, "Why do you want your freedom?" To which Hayden answered, "Because I'm a man."[21] Hayden would go on to become a lecturer for the American Anti-Slavery Society. He would also become a state legislator in Massachusetts. However, Fairbank was tried for Hayden's escape when he went back into Kentucky to try and free other enslaved humans. He was put into prison for five years and then was pardoned and released when Hayden paid his master for himself.

Fairbank came out of prison and resumed his practice of freeing slaves. He also met and became engaged to Mandana Tileston. Fairbank was kidnapped in Indiana and taken to Kentucky by law officials and again imprisoned for what would be over 12 years. Miss Tileston remained true to Fairbank and helped supply him with the necessities while he was in prison. A former bondswoman, Tamar, that Fairbank had helped escape, also provided him with supplies while he was incarcerated.

In 1864 Fairbank was released from his Kentucky prison. His health had deteriorated so much while in prison that when he got out Levi Coffin didn't even recognize him. Fairbank married his faithful fiancée. However, her death 12 years later wrecked Fairbank's already unstable physical and mental health.[22] He lived on for over two decades but he was broken spiritually and physically. He died in near poverty.

Steamboats plying Arkansas waters provided great opportunities for escape for bondspersons in this state, as did those in neighboring Missouri. Arkansas and her Mississippi waters were between two of the major steamboat terminuses of the time: New Orleans, Louisiana, and St. Louis, Missouri. Steamboats also ran on other rivers in the state such as the White River and Arkansas River. The steamboats had replaced the hand-propelled keelboats that had moved freight into the interior of Arkansas and along the Mississippi River on her eastern boundary.

It has been estimated that as many as 20,000 free and enslaved Black persons were employed on various steamboat lines in the 10 years prior to the Civil War. Men were used as deck hands, boiler attendants, waiters and other positions on the boat. They also loaded and unloaded cargo at the various landing docks up and down the rivers. Dredging the riverways was also done by free and slave labor. Women were often employed as chambermaids and in other occupations. The fact that free and slave Blacks intermingled on these boats would often make for opportunities for escape. An enslaved bondsman could see free Blacks and free white workers and wonder why he or she wasn't free and take steps to remedy their situation. In fact, working on the steamboats was so desirable among the enslaved population that often times a slave owner would tell his slaves they had been leased to a steamboat to keep them from trying to escape when in fact they had been sold to a planter in a faraway place.[23]

By 1860 well over half of the south's two million bales of cotton bound for the textile mills of Liverpool, England, Le Havre, France, and New York City came down the Mississippi River to New Orleans. These bales, weighing some 400 pounds a piece, had to be lifted, carried and rolled from the port landings onto the decks of riverboats mainly by free and enslaved Black laborers. The Arkansas delta area produced many of these cotton bales.

Life on the river and the steamboat trade could be very dangerous for the free or enslaved Black laborer. People drowned and the weight of the bales could crush a person and severely injure them or cause death. They were subjected to the elements, which could cause sickness, but many still preferred life on the river and its flexible style of living and its mobility. Very often the steamship personnel went out of their way to hire African Americans, be they free or slave, because they often had the advantage of being able to speak English, which the newly arrived immigrants from Europe did not.

While some enslaved Blacks worked on the steamboats for many years and in some cases (such as if they were working as waiters) received tips. These tips held out the hope of buying ones own freedom or of providing a travel fund for escape, which was always a possibility if an opportunity presented itself. Henry Crawhion, a bondsman who was leased to work on the steamships by his master almost as soon as he was of an age to work, toiled faithfully for many years in the steamship trade. He became familiar with how the schedules and industry worked. This helped him when he eventually saw a chance to make a clean get-away and escaped. He made his way to Canada for his eventual freedom.[24]

Free blacks often played a part in helping their enslaved brethren escape. They knew which river boat pilots looked at free papers with a suspicious eye and which pilots were only concerned with filling positions on their boats. Slave owners in their newspaper advertisements often warned steamboat captains not to employ or harbor any slaves making an attempt to escape. As in Missouri, Arkansas slave owners were very reluctant to hire out their bondsmen or bondswomen to steamboats that touched ports in free northern cities for fear that their bondspersons would make an easy escape. Woodcutters in the interior of Arkansas, along river-ways, saw opportunity, as did their brethren in Missouri, to make escapes on steamships. Wood, the propelling fuel in the steamships, was very important and free and enslaved Blacks were a significant element in providing steamships with this vital commodity. Woodcutters were often near port landings of steamship lines and could easily intermingle with workers on the boat docks for potential escapes.

Bondspersons always had to be on the lookout for opportunities for escape when working on steamships. One enslaved steamboat laborer saw an opportunity when the boiler on his ship exploded. The bondsman made his escape with the ship's captain thinking he had been killed in the explosion.[25]

The steamboat became an important part of Arkansas life and the prime mover of commerce. Railroads made a belated appearance in the state in the 1870s. By 1859 there was more than one steamboat a day docking at Little Rock, the state's largest city.[26] Escaping bondsmen saw that it was often a faster getaway when the steamship was used and the more distance between them and the place where they escaped from often meant a successful escape rather than capture and return to the brutality of slavery.

A bondsman named Williamson Peace was described as a mulatto who could easily pass for white and even had blue eyes. He lived in Tennessee for the first part of his life with his mother until his first master, an Englishman who had been a sailor, passed away. Peace's next master was the grandson of the English sailor. This grandson was only five years older than the 18-year-old Peace. The grandson then sold off his slaves in Arkansas and moved off his 150 acre cotton farm. The grandson took Peace with him to mine for gold in California. There he got sick and Peace nursed him back to health. The grandson promised to free Peace and his mother if Peace would accompany him back to the south. On a ship trying to make it through the Isthmus of Panama they were blown off course to Acapulco, Mexico, where they ran aground. They then hired horses at Acapulco, and rode by horseback to Mexico City and then to Vera Cruz. From Vera Cruz they took a schooner to New Orleans. Once they were in New Orleans Peace worked in a saloon for some time. Then the grandson went back on his word and sold Peace to a cotton plantation back in Arkansas. As was the case many times a slaver didn't keep his word to his bondsman. For some reason Peace's new master didn't like him and he told others that Peace thought he was white and that Peace would have to be whipped to let him know he was still a "nigger." The new master summed up a philosophy that many of his class believed, "niggers always should be whipped some, no matter how good they are, else they'll forget they are niggers." Another philosophical nugget from this good Christian planter about allowing people of color to attend church was, "(it was) perfect nonsense to have a preacher preaching to niggers: the driver was a good enough preacher for them."[27]

While on this farm Peace, in his own words, spoke about the conditions there:

> In Arkansas, on the river, or on the farm where I lived last, the people were treated worse than brutes. Horses and mules have food by them all the time, but the slaves had four pounds of fat bacon a week, and a peck of corn meal, — not enough to last some men three days. On this account it is that the slaves help themselves when they can get a chance. I don't see how any one can blame them for it. They are up at daybreak and work till dark and sometimes after dark, carrying cotton to the gin, and then have to prepare their food, or else at the first bell-ringing in the morning. Generally, in Arkansas, the men had good clothing so far as I saw, but there were some exceptions. Most I think of was, depriving them of the privilege of going off the place ... but on the plantations they do not expect to get out until they are dead. I never went to church while I was on that last farm: the people did not go.... In Arkansas they whip men with a leather strap about three fingers wide at the handle, and tapering down to two fingers at the end. It is about three feet long, and has a very short handle. I was told that several who were buried while I was there, had strap marks on them. I saw the overseer and the driver together give a man a terrible whipping in the night. The man had been promised fifty lashes, and ran to avoid them, but they caught him, and showed no mercy. They beat him over the head with the handle of the strap. They stripped him naked and drove four stakes in the ground to which they tied his hands and feet. I saw it done — I was looking through the palings. Then they whipped him with the strap and then with a piece of white oak made lumber. I saw his back, and it was all raw. The man was sent to work the next day, but he gave out, and was laid up from August until some time in the fall — until the cotton had been picked over three times. I have often seen men with their clothes sticking to their backs in the blood. The women who do out-door work are used as bad as the men."
>
> There was a great deal of excitement among the farmers there at one time about a woman on a plantation below, who had been whipped very badly and was then tied out naked all night in a swamp where the mosquitoes were very thick; there was a great deal said about it.

Peace also reported that he saw a great deal of oppression on the Tennessee plantation where he had lived.

Then Peace's new master had the blacksmith measure him in order to outfit him with a pair of stiff-legs. A stiff-leg was an iron ring around the ankle and one up on the thigh, joined together by an iron rod in the back. When put on a slave he or she cannot bend their knees and therefore cannot run away without great difficulty. Peace thought his master was going to fit him with these stiff-legs and then have him chained in the blacksmith's shop to work there. He knew the time to act was now and he left as quickly as possible with few provisions from the supper table. He slogged forty miles through an Arkansas swamp and got to the Mississippi River at two o'clock the next day. He had brought some clean clothes with him and changed and paid passage on the steamer. His almost white skin made it easy for him to pass as a free person. The distance the steamer could provide away from his master's plantation made him difficult to catch. Williamson Peace managed to catch a steamer headed north and he made it to Canada. He liked Canada — as he said, there "the colored man was regarded as a man." He said he would have to have his head pulled off before going back to Arkansas slavery.[28]

To make it harder for free Blacks to help enslaved Blacks escape, steamboat captains or the ship's clerk would often hold the papers of the freemen who were working on board the ship. This prevented any free African American person from slipping their papers to an enslaved person on the same or another boat. As mentioned before, some steamship captains became careless about this procedure especially if they needed someone to attend to the dangerous and very hard fireman duties. Sometimes, if a fireman quit at the last minute or ran off at a port the captain might not look at someone's papers too closely if he needed help right away.

Free Blacks working on steamers were of immense help to their enslaved brothers. They would vouch for them if they claimed they had "lost" their papers. If they had stowed away on the steamer their free brothers would make sure they had food and water and would protect them from being spotted. They would "show them the ropes" to help them gain their freedom to northern ports. Free Blacks even bought passage on steamers for themselves and their "slave" only to free the bondsperson once they got to the north.

In most southern states laws were passed that would heavily penalize any steamboat company providing employment or escape opportunities to enslaved Black persons. Even though these steamboats had a tremendous impact on the local economies, steamboats would bring supplies into the oftentimes isolated towns, such as in the interior of Arkansas, and also would carry out local farm commodities such as cotton for much-needed cash. If caught helping a slave to escape frequently the steamship line would be required to reimburse the slave owner for the cost of his slave and possibly pay a fine. After the passage of the Fugitive Slave Act of 1850 steamboat captains became more aware of the penalties of harboring a runaway bondsperson and often local authorities became more vigilant in enforcing such laws. However, sometimes a steamboat captain took the chance of hiring a bondsperson when in desperate need of personnel.

A 35-year-old Arkansas bondsman named Ben was described in a runaway slave advertisement in the *Arkansas Gazette* newspaper as a stout and dark man and good looking and pleasant. However, Ben was undoubtedly a man who could take care of himself as he bore "several scars on his neck and arms" from knife cuts. Ben had six months of experience as a fireman on the steamboat, *Liverpool*. As mentioned before, the job of fireman on a steamboat was only for really strong individuals who had amazing endurance. Ben had been purchased by a Thomas Thorn of Little Rock. Ben made his escape from Thorn in May of 1839. Thorn thought Ben would again seek employment on a steamboat and would be heading towards Tennessee where he could rejoin his wife.[29] As in the case of Ben, not all escapes in Arkansas were to the north for freedom but some were to see family members in other southern slave states.

A bondsman named Fielding fled on a "dark bay horse" of "fine appearance" but he was looking to the steamboat to carry him away from bondage in 1848. Fielding, from Washington, Arkansas, in the southwest corner of the state, had been a cook on a steamboat and his owner thought he was trying to go back to that profession. Fielding, it was thought, probably rode the horse north by northeast to catch a steamer either on the Arkansas River or Mississippi River. Fielding had tasted freedom before when he escaped bondage in Pine Bluff, Arkansas, and lived as a free man for three years.[30]

As in Missouri, Arkansas also had her share of forged free papers and copies of slave leases to steamship. Often, the boarding houses and taverns near steamboat ports were places where bondsmen could receive and buy forged papers. Adding to the probability of an enslaved steamboat worker gaining forged papers was the fact that many masters let their enslaved bondsmen negotiate their own self-hire out to the steamships. Almost all of the masters that allowed their bondspersons to self-hire would only allow their slaves to hire out to steamers that plied below the Missouri River in slave state Missouri. However, some bondsmen and bondswomen built up trust with ship captains over an extended period of time who thought nothing of it when they saw the bondsperson on a steamer headed to a northern port.[31] Once in the northern port of a state that didn't allow slavery the bondsperson would make their escape to ultimate freedom, often in Canada.

A bondsman from Tennessee named John Warren used a forged pass to gain employment on a White River steamship in Arkansas. Warren had learned to spell a little when he was a youngster but did not know how to read and write. He bought some letters from a young white lad in Mississippi for 50 cents, a considerable sum at that time for a bondsman to have saved. Warren then used the letters to try and teach himself better to read and write. Warren received many whippings for minor offenses when he was younger but as he grew into a man he would fight back or run away. He had seen a drunken master and overseer give one poor man 550 lashes with a whip. When he was younger Warren had received 200 lashes from a slaver at one time. Warren was a good worker and the overseer hated to lose Warren's time in the fields when he ran away so the beatings came less often.

Meanwhile Warren kept trying to teach himself to read and write, mostly at night and on Sundays. He became frustrated by the fact that he had no one to show him how to even hold the pencil or to monitor his progress. It was illegal for a person of color to be taught to read and write. But through trial and error Warren kept at it and began to have confidence in his writing ability. After being absent one Sunday an overseer was going to whip him. However, Warren beat the overseer up and he decided it was time to leave. He hid out in the woods for two days and then walked to Memphis. Warren decided to see if his writing skills were good enough to forge passes for himself to work on the steamships. Warren wrote out some passes for himself to go to work in Memphis on the boats. He made his way down the Mississippi and up the White River to Jackson Port in Arkansas. Because people of color weren't thought to know how to read or write no one suspected Warren of writing these passes himself. Then he went back to Memphis on a steamer where he caught a boat to Cincinnati. From Cincinnati it was on to freedom in Canada. John finally settled in London, Ontario. He detested slavery and all its brutality and had no desire to ever go back to the south again. He noted that in Canada he was treated fairly.[32]

Sometimes when a bondsman or bondswoman was whipped and ran away the master would put all the slaves on half rations until the runaway came back to the plantation. This undoubtedly had an effect on the attempted escapes knowing that you were putting your brethren in a distressed situation. Many times if the bondsperson was caught after an escape attempt and brought back they would have to make up their lost time by working on Sundays, which was usually the only day the slaves had to rest.

Some bondsmen who had a working knowledge of the steamboat world would often head south to New Orleans. They knew that any steamer headed north would be watched with more scrutiny. However, they knew once they were in New Orleans they could catch a steamer to the north at any time. In New Orleans a bondsman could often mix in with a group of free Blacks on a ship and never have their papers asked for by the ship's personnel. The hustle and bustle of a large port area like New Orleans and the ever-changing crews made it easier to gain entrance as a crew member. Or, the bondsman could even hook up with a sailing ship headed for the Atlantic Ocean and a northern port. Sailing ships that cruised the oceans often had a hard time finding seamen to sail with them and again, sea captains, sometimes out of necessity, didn't look at a bondsperson's papers too closely if they needed to hire help right away.

Often a bondsperson trying to pass as a free person and getting employment on a steamer was determined by how they were dressed. If they looked the part of a slave with tattered or old dirty clothing that was a sure sign they were enslaved. However, if they had nice clothing appropriate for a free person to wear it would be easier to pass themselves off as an emancipated Black seaman.

However, bondsmen who attempted to escape by steamers were always at the mercy of bounty and slave hunters. These bounty and slave hunters prowled the docks of port towns looking for possible runaways. As the telegraph made its way to the Mississippi River Valley slave owners could alert steamboat landings for possible runaways. Flyers of runaways were sent to steamboat landings to help aid in the return of escapees. Slave and bounty hunters often searched steamboats from top to bottom for possible runaways. The steamboat captains had to comply with these searches so as to not offend any local laws or appear as if they weren't obeying the laws not to employ bondspersons attempting to run away from slavery. Also, the bondsperson portraying a free Black person had to worry about being betrayed by white crewmen wanting to collect a reward. Once docked, the prying eyes of levee police or other local law officers could end a potential escape.[33]

Manuel escaped from Little Rock on May 10, 1844, along with other bondspersons from a Mrs. Colbert on the steamboat *Export*. The *Export* was bound for Pittsburgh. It is not known for sure if this group tried to gain employment on the *Export* or if they posed as free Blacks or simply stowed away. Manuel apparently got off near Memphis, Tennessee, and his fate is not known. Perry and Nelson escaped from Big Creek Township in Phillips County in the summer of 1840. They didn't leave at the same time but their owner had little doubt they were working together. Perry was described as having "a rather pleasing countenance" and Nelson as being "free spoken." It was felt they would try to board a steamboat to facilitate their escape. It is not known if these two found their permanent freedom.[34]

Lewis, a youngster described as being "17 or 18 years old" but only "four foot six or seven," escaped from New Orleans in 1840 on the steamship *Winchester* but was discovered by Captain G. Washington and turned over to authorities and jailed in Arkansas. Henry, a bondsman from Phillips County, escaped in the fall of 1852 and it was thought he would use the steamboats to help him on his journey to freedom.[35]

It might be of interest to look at the life of mulatto bondsman Harry Bibb, sometimes known in slavery as Walton or Walter. Henry Bibb's life as a bondsman was very complex, with many attempted escapes. He tried to flee on a number of occasions into Arkansas from slavery in Louisiana. He was later held in bondage in Arkansas, albeit under unusual circumstances. Later in his life Bibb became an important voice in the anti-slavery crusade in the northern United States and Canada.

Henry Bibb wanted to run away from slavery even at an early age. Bibb recorded that even at a young age he was subjected to whippings and was often forced to work long periods of time without enough to eat or without proper clothing to wear. Bibb told of even being no more than a child and laying his weary body down on a dirt floor as he had no bed to lie upon. He also had to do the bidding of a slave owner in all kinds of weather, including December, without even shoes to protect his feet.[36]

Bibb was often punished as a child for minor offenses and took to running away, for which he was punished even more. Then he got the idea of taking a bridle with him when he ran away. He would then tell anyone who spotted him in the woods that he was chasing an "old mare." Bibb, like many bondspersons, took to running away to avoid harsh and unfair punishment.

Bibb made up his mind to try and escape to Canada. As Bibb grew up to teenage years, however, his attention turned to the fairer sex. He met a tremendous bondswoman named Malinda. She was enormously talented and hard working. Her mother was a free Black woman and they often met at her mother's house. Bibb became extremely conflicted as he knew marriage would make his dream of escaping slavery very difficult.

Bibb was beginning to fall head over heels in love with this fine young lady. He did need to know how she felt on two important subjects: escaping slavery and the Christian religion. Henry was a devout Christian and wanted to try and live his life according to those principals. This was a demanding thing to do as an American slave.

Much to Henry's delight she agreed to "marry" him even though she had other suitors more agreeable to her mother. Malinda also wanted to escape slavery and was interested in the Christian religion. Even though marriage among slaves wasn't recognized by law Henry and Malinda married according to slave customs and lived as husband and wife. Henry managed to get sold to Malinda's master so that the two could live together. Soon they had a child together, a beautiful baby girl.

However, when the two lived on the same plantation Henry had to watch as his wife was whipped and insulted for the pettiest of reasons. He had to watch as the white mistress would slap his little daughter's face when she cried at an inappropriate moment. These indignities were almost too much for Henry to bear. He knew he would have to escape to Canada or the free north and then come back later for his wife and child.[37]

Bibb planned his escape. He got hold of a suit and managed to save two dollars and 50 cents. The Bibbs were residing in Kentucky at the time and Henry asked his master if he could go to the north of the state to find work as they were paying high wages there. His master liked the idea and wrote out the proper paperwork for him to travel. Malinda was conflicted to see him go but understood this was the first step to their being a free family.

Henry planned to escape by steamship. When Bibb got near the steamboat landing he put on his suit. It would be the first time he had ever ridden on a steamboat and he was apprehensive as even in the slave quarters they had heard about the explosions of the boilers on these boats. Steamboats at this time often had their boilers explode, killing not only members of the crew but also the passengers. It was night time and being a mulatto it was hard for anyone to tell he was a bondsman and with his suit on he fooled everyone. He got onto the boat with the crowd and stood away from the lights on deck. When a boatman left his hammock to go on duty Bibb asked him if he could lay in it and the boatman said he could for 25 cents. Bibb gladly paid the price and made sure no one saw his facial features. Bibb managed to get very little sleep worrying about getting caught or having the boiler explode.

When daylight came the steamer had made it to Cincinnati much to his delight. Since it was past sunrise Bibb waited until almost everyone had left the boat. He then coolly strolled off the steamer as if he owned it and went up the street, no one the wiser. Cincinnati had a sizeable free Black population and Bibb found a free Black man who was sympathetic to Henry's plight.[38]

Bibb told the African American man of his wish to go to Canada and the man pointed him to the house of a white abolitionist who would help him. At that point Bibb had never heard of an abolitionist. Bibb was astonished that a white person could be kind as he had only known white slavers and their whips and chains. The abolitionists fed him and sent him on his way. Bibb made it to Perrysburgh (now Perrysburg) near Toledo in northern Ohio, which had a large contingent of escaped slaves. He stayed there all winter chopping wood for a living. He bought a beard to wear for a disguise when he went back to get his family. He also purchased dry goods, which he peddled on his way back to Cincinnati to provide income for himself.

He made his way by steamboat to Kentucky and found his wife and family. They decided it best for her to escape on Saturday night as her master was watching her closely since Henry had escaped. Bibb went back to Cincinnati to wait for his wife but when men posing as abolitionists got $300 to turn him in, his hopes to reunite the Bibb family became untenable. He was a slave again. As they were taking him back to captivity Bibb managed to escape again and he went and saw his wife. That whole area was looking for Henry and he thought it best to leave the area as they were watching his family. He caught a steamboat for Cincinnati and then made it all the way to Canada. Unfortunately, Malinda, who was to attempt an escape and join him, was unable to do so. Henry went back to Kentucky to try and retrieve his family but was recaptured and put in a prison. While in the Kentucky prison some other bondsmen surreptitiously asked him through the bars how he got to Canada. Henry was only too happy to tell them and some of those he instructed made their way to the great white north. Several of the other prisoners who were white befriended Henry and suggested he learn how to read and write so as to be able to forge his own papers to be able to work on the steamboats. From the steamboats he could get his family and then head north to freedom.

A cruel and vicious slave trader by the name of M. Garrison bought Bibb and his wife and child to take them to New Orleans along with other bondspersons to sell. He was able to buy Bibb at a discount because of his reputation as someone who would attempt to escape. Also, because of Bibb's intelligent manner, many thought he could read and write. This however, was not true — Henry at this time could not read or write. His wife and child were also considered damaged goods because it was thought Bibb would have told her how to escape to Canada. The slavers were afraid she would pass this information onto other bondspersons.

Garrison was a sexual sadist whom Bibb had heard remark on several occasions that he would rather paddle a female slave than eat when he was hungry — that it was music for him to hear them scream, and to see their blood run.[39] The slaver took Henry and his family south in the fall of 1839. Garrison would buy attractive mulatto bondswomen in Kentucky and sell them to brothels in New Orleans or as concubines for slavers. Garrison also like to brutalize and torture slave men and women when they were in chains and unable to fight back.[40]

Bibb was put on the slave market in New Orleans where slaves were often stripped for examination. If a bondsman looked "dark and rough" they would be washed with greasy dish water to look slick and lively. When a bondsperson was interviewed by a prospective master they were to answer in a positive and lively manner — such as if they would be asked if they would try to escape. If the bondsperson was not bought they would be paddled for not projecting a positive enough countenance. The whip wouldn't be used because it would leave marks that would concern a prospective buyer, so a paddle was used in these situations.

In his book *Soul by Soul: Life Inside the Antebellum Slave Market* Walter Johnson gives a very gritty description of the slave markets in New Orleans. Johnson states:

...(the original slave market was) a few short blocks from the levee, past the cathedral, and the gin houses and sailor's tenements that served the nearby docks. After the 1840s there was also a slave market further uptown, amidst the shooting galleries, cock pits, barbershops, and bootsellers of the city's central business district ... these markets were really clusters of competing firms, each of which, in turn, maintained its own yard for keeping slaves-"slave pens" in the parlance of the trade ... the streets in front of the pens were lined with slaves dressed in blue suits and calico dresses ... as many as a hundred slaves might occupy a single block ... business was advertised by the painted signs hanging overhead: "T. Hart, Slaves," "Charles Lamarque and Co., Negroes." The walls surrounding the pens were so high-fifteen or twenty feet.... Inside those walls the air must have been thick with overcrowding, smoke and shit and lye, the smells of fifty or a hundred people forced to live in a space the size of a home lot.

When not on the outside the slaves were forced to live in what were in reality jail cells with bars. Some of these buildings would be made out of brick and stood three stories high.[41]

Garrison was trying to sell the Bibb family together — not out of any concern for them but because no one wanted Henry. Many thought because of his intelligence he could read and write, which he could not at this time, and this was a negative in the slave world. His wife, however, was very attractive and very accomplished and she was much sought after. The slaver thought he would get much more for the whole family if he sold them all together. However, there were no takers for the Bibb family. Garrison then instructed Henry to go out in the city of New Orleans and try to find a buyer for himself and his family. He knew Henry wouldn't try to escape when Garrison had custody of his family. He was to go to the hotels, boarding houses and other places that might buy his whole family. Henry did this with much earnestness, wanting to keep his family together, but did not meet with any success.

He finally found a man by the name of Francis Whitfield who would buy him and his family. Henry was hoping that this man, a deacon in the Baptist church, might be a humane person. The Bibb family went to the deacon's plantation, along with other enslaved laborers, in Claiborne Parish in Northern Louisiana along the border with Arkansas. When they got to his place Henry noticed the deplorable conditions in which the bondspersons on the place were living and the slaver's desire to cruelly punish his slaves for any minor reason. The deacon, observing Henry's intelligence, had wanted him to act as an overseer. The deacon had paid top dollar for Henry — $1,200, however his history for running away was not known to Whitfield. The deacon also paid $1,000 for Malinda and their child. But Henry's aversion to using the whip on anyone quickly put any idea of making him an overseer or driver to rest.[42] Henry at first worked mainly around the house. The deacon was a cruel taskmaster, nearly starving his workers and not even allowing a church service for a bondsperson who had passed away.

Henry made his first escape from the deacon on a large brown mule with a saddle and bridle; he also took a double barreled shotgun with him. Henry had with him a good supply of clothing, jeans and blanket coats. Whitfield threatened Malinda into telling him where Henry was going and she told him to Trimble County, Kentucky, where he had lived before or to a free state. Whitfield was certain that Bibb would go through nearby Arkansas and he ran a runaway slave advertisement in the *Arkansas Gazette* on September 2, 1840, and on October 7, 1840. So it may be assumed Henry was gone for at least the length of time between the two dates of the newspaper advertisements. In the advertisement Whitfield described Henry as "a bright mulatto, five feet eight inches high, twenty-four years old, quite intelligent, converses, reads, and writes well." In the ad, Whitfield called Henry by his slave name of Walton or Walter. Whitfield offered a reward for Bibb of $100 if taken from a state other than Louisiana or Arkansas. If captured in either of these two states the reward would be $50.[43] Bibb claimed that at this time he could not read or write. He practiced writing at night and on Sundays but had no knowledge of what the letters meant. His wife, seeing him practice writing and being illiterate herself, probably thought he could read and write. It seems for certain if he could write and read as well as the deacon thought he could he would have written himself a pass. Bibb was captured and brought back to the plantation.

Another time, Bibb left the Whitfield place to go to a prayer meeting at another plantation. When he got back Malinda said she had heard that he would get 500 lashes for going off without permission—surely enough punishment to kill him. Henry knew he would have to try and escape again. He took a mule and a bowie knife with him this time. However, the mule made so much noise when around people or other animals that Henry actually brought it back to the plantation lest it would give him away. When he came back he took Malinda and his child with him. They made it to an island in the Red River but were attacked but a pack of wolves. Henry made a charge with the bowie knife and drove them away. The small family tasted freedom for a few days but was captured by bloodhounds and slave hunters. Bibb and his wife were punished viciously with all of the other bondsmen looking on. Henry was stripped naked and spread-eagled on the ground and whipped so that every inch of his body was raw. He was unable to work for some time. The deacon then put a cruel device on Henry that consisted of an iron collar with prongs extending above his head and a bell on top. Henry had to sleep while in stocks or with heavy chains put on him.[44] After about six weeks the contraption was taken off of Henry.

Not too long after this latest episode Henry made plans with another man named Jack to escape the deacon's plantation again. His ultimate goal was to escape and then try and come back for his wife and child. Jack also had the reputation as someone who was always trying to escape bondage. The two men would head for Little Rock, Arkansas, with hopes of catching a steamboat. By this time Bibb had become a seasoned traveler on the various steamboat lines. With the northern star to guide them they made their escape. Henry had taken with him a gun, bowie knife and a new suit of clothes.

They generally traveled by night to escape notice and then hid out and rested during the day. When their food ran out Jack attempted to get more provisions. He endeavored to go onto an Arkansas plantation cook house and tell a fellow bondswoman that he was escaping slavery and ask her if he could have something to eat. Unfortunately she yelled out, "Here is a runaway Negro." Henry and Jack made a quick getaway as the plantation owner and his minions began looking for the pair.[45]

Next time Jack wanted food he bypassed any human contact and took six small piglets from a farm and captured a wild turkey. They singed off the hair from the piglets and prepared the meat. When the two had eaten their fill they were surprised by five slave hunters. This whole area of Arkansas had been plastered with wanted posters for the pair. However, since neither Jack nor Henry could read, the posters went unnoticed by them. The slave hunters told Henry that the posters had the notation that the two were wanted "dead or alive." If they had resisted they both would have been murdered on the spot. Apparently, the deacon was tired of these two runners and didn't care if they were returned alive but he certainly didn't want them to taste freedom. It is interesting to note that apparently Whitfield didn't run any advertisements for the runaway Bibb on his last two escapes, as no advertisements could be found.

When he was returned Bibb was punished again and had the contraption put on his head. The deacon was determined to sell Bibb as he never wanted any of his bondspersons to escape from his hellhole of a plantation. Henry was treated in a most inhumane way. Remarkably, a group of professional gamblers led by Thomas Wilson rode by the deacon's plantation only to see Henry at the cotton gin with the ungodly contraption on his head. They became intrigued by it and the slave who wore it. They then bought Henry at a discount to try and resell him later for a profit.[46]

After they had purchased him the gamblers took the contraption off Henry's head and dressed him up and took him to Texas. They knew that if they dressed him well and took the contraption off he would bring a better price. Henry acted as their servant and they even paid him! They gave Henry plenty to eat and even took pity on him for his having to leave his family. Wilson and the group even went back to the deacon's plantation to buy Bibb's wife and child but the stone-hearted deacon would not sell them out of spite. The gamblers couldn't believe the deacon's inhumanity. Henry Bibb would never see his wife or child again.

Wilson and his company of gamblers, along with Bibb, went into Arkansas and raced horses and made wagers, played at all gaming tables and gambled at every occasion. In Fayetteville, Arkansas, they almost lost Henry in a wager on a horse race. Bibb called them blacklegs, which would indicate they were not always honest in their wagers or with their gaming paraphernalia. Henry drove the wagon that contained their clothing and gambling equipment. He tended their horses and blacked boots for hire. The gamblers made a deal with Henry that if he could get someone to buy him whatever profit they made they would split with Henry. They told Henry that the best way to do this was for him to "act very stupid in language and thought, but in business ... be spry."[47] They traveled about the state of Arkansas and made their presence known at every horse race and gaming table they could find.

Wilson and the gamblers next went into the Cherokee Territory for a huge horserace. While in the "Indian Nations" Bibb met up with a wealthy Cherokee man who owned slaves and Henry determined that he was a good man. Bibb also thought it would be easier to escape out of the Cherokee Territory rather than one of the slave states with their cruel patrollers. Henry and the Cherokee man hit it off very well and it was determined that the man would buy Henry from the gamblers. The gamblers, true to their word, sold Henry to the Cherokee man and split their profit with Henry. The gamblers told Bibb how to get to Canada from the Indian Nations and Arkansas.

Bibb was treated with respect by the Cherokee gentleman. Henry acted as a personal servant to him and right off the bat the Cherokee entrusted Bibb with $500 and the care of his horses. Of course, thoughts of escape ran through his mind but Bibb didn't want to disappoint the man. The Cherokee man was a farmer who raised corn and tobacco and had many slaves.

Bibb noticed there were no overseers and the bondspersons in the Cherokee lands had enough to eat and wear. They allowed for religious instruction and their church pews were not segregated. They also didn't split up families as often as they did in other slave states.[48] Bibb had so much respect for his Cherokee master that he made up his mind to not attempt any escape until the man had passed away. His Cherokee master was in poor health. Henry tended to him and tried to make his last days as comfortable as humanly possible. Finally the great Cherokee farmer died. It was ironic to Bibb, a pious Christian, that he never found any Christian charity among any of the white slaveholding Christians who owned him. He did find compassion and was treated like a man among the pagan gamblers and a man of Cherokee heritage.

Bibb made his way out of the Cherokee Territory and then into Arkansas. He traveled as much as possible along the boundary of the Cherokee and Arkansas borders. He slipped into Missouri and headed in a Northeast direction. He traveled mainly at night trying to avoid anyone. Bibb mentioned that he was always more fearful when out on the open prairies as it was easier for a man to sneak up on you. On several instances he saw three men on horseback whom Bibb felt were looking for him. Henry, a light-skinned mulatto, was dressed in nice clothes. He was sometimes able to pass as a white man and did on some occasions and was allowed to stay at public houses. At these times Bibb was always able to act with extreme confidence and with the air that he belonged. He finally made it to the capital city of Missouri, Jefferson City, hoping to catch a steamer to St. Louis.

Bibb knew it might be difficult for him to get on the steamer lest the clerk might ask him for his papers to prove he was a free Black man in case he couldn't pass for a white man. He was dressed too nicely to be taken for a slave laborer. So he went into town and purchased a trunk. When a group of white passengers went on board he carried the trunk on as if he were one of their servants. When the ship got under way he went down on deck and found a group of passengers whom Bibb identified as Irish. They were in a festive mood telling stories and Bibb bought several rounds of drinks which ingratiated him with this group of passengers. When a bell was rung for the passengers who didn't have tickets to come forward, Bibb asked one of his newly found friends if he would mind going to the clerk and purchasing Bibb's ticket. Henry paid the man for the ticket and the transaction was completed without a hitch. When the clerk came by for the tickets Bibb's ticket was taken and no questions were asked.[49] The group reached St. Louis, Missouri, and Bibb had to find a ship bound for a free state.

He found a steamer going to Pittsburgh, Pennsylvania, and he inquired of the steward on the boat about the rates and fortunately he found a free Black man who had helped him escape before to Canada. He boarded the vessel and when it docked in Ohio to refuel he got off to head north. However, he was out of funds at this point and had to work in a hotel to earn money to make it even farther north. Even though the hotel manager stiffed Henry on his wages Bibb was able to shine boots to earn a living but did not make enough to move on. He left the hotel rather hurriedly when he saw the gambler Thomas Wilson in the establishment! Henry panicked; he wasn't sure how the gambler would react to seeing him and he didn't want his last possible hope of freedom go for naught. He knew that if Wilson had recently had a run of bad luck at the gaming tables he might turn against his onetime friend and try and raise a stake by selling Bibb back into slavery.

Fortunately, Henry met a man he had known in Perrysburgh, Ohio, who convinced him to go back into slave state Kentucky. The white man, named Smith, was going to buy a large herd of horses. Bibb went with him to Kentucky. The plan went without any problems only Henry saw a steamboat captain whom he had seen two years earlier when he was in chains. The steamboat captain didn't recognized Bibb without the irons and with the air of a free person.[50] After earning enough money from Smith, Bibb was able to attend school and make plans to try and retrieve his wife and child. He went to Detroit to attend school, which lasted only three weeks, but Henry was finally able to learn to read and write.

Bibb's situation as a slave in Arkansas was somewhat typical although his occupation as a servant to a group of professional gamblers was not the norm. His time in Arkansas as a bondsman was typical in that he came from another state and was not born in the state. Bibb's unsuccessful escape attempt from Louisiana into Arkansas was not unusual. Of the 615 runaway slave advertisements still in existence and run in Arkansas newspapers from

1820 to 1861 almost half of the escapees listed states other than Arkansas as their state of origin.[51] Plus, like Bibb, many Arkansas slaves were not native-born but were brought into the state. The stereotype of the slave being born and living his whole life on one plantation and in one state was for many not an accurate representation of life as a bondsperson. Bibb's life certainly reflects this fact. Henry had lived or had been in six slave states and one territory that allowed slavery. He had been born in Kentucky and had spent time in Tennessee, Missouri and Texas. He had resided not only in Kentucky but also in Louisiana, Arkansas and the Cherokee Territory of the Indian Nations now known as Oklahoma. Also, when he had escaped he had lived in Ohio and later in Canada. When Bibb attempted to flee the horrors of plantation life in Louisiana he made it as far as Arkansas. This escape mirrored the experiences of many bondspersons: when attempting to break away from slavery in the deep south they made part of their escape through Arkansas and unfortunately many were captured in this state, as was Henry Bibb. Bibb's story is also indicative of the many times bondspersons attempted to escape only to be returned to punishment and continued bondage.

After his short stint at schooling Bibb went on the lecture tour with others telling of the horrors of slavery. He went about Ohio, Michigan, New England and New York City. Mobs sometimes threatened him and those with him, especially when they were close to Ohio's borders with slave states. Many times slave supporters would try and silence Bibb and others who spoke out against the cruelty and injustice of slavery. Henry tried to recover his wife and child but was unable to do so. He found out she had become the mistress to her white slave master.

Bibb often times wrote and told other bondspersons how to escape and warned them to not be victims of unscrupulous imposters on the Underground Railroad. It was often the practice of certain white folks or even free Blacks to tell an enslaved human that if they gave them money or performed an illegal act such as theft or even murder they would help them escape bondage. Bibb's advice was, "If any professed friend refuses to aid you or your friends in making their escape from slavery, unless they are paid an extravagant price for it, they are not to be trusted: no matter if they are white or black." Bibb was concerned if a bondsperson had to pay someone to help them escape, if a slave or bounty hunter offered this Underground Railroad "conductor" more money what was to keep the "conductor" from turning the bondsperson in for a better offer?

In 1848 Henry was in Buffalo, New York, speaking at a free soil convention. On the platform with Henry Bibb were Frederick Douglas and Samuel Ringgold Ward and others.[52] These were very important programs and speeches to make the northern free states aware of what conditions were like on slave farms and plantations and for urban slaves. These lectures and programs made the people of the north understand why it was so important to help and support bondspersons fleeing these conditions and to help bring about the end of American slavery in the south.

Douglas, of course, became the premier spokesman for the abolishment of slavery in America. He had escaped slavery in Maryland posing as a free Black sailor. He had the papers and wore the uniform of a seaman and was able to make it north. With the publication of the first version of his life's story in 1845, Douglas became an instant sensation on the abolitionist lecture circuit. Samuel Ringgold Ward also had an interesting story to tell. At the age of three years old Ward became very ill as a slave in Maryland. His master wanted to sell Ward and his mother and father to the highest bidder—possibly to Georgia where the market for slaves was very good—without any regard to keeping the family together.

The venerable Frederick Douglas. Douglas was the best known Black lecturer and writer in favor of the ending of slavery in America. His eloquence impressed everyone. When Douglas shared his speaking platform with Henry Bibb that gave Bibb instant credibility. Bibb's life story of being a slave and trying to escape into Arkansas and residing for a time in Arkansas was a moving testament to the horrors of that institution. Bibb was probably one of the few Black lecturers on slavery at that time whose family and himself had been put up for sale in the large slave market in New Orleans and who had survived being a slave on a Deep South plantation. Bibb went on to establish the first Black newspaper in Canada, and it became a very important voice against American slavery (State Historical Society of Iowa, Des Moines).

However, Ward's master knew that if Samuel died or appeared very sickly he would bring next to nothing. Ward's father was a large strong man and the master knew that the young child, if healthy, would bring a good price. The days went on and Samuel remained in poor health. However, he began to improve. Normally a mother would be happy but not in this case. Samuel's mother knew when the child got better the family would be torn apart and sent to a strange land. She knew they must escape. The young family left one night for free state New Jersey.

A young scion of a nearby plantation saw the escaping family. He arrogantly barked for the Ward family to return to their master. Samuel's father wasn't going to let this son of privilege keep his family in bondage. He promptly beat the young man to within an inch of his life and the young family found their freedom in New Jersey and then New York. Samuel Ringgold Ward learned to read and write and grew into an impressive man.[53]

In 1847 Henry Bibb met a refined lady, Mary Miles, who had been raised in the Quaker religion by her free African American parents in Rhode Island. She became a teacher in Albany, New York, Philadelphia and later in Cincinnati.[54] They married in 1848. Since slave marriages were not recognized in the United States it was not necessary for Bibb to obtain a divorce from his previous wife.

Henry Bibb had his life story printed in 1849 and he became a fixture on the abolitionist lecture circuit. However, in 1850 the Fugitive Slave Act changed all of this in his life. All former slaves living in the north were subject to being recaptured and returned to their southern masters. Frederick Douglas commented on this matter from his home in Rochester, New York: "fugitive slaves who had lived for many years safely and securely in western New York and elsewhere, some of whom had by industry and economy saved money and bought little homes for themselves and their children were suddenly alarmed and compelled to flee to Canada for safety as from an enemy's land ... and take up a dismal march to a new abode, empty-handed, among strangers."[55] Douglas, whose freedom had been bought, felt safe to stay in the United States but Henry Bibb and Samuel Ringgold Ward and many others, who were technically fugitives, felt they had better flee to Canada for good.

However, Henry didn't feel he was defeated. In Canada he started printing a publication entitled *Voice of the Fugitive*. It became very popular and influential. Bibb also went back into the United States on occasion to give very effective and persuasive speeches.

Henry's publication came to have an almost taunting aspect to it as he boasted, "Fugitive slaves are constantly arriving here from all parts of the South," and he later bragged, "we can run a lot of slaves through from almost any of the bordering states into Canada, within 48 hours, and we defy the slaveholders and their abettors to beat that if they can." Henry called the south the "land of whips and chains." He would advise slave owners by name to stop hiring slave hunters or employing any more bloodhounds on a certain bondsperson as they had already reached Canada. Letters from former fugitives to their ex-masters would be printed in the paper. Bibb's language in his publication was satirical and vivid and abolitionist newspapers in the United States were overjoyed to reprint his columns in the newspapers in the north.[56]

Many white abolitionist leaders at this time were suggesting that slaves should be purchased from slave owners in Arkansas, Missouri and other slave states and be sent back to Liberia in Africa or other such schemes to obtain emancipation from slavery. Henry Bibb maintained that, "We shall also persuade, as far as it may be practiceable, every oppressed person of color in the United States to settle in Canada, where the laws make no distinction among men, based on complection, and upon whose soil 'no slave can breathe.'"[57]

While publishing the *Voice of the Fugitive* Henry learned that the cruel and abusive slave trader M. Garrison who had once owned him and his family had been shot twice in the head by a fellow slaver. Henry wrote in the February 26, 1851, edition of his newspaper that the way Garrison passed away was "the way such characters generally settle their difficulties before they leave the world."[58]

Bibb went on publishing the *Voice of the Fugitive* for several years, espousing freedom for southern blacks. He began spending more and more time in America on the lecture circuit probably as his reputation began to grow. He used the funds he received on the lecture circuit to keep his newspaper in print and also to support Mary Bibb's school for the children of the newly freed men and women of Canada. The Bibbs also became involved in an organization called the Refugee Home Society to aid the Blacks newly arrived in Canada. They also received aid from American Missionary Association for their projects. Mary Bibb took under her wing a young Black woman named Mary Ann Shadd.[59] The Bibbs encouraged Shadd to open up a school in Canada. Both the Bibb and Shadd schools encountered financial difficulties and underwent several transformations. Shadd also began to publish her own newspaper, the *Provincial Freeman*. Unfortunately the Bibbs and Shadd began feuding over the funding of their various projects.

In 1853 tragedy struck Bibb's enterprise as fire burned the newspaper offices to the ground. The newspaper had grown to the point where Henry had begun to think about expanding its operation. As Henry was thinking about rebuilding the newspaper he was struck by what they called at the time "brain fever" and he died in 1854.[60] One of America's most exciting anti-slavery proponents of the Black exodus to Canada was silenced.

After Henry Bibb's death thankfully the bad blood between the Bibbs and Shadd came to an end. Shadd married a man named Cary. Bibb's widow, Mary Miles Bibb, married Mary Ann Shadd Cary's brother-in-law, Isaac N. Cary. Thus the feud came to a peaceful end. Henry Bibb went on to become recognized as one of the important leaders in the escape to Canada by enslaved Blacks.

6

Arkansas: Fleeing from Farms and Plantations

> "Dem white folks didn't care nothing 'bout how
> de slaves grieved when dey tore up a family."
> — *Former bondswoman Katie Rowe*

A slave owner unwittingly helped to free her 12 Arkansas bondspersons by taking them out of the state. In 1846 a Mrs. Oliver from Maryland inherited from her father, a resident of Arkansas, a dozen enslaved humans. In May of 1847 she traveled to Arkansas where the bondspersons resided and then took these valuable persons back to Williamsport, Maryland, with her and her children. While Mrs. Oliver and this group were traveling to Williamsport they passed through Pennsylvania.

After five months in Maryland all of these Arkansas bondspersons fled the Oliver residence and headed northeast into Cumberland County in Pennsylvania. These bondspersons planned an extremely well thought out escape strategy to free that large a group at one time. The Oliver family hired a slave hunter who tracked them to this county in the Keystone state only to have the trail go cold. After they left Maryland this Arkansas dozen hooked up with the Pennsylvania Underground Railroad. In fact, the bondspersons were being hidden by members of the Pennsylvania Underground Railroad in Daniel Kaufman's barn until conductors Philip Breckbill and Stephen Weakley could move them on their route north.

The 12 from Arkansas proved to be too crafty for the slave hunters and they made a full escape, never to be recovered. The Oliver family filed suit in Pennsylvania to recover the cost of their enslaved humans from Kaufman, Breckbill and Weakley. The jury in the first trial voted ten members for the plaintiffs and two members for the defendants. In the second trial only Daniel Kauffman was found guilty and damages of $2,800 were awarded to the Oliver family.[1]

This was a hefty amount to levy against an individual during this time period. The jury, in all probability, felt that it had been proven beyond a shadow of a doubt that the bondspersons were hidden in Kaufman's barn but that it wasn't proven that Breckbill and Weakley had played a part in the escape. Cases like these and the large amounts, for this time, of awards given by the courts often had a chilling effect on members of the Underground Railroad and those who would try and help an escapee from American slavery.

It is worthy to note that Judge Grier in this case of *Oliver v. Weakley et al.* made mention of another case he had tried involving a runaway bondsman entitled *Van Metre v. Mitchell*. In that case Judge Grier had made reference to some relevant instructions to the jury in cases involving escaped slaves. In these instructions Judge Grier had stated to the Pennsylvania jury, "No theories or opinions which you or we may entertain with regard to liberty and human rights, or the policy or justice of a system of domestic slavery, can have a place on the bench or in the jury box. We dare not substitute our convictions or opinions, however honestly entertained, for the law of the land." In this same case of *Van Metre v. Mitchell* Grier's opinion went on and made an interesting analogy, albeit a somewhat fallacious one, regarding escaping slaves. In this opinion Judge Grier went on to say, "The extradition of criminals or slaves, escaping from one country to another, has generally been considered as a matter of comity and not of right; and the common law and law of nations which refuse to deliver up persons guilty of mere political offences, most probably have borrowed this principal from the Jewish Code (Deut. xxiii. 15).... The institutions of the Jews, while they tolerated slavery, and would not permit the harboring or concealing of the slave of one Jew, by another nevertheless forbade their extradition when they escaped into Judea, from a Gentile or foreign nation. And therein our own laws are assimilated to theirs. While we would not deliver up slaves escaping from a foreign nation, the people of these United States, as one people, united under a common government, have bound themselves by the great charter of their Union, to deliver up slaves escaping from one state to another."[2]

Judge Grier was referring to the Jewish code as declared in Deuteronomy 23:15. The King James version of the Bible was quoted by Grier and reads, "Thou shall not deliver unto his master the servant which is escaped from his master unto thee." In his opinion Grier didn't go on to quote verse 16, which states, "He (the slave) shall dwell with thee, even among you, in that place which he shall choose in one of thy gates, where it liketh him best: thou shall not oppress him." These Biblical quotes, as they make no mention of internal Judean slaves as opposed to external slaves from other countries, seemed to contradict Judge Grier's whole notion of turning over escaped slaves to their masters. In fact they seem to say it is biblically correct to hide or allow escaped slaves to reside in your own county. Another argument that falls on its face is the one that states it is okay to return internal slaves from other states but not those from other countries. The two large countries that bordered the United States at this time, Canada and Mexico, had outlawed slavery in their countries over two decades before Grier's decisions. There was no chance that slaves would escape into the United States from either of these two nations. The only question of escaped slaves in the United States concerned internal slaves not external slaves. By Jewish custom slavery was allowed but it was so different than American slavery that it was ludicrous to compare them. Judge Grier was known as a "doughface"— a northern man with southern sympathies.

From 1840 to 1860 Arkansas saw a dramatic increase in enslaved humans. In 1840 the state had 19,935 slaves; by 1850 it had 47,100 slaves; and by 1860 it had 111,115 slaves.[3] This sizeable increase from 1850 to 1860 in the number of enslaved humans in Arkansas was mainly due to the establishment of large cotton plantations in the delta area and elsewhere in the state. Most were not native-born but brought in from other slave states or from the various slave markets such as the markets in New Orleans or St. Louis. Arkansas' rural nature was also reflected in the fact that few of her slaves lived in towns. Little Rock, the state's capital and largest population center, had only 3,727 residents by 1860. Enslaved humans who lived in towns generally were used as servants, butlers, maids, artisans and craft persons or they were hired out by their slave masters. In 1850 the average slaveholder in Arkansas owned 7.8 humans and this average increased to 9.6 humans by 1860.[4]

Albert Pike, a controversial Whig politician in Arkansas, who was also a well-known newspaperman and attorney, owned slaves. Even though Pike was born in Boston, Massachusetts, and lived in the bay state until he was 21 years of age, turned his back on the abolitionist ways of many in his native state. Rebecca was a bondswoman described in the *Arkansas Gazette* as "tall and good looking, with sharp features; high cheek bones and a large head of hair." Rebecca was 22 years old and a mulatto and managed to escape the control of this future Confederate general. She had originally come from Alabama and Pike felt she had left the state of Arkansas and he increased the size of the reward for her capture from $50 to $80.[5]

Charles, a bondsman living 12 miles northwest of Helena, Arkansas, escaped on January 30, 1840. He was described in the newspaper as "when walking gate rather brisk ... has a scar one side of his forehead produced by a fall. This boy has been lurking during his absence in the neighborhood of Captain Benjamin Porter's place, 5 miles above Helena and from there to the point (mouth of St. Francis River) he was routed near Porter's on last Monday week. I have reason sufficient reason to satisfy me that he has been harbored, concealed, and assisted if not persuaded to leave me, by bad disposed Negroes in the neighborhood."[6] Elisha Burke, like most slave owners, could not believe anyone would want to leave their slave ownership. Burke assumed it must be "bad disposed Negroes" that would entice Charles to leave the Elysian fields of the Burke homestead. However, what is interesting is that slaver Burke acknowledges that it was a network of "Negroes," probably an informal network, who were helping bondsmen like Charles when they escaped — not a white Underground Railroad apparatus in Arkansas.

Some bondsmen took with them firearms to aid in their escape. There was little doubt that the two bondsmen, Cary and Jack, were very serious about escaping slavery and making it all the way north to freedom even if they had to fight their way out of bondage. They took with them a rifle and a shotgun and changes in clothing. They were possibly aided by other Blacks. Cary was described in his slave advertisement as a "very stout made fellow, about 5 feet 6 or 8 inches high, heavy beard, full faced, and wears large whiskers, he is about 28 years of age, and has a crooked thumb on one of his hands." Jack was about "18 or 20 years of age, 5 feet 3 or 4 inches high, quick spoken, has a large nose with a scar across it near the forehead...." The two were going to head across the mountainous region of Arkansas to get into Missouri. This was a very difficult passage to freedom because of the rough terrain of the area.[7]

Campbell, "about 30 years of age," and Reube, "about 40 years of age," escaped from Hot Springs County July 10, 1842, armed with "rifle guns ... a pistol." Reube was described as "quite a sensible fellow." They left on a Sunday when presumably it was easier to slip away. It is believed they were headed for a free state. However, it was stated "one of them being a pretty resolute fellow, it is likely that they may resist an attempt to take them unless there is a show of competent force to overpower them."[8]

Even Arkansas' first governor was not immune from having a bondsperson escaping underneath his nose. Amanda Foster (her married name), a free Black nurse, obtained employment with Governor James Sevier Conway. Amanda was a nurse to Conway's children. Foster used her "free papers" to help a young fugitive slave girl escape from Arkansas. Foster left Arkansas in 1837 and went back to her native New York where with her husband the Rev. Jacob Foster she helped form the Foster Memorial AME Zion Church in Tarrytown, New York. This became a haven for escaping slaves bound for Canada.[9]

Conway was in poor health after his term of office ended in 1840 and he retired to his plantation in Magnet Cove in Hot Springs County some 50 miles south of the state capital. Conway had purchased a bondsman from Daniel Coody near Fort Gibson in the Cherokee Nation. The 20-year-old bondsman named Carter had apparently worked in Coody's house but became a field laborer on the ex-governor's plantation. Carter left Conway's plantation on a fine-blooded sorrel mare equipped with a compass and a map of Arkansas. Carter left dressed in fine clothing. However, the governor learned that Carter was later dressed as an "Indian" and believed he would head back to the Cherokee Nation.[10] Apparently Carter felt more at home in the Cherokee Nation.

Conway wasn't the only governor touched by escaping bondsmen. Territorial Governor John Pope had a bondsman named Austin. Pope was well connected as he was a cousin to George Washington and was related by marriage to President John Quincy Adams. Austin was sold or transferred from Pope to E.H. Waldon. Waldon had Austin working on the farm of a Colonel Thorn. Thorn had a farm two miles below Little Rock. On September 29, 1841, Austin escaped from Thorn's farm.[11] What makes this even more interesting is that John Quincy Adams, after leaving the White House as president, was elected to congress from Massachusetts. While a congressman Adams became the leading advocate in that body to try and pass legislation to outlaw slavery. Family gatherings must have been interesting. However, Adams and Pope had gone their separate ways long before that when Adams refused to name Pope secretary of state but instead chose Henry Clay for that prestigious position.

Another important figure in Arkansas politics and economic life was the editor of the *Arkansas Gazette*, William E. Woodruff. Woodruff also had trouble keeping his enslaved humans at home. In November of 1841 John ran away from Woodruff. Woodruff said that John was addicted to "intoxication." Woodruff must have thought John would head for a free state and his ultimate freedom as his reward for the return of John was $50 if found in a slave state and $100 if found in a free state. Woodruff thought John had escaped with three or four other "Negroes."[12]

Another of Woodruff's bondsmen, Moses, was described as a "notorious liar, and quite boisterous when intoxicated. He has a variety of good clothing and bedding...." Woodruff was very worried that a free Black or mulatto had helped Moses in his escape. He was also concerned that it might have been a white person who had "seduced" Moses to leave. The editor slaver offered a reward of $150 for the capture of Moses and $100 for the capture of anyone who had aided in Moses' escape.[13] Another of Woodruff's bondsmen had an out of the ordinary escape, which is described in Chapter 7. Woodruff owned 14 slaves and between 1841 and 1857 they had made four escape efforts that we know about. This would appear to be a somewhat high number of escape attempts for one slave owner. In his editorials Woodruff was solidly behind the system of slavery and he wanted to curtail or abolish all rights of free Black persons.

English was not always the first language spoken by American slaves. French and Spanish were first languages spoken by some and some had only broken English. One wonders if this didn't greatly hinder them on their quest for freedom. Some were able to escape but it is not known how long or how far they got on their journey. Alexander escaped from a farm close to the Arkansas Post on May 31, 1841. He had a scar made by a knife on his face and he covered the scar by wearing whiskers. Alexander spoke French fluently but he spoke only broken English. It is not known how far away he got from his place of bondage. It can be reasonably concluded that Alexander was probably from Louisiana originally where in some parts of that state French was spoken as a first language, especially during this time in history. William Johnson, another bondsman who escaped from below New Orleans and spoke only broken English, was captured in Arkansas and held in the Chicot County jail. Again one wonders if the language barrier aided in his capture. Peter, about 40 years of age, and with ears that were bored to wear earrings, ran away from his residence about a mile and a half from Hot Springs, Arkansas. Peter was described as a good carpenter who played the fiddle. He spoke Spanish and only broken English. His owner said "Any man is at liberty to whip this fellow, as I myself have never done it."[14]

A bondsman named Joe cultivated the look of a Native American. Because of Arkansas' history with the Native Americans a number of bondspersons there tried to pass themselves as "Indians" when they were attempting to escape. Joe let his straight hair grow long and tried to dress like a Native American as much as possible. He ran away on several occasions with this look. Other bondspersons in Arkansas who wanted to escape would often develop this look of a Native American to escape bondage. Joe was residing on a farm 10 miles west of Helena, Arkansas, when he took off in the winter of 1842 looking as much as possible like an "Indian." When Jordon ran away from bondage in Dover, Arkansas, in the spring of 1850 he bore a strong resemblance to an "Indian." It was said Jordon would try and pass himself off as an "Indian" or free person. Winn, described as "a bright mulatto," escaped in May of 1853. It was noted in his slave advertisement that Winn had "been trying to pass himself sometimes as a Choctaw and white man, half breed...."[15] It was not sure if these escaping bondsmen were trying to make it to the "Indian Nations" where it was thought that the treatment of bondspersons would be better or if they were merely using this ruse to get to permanent freedom in Mexico or Canada.

Slaves in the American system of slavery had no rights. It was impossible for them to petition the courts for even the most outrageous maltreatments. In some forms of slavery throughout the world slaves had basic rights and a means to address grievances. In some slave systems ombudsmen were appointed to look after the welfare of the slaves. In the American system almost nothing was ever done by any governmental or Christian church to assure that slaves were treated with even the minimum of human dignity or decency. There were almost no laws passed in slave states to protect the human rights of slaves. If there were a law or two passed to protect slaves they were routinely ignored — even requests by masters to free slaves upon their death were often disregarded by the heirs or executors of their estates. There were thousands of laws passed in slave states to protect white citizens against slaves but almost no laws passed to protect slaves from being brutalized. In some cases slaves were ill fed, ill housed, robbed, spouses and daughters brutally raped in front of fathers and husbands, children kidnapped from parents and brutalized, and submitted to whippings and beatings with no means for justice for the enslaved human beings. One historian wrote of slavery in Arkansas, "But while whipping was common, it is doubtful that it was usually as brutal as often alleged." I guess it depends on whether you were the one wielding the whip or the one getting whipped. If you were the one administering the whippings they might not seem so brutal. Would this historian feel the same way if it was his wife or child being whipped?

Sometimes the injustices administered to slaves became too much to bear. Driven by inhumane treatment many bondspersons snapped. If the prospect of running away didn't seem likely, oftentimes in a rage a master or overseer paid with their lives. Nearly every year in almost all states in the south bondspersons were charged with murdering their owners.[16] Arkansas was not an exception to these murderous rages.

It was unusual for a bondman to kill a white master and get away with the crime but in a FWP interview Plomer Harshaw reported that a white master Jim Stanley, who owned a neighboring plantation, was murdered by one of his slaves. Stanley put one of his slaves in chains, much to the dislike of the bondsman. The bondsman even had to work with the chains on. After the work was done for the day Stanley took to his porch and was rocking a baby in a rocking chair. The aforementioned bondsman took an axe and chopped Stanley to death while other slaves looked on. Stanley never knew what hit him. The slave patrollers took up chase but never were never able to catch the murderer. Harshaw stated they never saw that bondsman again and presumed he got clean away.[17] One bondsman who killed his master, a Colonel Reedy of Clarendon, passed himself off as a Native American and headed for the "Indian Nations" and was hotly pursued by a posse.[18] Lucretia Alexander, a former slave, claimed in a FWP interview that "You know in slave times, sometimes when a master would git too bad the niggers would kill him — tole him off in the woods somewheres and git rid of him. Two or three of them would git together and scheme it out, and then two or three of them would git him way out and kill 'im."[19] There were others that killed their masters in Arkansas and were caught and were burned to death without benefit of a trial.

Killing a master was almost a certain death sentence; however, killing an overseer could be a different matter. By 1860 Arkansas had over 1,000 persons who listed their occupation as overseer. There were more slave overseers in Arkansas than school teachers.[20] The overseer was directly responsible for the amount of work slaves did day in and day out. Very often it was the overseer who performed the whippings or punishments meted out to the slave workforce. A lot of these overseers were very young, in their late teens and early twenties, and there was a tremendous amount of turnover in the occupation.[21] Many of these Arkansas overseers came from lower social and economic strata and were moving west and had no local ties. Oftentimes, being very young, their judgment on how to handle people was not good. Very often these overseers' mistreatment of slaves was the reason many bondspersons attempted to escape. Because of this they were somewhat expendable and no one thought much of it if they just disappeared. In a FWP interview Joe Ray revealed that his father John had killed an overseer who tried to lash him. His father was never punished, just sent off to another slave plantation for a while away from his family.[22] It was obvious that the master decided that the cost of a good slave, around $1,500 (in present day money around $75,000) or more was too much of an economic loss to be punished by jail time or death and just ignored the murder of the overseer. If you put a price tag on the slave you also put a price tag on the white overseer.

Very often the overseers weren't murdered but were intimidated. Ms. Irene Robertson in a FWP interview stated that her mother-in-law was a slave and worked as a field hand. Her mother-in-law told her, "One day the overseer was going to whoop one of the women 'bout sompin or other and all the women started with the hoes to him and run him clear out of the field. They would have killed him if he hadn't got out of the way."[23] However, in many instances the killing of a white person by a Black person, slave or free, in antebellum Arkansas brought a death sentence — often times carried out by a mob of angry whites. On August 11, 1859, a bondsman crushed the skull of overseer Robert Bickers on the farm of J.W. Carpenter near Helena, Arkansas. The bondsman hid in the hayloft of the plantation barn until hunger got the best of him. He was captured and hanged immediately. His body was kept hanging for a day so as to warn other slaves not to commit any violence against any whites.[24] Pauline Howell stated in an incredible narration that her maternal aunt was sold because she had killed two overseers. One of the overseers was whipping her with a black snake whip and she grabbed the overseer's private parts and pulled them out by the roots. She did that because she knew that would be a slow death. The other overseer she killed was by the same method. Pauline's mother said that overseer was the "nicest little soft man." Her mother said that he just climbed the walls that night because he was in so much misery.[25] However, there were many more slaves killed by whites in the South than whites killed by slaves.

Ellen Cragin's mother was beaten when she fell asleep at the loom where she was weaving. She fell asleep due to the long hours she was made to stay at the loom. Her owner's son was whipping her when Ellen's mother's fought back and knocked him down. She knew she would need to escape. So she took off on a cow and went all the way from Arkansas to Atchison, Kansas. It wasn't until after the Civil War that Ellen was reunited with her mother.[26] Ella Johnson escaped with her mother and other children from Helena, Arkansas. They had a cruel master. Their father had escaped and joined the Union Army but was killed in the war.[27]

Probably one of the most sickening aspects of American slavery and a reason many bondspersons tried to escape out of this horrible institution was the break-up of families and in many cases the virtual kidnapping of children without any recourse by the mother or father of said child. Former bondswoman Katie Rowe described one disturbing scene in which a group of Black slave children were playing. A man owed a debt by the white master of these children came upon the children. The white master had listed these children as collateral on a debt that he was unable to pay. The master told the man to pick out any child in order to pay off the debt and to give the master the debt papers when the child was taken. The man simply swooped up a Black slave child and rode off. The mother of this child saw the scene and of course was completely heartbroken. Ms. Rowe also made the comment at the beginning of the chapter about the horrible break-ups of families.[28] These were the actions of what some historians call a "benevolent system."

Ms. Rowe also told one of the great karma stories of slavery. She stated that at one time she lived near Washington, Arkansas, near the Bois d'Arc Creek. Her master here was a cruel and arrogant physician named Dr. Isaac Jones. During the Civil War Jones, who was vicious and evil, told his slaves that he would kill them with his shotgun before he allowed the Union Army to free them. It was estimated that Jones owned over 200 enslaved humans at this time. On his plantation Jones had a steam driven cotton gin with a boiler. The gin box had a long belt running through the side of the gin house and out to the engine and boiler in the yard. A bondsman named Brown was the mechanic for the steam gin and he ascertained that the boiler had a crack in it and should be shut down so that repairs could be made on the boiler.

When Jones came out and saw the gin shut down he became furious. He told Brown to fire up the boiler. Brown advised against it as the boiler was cracked, but to no avail— after all, the good doctor knew everything. Jones said to Brown, "Cuss fire to you black heart! The boiler is all right! Throw on some cordwood, cuss fire to your heart!" As soon as the boiler had built up a head of steam it exploded with the good doctor standing in front of it. Jones was blown to pieces and they just found little chunks of his clothes and small parts of his body to bury. Fortunately, Brown survived as he had been smart enough to stay far enough away from the boiler when the blast went off.[29]

The rivers of Arkansas supplied an escape path even when passage on steamboats could not be secured. Bondsman Jim escaped in June of 1842 by paddling a canoe down the river. It was thought he might be heading for Tennessee. Bob left on a skiff down the Arkansas River on July 30, 1844. In the early summer of 1845 Mat took off in a skiff on the Arkansas River about 18 miles from Little Rock.[30]

Anderson escaped in August of 1842 with what was described as a "Choctaw rifle." He was described as a man with an "open ad [sic] intelligent countenance." Anderson had just come from Virginia and it was thought he might be trying to get back there presumably to see family, or, it was thought he might head for freedom in Ohio.[31] Tom and Jim escaped from near the Arkansas Post in August of 1842. It was thought they were heading to Batesville, Arkansas, where Tom had a wife. The two had been purchased just two months prior in New Orleans.[32]

Three families with two extra children, 13 enslaved humans, managed to escape bondage. The advertisement for this escape was run in April of 1843, the product of a convoluted purchase. It was believed that they had made it to Texas. It was not known if they were trying to get into Mexico. Officials were not sure if the bondspersons had taken off on their own or if they were in the possession of a dishonest agent of the former owner.[33]

Talton ran away from a Conway County farm headed, it was thought, towards Little Rock in May of 1843. However, Talton still had a chain attached to his leg which of course would impede getting away from bondage.[34] Bob escaped from Bossier Parish in Louisiana and was one of the large numbers of out-of-state runaways in the state of Arkansas. Bob was easily identified as he had had his ears cut off.[35] This was probably done to identify him as a runaway. Many slavers liked to mutilate their human property in some way to denote they had tried to run away and had been recaptured. However, this was very shortsighted as it told any prospective buyers that this bondsperson had attempted to escape bondage, which would reduce their "market value" if an attempt to sell the bondsperson was made.

Wilkes had escaped from De Soto Parish in Louisiana. He was described as stout. It was thought that he was making his way towards Batesville, Arkansas, to be reunited with his wife. John took off from bondage late in 1845 with some extra clothes plus a lot of cash—$300 in silver and a five dollar gold piece. Slaver Farrelly was concerned that John could purchase free papers or attach himself to a white person who would claim John as his own as they made their way to freedom. Farrelly not only offered a very liberal reward of $150 for John's return but also one-third of the amount of money found on John.[36]

Daniel Hall escaped from inside the city of New Orleans around 1840. He managed to get through slave state Louisiana. As many who escaped from slavery in the Bayou state did, he made his way through Arkansas. He then managed to navigate his way through Missouri without much trouble. Many thought that when runaways were able to get to a free state they were liberated. However, this proved to be a thorny issue as in many cases those in the north wanted slaves to stay down south and not come up to the northern free states. Daniel encountered many difficulties while in the heart of Illinois. He thought for a while his attempt at freedom had come to an end. He ran into a bunch of pro-slavery men in central Illinois and was lucky to flee their clutches. Mr. Hall finally was able to escape from the United States and to make it safely to Canada. He worked hard and was able to purchase 50 acres of land near Colchester.[37]

There were many slave advertisements in Arkansas newspapers purchased by sheriffs and jailers for captured runaways. The act of running away was a criminal act by an Arkansas slave. However, prior to 1849 there were no state punishments for this act. Arkansas slaves were deemed runaways when they were found over 20 miles from home without a proper pass. Prior to 1849 if a runaway was captured and not claimed by their owner they would receive life imprisonment. In reality, after 15 months the bondsperson was sold in order to pay the expense of imprisonment and the remainder of the money put in the general county fund. After 1849 the runaways were kept in county jails for six months and if they were unclaimed by their owners they were transferred to the Arkansas state penitentiary. Advertisements were to run for a year. If owners claimed the bondsperson they were to pay the expense of their upkeep while incarcerated.[38]

William Smith seemed to believe that "his man Sam" wouldn't leave on his own but had to have been "enticed away by some white person." Sam was 25 years old and described as being "a bright mulatto." Sam escaped on a "common sized gray horse."[39] William escaped on a little bay mare on September 6, 1845. He was described as a "very bright quadroon." Andrew and Jackson left with an old U.S. musket when they escaped eight miles below the city of Little Rock. Their owner stated in the advertisement, "It is probable said boys may have been decoyed, or enticed away by some white person." Three miles above Napoleon, Arkansas, on the Mississippi River on May 9, 1847, James Hibbard described in his slave ad that Cato had run away from his plantation. Cato had been raised in the "Indian Nation" and spoke little English but mainly "Indian Language." Hibbard surmised that Cato had been decoyed away by a white man who spoke the same Indian language as Cato, and Hibbard offered rewards not only for Cato's return but also for the "conviction and punishment of the thief." Henry and Peter and Barnaby, described as "30 years old and 4 feet 6 inches" left in the late summer in 1850 from Lafayette County and were suspected of being decoyed by some white person. Rewards were offered for these three and a liberal reward if the white person was apprehended and convicted.[40]

Many slave owners thought that the only reason their bondspersons would run away from their farm or plantations was if they had been decoyed or enticed away by a white person or free black person. Many slavers were in denial and they thought their slaves were extremely contented with their lot in life on their farm or plantation. However, there were instances where slaves were enticed or decoyed off plantations. Sometimes whites would tell a bondsperson they could escort them to freedom and get them to flee the farm or plantation. The white person would simply take the unsuspecting slave to another region and sell them to a slave trader or slaver looking for a bargain.

The penalties for a white person or free Black helping a slave escape in Arkansas were rather severe. After 1838 the penalty for enticing a slave to flee his or her master in Arkansas was from two to five years confinement in prison. For stealing a slave the penalty was five to 25 years of confinement. In Arkansas society it was thought that those who would aid a bondsperson in escaping bondage were one of the lowest forms of humanity. It appears there were verified accounts of this activity but there were few convictions.[41] One conclusion that could be entertained is that the slave owners in Arkansas in their newspaper runaway advertisements overestimated the assistance of others in the escapes of their slaves and that in fact their bondspersons had a desire to leave slavery either for permanent or for temporary freedom.

Another tactic used by some was called "Negro running." In this illegal endeavor a Black man was in cahoots with a white man. The Black man was "sold" to a slave owner. Soon after the "sale" the white seller was assisting the Black man in escaping from the slaver. The money the white seller made was split between the two and the process was repeated again.

As mentioned before, there appears to have been little activity in Arkansas by any that may be considered an organized white contingent of the Underground Railroad. However, on occasion whites did try and aid slaves to escape. On March 19, 1847, Anderson escaped from Montgomery County, Arkansas. He also took along two derringers with "5 inch barrels." Anderson hired himself out on various steamboats. However, on May 18, 1847, Anderson was captured and put into the jail in Johnson County, Arkansas. Anderson was fastened to the floor in the upper room of the jail by a log chain. On July 12 of that year a courageous white man went to the upper room of the jail and released him from his chains and carried the five foot eleven inch Anderson downstairs and off to freedom. One wonders if this white man was someone who had befriended him in the steamboat trade or possibly was an official of the steamboat line who viewed Anderson as a valuable employee. The white man was described as a "villain" and a "scoundrel" in the slave advertisement. An ad was run on April 3 after Anderson had first run away offering a $100 reward for him plus all necessary expenses. In another ad, run on July 22 after Anderson had been aided in his escape from the Johnson County jail, the reward was upped to $500. A $300 reward was offered for the white man who aided Anderson in his escape. Hardin escaped from between Dardanelle and the Sulphur Springs in Arkansas in July of 1858. It was believed that Hardin had with him a silver watch, black dress coat, brown pants with blue stripe, calico shirt, yellow with broad stripe and a "Colt 5 shooter." It was also thought Hardin may have some money with him. Slaver F.C. Kendall believed that Hardin had been given a written pass by a white abolitionist. In August of 1858 another advertisement was run for the return of Hardin, so it can only be hoped that if Hardin had a pass or not he made good with his escape.[42]

Fielding ran away in the spring of 1848 from Washington, Arkansas, and would have been a difficult man to bring back to bondage. He was well dressed and had a variety of clothing with him. Fielding was described as being "slow of speech" but was actually "quite intelligent." He had worked as a cook on the steamboats and it was felt he would make his way from Washington in southwest Arkansas to either the Mississippi or Arkansas River to gain employment on the boats. What would make Fielding even more difficult to capture was the fact that he knew how to read and write and was perfectly capable of writing his own "passes" to work on the steamboats or even to write his own "free papers." Although he was only 22 years old Fielding had escaped from his previous master in Pine Bluff and for three years had passed himself off as a "free man" named John. Fielding had left on a beautiful, dark bay mare.[43]

Wilks and Ranson left on a bay mare and a black pony in the early summer of 1849. It was thought they had a pass with them so they could move about in Arkansas. However, their escape didn't end well. Wilks was captured in September of that year in Arkadelphia. It is not known how far away Ranson was able to get from his place of bondage.[44]

There was a very interesting escape in Arkansas by bondsman Nelson Hackett (sometimes spelled Hacket) in 1841. This episode, as did the Anderson case in Missouri, had international implications and even though Hackett had very little help in his own escape it could have derailed many of the activities of the Underground Railroad throughout the north. Hackett was the valet and butler to a wealthy slave owner named Alfred Wallace. Hackett left bondage with a beaver overcoat, a gold watch, a saddle, and a racing mare. He made his way through northern Arkansas traveling only at night and living off the land. He found a Black man who ferried him across the Mississippi River to Kentucky. Hackett made it from the bluegrass state to Chatham in Canada using mostly his own wits.[45]

Slave master Wallace followed Hackett to Canada with a peace officer from Washington County in Arkansas. Wallace demanded Hackett be extradited back to the United States for theft of the horse, watch, overcoat and saddle. To their credit the Canadians refused. Wallace then went to Michigan and at his behest the acting governor of Michigan demanded that Hackett be extradited for theft. However, the governor, General Sir Charles Bagot, refused extradition reasoning that no crime had been committed in Michigan. Not to be deterred Wallace had the governor of Arkansas, Archibald Yell, ask for extradition to the state of Arkansas for theft; no mention was made of Nelson Hackett's condition of slavery. On November 26, 1841, a Grand Jury in Arkansas indicted Hackett for grand larceny and on that basis, a request was made to the Canadian authorities for the extradition of Hackett.

Bagot then recognized that Hackett had committed a crime of stealing the gold watch and saddle. As mentioned before there was much discussion in abolitionist circles in the United States as to how much property was reasonable for a bondsperson to take with them when they left bondage. Certainly after a lifetime of servitude they would have, had they been free, accumulated a certain amount of cash and property. Shouldn't they be allowed a certain amount of property or cash when they escaped? The Canadian government decided that the taking of the horse and coat were reasonable expectations of a slave escaping. However, the taking of the gold watch and the saddle were not necessary to the escape of Nelson Hackett and they considered it theft. The government said they were unwilling to see Canada become "an asylum for the worst characters provided only that they had been slaves before arriving here." The Governor General ordered surrender on February 8, 1842, and Hackett was rowed across the Detroit River bound and gagged and turned over to American authorities.[46]

Hackett had begged Canadian authorities to allow him to stay in Canada or else he would be "tortured in a manner that to hang him at once would be a mercy." On the way to Arkansas Hackett managed to escape while in Princeton, Illinois, but he was captured two days later when a farmer from whom he sought food turned him into authorities. The Canadian *Western Herald* reported that the legal and other fees incurred by Wallace had come to some $1,500, far more than Hackett's value as a slave. Wallace said his motive was to "deter other slaves from running away." Ironically Hackett was never tried for his alleged crime. It was reported by another escaped bondsman that upon Hackett's return to Arkansas he was bound and whipped several times— the first time in front of other slaves, as was often done in the belief it would deter other escape attempts. It is thought that Hackett was then sold to someone in central Texas. A British abolitionist society tried to purchase Hackett but could find no trace of him after the Texas transaction.[47]

Public opinion in Canada West, with United States abolitionists and the British Colonial Office on the Hackett case was one of dismay. Many abolitionists in America were frightened that slave owners would come to Canada and claim that their bondsmen had stolen the clothes off their backs or that they had stolen themselves and therefore they should be extradited back to slavery in the United States and stand trial as thieves. The British, with strong anti-slavery feelings in the isles, were very committed to a new treaty with the United States dealing with extradition of American slaves.

Lord Alexander Ashburton of Great Britain and United States Secretary of State Daniel Webster in 1842 signed the Ashburton-Webster Treaty. The treaty, while an agreement mainly concerned with Canadian and United States boundary disputes, also dealt with extradition matters. Noted British abolitionist Thomas Clarkson was concerned that the extent to which American slaves and abolitionists were affected by the agreement hinged on the interpretation of the word "robbery." The Canadians stated in the treaty they would return anyone to the United States who had committed a crime that would be punishable in Canada. It is interesting that Clarkson didn't think the crime of forgery would ever apply to American slaves as he felt they were all illiterate. He obviously was unaware of the fact there were a small number of American slaves who were capable of writing and forging "work passes" on steamboats or elsewhere for work or had free papers forged either by themselves or by others. Lord Ashburton was in sympathy with the abolitionists as he met with officials of the American and British anti-slavery societies. The British authorities vowed they would follow the narrowest view of the obligations under Article 10, concerning extradition of criminals from Canada to the United States, and that slave owners would face difficulty in recovering their chattels from this British colony.[48]

The important news out of this treaty was that no American slave was ever extradited back to the United States under its provisions. The Canadian government would remain allies to the United States bondspersons and abolitionists until American slavery was ended.[49]

Edmund, who escaped from oppression in Hempstead County, Arkansas, was trying to get to freedom either in Missouri or Illinois. Edmund was said to read well and speak quickly. Lewis was described as a "first-rate blacksmith" and "an intelligent fellow." Lewis had $500 or $600 with him when he left Conway County. A reward of $100 and one half of the money found on him was offered for his return. A postscript on this advertisement advises that if any person apprehends Lewis they should put him in irons.[50]

Anthony was a housepainter by trade who ran away from Pulaski County and it was believed he headed west to see his wife in Johnson County, Arkansas. It was thought that from there they may head west into "Indian country." Wilson was another blacksmith who took off from Saline County with a variety of clothing.[51]

Women also tried and were successful at escapes but not in the same numbers as the males. As has been noted by historians John Hope Franklin and Loren Schweninger, most of the bondspersons who tried to escape bondage were young male field hands in their late teens and early 20s. They usually fled by themselves or in small groups. Females usually had harder times trying to escape as they were often caregivers to children, the infirm or the elderly. With these duties they often felt obligated not to leave. Also, many times females had job assignments that made it more difficult to get away from bondage.

The number or percentage of women who attempted to escape slavery, as is true of much in this field of study, is subject to a large amount of interpretation. In the National Park Service's Network to Freedom study titled "Fugitives from Injustice: Freedom-Seeking Slaves in Arkansas, 1800–1860," Professor S. Charles Bolton, using just slave advertisements as his source for his database comes up with the figure for females escaping between 1820 and 1836 as being 18.2 percent of the total escapees. However, between 1836 and 1861 this figures drops to a low of 7.5 percent of total escapees. This is a considerably lower number than any of the other periods of studies we will look at here.[52]

In Franklin and Schweninger's database in their book *Runaway Slaves: Rebels on the Plantation*, they looked at the slave states of Virginia, North Carolina, Tennessee, South Carolina, and Louisiana. In the first period from 1790 to 1816 the percentage of females runaways were: Virginia 15 percent, North Carolina 18 percent, Tennessee 21 percent, South Carolina 23 percent, and Louisiana 11 percent. In the next period, from 1838 to 1860, the percentages of female escapees were: Virginia 9 percent, North Carolina 14 percent, Tennessee 12 percent, South Carolina, 19 percent and Louisiana 29 percent. This works out to be an average of 19 percent of escapees who were female.[53] Another study in Kentucky and its borderlands by J. Blaine Hudson, *Fugitive Slaves and the Underground Railroad in the Kentucky Borderland*, gave female escapee figures of pre–1850 at 20 percent and from 1850 to 1861 of 27.4 percent.[54]

The Franklin and Schweninger study used only slave advertisements for its database as did the National Park Service–Bolton study. The Hudson Kentucky borderland study used slave advertisements plus newspaper articles, jail notices and court reports for its data base. The National Park Service–Bolton study stated that only 7.5 percent of the escapes from 1836 to 1861 in Arkansas were female — the lowest figure of all the studies for a specific period.

Nancy who was "30 years old" but looked younger escaped from Jefferson County, Arkansas, in January of 1851. Nancy was only four feet tall and her owner thought she had been stolen or enticed away by some white man. Susan tried to elude bondage and her arrest but was captured in Pulaski County in July of 1851 and jailed in Little Rock. Some bondswomen fled with their husbands. Hannah left with her husband Bill in October of 1853 from Washington, Arkansas. It was believed they were seeking freedom by heading to the Choctaw nation. Jinny escaped from bondage in Little Rock on November 30, 1849. It was noted that she was very bold and spoke and laughed loudly. Polly also tried to escape with her husband. She had a diverse history. She was from Virginia and was purchased by a Mr. White who was a dealer in human beings. She was then taken to the large slave market in New Orleans and then sold to Mr. Brach. She and her husband fled bondage from there but were captured in Arkansas as they attempted to head north from Louisiana. They were jailed in Chicot County in Arkansas. From Polly's manner of talking the sheriff thought she would be a good "house servant" and she had no markings from whippings.[55]

It is interesting to note that many females in slave states and slave territories escaped not for ultimate freedom in Canada or Mexico but to be reunited with loved ones or to act as caregivers for relatives or friends in other slave areas. The maternal bonds of motherhood or the nurturing nature of the Black females often caused them to seek those who needed their special touch, regardless of the consequences. Joseph Samuel Badgett related that his mother was a slave in Arkansas and she would go visit friends or relatives in times of need on other slave farms. She would never ask for a pass from her master because she was too proud to ask for anything. Her master probably would have granted her a pass as she was well liked by him and everyone. The slave patrols supposed that any Black person on the move in a slave state like Arkansas was a runaway. Badgett reported that his mother was whipped often as she was never able to produce a pass when stopped or challenged by a slave patrol. She wore the scars of her whippings like a badge of honor until the day she died.[56]

In May of 1851 George escaped a plantation near the Post of Arkansas with another man named Harrison. George's goal was not to find his eventual freedom but to head to Little Rock where his wife was in bondage at a Dr. Watkins.' George had recently been sold away from his wife and just wanted to be reunited with her. Ned was sold away from Clark County, Arkansas, to a slave owner in Natchitoches Parish, Louisiana, in April of 1840. By August of that year Ned had escaped the plantation in Louisiana to head back to Clark County, Arkansas, to be near relatives and friends. Tom also escaped from the Arkansas Post in the fall of 1842. He had been sold at the slave market in New Orleans just two months prior to a slave owner at the Arkansas Post and he longed to see his wife again. He had a wife in Batesville, Arkansas, and he was heading there to be reunited with her.[57]

The breakup of families was often a prime motivator in the escape of slaves. A bondsman from Arkansas named Robert Herman escaped from this condition in 1853. He had to travel through the rough terrain of the Ozark Mountains to seek freedom. He managed to elude all of the slave patrols and slave hunters in Arkansas and made his way into Missouri. Herman encountered more of the rugged terrain of the Ozarks and extremely heavily wooded areas in southern Missouri. While in that state Herman teamed up with another bondsman who was making his escape. Again Herman and his new comrade managed to escape detection from all of the slave patrols and slave bounty hunters in Missouri. The duo made their way across the Mississippi River into what they felt would be surefire freedom once they crossed the great river into Illinois.

However, while in Illinois their condition as runaways was discovered and they were jailed for six weeks while local law officials tried to return them to their owners. Herman was smart enough and passed this information onto his colleague — not to give any information to the local police officers about where they were from or what their identity was. The two escaped bondsmen did this. No matter how often they were questioned Herman and his mate would give no information as to their true identity or the locations where they had made their escapes. The local police became exasperated. Since they had no knowledge of where the two bondsmen were from or even their names no officials from their home states could be notified for their return. The Illinois lawmen could not match up any flyers of runaway slaves to Herman or his confederate. No identification was ever made of the two and the local police captain grew tired of the expenses of feeding and housing the escapees.

The local marshal was going to sell Herman and his mate to recover jail costs. They were hauled into a local court for this to be done. However, when the two bondsmen were brought before a judge this freedom-loving member of the judiciary freed them. Herman and his fellow escapee made their way out of Illinois with possibly a stop in Chicago. Then the duo went onto the Underground Railroad and found freedom in Canada.

After being freed and well onto his way to freedom, Robert Herman remarked that if his master Richard Thurston of Van Buren, Arkansas, had allowed him to stay with his wife and child in Van Buren he would have never escaped and would have remained a slave forever. But, when he was separated from his family he knew he would have to seek total freedom in Canada.[58]

Arkansas played a minor role in one of the most disheartening and famous slave escapes on the Underground Railroad. Margaret Garner was a bondswoman with four children living in Kentucky. Margaret, along with 16 other bondspersons escaped from the bluegrass state below Covington. It was January of 1856 and a large sled and two horses carried the crowded crew on their way to freedom. The Ohio River was frozen and the group walked across the river. Daylight was coming upon Cincinnati and the city was rousing from its sleep. Pedestrian and horse and carriage traffic began to come alive as the large group came upon the "Queen City." It was decided to split up the group so as to not attract as much attention. Nine of the group made their way uptown and located comrades who hide them all night. They were soon put on the vibrant Cincinnati Underground Railroad system and they made it all the way to Canada.[59]

Margaret and her group of eight went looking for her cousin Elijah Kite. They were not sure of the way and asked for directions to Kite's residence. This would turn out to be the fatal flaw in their escape plan. They reached the Kite home and he made them comfortable. Kite then went to Levi Coffin's house at Sixth and Elm in Cincinnati for instruction on advancing the group on the Underground Railroad. By the time Kite got back to his house it was surrounded by Margaret's master, Archibald Gaines, and a slave posse trying to capture her and the other bondspersons. It is believed someone whom the Garner group asked for directions had told the Gaines group of the location of the Garner party.

Margaret had been a fugitive for only 12 hours. A posse of 11 men surrounded the house. Deputy George Bennett demanded the group give up and surrender. Kite's neighbors and other people both Black and white came out to see what the excitement was about. Some of those inside the Kite house hoped that possibly a large mob would appear and disable the Deputy and his men, but Margaret and her group would have no such luck.[60]

The posse rushed the house and battered down the door. The bondsmen inside the house fought bravely, wounding two of the posse. Margaret's husband fired several shots, wounding one of the officers. Margaret was absolutely desperate and had told everyone she would kill her children and herself before she would go back to slavery. She took a butcher knife and with one swift stroke cut the throat of her beloved little two-year-old daughter Mary. She then picked up a shovel and tried to end the life of her ten month old daughter Priscilla but the posse caught Margaret and put her under arrest.

The Garners and the rest of their party were put in jail and then put on trial. The Cincinnati newspapers noted that the Garners had on inadequate clothes and did not have on proper shoes for the winter time.[61] This would be one of the harshest winters in Ohio history in the last 60 years and many who followed the trial in Ohio would realize how poorly American slaves were housed, fed and clothed.

The defense for Margaret Garner was that she had once been in Ohio and so she should be considered a free person as should her children. Her lawyers knew they had little chance of winning the trial. During the trial her defense attorneys came up with the idea that Margaret should be charged with murder and that the others in her group should be tried as accomplices. They knew they had little chance of keeping the bondspersons in Ohio and it was thought that the murder charges would at least keep them in the buckeye state. The strategy was to have her charged with murder and then tried. She would be undoubtedly convicted and then pardoned by the governor of Ohio and kept away from slavery. However, after a two-week trial in which the Garner defense team tried to get the Fugitive Slave Law declared unconstitutional the judge handed Garner, her husband and her children back to their master Archibald Gaines.[62]

Gaines took Margaret her children and husband and the others back to Kentucky. Gaines was to keep Margaret available to be served papers if she was to be charged with murder in Ohio. If she was to be charged with murder then he was supposed to turn her over to Ohio authorities. However, the slaver didn't keep his word to the Ohio judge and he kept moving Margaret about Kentucky so she couldn't be served any papers. The case did attract much attention among the abolitionists in the United States and the freedom seekers who had made it to Canada and of course the slavers in the south. Some in the slave states looked at this tragedy as a great victory for slave holders.

Archibald Gaines's brother Benjamin owned a cotton plantation in Arkansas at Gaines Landing in Chicot County. In March of 1856 Gaines put Margaret and her children, including her other daughter Priscilla, on the steamboat *Henry Lewis* bound for Benjamin Gaines' plantation in Chicot County. On March 7 the *Henry Lewis* collided with another steamship, the *E.H. Howard*. As one might imagine chaos broke out on the steamship. Margaret was holding Priscilla in her arms and Margaret was saved by the Black cook on the steamship. Priscilla however was never recovered and of course there was speculation as to whether Margaret had let this daughter drown rather than live in the hellish domain of the American slave.[63]

It is interesting to note that the Margaret Garner case was followed closely by the former American slaves in Canada. They could truly understand Margaret's frightful dilemma. Mary Ann Shadd's newspaper, the *Provincial Freeman*, on April 5, 1856, carried the story of Margaret Garner's shipwreck on the way to Arkansas. It is possible Shadd reprinted this from a Cincinnati paper. A portion of the article is reproduced here with its original spelling and punctuation:

> **The Slave Margaret**
>
> The following circumstances took place on board the Henry Lewis, at the time of the collision with the E.H. Howard, whilst on her downward trip to Gaines's Landing, with the fugitive slaves, Margaret and her children.
>
> When the accident occurred to the Henry Lewis, the negroes were in the nursery (as a place between the cabin and steerage in the stern of the boat is called), ironed by couples. After the disaster, they were heard calling for help and to be relieved of their handcuffs, Some one happened to be on hand to save them. Margaret had her child — the infant that she hit on the head with the shovel when arrested here — in her arms, but by the shock of the boat that came to the assistance of the Lewis (as one story goes) she was thrown into the river with her child and a white woman who was one of the steerage passengers, and was standing by her at the moment. This woman and the child drownded, but a black man, the cook on the Lewis, sprang into the river and saved Margaret, who, it is said displayed frantic joy when told her child was drowned, and said she would never reach alive Gaines's Landing, in Arkansas, the point for which she was shipped, thus intimating a desire to drown herself.
>
> Another report is that as soon as she had an opportunity, she threw her child into the river and jumped after it. Still another story has it that she tried to jump upon the boat alonside, but fell short. It is only certain that she was in the river with her child, and that it was drowned, while she was saved by the prompt energy of the cook.[64]

Gaines had Margaret stay in Arkansas for March and April but she was returned to Kentucky for a short time. Then Margaret and the remaining Garner family were taken to New Orleans.[65] Margaret lived only for a short time and died of typhoid fever in 1858. Her poignant life was turned into a Pulitzer Prize–winning novel *Beloved* by author Toni Morrison. An opera and movie based on this story have also been produced.

It is also of interest to note that the *Provincial Freeman* ran a long and edifying speech given by Martin Robinson Delany earlier in 1855 entitled the "Political Aspect of the Colored People of the United States." In this speech Delany, onetime editor of the famed black abolitionist newspaper the *North Star* and a Harvard educated medical doctor, gave a detailed analysis of this subject matter in many of the free and slave states in the nation. On Arkansas and Texas he stated that, "In neither of these states has the free colored man any privileges, but those permitted by the merest sufferance."[66] And of course, as previously stated, the free Blacks in Arkansas in 1859 were run out of the state or they would be returned to the condition of slavery if found in the state. The loss of free Blacks in the state of Arkansas made it even harder for the bondsperson to escape the condition of slavery in the state.

E.J. Smith seemed puzzled that his "Negro Boy Bob," as he described him, "left my premises about the first day of June (1850)." What was confusing according to Smith was the fact that Bob had been raised in Hempstead County, Arkansas, had a wife, children and many relatives in the area. Bob was described as "lively and fond of music, and plays upon the banjo." Even though Bob had some whip marks on him Smith seemed to have a genuine fondness for Bob and was more concerned that Bob had been kidnapped rather than that he had run away. Smith stated that Bob "may have fallen into bad hands, and [been] conveyed off and sold in an adjoining state." Smith pleaded that if Bob were in the hands of an honest man he would like to hear from him. However, Smith was enough of a realist to know Bob could have left on his own. He later stated, "If not stolen, he in all probability has gone to some of the neighboring Indian nations, and may have obtained forged free papers, and attempt to pass himself as free, or he may be hovering about some city or town not far distant." Then Smith said almost plaintively and as if he was more interested in hearing from Bob or seeing if he was okay than in recapturing him, "I hope the patrol and police of the county will look out for him.... Any information in relation to said boy, will be thankfully received." What is also of interest is the fact that Smith waited nine months from June of 1850 when the escape occurred to March 7, 1851, before the advertisement ran in the newspaper for the return of Bob. It is obvious that Smith thought Bob would return on his own before that date and that was why he was concerned Bob had fallen into "bad hands." Also demonstrating Smith's concern was the fact that he ran ads in a number of newspapers covering a wide area. They included the *Cherokee Advocate*, *Choctaw Telegraph* in the "Indian Territory," and papers in Memphis, Tennessee, Shreveport, Louisiana and Natchez, Mississippi. It is obvious Smith didn't think Bob was trying to head north for his escape to a "free" state or to Canada.[67]

Bartlett was one of the most committed runaways. The slaver Victor Thompson who lived 25 miles from Memphis, Tennessee, moved to Texas. Bartlett, who was 40 years old and suffering tremendously from rheumatism, also walked on crutches. He decided to leave Texas and work his way back to the Memphis area all the while walking on crutches. Unfortunately, Bartlett was captured in Chicot County in Arkansas in the extreme southeast corner of the state.[68]

Isaac escaped slavery on the morning of February 28, 1851. Apparently Isaac was captured and then jailed in Arkadelphia. He broke out from the jail with a white man named Pattison. It was thought Isaac would head back to Alabama where he had come from before being in bondage in Arkansas.[69]

R.C. Smith in his FWP interview stated that prior to the Civil War slave owners in Arkansas had trouble with the Underground Railroad and he claimed that nearly everyone lost one or two slaves. In particular, a Judge West from Fayetteville had in Smith's words a "sight of vexation about that time." West was known to be very hard on his slaves and was prone to have them run off. West lost one of his men who went north and Judge West could not recover the bondsman. Another of West's bondsmen was not so lucky. He stole a horse and a fine broadcloth suit of clothes and made his getaway. He made it to freedom. Smith thinks if the man had sold the horse and the suit of clothes he might have remained a free man. However, West was able to have the bondsman identified because of the horse and the suit. The unfortunate escapee was returned to West.[70] It is interesting that Smith used the words Underground Railroad even though he gave no example that anyone helped these runaways in their escape.

In Scott Bond's FWP interview he told a harrowing tale of an Arkansas bondsman who was attempting an escape, as he had several times before, when the patrollers set their hounds on him. He ran for two days with the dogs on his heels. He managed to double back over his tracks to give himself some time to rest. However, the dogs always managed to pick up his scent and be on his trail again. But the chase went on and the bondsman, finding that he couldn't escape, ran deliberately into a blazing furnace and was burned to death rather than allow himself to be caught and suffer the torturers that awaited him.[71]

In Chicot County, Arkansas, Lilbert had run off from his plantation. His slave master George W. Johnson wasn't sure if Lilbert had run off or if he was stolen or decoyed by a white man named House. Johnson wasn't sure of House's first name and listed several possible first names, Jefferson House, G.A. House or M. House. House was described as 45 years of age, talking very slowly and drawling and having rheumatism and being "apparently a little deaf when spoken to." Lilbert was described as being 25 or 26 years of age, six foot one or two inches high, "straight hair ... has a fine set of teeth, and plays the violin very well." Johnson offered a reward of $300 for the return of Lilbert to his plantation, together with the apprehension and conviction of House.[72]

In Little Rock the sheriff of Pulaski County, B.F. Danley, had jailed a bondsman named John. John had been captured by a man named Purdom. John interestingly had a paper purporting to be a pass authorizing John to pass and repass, and to work where he could get employment. However, one wonders if John's story fell apart when he told the sheriff he belonged to an O.D. Hogins of Johnson County but his pass was signed by a C. Baremoore. It was not known if this was a legitimate pass. Also, it is not known whether John did the forgery himself or if he had purchased the forged document from someone. George also had a pass signed by a Colonel Coffee whom George claimed as his master. However, after further interrogation George said his master was a John Wade from fifteen miles back of Lake Providence, Louisiana. George was captured and jailed in Phillips County.[73]

A Georgia slaver thought his bondswoman Dilcey Ann and a white man she left with would be headed for Arkansas. The pair left in February of 1852 with a horse. A very liberal $500 reward was offered for the return of Dilcey Ann and the capture of the white man she left with.[74]

As mentioned before many slavers thought their chattel would not run off unless stolen or decoyed by some white person. Many times these slavers were badly mistaken. However, on some occasions this did happen. Slave stealers like Fielding G. Secrest infested the White River swamps of Arkansas stealing slaves until he was finally caught. However, the slippery Secrest managed to escape from the jail in Little Rock. The *Arkansas Gazette* newspaper in their April 4, 1835, edition felt it was one of Secrest's fellow slave stealing comrades who helped him escape.[75]

Some slave stealers would act as if they were looking for lost horses in an attempt to come into contact with the enslaved humans of the region. They would then engage the bondsperson in a conversation and try and get them to come with them.

The boastful John Murrell is one of the best known of the slave stealers in this region. It is hard to judge where Murrell's actual outlawry begins and his "legend" ends. But undoubtedly he made off with his share of slaves and as was the case with men like Secrest and Murrell they also stole not only bondspersons but the best horse flesh and mules they could find.

In 1840 there appeared to be a group of thieves stealing both slaves and livestock in the Arkansas area. On April 15 of that year an advertisement was run in the newspaper offering a generous $150 for a bondsman named Jack, sometimes called Jackson. The ad stated that "It is quite probable that said boy has been stolen, or decoyed away by some white man, as one or two suspicious characters were seen, for a few days prior to the said boy's leaving, in the neighborhood, and as there is an extensive clan of Negro and horse thieves operating through the county, we are firmly of the impression said boy has been taken by some of them." However, Jack took with him a rifle and one has to wonder if he didn't take off on his own. Would you want to attempt to sell a bondsperson to a slaver when the bondsman was in possession of a firearm? The reward was for the return of Jack and the conviction of the white man or white persons who took Jack. The reward for the return of just Jack was for $25 if taken in the county or $50 if taken out of the county or out of state.[76]

In December of that same year four bondsmen were believed to be stolen from Pecan Point on the Red River. They were seen passing through the Choctaw Nation with three well armed white men. It was thought that they were heading to the Cherokee Nation as one of the white men could speak some Cherokee and, it was thought, another Native American dialect. Three mules were also missing and were believed to have been taken with the bondsmen.[77]

Wilcher, a blacksmith by trade, managed to escape bondage August 9, 1852. Wilcher resided 20 miles south of Fort Smith, Arkansas. Joe, who had been heavily whipped in his life with plenty of scars on his back to show for it, ended his bid for freedom when he was jailed in Little Rock in September of 1852. What is interesting is Joe was wearing a well-worn steamboat pilot's frock coat. Jim escaped with a double-barreled shotgun but was apprehended without incident. Jim was described in the sheriff's advertisement as being able "to read a little and appears to be very intelligent." Jim's attempt to find freedom ended in the Pulaski County jail in Little Rock on September 7, 1852.[78]

Daniel escaped slavery three miles below the Arkansas Post. It was said Daniel, who could read but not write, was fond of "argufieying." Daniel had a special talent that he used if he needed to get some time off from work. Daniel could throw his left shoulder out of place, giving the impression of a horrible injury. If taken out of state a reward was offered of $100 for the return of Daniel. However, the slaver offered a huge reward of $500 for the conviction of anyone harboring Daniel.[79]

As stated before it was common for bondspersons trying to escape from other slave states to try to make their way through Arkansas but get captured in the state. Wedlock tried to escape from Yazoo City, Mississippi, in August of 1854 but was captured and incarcerated in the Desha County jail. Also in the Desha County jail was another runaway from Bourbon County, Kentucky. Jack, who formally resided in Jackson, Mississippi, was jailed in Phillips County, Arkansas, when captured. Jack had scars on all the fingers of his left hand caused by a cotton gin saw. The May 3, 1855, edition of the Democratic Star had notices of captures of three runaways from out of state. These were Rafe from Coahoma, Mississippi, James from Millikens Bend, Louisiana, and Alexander from Nacogdoches, Louisiana. Oscar, who was nearly white, escaped from Louisiana but his master thought he had been enticed off by a free white man. A reward was offered for Oscar and the thief who allegedly took him.[80]

Samuel, described as a "bright mulatto," and his wife Sally escaped from bondage in Little Rock during the spring of 1855. Sally, who was nearly white, passed herself off as a white woman and the owner of Samuel. It is thought they made their way to freedom with this ruse.[81]

Tom escaped from bondage in February of 1857 from Little Rock but the slaver who owned him felt he would remain lurking about the Arkansas capital city. Another Tom escaped from Ben F. Danley in the summer of 1858 and it was felt he would be also hanging around Little Rock However, this Tom had been a hand on the steamboat *Quapaw* and perhaps he was staying around the vicinity of Little Rock to find work on another steamboat. Dick was captured and put in the Pulaski County in Little Rock in the winter of 1858.

Dick was riding a black horse when he left Hillsborough in Union County in Arkansas but this didn't prevent him from being captured.[82]

Callie Washington remembered her master Sam Terry and his wife Miss Ann as having no children and they let her live in the big house with them when she was a child. She said Terry would not have an overseer because they were too mean to the slaves. She remembered Terry as having a big farm with "a heap of slaves." The only whippings she remembered Terry administering was when any bondsperson tried to run off. Even though the treatment of the slaves on the Terry place seamed to be mild when compared with others the bondspersons still yearned to be free. Ms. Washington remembered many slaves running off but she wasn't sure if they headed north for freedom. She did remember that most of them must have been successful in finding their destination as most never came back. By the time the Union Army came to their section of Arkansas she said most of the bondsperson had made their way to freedom.[83]

Jane and William Brown decided to escape for freedom from bondage in Arkansas. Mrs. Brown was very pregnant and not able to work but her master still made her go out to the fields. The couple decided to run away. Their first night out they were sleeping in a canebrake and a small panther attacked them. William had a bowie knife with him and killed the predator. Mrs. Brown delivered her baby out in the canebrake.

The Browns went back to their master and made a deal with him. They wouldn't try and escape any more if they would allow Mrs. Brown to stay inside out of the fields and take care of her children. Mrs. Brown was very able to conceive very fast and slavers prized "fast breeders." She produced 10 children, which made her slave master a rich man.[84]

Sam was described as "very likely and intelligent; and apparently of good disposition." He made his run for freedom in the spring of 1859 around the Little Rock area. The slaver thought Sam might have been "decoyed off by some white man." The slaver did not think Sam was making his way north but was "lurking about the country."[85]

In March of 1860 Willis ran away from the James Finley farm in Union County, Arkansas, near Hillsborough. Willis was about 28 or 29, about six feet tall and weighed about 180 pounds. Willis had a scar under his right jaw which he cryptically said was caused by the "King's Evil" when he was a boy.[86]

As the Civil War came upon Arkansas in 1861 the fortunes of the escaping bondspersons often depended upon the successes of the Union Army or their defeats. The War of the Rebellion rose and fell several times in Arkansas. It produced many displaced people among the Black community in Arkansas as it did elsewhere. Many enterprising bondspersons made their way to the Union lines for freedom. It has been estimated that some 5,000 Arkansas African Americans served the Union Army. The African American soldier in the Union Army faced many dangers including being captured by Confederate forces who many times executed any Blacks found in a Union uniform.

Although Confederate General Ben McCullogh defeated a small Union force at Wilson's Creek in southwest Missouri the efforts failed to produce a real victory for the Confederate forces in Arkansas. At Pea Ridge Union Brigadier General Samuel Curtis drove the Confederates from the battlefield. Curtis cut down trees on the roads to slow the Confederate Army down and at one point when ammunition was low he ordered a bayonet charge. Curtis had 203 men killed in the battle and had 1,148 men missing or wounded.[87] In this retreat the rebels left most of Arkansas virtually in the hands of the Union forces.

In the vacuum left by local Arkansas law enforcement it was possible for some bondspersons to simply slip away and seek shelter in Union lines. Some of these bondspersons were put to work as military support persons in a wide variety of positions such as building roads, teamsters, burying the dead, building military fortifications, cooking and washing for the Army. Others were put into camps where oftentimes disease ran rampant. Some were of course put into all Black military units some of which had been organized in Kansas and saw combat. Early in the war the Union Army wasn't sure what the legal status of these bondspersons was to be. Many times the status of these bondspersons' freedom depended on the actions of the local military commander.

Curtis marched his army to the Mississippi River around Helena, Arkansas, and it was estimated that some 2,000 slaves followed him into this important river city. The Union Army's plan on the frontier was to control the Mississippi and to cut the western Confederate states off from the eastern Confederacy. General Thomas Hindman raised another Confederate Army in northwest Arkansas and posed a threat, although his army was poorly trained and poorly supplied. Union General James G. Blunt commanded the Army of the Frontier and defeated Hindman's forces at the Battle of Prairie Grove in Arkansas. Hindman had found good positions for his men in the Boston Mountains and his men fought well. In a letter to Major General Henry Halleck, General-in-Chief Samuel Curtis wrote of the Battle of Prairie Grove noting that Hindman had positioned his Army well. Curtis went on to write, "The loss on both sides is heavy, but much greater on the side of the enemy, our artillery creating a terrible slaughter...."[88]

By 1863 the Union Army managed to control much of the state including the important towns of Fort Smith, Fayetteville, Little Rock, Pine Bluff and Helena. In many cases bondspersons found freedom not a thousand miles away in Canada or Mexico but a few miles away when they crossed into the advancing blue Union lines.

It is interesting to note that in the National Park Service's collection of Arkansas newspaper slave runaway advertisements that ran from 1862 to 1865 (during the Civil War) there were in this collection 50 advertisements from only two newspapers. There were no advertisements for 1861; it is suspected that none were recovered. Of these slave escape advertisements five appeared in the *Arkansas Gazette*, which was a Little Rock newspaper. None appeared in the *Arkansas Gazette* after August 22, 1863. The other 45 all appeared in the *Washington Telegraph*. This newspaper was located in the southern part of the state and as such was out of Union control for a significant part of the war and in fact was the only newspaper in Arkansas to be in operation throughout the whole of the Civil War.

As one might expect, runaway attempts from 1861 to 1865 often involved trying to get to Union lines or were in some way connected with the Civil War. In September of 1862 Peter tried to find his freedom and his master offered a reward. Peter allegedly had a pass from Mrs. Susan Cole of Clark County, Arkansas, to go to Confederate General Hindman's command to aid that cause. Peter worked at the Anthony House for some 18 to 20 days and then left to find his freedom.[89]

Frank made his escape from bondage in June of 1863; he was described as having an "intelligent countenance." Frank left with a horse and was also wearing what was depicted as a "grey soldier's cap." We can only suspect that this was a Confederate soldier's cap. In December of 1864 a husband and wife team named Adolphus and Angeline escaped bondage from the Dallas, Texas, area. It was believed they were headed to Princeton, Arkansas, where they would try to "make their way to the Federal lines in that vicinity." Jack was a good cook who had escaped from his master in Center Point, Arkansas. Jack's master said he could tell a plausible tale and would say he and his master were captured by Federal troops and Jack managed to escape. It was thought Jack would head for Texas.[90]

However, during the Civil War bondspersons wanted to escape their appalling living and working conditions as they had before the War. Two bondsmen, Louis and Milford, were making their way during late summer of 1863 to Texas, possibly with Mexico as their ultimate destination, when they were captured and jailed in Hempstead County, Arkansas. They said they escaped to get away from their cruel overseer.[91]

Of course as the Civil War ground on the Union Army and finally President Lincoln tried to clarify the status of those held in bondage. In the summer of 1862 the Second Confiscation Act was passed which stated any slaves who were owned by masters disloyal to the United States were to be considered free. General Curtis, commander of all Union forces in this area, issued Special Order 1251 which gave freedom to all slaves who entered his Union lines. If these now former slaves were not needed in the war effort Curtis would give them passes through the Union lines to go live in the north. As noted before, Curtis' overly aggressive views on freeing the slaves came into conflict with the governor of Missouri, Hamilton R. Gamble, and others. Later in 1863 Gamble also objected to Curtis' policy of confiscation of property of wealthy rebel farmers and planters. Curtis even sent some wealthy rebels out of Union territory into Confederate lines. Curtis and Gamble, both good Union men, were at each other's throats. As Abraham Lincoln wrote in a letter, he couldn't remove the governor but he could replace Curtis. Because of this Curtis was removed from his command of the southwest in Missouri and Arkansas.[92]

On January 1, 1863, President Lincoln issued his defining Emancipation Proclamation. In this, Lincoln stated that on this date "all person held as slaves within any state, or designated part of a state, the people whereof shall then be in rebellion against the United States, shall be then, thenceforward and forever free...." Later in the proclamation Lincoln mentions Arkansas as being in rebellion against the United States.[93]

David Todd was a Congregational minister from central Illinois and was a graduate of Oberlin College's abolitionist-minded seminary. David traveled to work at a school in Arkansas that had been set up to help the newly-freed bondspersons near Pine Bluff. In June of 1864 David reported much sickness in his camp including measles, mumps, whooping cough and of course dysentery. He complained about the poor condition of the water in the area.

Because the Union Army was in the midst of its unsuccessful Red River Campaign in Arkansas, David said the Confederate guerrillas felt emboldened and had killed "five negroes" only a few miles from the Pine Bluff federal refugee camp.[94] The Confederate Army began in that year to advance and by July they were within 20 miles of Pine Bluff. Because of sickness and the threat of a Rebel attack most of the teachers had left the school. Only David Todd and another teacher, a Mrs. Thomas, remained.[95] Sometimes when the Confederates would overrun a school or camp like this that taught Blacks to read and write or try to improve their condition the Rebel soldiers would kill the white teachers.

David Worcester reported in a letter from August of 1864 from Island #63 below Helena, Arkansas, that there was a good crop of cotton growing on the island by its colony of freedmen. The island was being defended for the Union by two companies of "colored soldiers."[96]

The Union Army in Arkansas replaced Curtis with Major General Frederick Steele, a dandy with a high-pitched voice. In 1864 he attempted to drive the Confederates out of the whole state of Arkansas and then move into Louisiana and Texas. Steele was to hook up with General Banks' substantial army around the Red River area and destroy the Confederate Army of General Edmund Kirby Smith.

However, the campaign floundered and the Federals suffered some major casualties. The Confederates counterattacked and gained control of much of southern Arkansas. On his way back to Little Rock, Steele's column was attacked by Marmadukes' Confederate horsemen around Poison Springs. When many of the Black troops surrendered, the Rebels killed them without mercy. The whole Red River operation was considered a failure by the Union Army. The news was not well received in Washington, D.C., as 1864 was an election year and news like this from Arkansas was not the tonic Lincoln's Republican Party wanted.[97]

This of course made any attempt to escape by bondsmen more difficult. Some Arkansas slavers took their human chattel into Texas to help preserve their capital. Some slave owners threatened to kill their bondspersons, like the before mentioned Dr. Isaac Jones, if they tried to go for the Federal lines. Molly Finley said in her FWP interview that her master Captain Baker Jones sent his slaves to Texas when the Yankees got close to his farm but first he buried two barrels of money in a big iron chest on his farm in Arkansas.[98] It was suspected Jones planned to come and get the money-laden barrels after the war had ended. One wonders if Jones buried United States coins and currency or Confederate money. Mary Ann Brooks in her FWP interview stated that her master Dr. Arthur Brewster moved his slaves from Arkansas to Texas during the war as did other Arkansas slavers.[99]

As the Civil War in Arkansas ground down to its conclusion bondspersons flocked to Union lines. The Union Army began to enlist many of these former slaves into their ranks. As early as April of 1863 the 1st Regiment of Arkansas Vols. of African Descent was formed. Late in 1864 six Black regiments were raised in Arkansas and formed into the Second Arkansas Volunteer Infantry Regiment (African Descent). The Second Arkansas (African Descent) had participated in the defense of Helena, Arkansas.[100]

For much of the Civil War, as in Missouri, guerrilla bands from the north called Jayhawkers and from the south called bushwhackers caused havoc among the civilian population. Harry (Jim) Johnson tells of a harrowing experience he had. As the war wound down in Arkansas he was kidnapped by bushwhackers and taken to southern Missouri where one assumes the bushwhackers were trying to sell him but could find no takers. He was treated okay and just sat around a house all day while the bushwhackers talked of killing Yankees. Somehow he was brought back to his master, a man named Graham. Graham took Johnson to Texas as a slave even though the war was over. Johnson worked in Texas for two years as a slave, not knowing he was in fact a free man.[101]

The military situation in Arkansas had deteriorated in 1864–65, but the Confederate hold on southern Arkansas was at best tenuous. The Union Army and Naval gunboats kept control of the important Mississippi River in Arkansas. With the Union victories in the east and the Confederate economy in chaos the war came mercifully to an end. The bondspersons were free at last in the whole of the state of Arkansas.

7

Western Frontier and the Indian Nations (Oklahoma)

"Sometimes someone would come along and try to get us to run up north and be free. We used to laugh at that. There was no reason to run up north. All we had to do was walk, but walk south and we'd be free as soon as we crossed the Rio Grande. In Mexico you could be free."

— *Felix Haywood former bondsperson from Texas*

Some of those trying to find freedom by fleeing from the Dixie slavocracy via the western frontier of America in the 1840s and 1850s faced many problems in securing a successful escape, such as the lack of roads and bridges. Also, since much of the area was newly and thinly settled there was always a lack of food and many times the availability of water was a problem.

It is a romantic notion that it is possible to escape to the frontier with nothing more than the clothes on your back and with your skills of living off the land. The reality was much different. Even those who came well prepared to the western frontier at times faced starvation. John Todd, the erstwhile Underground Railroad master in Tabor, Iowa, reported that soon after he moved to Tabor he and his family faced starvation. He had lived in western Iowa for four years but starvation was still a reality to these frontier families. Fortunately, out of the blue a widow woman gave the Reverend Todd 50 cents with which he went and bought two bushels of corn and had it milled. This was what his family subsisted on for many days.[1] John Stewart, zealous Kansas Underground Railroad conductor, related how near starvation he and his family were at times on the frontier. John C. Frémont would leave on his mapmaking journeys with ample supplies of flour and other edibles. He would also have guns and an array of equipment with which to slaughter animals for eating on his expedition. However, in the autumn of 1843, Frémont staggered into the Pawnee Mission in Nebraska almost at the point of starvation.[2] The Pawnee had to feed Frémont or the Republican Party might not have had him as their abolitionist Presidential candidate in 1856. All these individuals left their homes in the east well provisioned, but almost met with starvation on the frontier. How could one expect the bondspersons with no supplies to make it on the frontier with the long distances to freedom without facing the reality of starvation?

Also, on the frontier there were wild animals that had to be contended with and without weapons this could be very problematical. Bands of brigands that were pushed to the outer limits of civilization also had to be contended with by those trying to escape slavery. Without a doubt, many bondspersons lost their lives trying to flee on the frontier either by starvation, illness caused by a lack of food, or the extremes in weather that could cause dehydration or in the winter hypothermia on the central plains.

It was thought that bondsman John, who was originally from Virginia and came out west with his master to Tennessee, in the area around Nashville, was trying to make it to the frontier. He escaped from the volunteer state in the summer of 1842 but didn't head north. He headed west presumably to make it to the western frontier or possibly to the Indian Nations. However, he was captured in Phillips County in eastern Arkansas and was jailed before he could reach freedom farther west. John claimed he was a free Black man but of course no one checked out his assertion. Harry escaped from Carter County, Kentucky, in November of 1840. He didn't head north to Ohio, which was a relatively short distance away — only about 50 miles from Carter County. Instead he headed south and west. Unfortunately he was also captured in Phillips County, Arkansas, over 600 miles from his home. It was not possible to ascertain if he was trying to visit relatives or friends in Arkansas, Texas or the Indian Nations. Perhaps he was just trying to find freedom on the western frontier.[3]

America was on the move in the 1840s and 1850s. Slave owners thought nothing of taking their human property with them on their treks across the Santa Fe Trail, Oregon Trail, to the California gold fields or to the Great Salt Lake region. Followers of Brigham Young went to Utah where slavery was legal, although census figures show there were only a couple of dozen slaves in the state by 1850. Many times these journeys to the far west provided escape opportunities for the bondspersons.

There were a lot of questions concerning James' attempted escape in June of 1854. He was owned by a Mr. E from Washington, Arkansas. James and his master were on their way to Fort Smith, Arkansas. Somewhere along the way James escaped before they got to Fort Smith. James headed west — it is not sure if his idea was to head to the Indian Nations, to freedom in Mexico or even further west, possibly to California. Also, another possibility was that James just saw the opportunity to escape and took it without any clear-cut plan. Somewhere along the way he was picked up by a Mrs. Holiday and, one assumes, the emigrant party with whom she was traveling on her way to California. Whether this was part of a plan or just happenstance is not known. What is known is that Mrs. Holiday dropped James off in the custody of Major Enoch Steen, commandant at Fort Belknap in northern Texas. Was this an escape plan that went bad and the two had some differences and Mrs. Holiday turned James over to the authorities? Perhaps James left Arkansas and went west following the Indian Nations and Texas borders on his way to Mexico and was lost, possibly near starvation. This scenario has Mrs. Holiday and her party taking pity on James and taking him to the nearest civilized outpost, which would have been at Fort Belknap, Texas. We don't know what the whole story was behind this intriguing escape attempt. All we know for sure is that James ended up some 340 miles west of his home in Washington, Arkansas, at Fort Belknap, Texas. This was accomplished having been dropped off there by a Mrs. Holiday into the custody of a Major Steen.[4]

In 1854 a Mississippi slave owner was heading west to join the Mormon migration to Utah. He had six enslaved humans with him and was attempting to cross the Missouri River at the busy crossing at Nebraska City, Nebraska Territory. This hectic river crossing saw wagon trains and emigrants heading out to California, Oregon and Utah. Because of the large number of wagons, the rush of emigrants and the large amount of freight heading out west it would take a few days to negotiate the river crossing. The Mississippian became impatient and decided to cross the Missouri River farther north.[5]

The slave owner with his family and bondspersons had three covered wagons and a carriage in his caravan and he settled into to Tabor, Iowa, as night fell on the prairies on July 4, 1854.[6] Although Tabor had just newly been settled its inhabitants from Oberlin, Ohio, were rabidly anti-slavery in sentiment. The slave owner underestimated their resolve.

When the slaver sent two of his bondspersons to the public well in Tabor they were contacted by Samuel H. Adams, a resident of the town. It was determined that five out of the six wished to escape slavery. An older woman was felt to be so loyal to the master that she would not even be offered the chance to escape for fear she would inform the slave owner. Those that wanted to go forward were two children with their mother and father and another adult male.

July 5 on the prairie of southwest Iowa the slaver who was used to having his breakfast ready, his horses fed and ready to go, the water drawn for his family, arose and found an eerie silence greeted him. He knew immediately what had happened and he knew it would do him no good to ask the residents of Tabor, Iowa, what had happened to his "property." The Mississippian went outside of town and assembled a slave hunting posse. Many of the residents from outside of Tabor hailed from southern states and they joined the slave hunting posse with gusto.[7]

Samuel H. Adams. A Mississippi man wanted to take his six enslaved humans with him to the territory of the Great Salt Lake Valley in Utah where slavery was legal. When the river crossing at Nebraska City was going to involve a three day wait he headed north but had to stay the night in the strong abolitionist town of Tabor, Iowa. The Underground Railroad in Tabor was on full alert and the bondspersons were contacted and they wanted their freedom. Samuel H. Adams took two enslaved children with him as he crossed a large cottonwood tree that had fallen across the Nishnabota River. Five of the Mississippi man's slaves escaped from him to find freedom (courtesy Todd House Museum and Tabor Historical Society, Tabor, Iowa).

The slave hunt was organized. Groves, thickets and areas of tall prairie grass were especially looked at as was every nook and cranny that might offer a hiding place.

Some of Tabor's sympathizers infiltrated the slave posse and of course looked in the areas they knew the "train" was hiding. The bondspersons and the conductors on this Underground Railroad train managed to get a good distance away from Tabor and the posse while this "hunt" was in progress.

They were making good time and had already crossed the Nishnabota River, one of the major obstacles for moving eastward. A large cottonwood tree had fallen across the Nishnabota creating a nice "bridge" and making its crossing a little easier as long as one kept one's balance. Deacon Adams of the Tabor Underground Railroad carried two of the children as they crossed this "cottonwood bridge."[8]

The group was heading to Quincy, Iowa, where they had hoped to find a place to rest and find food enough to carry them on the rest of their journey. The conductors encountered a strange man on the way to Quincy. After the strange man left them he got in touch with the posse and told them where the train was heading. However, the conductors became suspicious of the man's inquiries and they changed their course to Lewis, Iowa. Around Lewis the Tabor train was harassed by some proslavery men but they managed to escape.

The conductors managed to get the "train" to eastern Iowa where they handed the bondspersons off to some Wesleyan Methodists. These bondspersons were next spotted in church in Peoria, Illinois.[9]

The slaver and his posse managed to chase these runaways all the way to Detroit, Michigan. They were unsuccessful in catching them and the runaways made it into Canada and their freedom was secure. The Mississippian, not happy with the Tabor conductors, not only offered a $200 reward for the return of his slaves but also offered a $50 reward "dead or alive" for the Tabor Underground Railroad conductors. The slaver offered to kill the Tabor men personally if he caught them.[10] However, the conductors made it back to Tabor safe and sound with their friends and neighbors only too happy to protect them. The slaver later proved he was prone to violent action. With most of his wealth gone and his bondspersons escaped, the Mississippian had to settle in nearby Mills County, Iowa. When the slaver found out one of his Mills County neighbors, Cephas Case, had aided in the escape of his slaves he attacked the man with a black cane. Another neighbor intervened before serious injury could occur.[11]

There were other escapees who made their way to the Tabor Underground while traveling out west with their masters. At another time a disoriented male slave was found in Nebraska City, Nebraska Territory. The bondsman was very hungry and was not sure of his present location. It could very well have been that this bondsman came out west with his master and became separated from his party in Nebraska City. The river crossing at Nebraska City was a very chaotic affair with the crush of people and traveling groups wanting to make this necessary river crossing. Livestock had to swim across the wide Missouri River and then be rounded up again on the other side of this waterway. Very often the travelers would have to wait several days before their wagons and other goods could be transported across the river on the ferry. It would be easy to become separated from the group with which you were traveling.

The slave, when he inquired where he might be fed in Nebraska City, was informed that the people across the river in Civil Bend, Iowa, were more likely to help "his kind." He made it across the river, now extremely hungry. He saw various white people but was still hiding out in fear they would turn him in to the authorities.[12] However, hunger finally got the best of this bondsman and he approached a Mr. Ricketts who was walking by his hiding spot. Ricketts promptly took him to his house and fed him a feast of corn bread, meat and potatoes. Ricketts then turned the bondsman over to the local Justice of the Peace, Doc Blanchard. Blanchard was in charge of the Underground Railroad station in Civil Bend and promptly forwarded the young man on to Tabor, where he was able to facilitate his freedom route to Canada.[13]

Aunt Hannah Moore was a bondswoman who was to accompany her mistress to California from Missouri. Thousands had left Missouri in the decade of the 1850s to find their fortune in the golden bear state. Many took their bondspersons with them. Aunt Hannah Moore managed to escape her mistress who was going to California by a very circuitous route.[14]

Aunt Hannah Moore had lived under the ownership of a half a dozen masters, five of which were more reptilian than human. Aunt Hannah never knew her mother or father. She thought her mother had been a white girl who had been impregnated by a Black man and as such was outcast from all society. Almost from birth she was ripped from her mother and the earliest recorded memory of her was when a small white boy was carrying her in a bundle down the road and a man by the name of Scott bought her from the boy for a horse. Scott sold her to a man named Hackler who treated her in a most brutal manner even as a child. When she got older she was stripped naked and whipped by Hackler. His wife treated her almost as badly.[15]

However, after Hannah turned 25 the couple found religion and the beatings stopped. Although the good Christian woman Mrs. Hackler wanted the beatings to continue, Mr. Hackler would not allow them to. Mr. Hackler then passed away. It was determined by Mrs. Hackler and her heirs that if Hannah took diligent care of her she would receive her freedom as a just reward. When Mrs. Hackler passed away Hannah, after decades of care for this gruesome pair, was not given her freedom but was sold along with her son to the profit of the heirs.[16]

She was sold to a Landers and then to a McCaully. McCaully and his wife were a loathsome couple who didn't feed their bondspersons with any regularity. McCaully tried to rape Hannah on several occasions. Both McCaully and Mrs. McCaully would tie Hannah up and beat her to the point she was coughing up blood. The McCaullys liked to find children of free Blacks and then kidnap the children and sell them into slavery. The free Blacks of course had no rights and their pleas for justice were ignored and the McCaullys made a nice bundle of cash off these transactions. Aunt Hannah reported that one such youngster pleaded with everyone that he was a free Black child who had been kidnapped in Arkansas and brought to Missouri. But no one listen to the boy's pleas and he had to live his life out as a slave.[17]

McCaully sold Aunt Hannah to a man by the name of Moore. Moore and his wife treated Hannah with dignity and she had enough to eat and plenty of nice clothes to wear. She lived with them for 10 years. Of all her "masters" the Moores treated her the best but these were the people Hannah escaped from. This gives credence to the idea that it wasn't the people who were treated the worst who escaped but those who had the opportunity to escape. Aunt Hannah Moore would soon have the opportunity to escape.

Soon after the Gold Rush in California Mr. Moore trekked to the west coast and unlike many who went out there he did reasonably well in some sort of enterprise. After several years, in 1854 he requested that his wife Mary Moore and Aunt Hannah join him in California. Mrs. Moore and Aunt Hannah readied for their trip out west but first Mrs. Moore would visit relatives in Philadelphia. Once in Philadelphia she felt Hannah posed no threat to run away after years of faithful service. However, Hannah not knowing what escape opportunities the trip to California would provide, seized the moment in Philadelphia. William Still's Vigilance Committee with the help of white abolitionists provided her with the opportunity to escape.

Aunt Hannah was 57 years old when she was in Philadelphia and made it known to an abolitionist shopkeeper that she wanted out of bondage. Arrangements were made over the objections of Mrs. Mary Moore, of course, and Aunt Hannah was whisked off to freedom. She lived her remaining years in some sort of normalcy. She was able to marry a man named Thomas Todd. Todd had worked diligently for a Quaker gentleman for many years and the man left him a comfortable inheritance and with his and Aunt Hannah's savings it was not necessary for Todd and Aunt Hannah to labor anymore. Aunt Hannah became a rock in the AME Bethel Church in Philadelphia and lived her remaining years deeply respected by everyone around her.[18]

As Americans trekked across the plains their jumping off points into the unknown "Great American Desert" were varied. Sometimes starting from Franklin and Arrow Rock in Missouri on the Santa Fe Trail, also from Westport, Independence and St. Joseph in Missouri and Nebraska City in the Nebraska Territory and from many points in the Kansas territory. These Americans journeyed to Oregon, California, Utah and points in between and in what would become Washington State. Many of these traveling pioneers were from the south and brought their bondspersons on their journeys. The bondspersons who managed to escape made their way through the Underground Railroad apparatus in Kansas, Nebraska and Iowa. To try and escape by oneself several hundred miles farther west in the "Great American Desert" away from these departure points would have been suicidal, as the lack of food, the presence of predatory animals and sometimes equally dangerous humans would have been very perilous.

Also, the political conditions and realities for the slaves in the west were very negative. The Nebraska territory with its welcoming Platte River Valley received thousands of travelers on the Oregon Trail and to the California gold fields. But the territory of Nebraska didn't outlaw slavery until three months before the Civil War. A bondsperson would have a better chance of surviving these trips by making the trek out west and taking their chances on the west coast. Although California and Oregon and the territory of Washington outlawed slavery there were dozens of examples of these laws being flouted. Utah, Nevada and New Mexico territories allowed slavery. Colorado, Nebraska and the Dakota territories were under the doctrines of popular sovereignty where the residents would vote whether they allowed slavery or not.

Blacks did manage to participate in some numbers in the California Gold Rush. Undoubtedly some of these were bondspersons who managed to escape their masters going west. Many of these overland companies, wagon trains headed for California, had Blacks with them. One described its roster as 105 men, 15 Negroes and 12 females.[19] It is interesting to note that the roster didn't designate between free and slave Negroes as was often done at this time. Oftentimes as one got further away from so-called "civilization," where manpower was in short supply the fact that a person was Black, Hispanic or Native American mattered little when a task was before a group of people. Fighting the elements, battling aggressive, voracious animals or unfriendly human beings it mattered little what your ethnic background was; what was more important was whether you could get the job done. Of course if you were Black and moving out west with a wagon train and trying to escape slavery you would be wise to tell those around you that you were a "free" Black person.

Once in California bondspersons were encouraged by free Blacks to escape slavery. Peter Lester, a Black abolitionist from Philadelphia, would invite those of African descent in California who were still held in bondage to his home to tell them of their rights as free persons. A number African Americans had become wealthy in the California gold fields either by striking it rich mining gold or by providing services to the miners, acting as restaurant owners, barbers or boarding house owners. Because a number of Black miners had found large gold deposits there grew legends about Black miners having mystical powers in finding gold. Peter Brown, a Black miner, enthusiastically wrote to his wife in Missouri that he had "cleared $300. California is the best country in the world to make money.

It is also the best place for black folks on the globe. All a man has to do is to work, and he will make money."[20] In many cases white miners tried to exclude Blacks from the gold fields because they had success there.

For slaves being held in bondage in Arkansas and other southern slave states the "Indian Nations" and Mexico made an inviting destination for freedom. On September 15, 1829, Mexican President Vicente Guerrero signed a decree banning slavery in the young Mexican Republic. However, Guerrero, who was part Black and Mexican, yielded to pressure and exempted Texas from this ban. However, after a few months the Mexican government banned the introduction of slaves into any region of the republic including Texas. Many Texas slavers began to call their slaves "indentured servants who were bound to them for life" in order to bypass Mexican laws. If they went below the Rio Grande River where Mexican laws on slavery were enforced sometimes they would write contracts that their slaves owed them money and were bound to work it off. The amount of money the slaves were paid was so low that they would never be able to pay off the "loan." The Mexican government was wise to these schemes and outlawed them as soon as they were aware of them. By 1831 the Mexican government had rejected treaties which called for the pursuit and reclamation of fugitive slaves from the United States.

It was said that the Mexican government even encouraged runaway slaves to settle in northern Mexico and establish colonies. The Mexican government was fearful of interventions by the slave-holding interests in the United States government. They thought by having this "buffer" of fugitive slave colonies on their northern border these former slaves would fight to the death against any United States incursion into Mexico lest they be taken back into slavery. The Mexicans called these Black former slaves "Mascogos."

In 1836 Texas gained her independence from Mexico and became a republic that allowed slavery. Now, if fugitive slaves wanted to gain their independence they had to travel hundreds of miles to the south into Mexico. For some 30 years on many occasions the United States government, on behest of her slave-allowing states, tried to get the Mexican government to sign treaties to return American slaves who had run away from southern slave holders. But to its credit the Mexican government resisted and refused to allow the return of American fugitive slaves or the pursuit of runaway American slaves into Mexico. Thus, Mexico became a tremendous destination for runaway American slaves on the southern fringes of Dixie.[21] During this time Mexico always welcomed these seekers of freedom with open arms. By 1857 the Mexican Congress passed Article 13 which stated that any American enslaved person was free the minute they set foot on Mexican soil.

Felix Haywood, a former Texas slave, said in his Federal Writers Project interview that "Sometimes someone would come along and try to get us to run up north and be free. We used to laugh at that. There was no reason to run up north. All we had to do was walk, but walk south and we'd be free as soon as we crossed the Rio Grande. In Mexico you could be free. They didn't care what color you were, black, white, yellow, or blue. Hundreds of slaves did go to Mexico and got on all right. We would hear about them and how they were going to be Mexicans. They brought up their children to speak only Mexican."[22]

When runaways from Arkansas or the Indian Nations made it to Mexico it was sometimes hard to tell their original point of departure — whether they had come from these two areas or from Texas. It has been projected that by 1850 some 3,000 slaves had made it to freedom in Mexico. It was thought that 90 percent of these bondspersons were men between the ages of 20 and 40 years old. Estimates put the varied ages of the runaways between five months old to 60 years old. It was also projected that between 1851 and 1855 another 1,000 bondspersons had found freedom in Mexico.²³ However, it was indistinguishable how many of these freedom seekers were from the Indian Nations, Arkansas, Texas or elsewhere.

A bondsman was trying to find freedom in Mexico on a humid afternoon in February of 1855. The slave was caught by an Anglo but the determined bondsman got away. The Texan then took out a handgun and fired at the fleeing bondsman but every shot misfired, leaving the escapee unscathed. Then, the resident of the lone star state took out his rifle and fired at the elusive bondsman three times but to no avail.

The Texan had a dog that then pursued the fleeing slave but the bondsman also had a dog that fought back and got the best of the Texan's dog. He kept on going step by step longing for freedom heading for Mexico. While being chased the bondsman lost his coat, his boots and his pistol. The Texan noted correctly as the bondsman ran away from him that if the bondsman got across the Rio Grande River the Mexicans would take care of him and provide him his freedom.²⁴

The trip across the wide expanse of West Texas to Mexico could be very daunting. Very few bondspersons knew the way to Mexico across this huge stretch of West Texas and nomadic Apaches and Comanches were known to attack whites or Blacks who ventured into their spheres of influence. These tribesmen, if they didn't kill the escaping bondsperson, knew the economic value of the slaves and would sell them to the Cherokee and Creek. Doubtless, many freedom seekers lost their lives to these attacks or due to lack of water or food in this area known for droughts and water shortages.

The Tejanos, those of Mexican heritage residing in Texas, often aided fugitive slaves on their way to Mexico. They were accused of "tampering with slave property" and of coaxing slaves to run away and of aiding out-of-state fugitives from Arkansas, the "Indian Nations" and other slave states. The Texas government encouraged all citizens and slaveholders to prevent Tejanos from communicating with Blacks. Local laws were passed to keep Tejanos out of slave-holding communities. It was feared that Tejanos would assist bondspersons in escaping or revolting.²⁵ The slave-holding interests in the United States became so frightened of the number of slaves escaping to Mexico that the United States Army posted 20 percent of its forces on the United States–Mexican border to prevent fugitive slaves from entering into Mexico. Even the great Sam Houston had two of his "best slaves" flee to freedom in Mexico.

A large group of slaves were attempting to get into Matamoros, Mexico, when the sheriff of Gonzales, Texas, Claiborne Stinnett, intervened and tried to stop the crossing. Earlier in 1836 a sizeable contingent of slaves had retreated with the Mexican Army into Matamoros and had created a Black colony there. The sheriff was killed while trying to stop this large escape attempt and there are estimates about the number of bondspersons who made it into Mexico. In some places numbers as high as 30 bondsmen made it into Matamoros to join their former enslaved comrades.²⁶ Stinnett's widow Sarah, described as a graceful, kind, blonde-haired beauty from Illinois had moved to Texas with her first husband. She had seen him killed and scalped by hostile Native Americans. Her second husband, her brother and her two children were captured by Comanches who killed her husband, brother and her infant child. Stinnett was her third husband to be killed in Texas.

The slaves of the 1842 slave "revolt"²⁷ in the Cherokee Nation had Mexico as their destination. In the late fall of that year more than a score of bondsmen owned by the Cherokee tribe around Webbers Falls took some horses, mules, rifles, ammunition and other supplies as they traveled southwest across the open prairie headed for Mexico. At a predetermined hour and on the signal of a particular song these supplies were acquired and the trek to Mexico started. It is interesting to note that most of these escaping Cherokee bondspersons were owned by Joseph Vann. Vann owned many slaves and also a steamboat and ferry operation in which many bondspersons were employed. Perhaps these Cherokee bondspersons had seen a wide variety of humanity and regarded their situation as unacceptable. Some historians have speculated that these Cherokee slaves had seen the freedoms allowed the Seminole Blacks, such as the right to own guns and property and desired to improve their situation. What is also interesting is the role that free Blacks may have played in this "revolt." After the "revolt" had played out its course laws were passed to remove free Blacks from the Cherokee Nation who had not been freed by Cherokee citizens. It was feared that Blacks who had been freed by whites were abolitionists who aided their fellow Blacks in escape attempts.[28]

In the course of this episode of flight these bondspersons were joined by slaves from the Creek tribe bringing their total to over three dozen freedom seekers. The Creeks organized a party to bring back the fleeing bondsman. The Creeks caught up with the Black men and a skirmish ensued. The Blacks entrenched themselves and two were killed and 12 were captured. The rest of the bondsmen managed to escape and head for the Rio Grande.

However, only 15 miles from the battle site the surviving bondsmen met Billy Wilson, a Native American from the Delaware tribe, and a white man, James Edwards. These two had in their custody eight slaves of African descent — one man, two women and five children. These eight had escaped their original owners but had been captured and Edwards and Wilson were returning them to the Choctaw tribe. The escaping bondsmen took possession of the eight and they killed Wilson and Edwards. The eight plus the remaining 25 once again headed south to Mexico.

On November 17 of that year the National Council of the Cherokees was meeting at the capital of the Cherokee people in Tahlequah. The council with the approval of their leader John Ross passed a resolution appointing Captain John Drew and a company of 100 "effective men" to pursue, arrest and deliver the escaping bondspersons to the army commandant at Fort Gibson.

The Drew party began to track the fleeing slaves. They came upon the site of the battle between the bondspersons and the Creeks. Then they came upon the murdered bodies of Edwards and Wilson. Two days after finding the murdered bodies they came upon the escaping slaves some 280 miles from Fort Gibson. They captured 31 of the bondspersons including the eight escaping from the Choctaw. Two of the escapees were out hunting and avoided capture and presumably made it onto Mexico.

Drew turned over to the Cherokee all but five of the Cherokee escapees. Five were determined to be the killers of Wilson and Edwards and they were turned over to the sheriff of the Canadian District of the Cherokee Nation who would hold them for the commandant of Fort Gibson until they could stand trial for murder. One of the Choctaw escapees named Hardy was also turned over to the commandant of Fort Gibson for unknown reasons. Drew kept the two Choctaw women and five children in custody. Thus the "slave revolt" of the Cherokees ended.[29]

Morris Shepard noted in his FWP slave narrative that in the years after the "Cherokee slave revolt" Cherokee patrollers in the Cherokee Nation were very vigilant and always on the lookout for runaway bondspersons. He described how "We had to have a pass to go any place to have singing or praying, and den they was always a bunch of patterollers around to watch everything we done. Dey would come up in a bunch of about nine men on horses,

7—*Western Frontier and the Indian Nations (Oklahoma)* 171

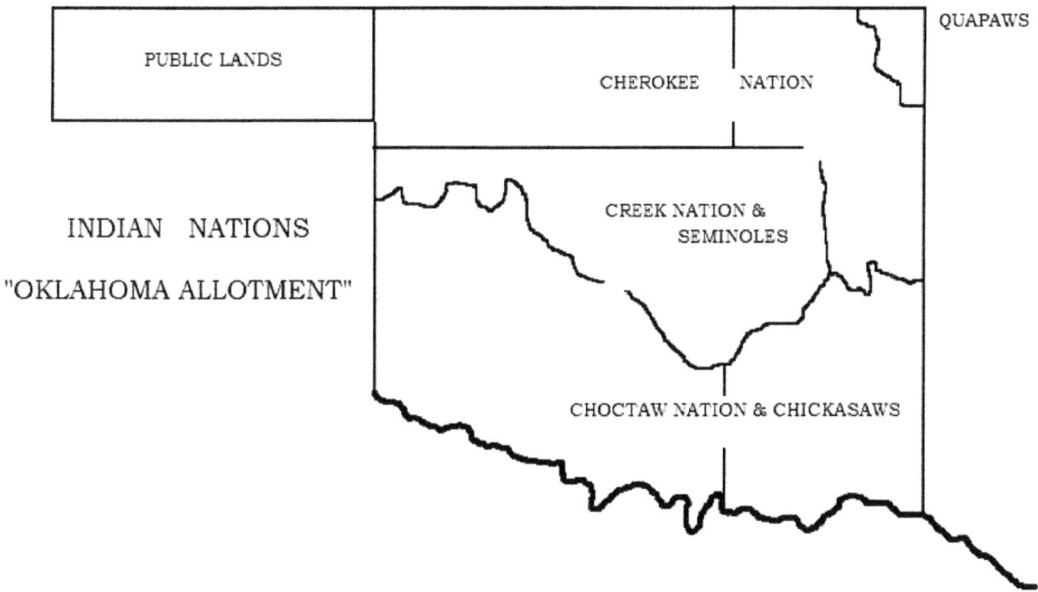

This was how the area of what was known as the Indian Nations was partitioned in the early 1850s. The area has since become the state of Oklahoma. By the middle of the decade the Choctaws and the Chickasaws had their land divided, with the Choctaws getting the eastern half of the district. The Seminoles were the last tribe to come to the Indian Nations and were put into the territory given to the Creeks, the Seminoles' bitter enemies. Because of their location sometimes the bondspersons wishing to escape from the Choctaw, Chickasaw, Creek and Seminole Nations would head to the south on their freedom treks. The Cherokee bondspersons, especially after Kansas was settled to the north of the Cherokee lands in 1854, tended to try and escape to the north (James Patrick Morgans Historical Illustration & Photograph Collection).

and look at all our passes, and if a Negro didn't have no pass dey wore him out good and made him go home. Dey didn't let us have much enjoyment."

Shepard also reported that one night a "runaway Negro come across from Texas" and he had bloodhounds chasing him. Shepard went on to describe, "His britches was all muddy and tore where de hounds had cut him up in de legs when he clumb a tree in de bottoms. He come to our house, and Mistress said for us Negroes to give him something to eat, and we did. Then up come de man from Texas with de hounds…. Mistress try to get de man to tell her who de Negro belong to so she can buy him, but de man say he can't sell him, and he take him on back to Texas wid a chain around his two ankles. Dat was one poor Negro dat never got away to de North, and I was sorry for him 'cause I know he must have had a mean master, but none of us Shepard Negroes, I mean the grown ones, tried to git away."[30]

As in many slave areas the "Nations" weren't immune to abuses by the slave patrollers with attempted runaways. In her FWP interview Kizlah Love told of an abusive patroller in the Choctaw Nation. Love thought the world of her master Frank Colbert and mistress and called Colbert and his wife the best folks who ever lived. However, Frank Colbert had a half-brother Buck Colbert who was the embodiment of evil. Buck used every excuse he could to whip bondspersons and once even killed his baby's slave nurse when she couldn't get his child to stop crying. When Buck was on slave patrol duty the unfortunate bondsperson he would stop might have a legitimate pass, but Buck would tell the bondsperson, who couldn't read the pass, that he had overstayed his time and was late and then "he'd beat 'em (al)most to death. He'd say they didn't have any business off the farm and to git back there and stay there."³¹

The Choctaw Nation, as did the other Native American tribes in Oklahoma or as it was known then, the Indian Nations, had missionaries who taught their children in their schools. Many of these missionaries preached against slavery. However, their own need for physical labor to sustain their mission often led them buy slaves. These missionaries had as benefactors many who were slaveholding Choctaws. This provided a conundrum in that if they preached against slavery they could very well loose their teaching positions. Most of these white missionaries just kept quiet and did little to help any bondspersons escape or change their conditions. Choctaw law forbade the teaching of bondspersons to read or write or to sing hymns or to sit at a table with their masters.³²

A Seminole leader named Wild Cat or Coacoochee had established a Mexican border settlement in 1850 of Native Americans, mostly Seminoles, a large number of Kickapoos, and escaped Black bondspersons. Coacoochee had chafed under control of the Creeks in the "Indian Territories" and wished to start his own settlement without interference from the whites or Creeks. This settlement was in the Santa Rosa Mountains 80 miles southwest of the Rio Grande River in the community of Piedras Negras. In an article in the *Houston Telegraph* editor W. Secrest reported that Wild Cat had under his control 1,800 escaped slaves; 500 were from Texas and the rest were mainly from Arkansas. These numbers were probably exaggerated. The article went on to say that at a rate of several hundred a year escaping bondspersons were fleeing the United States at Eagle Pass and Laredo, Texas.³³ Fort Duncan in Eagle Pass, Texas, turned a lot of their resources to hunting escaped slaves before they reached the Rio Grande. Lehman's ranch north of Eagle Pass, Texas, became a favorite crossing place for the fleeing bondspersons. Bondspersons trying to elude the slave hunters' dragnet along the Mexican border often found a friendly hand-pulled skiff waiting for them to pull them to freedom across the Rio Grande.³⁴

In the summer of 1850 a group of 180 bondspersons led by Jim Bowlegs left the Seminole Territory bound for Mexico. They were chased by white and Creek slave hunters. Near Fort Arbuckle the Bowlegs group was attacked by the slave hunters. A firefight resulted and several of the Black resisters were killed. Most of the group was captured but a number made it to the Mexican outposts of Coacoochee and John Horse. Those that were captured were taken back to the Seminole territory in the Indian Nations.³⁵

There were several colonies in the Mexican state of Coahuila that had as inhabitants members of the Seminole tribe and their Black comrades in arms, the Mascogos. These include El Moral near Monclova Viejo and Hacienda de Nacimiento near Muzquiz. The Mexican government considered Coacoochee and his people to be Mexican citizens.

In October of 1855, alarmed at the number of slaves escaping into Mexico, Texas slaveholders raised $20,000 for an expedition to attack Coacoochee's stronghold. The Seminole leader had been busy arming his escaped slaves and disaffected Native American followers. Texas Ranger Captain James H. Callahan and 130 men ostensibly sent to "chastise hostile Indians" went to assault Coacoochee's positions but they were defeated handily by a combined force made up of escaped Black bondsmen, Native Americans and Mexicans. Texas Ranger Callahan's defeated outfit returned to Texas.³⁶

Earlier in 1851 Coacoochee and a force of 60 men, about 20 of whom were escaped former slaves, defeated an army under Jose Maria Carbajal. Carbajal was ostensibly a revolutionary but he financed his movement by capturing escaped slaves and reselling them back into slavery. Carbajal had with him some 300 or 400 American filibusters and adventurers.[37] Coacoochee and John Horse would see their fair share of filibuster activities from Texas while trying to establish their freedom colony in Coahuila. A filibuster was someone who engaged themselves in an unlawful military enterprise into a foreign country to incite and support a revolution without the backing of their own government. In the mid–19th century these illegal soldiers or filibusters or "freebooters" as they were sometimes known usually came from the United States to foment insurrections in Mexico or other Latin American countries. They were usually motivated by the thrill of adventure and the hope of monetary gain. They usually stole everything they could get their hands on when they entered a foreign country and often committed murder.

It was thought that the escaped bondsmen, Seminoles and others in Coahuila, Mexico, had participated in 40 campaigns, expeditions and mobilizations between 1850 and 1861. Eight of these were against forces of white filibusters who mostly had slave hunting as their purpose and the rest were against hostile Native American tribes such as the Comanche.[38]

Unfortunately Coacoochee died in January of 1857 of smallpox. An epidemic hit this community and 53 people died.[39] Many of the Seminoles of Native American heritage returned back to Oklahoma. However, the Black Seminole knew they couldn't leave Mexico without being returned to bondage so they remained.

Another of the Seminole leaders in Mexico was John Horse, sometimes known as Juan Cavallo or Juan Caballo or Gopher John, a Black man with mixed ancestry. The Seminoles accepted Horse as one of their leaders and of course the recently emancipated slaves in Mexico looked upon him as a role model. Horse would grow into a man of remarkable accomplishments. John first came to the attention of the United States Army in 1826 when as a gangly youth of 14 at Fort Brooke near present day Tampa Bay in Florida. Fort Brooke was garrisoned by soldiers from the Fourth United States Infantry and this was a proud unit with some of its officers graduating from West Point. Horse noted that the officers and some of the new recruits from Europe considered a Florida terrapin that burrowed into the ground a delicacy. John went and captured two of these elusive creatures and sold them to the officers' mess for 25 cents—a princely sum for the time. The next day he did the same thing—sold two more turtles to the officers' mess; he did this for 10 days and had a tidy sum of $2.50. The terrapins had been put in a pen to fatten up. However, someone discovered that Horse had simply been re-selling the same two turtles over and over again. The officer in charge was furious and was ready to give Horse a sound whipping and sell him back into slavery for his insolence. However, Horse, who spoke English very well at this time, launched into a humorous tale of how he pulled off this caper, much to the amusement of the officers. He was spared any punishment and earned a nickname of "Gopher John" due to the burrowing characteristics of his "captured turtles."[40]

However, nine years later "Gopher John" was no laughing matter. He had grown into an extremely brave warrior and participated in the ambush and killing of over 100 United States soldiers in the southeastern part of the United States. These soldiers wanted to remove the Seminoles from Florida and take them to the Indian Nations in present day Oklahoma. A guerrilla war broke out among the Seminoles and the United States Army. Horse accounted himself extremely well and was made a "war chief" by the Seminoles. It was highly unusual that a non–Seminole would be made a war chief. The Seminoles had also given sanctuary to a large group of escaped slaves from Georgia who were absorbed into John Horse's war battle group.

The United States forces managed to capture Horse and also his long-time fighting ally Coacoochee and put them into a hellhole of a prison at Fort Marion in St. Augustine, Florida. The pair after a while managed to escape and fight for another day.[41]

In 1837 at the Battle of Okeechobee in which Colonel Zachary Taylor, who would later become President of the United States, led a force of over 1,000 men and sustained much higher causalities than a much smaller Seminole force. John Horse participated in this battle. The Seminoles left the battlefield to the United States forces. This guerrilla war would drag on for five more years. However, John Horse became concerned with the safety of his wife and children as the guerrilla war dragged onward into 1838. In the spring of that year John gave himself up to United States authorities and he and his family were removed to the Indian Nations. While in the Indian Nations some of the Seminoles quarreled with the much larger Creek tribe. John Horse and Coacoochee decided to leave the Nations and set up in Mexico where the political climate was somewhat better and they felt they and the Seminoles and Blacks would be better treated.

John Horse was a man of many talents. He was a crack shot with a rifle. He had great linguistic skills and was often the interpreter for the various cultures and languages that he came into contact with during his eventful life. John became a doctor or medicine man for his people. He learned about herbal medicines and folk remedies from the African and Native American people he had been dealing with at this time.[42] John was a master strategist during wartime and a master psychologist during peacetime. While in Mexico John urged that the escaped slaves and Seminoles go out of their way to get along with the Mexican people. In this way they would always be welcomed in this country and strife between these various ethnic groups was kept to a minimum. When the Black escaped bondsmen, Seminole, or Mexican members of his community fell onto hard times John knew they would be too proud to take handouts. John would organize a community-wide party with plenty to eat, such as a hog or calf, for everyone in his group. This way the disadvantaged could eat heartily and take the leftover food home without feeling like they were taking a handout.

Slave hunter Warren Adams from Texas managed to kidnap a wounded John Horse when he was in Mexico.[43] A ransom was set up to free John Horse and he made it back to Mexico.

By 1861 on the eve of the American Civil War it has been estimated that over 10,000 bondspersons managed to successfully escape into Mexico. Although several large groups of fleeing bondspersons had made it to Mexico the majority came by themselves or in small groups. Many of them made it to the special colonies set up by John Horse and Coacoochee, in Matamoros and other points in Mexico. For the most part these escapees were treated with dignity and respect by the native Mexican population.

The state of Texas had offered rewards of up to $600 U.S. depending on how close the bondsperson was to Mexico for the capture of any runaway. But even these high bounties had little effect. The state of Texas also encouraged slave hunters to go into Mexico to kidnap slaves and bring them to the American side of the Rio Grande for large rewards. "The Act to Encourage the Reclamation of Slaves, Escaping Beyond the Limits of the Slave Territories of the United States" provided for a bounty of one third of the value of a former bondsperson kidnapped in Mexico and brought back to the United States. However, even this measure had little effect on the number of slaves brought back to the United States.[44] These bounties in present day money could be as high as $30,000. Few of these bounties were claimed probably because the Mascogos were armed and willing to fight for their freedom and not easily taken back into slavery.

Slavery in Oklahoma or the Indian Nations was a very complex issue. However, many of those held in bondage in the Indian Nations wanted out of their situations as did their brothers and sisters in the rest of the slave-holding regions in America. To understand the situations of those in bondage in the Indian Nations a brief discussion of how they got to Oklahoma is useful.

The Cherokee tribe developed their tribal government into a constitutional system modeled after the United States. They had a newspaper and a written language and many of the vestiges of the white civilization that surrounded them in Georgia. Unfortunately they had also adopted the practice of enslaving African people. However, when gold was discovered in the northern part of their Georgia lands in the 1820s, white gold hunters flooded the area. The Georgia legislature passed a series of repressive laws and the Cherokee lost many of their rights as an autonomous nation.

The Cherokee sought protection through the United States Court system but were denied justice. The situation became almost unbearable. The United States government signed a treaty with a minority wing of the Cherokee people that accepted the removal of the Cherokee people to the land that is now the present day state of Oklahoma. Those that signed the treaty for removal to what would become known as the Cherokee Nation were known as belonging to the "Treaty Party" and several of the signers would be mysteriously murdered. In 1838 the United States Army forcibly removed the Cherokee from Georgia to present day Oklahoma in what became known as the "trail of tears."

The other four of the Five Civilized Tribes, the Creeks, Chickasaws, Choctaws and Seminoles, were also removed from southern states to the present day lands of Oklahoma. The Creeks were located in Alabama and eastern Georgia and resisted Federal attempts to remove them but ended up being forced into Oklahoma in chains and shackles. The Choctaws were located primarily in Mississippi and accepted the removal to the "Indian lands" as inevitable. The Chickasaws from Mississippi were a small tribe related to the Choctaws. They used the Choctaws as a model and entered Oklahoma voluntarily.

The Seminoles had been fighting a protracted guerrilla war with the United States Army in Florida. Some think the United States government was interested in fighting the Seminoles because they provided a haven for runaway bondspersons from the southern slave states. Many slave-masters in the southeast portion of the United States wanted the Seminoles removed from Florida to the "Indian lands" of Oklahoma. However, when their great leader Osceola was captured while negotiating under a flag of truce during the Second Seminole War, many in the tribe became despondent and wanted to leave Florida. When other leaders such as John Horse left for Oklahoma many in the tribe did likewise. By 1842 the Seminoles, the last of the civilized tribes, were in the Indian Nations of present day Oklahoma.

Originally the Cherokee, Choctaws and Creeks owned title to most of the land in present day Oklahoma. In 1825 a treaty was signed with the Choctaw and in 1828 with the Cherokee.[45] There were other Native American tribes in the Oklahoma territory at this time — the Senecas, the Quapaws, the Wichitas, the Shawnees and Osages. At times other tribes also occupied lands for short periods of time.

The Chickasaws and Choctaws shared land but by the mid–1850s they dissolved their union. The Choctaws had the southern portion of the state and part of it was partitioned off for the Chickasaw tribe. The Creek had settled land but then the United States government wanted the late entering Seminoles to share their land with them. The Seminole had already squatted on land owned by the Cherokee near Fort Gibson. The Seminoles had taken possession of a number of slaves from the Creeks during the Creek Civil War in 1813–1814. The Seminoles didn't always look at their Black slaves as chattel and they had developed a tributary relationship with them. This often angered the Cherokee and Creek slaveholders. The Seminoles were afraid the Creek would try and recapture the African American Seminoles. Finally the Seminoles were given their own separate Seminole Nation in 1855.

Some of the Native American slave holders became very wealthy living in the style of their Dixie brethren. These Native Americans laid out extensive plantations and built richly furnished mansions. John Ross, a leader of the Cherokee tribe, owned a huge white house at Park Hill near the town of Tahlequah. This grand mansion was dubbed Rose Cottage and could accommodate 40 guests in style. Captain Robert Jones, a Choctaw, owned six cotton plantations. One of Jones' plantations, Lake West, had some 5,000 acres and had 500 enslaved humans on it. Jones' holdings were so large that he often made direct shipments of cotton to the textile mills in Europe in places such as Liverpool, England.[46]

The slaveholders tended to dominate the political and economic life of the "civilized" tribes. However, the slaveholding Native Americans in the Five Civilized Tribes were only 2.3 percent of the total members.[47]

Many of the Native Americans in the Five Civilized Tribes had severe reservations about the practice of slavery. Numerous members of these tribes thought this custom of mirroring the white culture, especially in the practice of slavery, was a bad idea and out of harmony of the tribes' core belief system.

The Cherokee had a system of patrollers and did not allow their slaves to own any kind of property such as horses or firearms. The Cherokee also didn't allow any of their people to teach the bondspersons to read or write. Some of the white Christian missionaries who were attached to the Cherokee Nation felt that since they were not citizens of the Cherokee Nation that they could teach the bondspersons this valuable skill. However, the National Council of the Cherokee passed an act on October 24, 1848, that made it illegal for anyone to teach the slaves to read or write.[48]

The Creek also didn't allow their chattel to own property. It was recognized that the Chickasaws regarded their slaves in the same manner as the whites.[49] However, a major bone of contention between the Cherokee, Creek and the Seminoles was the Seminoles' attitude towards their bondspersons. The Seminoles allowed their bondspersons to live in separate villages and raise their own livestock and crops. The Seminoles allowed their bondspersons to own horses, property and to carry firearms. They required their slaves to pay them a reasonable tribute once a year. Naturally many bondspersons gravitated towards the Seminoles' land. Unfortunately the Blacks in their separate villages had to suffer raids by slave hunters who were from both the Native American and white cultures. Often these slave raiding parties were quite large but the Seminoles would help the Blacks fend off these intruders.

Between 1845 and 1847 many slaves escaped from Arkansas, the Cherokee Nation and the Creek Nation onto Seminole land near Fort Gibson. These bondspersons claimed they were free and the soldiers from Fort Gibson would protect them until their claims could be proved or disproved. Some were even hired and paid to work erecting the stone buildings at the fort.[50]

Some bondsmen like Henry Bibb considered the "Indian Nations" as having a more laid back way of living and as such an easier venue from which to escape slavery. This view was shared by others. Polly Colbert was born a slave. Her masters the Holmes were a husband and wife who were half Choctaw. The Holmes had been sent back east as youngsters and had had extensive schooling. When Polly's parents both died the Holmes raised her as they had no children of their own. It was Polly's opinion that "...I think dat Indian masters was just naturally kinder any way, lestways mine was." She went on to say that the Patrollers in their district would not whip any of Holmes' slaves if they were caught off his property, "for he didn't allow it. He didn't whip 'em hisself and he sure didn't allow anybody else to either." Polly went on to report that although they went to the same church as the whites and Native Americans, the Blacks were segregated in their seating; they could, however, join in the services such as singing and giving praise testimony.[51] However, religious freedom wasn't given to all in the "nations." Nancy Rogers Bean, born a slave in the "Indian Nations," told that her master, a man named Rogers, had a brother who used to preach to the bondspersons on the sly and when he was caught Rogers whipped his brother "something awful."[52]

Slave owners in Arkansas and Missouri found that slaves who had been owned by the Native Americans were less desirable because they had been "spoiled." It was felt that slaves from the "nations" were unfavorable because they were difficult to control.[53] Mary Grayson who was a former slave said in her FWP interview, "I have had people who were slaves of white folks back in the old states tell me that they had to work awfully hard and their masters were cruel to them sometimes, but all the Negroes I know who belonged to Creeks always had plenty of clothes and lots to eat and we all lived in good log cabins we built ... each Negro family looked after a part of the fields and worked the crops like they belonged to us."[54] However, even though in many instances bondspersons were treated better in the "Indian Nations" they still had a desire to escape and taste freedom.

As in other slave areas many Oklahoma bondspersons would help their escaping brethren any way they could. Victoria Taylor Thompson was born a slave in the Cherokee nation. Her mother was Judy Taylor. Victoria told in her FWP interview of how her mother Judy would try and help fleeing bondspersons escape. Victoria said, "I hear mother tell about the slaves running away from mean masters, and how she help hide them at night from the dogs that come trailing them. The high fence keep out the dogs from the yard, and soon's they leave the runoffs would break for the river (Illinois River), cross over and get away from the dogs."[55]

In 1840 Roley McIntosh was elected principal leader of both the Lower and Upper Creeks. Both these two entities had differences that had been adjusted so McIntosh could gain control of both branches.[56] In her FWP interview Nellie Johnson reported about being a slave on McIntosh's farms, "I belonged to Old Chief Roley McIntosh ... I didn't know at the time that old Chief was my master, until my pappy tell me after he was gone. I think all the time he was another preacher ... the Negroes have all the horses and mules and tools they need to work with. They all live in good log houses.... Everybody could have a little patch of his own ... the old Chief never bothered any slaves about anything ... Old Chief just treated all the Negroes like they was just hired hands.... He (McIntosh) was gone off a lot of the time, too, and he just trusted the Negroes to look after his farm and stuff. We would just go on out in the fields and work the crops just like they was our own...."[57]

Not all the Creeks' slaves were as well treated as those on McIntosh's farms. Granderson resided at the Old Agency in the Creek Nation and sought his freedom in August of 1852. He was raised by a Colonel R.B. Mason and was known by many of the officers in the United States Army in that area. It was said he was easy and pleasant in his manners. His master was certain for some reason that Granderson had been furnished with free papers by some person or persons traversing the area. A "liberal reward" was offered for the return of Granderson. It is interesting to note that his master, who was so certain someone had supplied him with "free papers," offered no reward for the capture or prosecution of the person who gave Granderson these alleged "free papers." Later another advertisement was run for Granderson in late October of 1852. William was a "good blacksmith" when he escaped from a farm near Look-fah-tah in the Choctaw Nation. An advertisement was run for his return in January of 1853 and a reward offered. He left with a black horse mule, Spanish saddle, saddle-bags and other goods including a "six-shooter pistol." It was not known if Granderson and William made it to permanent freedom.[58] One of the complaints the slave holding Native Americans had in the "Indian Territories" was of the number of whites who had come into the territory unauthorized and had taken up residence. Many times their purpose in the territories was not known and many took to an illegal lifestyle or were just land squatters. Of course, many of the slave owners thought these whites had on their agenda being abolitionists or trying to steal slaves or providing slaves with a means to escape. This was thought to be the case in the Granderson escape. However, there was no proof to support any claims of Granderson being supplied "free papers."

The United States government goaded on by her states that allowed slavery was always very concerned that the "Indian Nations" would at some point abolish slavery and allow this territory to become a haven for runaway bondspersons. Some of the "Indian" agents attached to the tribal lands and some of the missionaries in the territory from southern states were concerned about the conduct of some northern missionaries with abolitionist tendencies. In 1856 the Creeks passed a law that abolitionists could not teach in their schools.[59]

The Cherokees and Choctaws were heavily influenced by the Congregationalists and their American Board of Commissioners for Foreign Missions. The Congregationalists had a long history of helping oppressed slaves win their freedom or escape on the Underground Railroad. Congregationalists had helped to defend the slaves who overtook the crew on the slave ship the Armistad and helped them win their freedom. Oberlin College, the most radical of all Congregationalist Church Colleges, regularly pumped out an annual crop of abolitionists only too willing to help bondspersons escape on the Underground Railroad. The Rev. S.A. Worcester was one of the abolitionist missionary leaders in the Cherokee Nation and a vocal proponent of removing slavery from the "Indian Nations."

Douglas H. Cooper, the Choctaw and also later the Chickasaw agent and former resident of Mississippi, wrote in 1854 to the southern superintendent Charles W. Dean in Fort Smith, "If things go on as they are now doing, in 5 years slavery will be abolished in the whole of your superintendency (Private). I am convinced that something must be done speedily to arrest the systematic efforts of the Missionaries to abolitionize the Indian Country. Otherwise we shall have a great run-away harbor, a sort of Canada — with "underground rail-roads" leading to & through it-adjoining Arkansas and Texas. It is no use to look to the General Government — its arm is paralyzed by the abolition strength of the North. I see no way except secretly to induce the Choctaws & Cherokee & Creeks to allow slave-holders to settle among their people & control the movement now going on to abolish slavery among them."[60]

The pro-slavery missionaries and agents mobilized to lessen the influence of the abolitionists in their midst. A Choctaw missionary and slave owner, the Rev. Cyrus Kingsbury, managed to create a controversy and get the Congregational American Board to separate its patronage from the Indian Nations missionaries. This patronage was replaced by the Presbyterian Board of Foreign Missions (Old School) which was more in sympathy with the slave holders. Also, in 1859 the Reverend Worcester died, making it easier for the pro-slavery agents and missionaries to impose their will on the churches and schools in the territory.[61]

By 1859 Cooper was able to write the southern superintendent, Elias Rector, that the missionaries, "now among the Choctaws and Chickasaws ... entirely repudiate the higher-law doctrine of northern and religious fanatics."[62] William H. Seward, then a United States senator from New York and later secretary of state for Lincoln and Johnson, had given a speech in March of 1850 in which a phrase he used became a doctrinal point for the abolitionist cause. In answer to pro-slavery men who promoted the idea that slavery was the acceptable norm because it was mentioned in the constitution, Seward claimed there was a "higher law than the constitution" in seeking to justify his opposition to the expansion of slavery into the new territories, in this specific case California. Seward reasoned that slavery was doomed and that the new territories were governed by a moral law established by "the Creator of the Universe."[63]

The Cherokees had formed a secret society called "Kee-too-wah" or the "Pins." These men wore two crossed common pins on their shirts or coats to signify their membership. Most of the members were full-blooded Cherokees who mainly wanted to encourage their people to keep the old ways and not take up the ways of the whites. Since most of the "Pins" did not own slaves and were in fact some what hostile to slavery the white agents became suspicious of their activities fearing they were some kind of abolitionist cover organization that might aid Blacks in escaping. Cherokee Agent R.J. Cowart reported the secret Cherokee organizations and the white men who he thought were abolitionists in the territory. He was unable to prove the Pins had aided in any escapes by bondspersons. Cowart became firmly committed to removing any white abolitionists from the Cherokee territories even if United States Cavalry or Dragoons were needed to perform this task. Cowart even talked to persons who complained of white men interfering with the institution of slavery in the Cherokee Nation. When Cowart asked the complainants to bring charges or witnesses to substantiate these incriminations to prosecute these men Cowart said "*none came.*" It appeared most of these white intruders were in fact just land squatters rather than abolitionists and their aid to any Black freedom escapes was probably minimal.[64]

The Pin Cherokees had made allies with the Treaty Party of the Cherokee. Stand Watie had been a figure in the "Treaty Party" that okayed the removal of the tribe to the West. His comrades John and Major Ridge and Elias Boudinot had been murdered as participants in this treaty. Watie managed to escape execution when he was warned of the impending act. Many thought that John Ross had engineered these political murders although he had always denied it. He and Watie had become rivals. However, the bitterness between John Ross, the "Principal Chief" of the Cherokees, and the Pin and Treaty factions continued throughout the years before the Civil War. There were murders and other acts of violence that marred the Cherokee Nation. This also affected the potential escapes of Cherokee bondspersons.

Chaney Richardson was born a bondswoman in the 1850s in the Cherokee Nation and told of how this feud between the "Pins" and the "Ross" faction affected the slaves in the territory. Chaney relates,

> When I was about 10 years old, that feud got so bad the Indians wan always talking about getting their horses and cattle killed, and their slaves harmed ... one morning my own mammy wont off somewhere down the road to git some stuff to dye cloth, and she didn't come back.

Lots of young Indian bucks on both sides of the feud would ride around the woods at night, and Old Master got powerful uneasy about my mammy and had all the neighbors and slaves out looking for her, but nobody find her.

It was about a week later that two Indian men rid up and ast Old Master wesn't his gal Ruth gone. He says yes, and they take one of the slaves along with a wagon to show where they seen her.

They find her in some bushes where she'd been getting bark to set the dyes, and she been dead all the time. Somebody done hit her in the head with a club, and shot her through and through with a bullet, too." Chaney not only lost her mother but her brothers and sister were also sold off by her master and she didn't get to see them until after the war.[65]

Because of this feud between the Cherokee factions of the Pins and the Ross people some bondspersons, especially in the late 1850s and 1860 and early in 1861 when the feud was at its zenith, were afraid to venture too far from their homes at night to try and escape from bondage. There was fear of being killed in retaliation for some unspecified act by one side or the other.

Lucinda Davis was held in bondage by members of the Creek Tribe in the nations. Apparently she was raised by the Creeks as it appears that Lucinda was sold when she was a small child. She could not remember her parents as a young child and no one told her about her parents as she grew up. Maybe because of her being sold her parents escaped bondage soon after Lucinda was sold. About the time of the Civil War Lucinda's master Tuskaya-hiniha was going blind and she helped him around. At this time she reported that most of his bondspersons began to "slip out and run off." After the Civil War was over Lucinda's parents came for her so they all could be reunited as a family.

When Lucinda was growing up around the Creeks she only spoke their language. She reported that when she heard English it sounded like "(a) whole lot of wild shoat in de cedar brake scared at something."[66]

However, just as some bondspersons wanted to leave the "Indian Nations" for freedom others sought refuge in the area. In late fall in 1850 two bondspersons from three miles from Brazoria, Texas, were trying to make it to the "Indian Nations." Jonas, described as having a quick step and speaking quickly, was also able to read and write. Jonas had with him a pocket compass and it was said he used the expression "dog on it" a lot. His compatriot was Sam who could play the violin very well. The pair had a short barreled shotgun with them. There was a $400 reward if they were captured out of the state of Texas and $200 if captured in the state of Texas.[67] In 1859 Dick had escaped during the summer from Pine Bluff, Arkansas. He had originally come from Georgia. Dick and a group of other freedom seekers were trying to make it to the "Indian Nations." It was not certain what their plans were after they reached the "Nations."[68]

Two bondsmen, Billy and Grandison, escaped from their Cherokee masters in 1840. They armed themselves with guns. However, in November of that year Creek slave hunters captured them about 20 miles above Fort Gibson without incident. The Creek slave hunters according to their law at this time managed to collect a $50 reward. Early in 1841 a suspicious white man by the name of Warren F. Foster appeared in the Creek Nation. Foster had with him a Black man as his slave whom he said he purchased from a Nelson Hill in Little Rock, Arkansas. Whether Foster decoyed the Black man away from his owner or if the Black man had run away on his own only to be captured by Foster is not known. The Creeks determined that Foster's bondsman actually was owned by W.E. Woodruff, the editor of the *Arkansas Gazette*, who, as we mentioned before, had trouble keeping his bondspersons on his property.[69]

7—Western Frontier and the Indian Nations (Oklahoma)

Some historians say that slavery amongst the Cherokee was at times little different than that of the whites. In 1860 a quartet of escaping bondsmen wanted out of slavery in the Cherokee nation. They made their way through the "Indian Nations," managing to flee from the Cherokee patrollers. They made it through the prairie lands of the Kansas and Nebraska Territories. They then crossed the Missouri River into Iowa. They were in the United States of America for the first time and out of the territories. Unfortunately, their troubles started in the "free" state of Iowa.

This quartet found themselves in Civil Bend, Iowa, near the Missouri River in March of that year. George Gaston, one of the leaders in the Underground Railroad in Western Iowa, found that the four bondsmen wanted to find total freedom in Canada. He took them by carriage to Tabor dressed in women's clothing, heavily veiled.

Two conductors were chosen to move this quartet farther north on the way to Canada. The conductors were to be Edward T. Sheldon and Newton Woodford. The four escapees and the two conductors were loaded into a sled. Although it was March there was still considerable snow on the ground and a sled would be a faster mode of transportation for this group.

The group in the sled was making their way from Tabor to the next Underground Railway station in Lewis, Iowa. After they had traveled a distance on their journey the sled was stopped to give the horses some rest and water at Mud Creek. Near Mud Creek stood a house on a hill and a little boy at the house noticed the sled. He crept down the hill to get a better look at the cargo of the sled. The little boy noticed that in the sled were humans escaping slavery and he went and told his father. The train was derailed in short order in Iowa when the little boy's father notified the local authorities of the escaping bondsmen. The four escapees and the conductors were arrested by local authorities in accordance with the Fugitive Slave Act. The white conductors were taken to stand trial in Glenwood, Iowa, and the bondsmen were taken to a farmhouse where they were loaded onto a wagon for transportation into Missouri. It was thought that the bondsmen would be easier to handle in slave state Missouri before they were returned to their slave masters in the Cherokee territory. The arrest of this train of the Underground Railroad was on a Saturday and an unusual trial date was set for the next day on Sunday. The majority of the townspeople in Tabor, Iowa, were involved in the Underground Railroad. Most of the Tabor people went to the trial of the two conductors, Edward T. Sheldon and Newton Woodford. During the trial a note was passed to one of the Tabor people asking him if he wanted to know where the bondsmen were being held. The Tabor man of course wanted to know.

Two Tabor people rushed from the trial and found the farm where the Cherokee slaves were being held. They saw them being loaded into a wagon. With the snow still on the ground they knew the wagon would be easily tracked. The two Tabor scouts headed back to Glenwood and the courthouse. By that time the trial was over and, remarkably, Sheldon and Woodford had been found not guilty. There would be little time to rejoice at this victory. The bondsmen had to be retaken and sent on the way to Canada before they reached Missouri. The Tabor people climbed into two sleds and hoped to catch up with the wagon carrying the bondsmen on this cold Iowa night.

During an all night chase the Tabor party managed to catch up with the wagon holding the slave posse and their cargo of human chattel. Guns were pulled on both sides but the Taborites prevailed and they recaptured the bondsmen. The four bondsmen were put on the Underground Railroad and they eventually made it safely to Canada.

The next year Tabor resident Loren Hume, who was an orphan being raised by George

Gaston, noticed one of the escaped Cherokee bondsmen back in Tabor. Hume asked him what he was doing in town and the man answered he was on his way back to the Cherokee territory to get his wife and bring her to freedom in Canada. Even though his first escape had been very difficult and he had in fact been recaptured and almost returned to slavery he took the chance so as to retrieve the person closest to him. Often the bonds of family proved to be stronger than the chains of American slavery.[70]

The fear of being removed from your family or friends manifested itself in many ways. Nancy Rogers Bean described a gruesome scene of her aunt who Bean said was a "fighting woman." She was put on the slave auction block to be sold to the highest bidder in the Cherokee territory and did not want to leave relatives and friends. When the bidding started for her Bean's aunt grabbed a hatchet and laid her hand on a log and chopped it off. She did this knowing no one would want to purchase her after this incident. This way she could stay among family and friends.[71]

Many of the Native Americans in the "Indian Nations" who owned slaves were often at the mercy of marauding whites who would steal their "human chattel." These Native Americans felt they had few rights in the United States courts of law as far as recovering their "human property" from any whites. The nearest court to adjudicate any proceedings was in Fort Smith, Arkansas. This often would require many days of travel to attend any kind of court proceeding, which would often dampen any desire to try and recover their "human property" because of the great expense and lack of success in the white courts to get favorable action. Native American leaders were very much dissatisfied with this system. They felt they were entitled to their own federal court system in the "Indian lands" but were denied at every turn. This sometimes caused confusion as to whether a bondsperson had escaped or had been kidnapped by a white for sale as a slave in another slave region.[72]

The Civil War brought chaos to the Indian Nations as it did to much of the frontier and the rest of the country both north and south. In 1861 Washington, D.C., did not send to the tribes the annual annuities owed them by treaty for fear of having the money fall into the coffers of the Confederacy. The Federals also sent most of the soldiers who had been in the "Indian Nations" to Fort Leavenworth in Kansas. This only played into the hands of the Confederacy as the tribes felt they had been betrayed and abandoned by the Federals in Washington, D.C., and left vulnerable to attacks by whites who coveted their slaves and other property. Albert Pike from Arkansas became the Confederate commissioner to the Native Americans in the territories. Pike was authorized to use large subsidies and gifts to sign up the Creeks, Chickasaws, Choctaws, Cherokees, Seminoles and other tribes to support the Rebel cause.[73]

Jefferson Davis understood the importance of the half million cattle that were in the "Indian Nations" and how they could help feed his rebel army. Also, if the "Indian Nations" were lost to the Confederacy the Union Army could use it as a base from which to attack Texas or Arkansas. Pike quickly signed up the Creeks, Chickasaws, Choctaws and even the Seminoles to the Confederate side; only the Cherokee held out. Many in these tribes felt that since those in Washington, D.C., had broken every treaty they had signed with the tribes maybe their lot would be better with the Confederacy. The Confederacy also promised the "Indian Nations" their own court system to resolve questions of ownership of their "human chattel." The leader of the Cherokees, John Ross, from his famed Rose Cottage with its half mile driveway lined with rose bushes, knew if they left the United States' fold the Cherokee would forfeit some five million dollars owed to the tribe for lands vacated in North Carolina, Georgia and Tennessee.[74]

However, Ross who was in his 70s, knew many of the Cherokee men and his principal rival, Stand Watie, wanted to side with the Confederacy and the other civilized tribes. Watie had already commanded a company of Cherokees at the battle at Wilson's Creek.

In September of 1861 Brigadier General Ben McCulloch, in order to ingratiate himself with Ross, wrote two letters to Ross as the "Principal Chief" of the Cherokees. McCulloch informed Ross that he would send Stand Watie and his men to the northern border of the Cherokee territory to protect Ross and the Cherokee people against Kansas Jayhawkers or other predatory whites.[75] It was Ross' wish to remain neutral in the war and a Proclamation of Neutrality was issued.[76]

However, Ross could not help but notice how many of his young men were leaving their homes to join Stand Watie and Ben McCulloch's Rebel Army. Finally in the fall of 1861 Ross capitulated to Pike's offers and signed the Cherokees on the side of the Confederacy.

After the Creeks signed the treaty with Pike and the Confederacy some wanted to stay with the Union or remain neutral. A Creek leader, Opothele Yoholo, was organizer of this neutrality movement and left for Kansas to join the Union forces and seek protection for the woman and children. Some 500 Blacks held in bondage by the Creeks and Seminoles and some 5,000 Creeks plus others from other tribes joined Opothele Yoholo in his trek north. Some of the Creek masters gave their bondspersons wagons, horses, guns and provisions to help them make it north.[77] Also, some Cherokees and Seminoles came north during the winter of 1861-1862. Refugee camps were set up but the Union government was slow to respond to this and many Native Americans perished during the winter conditions and from starvation.

Of course with the chaos of war there were left opportunities in the nations for the bondspersons to escape often with the help of the Union Army. Chaney McNair was born a slave and was nine or ten years old when she first saw Union soldiers in the Cherokee lands. The soldiers came and captured her master William Penn Adair. She said the Union soldiers took all of her master's 10 slaves and then went by horse and wagon and rounded up many more slaves from other plantations in the area to take them up north into Kansas. Chaney reported that they had plenty to eat on the way north, as she saw many of the Union soldiers robbing along the way and helping themselves to as much livestock as they could handle. However, securing water was a problem and she told of drinking muddy water from the creeks. Chaney said that Adair was kept prisoner for a while in the north but was finally let go. He, however, went and became a colonel in Stand Watie's Rebel Army. She went on to say she got "free" while she was in Kansas but stated, "We all know it was comin.'"[78]

Moses Lonian was a child slave to Louis Ross, brother to John Ross. Louis Ross was very rich and owned a lot of land and slaves and also held the position of treasurer to the Cherokee Nation from 1855 to 1859. Moses' father, although a slave, was the overseer to Ross' salt wells. This was a very profitable enterprise as these were the only source of salt in the Cherokee Nation and people came from all parts of the region to purchase the salt from these wells.

Lonian reported that when the Union soldiers came into Cherokee lands in 1862 Louis Ross was anxiously waiting for them. They fired warning shots at Louis Ross and he ran for cover in a river and almost drowned because he could not swim. As these soldiers had done elsewhere they ransacked the Ross plantation for all the valuables on it. Ross had not been kind to his slaves and they were in fear of him. When the Union soldiers told the bondspersons they would take them to freedom in the north they were reluctant to go.

They feared the Union soldiers would not be able to protect them and that Ross and the other slave owners would come back and severely punish them.

When the Union soldiers told the bondsperson they had made Louis Ross a rich man and they deserved some of his possessions the slaves were afraid to take anything for fear that the mere possession of the goods would cause them to be punished at a later date when the soldiers were gone. The soldiers took them to freedom in Kansas and told them to head for Fort Scott near the Kansas and Missouri border and left them to fend for themselves. The bondspersons were still in such fear of the slave owners that they ran off the 500 cattle the soldiers had given to them from the slave owners and they broke up other valuable property for fear the slavers would catch them with their property. The former slaves almost starved to death in the subsequent months and wished they had kept the property they had been given by the soldiers.[79]

After the Battle at Pea Ridge in Arkansas, Confederate General Albert Pike, who was in command of most of the soldiers recruited from the "Indian Nations," became very bitter at the lack of support from Richmond. The Confederacy had promised uniforms, guns, ammunition and equipment to Pike's troops and none of these things was forthcoming. Pike's Native American troops fought with bows and arrows and tomahawks at Pea Ridge because their promised armaments never had come from the Richmond government. Pike angrily brought his men back to the "Indian Nations" where he would also have trouble receiving pay for his troops.

Under Colonel William Weer not only Blacks in the Indian Nations were being recruited into the Union Army but now also Native Americans who found the promises out of Richmond to be as hollow as those often coming from Washington, D.C. It seemed to many the tide was turning and the Union was winning in the west.

Weer plunged into the heart of the nations and captured not only the Cherokee capital at Tahlequah but its leader John Ross. The Cherokee archives and other tribal valuables were packed up and sent to Washington, D.C., for safe keeping. Ross was imprisoned for a while then was released and lived in style back east in Philadelphia.

However, Weer failed to follow up this victory with any meaningful action and he took to serious drinking. Now a drunken lout, Weer lost control of his army and ranking Colonel Frederick Salomon and other officers took control of the command.[80]

Salomon took his white troops and left the region with the Native American troops guarding the Native American lands. Salomon left little instruction on what was to be done and the moral of the Union troops suffered. Nobody knew who was safe and Stand Waties' Confederates took control of the area again. The Black population was in a flux: Were they free? Were they slaves again? If they acted free certainly some slavers would come and punish them. Many Blacks had left the Indian Nations to live in refugee camps in Kansas or to join the Union Army.

The Federal government in Washington seemed to pay little attention to the area as they continually stripped Union troops from the area to fight at Shiloh or other battlefields farther east. However, early in February of 1863 the Cherokee National Council voted to join the Union cause for good and to free all slaves in their nation. By this time most of the Native American men of the five tribes were either fighting on the side of the Union or (a smaller number) still fighting for the Confederacy.

A few weeks after the Union victories at Gettysburg and Vicksburg the only battle fought in the Indian Nations during the Civil War was contested at Honey Springs near present day Muscogee, Oklahoma. The Union Army was victorious with the center of their line being held by the 1st Kansas, a Black Regiment. Commanding Union Major-General James Blunt stated for the record that the 1st Kansas "particularly distinguish[ed] itself" in the battle. Blunt went on to report, "Their coolness and bravery I have never seen surpassed; they were in the hottest of the fight, and opposed Texas troops twice their number, whom they completely routed."[81]

Lucinda Davis told that she would

> never forgit de day dat battle of de Civil War happen at Honey Springs! Old Master jest had de green corn all in, and us having been having a time getting it in, too. Jest de women was all dat was left, 'cause de men slaves had all slipped off and left out. My uncle Abe done got up a bunch and gone to de North wid dem to fight.... I was swinging de baby, and all at once I seen somebody riding dis way ... jest coming a-kiting and a-laying flat out on his hoss. When he see de house he begin to give de war whoop, "Eya-a-a-he-ah!" When he git close to de house he holler to git out de way 'cause dey gwine be a big fight.... We jest leave everything setting whar it is...
>
> Den jest as we starting to leave here come something across dat little prairie sho' nuff! We know dey is Indians de way dey is riding, and de way dey is all strung out. Dey had a flag, and it was all red and had a big criss-cross on it dat look lak a saw horse ... we git out to de big road and de rain come down hard ... den long come more soldiers dan I ever see befo.' Dey all white men ... dey have on dat brown clothes dyed with walnut and butternut...
>
> We can't git out on de road so we jest strike off through de prairie.... We git in a big cave ... and spend de whole day ... listen to de battle going on. We can hear de guns going all day ... here come de South side making for a geteway.... After while here come de Yankees, right after 'em.[82]

After this battle, although there were skirmishes involving both sides, the Union slowly began to take control of the Native American lands in Oklahoma. Stand Watie, now a general in the Confederate Army, managed to hold out even though the Confederacy provided him with almost no provisions. He supplied his Army by capturing Union supplies and he held out until June of 1865.

Most of the male slaves from the "Indian" lands had escaped during the war and had found freedom, usually in Kansas, or they had joined up with the Black Union regiments that were formed during the War. As the Civil War wound down in the spring of 1865 the lands of the Cherokee, Choctaw, Creek, Chickasaw and Seminole was one vast scene of desolation. This once prosperous region lay in ruins. However, the evil stain of slavery had been removed forever with the help of Black and Native American Union soldiers.

8

Conclusions

> Be free, oh, man! Be free.... My strong attachments to friends and relatives, with all the love of home and birth-place which was so natural among the human family, twined about my heart and were hard to break away from ... the fear of being pursued with guns and blood-hounds, and of being killed, or captured and taken to the extreme South, to linger out my days in hopeless bondage.[1]
> — *Former bondsman Henry Bibb lamenting the pros and cons of escaping from slavery. The absence from all friends and relatives were he to escape and the thought of never seeing his loved ones again weighed heavily on his decision. If he was caught the reality was that he may be killed or sent to the deep south to the mind and soul crushing reality of 14 hour workdays.*

In this work we have defined the Western Frontier from 1840 to 1865 as being on a line from the western border of Iowa in the north to the southern border of Arkansas in the south. Although some of these locations went from being territories to states, for the most part the area from Independence in Missouri to Council Bluffs in Iowa was the jumping off point for hundreds of thousands of Americans from the United States into the western territories. They headed for the Great Salt Lake Valley in the Utah territory, the famed Santa Fe Trail, the gold fields in California and later the gold fields in Colorado. They could head to the Oregon Territory where slavery was illegal or they could take a turn to the north into Washington country where slavery had not yet been declared illegal, at least for a while. South of Independence to the state of Arkansas on its western border you could leave the United States and head into the Indian Nations of the area we now know as Oklahoma.

It is interesting to note that Arkansas and Missouri were of course considered slave states while the Indian Nations allowed slavery. Kansas was to be a slave territory by wishes of the federal government and then become a slave state. Even in the Nebraska territory where the language of the famed Kansas-Nebraska Act of 1854 was the same as in the Kansas territory slavery was allowed. If the population of these two territories wanted slavery by voting that way they were supposed to be able to have it as a part of "popular sovereignty." The best-known newspaper in the Nebraska territory bragged that "The clanking of the chains of slavery may be heard upon her (Nebraska's) great plains."[2] The western frontier was no different than anyplace else in the United States. Where slavery reared its ugly head you had bondspersons who wanted to escape from it.

During the 1850s the focal point for the expansion of slavery in the United States became the Kansas territory. Many have said that the chances of Kansas becoming a slave state were problematic, but those of that opinion were unaware of the realities of the time. Granted, Kansas would never have become a large grower of cotton, rice, tobacco or sugarcane — some of the staple crops grown in the southern United States that were heavy users of slave labor. However, Missouri was a large grower of hemp, as was Kentucky. Hemp could easily be grown in the Kansas territory and, for that matter, the Nebraska territory. In 1873, a few years after the Civil War concluded, William Gilpin wrote, "There is a region of Missouri and Kansas of rapidly rising fame ... which we will define as the 'Region of the Hemp Culture' ... specially favored by nature, in its geographical locality, climate and superlative fertility this region has become the seat of a hemp culture."[3] Even during World War II hemp was grown in this region with great success.[4]

Hemp, which was used for the making of ropes, ship sails and other products had great commercial use in the United States in the 1850s and was even an export item. Rope was used a great deal in the growing of cotton to secure the huge cotton bales. Hemp slave plantations in Missouri were profitable and there was no reason such plantations in Kansas would not have been equally valuable. Lafayette County, Missouri, less than 50 miles from the Kansas border, was the county in the state of Missouri with the largest number of slaves in 1860. Lafayette County also had one of the largest rope making manufacturing plants in America. While the number of slaves used on large hemp farms was only about 20 to 30 — not the several hundred used for cotton plantations — these hemp farms could be extremely lucrative. The number of slaves in Kansas would have never been over 50,000 but it would have been politically useful to the southern slave states to be able to expand their slave empire into a territory such as Kansas. The addition of two more United States senators and additional congressmen would have been politically useful to American slavers in securing their grasp on the legislative branch of the United States government. The harvesting of hemp at this time was such a laborious process that usually only slave labor was used. It was almost impossible to hire enough free labor to harvest large amounts of the hemp crop.

So, the possibilities of the Kansas territory becoming a slave state were certainly plausible with the cultivation of hemp as its cornerstone. The early pro-slavery settlers were certainly serious about Kansas becoming a slave state. The initial slave constitution and laws passed by the pro-slavery Kansas territorial legislature were some of the toughest in the United States to protect slave property. When John Stringfellow, who was the speaker of the House in the territorial Kansas legislature, passed harsh measures to protect slave owners' rights in Kansas his brother Benjamin Stringfellow encouraged southern slave owners to move slaves into Kansas by saying, "now (the Kansas territory) have laws more efficient to protect slave property than any state in the Union."[5]

Some have estimated that the number of slaves in the Kansas territory was never over 200. But in looking at the amount of slave owners in Kansas the numbers would seem to be larger. Zu Adams and her father F.G. Adams gathered information in 1895 for the Kansas State Historical Society about "the slavery days" in that state. This information they gathered would indicate there were more slave owners in Kansas than previously had been thought. However, what is also evident is that many of these slave owners once they got to Kansas decided that the fact that so many of their bondspersons ran off to freedom meant that Kansas was not a good place for slave owners to try and hold their property. The slave owners moved into Kansas but many quickly left — often before they could be counted in any census. The activities of the bondspersons in escaping, plus the actions of men like John Stewart, James Montgomery, John Brown, James Abbott, Charles Jennison, John Kagy and

Aaron Stevens, left little doubt in the slave owners' minds that their "human property" was not safe from escape but also that the slave owners' lives themselves were in jeopardy.

John Brown's murderous rampage, killing and hacking to death of five slave owners on Pottawatomie Creek left little doubt that not only the slave owners' chattel was in danger of being freed by their own movement to the north, but also that the slave owner's life could easily be extinguished without the perpetrators being brought to justice. By 1859, when it was obvious to everyone that Kansas would not be a slave state, still over 5,000 Kansans out of a total of around 15,000 voted to support a constitution that allowed slavery. The hopes of establishing a slave state on the prairies of Kansas was a hard proposition to die.[6]

George W.S. Lucas, a Black man who had been with John Brown in southeastern Kansas, told Underground Railroad chronicler Wilber H. Siebert, that Brown had liberated 560 slaves in that region of Kansas. Lucas then went to Ohio and helped freedom seekers there in the late 1850s.[7] Kansas slave owner James Skaggs, who owned 27 humans saw that the Kansas territory was not conducive to slavery and took his chattel to Texas where he figured they would be safer.[8] Many other slavers entered the Kansas territory with high hopes only to be frightened away by the violence and the escape of their chattel. To many slave owners in Kansas the value of their slaves represented most of their accumulated wealth. They did not want to see their wealth run off to the north. They felt it better to take their "human property" out of the state due to the numerous slave escapes in that territory. Slave escapes in nearby western Missouri became so frequent that slave owners doubled the usual slave bounties from $100 to $200 to try and abate the flow of bondspersons out of the area to freedom in the north.[9] (In today's money $200 would be worth about $10,000). Usually in Missouri a bounty was offered of $25 if the escapee was captured in the same county they were from, $50 if the escapee was captured in the state of Missouri and $100 if the escapee was captured in another state or territory such as Kansas or Iowa.

It has been said that because the escapes of the freedom seekers and the activities on the Underground Railroad were not frequent enough in the United States, the Underground Railroad did not strike enough of a blow to slavery and the Civil War was necessary to end the horrible institution. Some say that if the Underground Railroad had been more effective in promoting slave escapes the Civil War may have not have been necessary.

However, one might disagree that in the Kansas Territory and on the western boundary of Missouri the escapes on the liberty line were so frequent and that the activities on the Underground Railroad were so common it was not possible for slavery to take a foothold in Kansas. Also, it became more and more improbable that western Missouri could support slavery. The freedom seekers and the Underground Railroad were a deterrent to end the expansion of slavery into the west. The large number of slave escapes from western Missouri and Kansas and then the freedom road into the Nebraska territory and then across the state of Iowa helped to convince the slave owners eager to establish that economic system in Kansas that their expensive "chattel" had no desire to stay in the condition of slavery and would rather find freedom in the north. Although the percentage of slaves were not large in number on the western frontier — probably less than seven percent of the total of bondspersons held in servitude in the whole of the slave states[10]— the escapes of bondspersons in the Kansas territory and western Missouri changed the whole equation of expanding slavery into the west. This stifling of the expansion of slavery helped to ultimately sow seeds for the destruction of that horrible institution in the United States.

Slavery was definitely on the upswing in the southern slave states of America. Between 1850 and 1860 the United States showed an increase in the number of human slaves by almost three quarters of a million new slaves added. Prices of slaves increased in this decade. From 1850 to 1860 there was a 23 percent increase in the number of slaves in the United States.[11] Slavery was growing by impressive numbers in the slave states of the United States. It was a growing institution and to be viable it needed continued expansion into the western frontier. Without this expansion slavery was landlocked in its present, confined states. Like any cancer, slavery needed to keep growing, it needed to keep opening into new lands. The congressional slave state delegations had managed to steamroll the legal apparatus in the United States and voted the harshest of measures against runaway slaves. The beast needed to be fed by opening these new territories on the western frontier to this monstrous institution. When any slave state senator or congressman did not vote in lockstep with those in the slave delegation, such as Senator Thomas Hart Benton, they were quickly removed from office. Abraham Lincoln wrote a remarkable letter in August of 1855 to his friend Joshua F. Speed, a slave owner in Kentucky. Lincoln wrote, "You say if Kansas fairly votes herself a free state, as a Christian you will rather rejoice at it. All decent slaveholders *talk* that way; and I do not doubt their candor. But they never *vote* that way. Although in a private letter, or conversation, you will express your preference that Kansas shall be free, you would vote for no man for congress who would say the same thing publicly. No such man could be elected from any district in a slave-state. You think Stringfellow & Co ought to be hung; and yet, at the next presidential election you will vote for the exact type and representative of Stringfellow. The slave-breeders and slave-traders are a small odious and detested class, among you; and yet in politics, they dictate the course of all of you, and are as completely your masters, as you are the master of your own negroes."[12]

It was only when the freedom seekers and abolitionists on the western frontier made the slavers pay dearly for the loss of their human property that the beast was finally slowed down. Slavery was defeated for the time being until the slave states began to leave the Union. Numbers of slave escapes are always hard to determine. Harrison Trexler in his book *Slavery in Missouri 1804–1865* quoted an undated newspaper article of the *St. Louis Daily Intelligencer*. That newspaper article stated that after the Kansas-Nebraska Act of 1854 was passed 10 slaves escaped in Missouri for every one before that act was passed.[13] We do know that more than 41,000 bondspersons escaped slavery in Missouri between 1860 and 1863, a figure of almost 30 percent of the total number of slaves in Missouri in 1860.[14] We can rightly figure a number of them joined the Union Army and that a good number were taken by their masters out of the state of Missouri to points further south. But we also must figure that thousands of bondspersons escaped to freedom to northern states and cities like Chicago and to Canada. Also, a great number of these escaping bondspersons stayed in Kansas as by 1870 the Jayhawker state had a Black population of over 17,000.[15] Only 11 years before the Kansas Territory had not allowed any free Blacks to even live in the state.[16] This loss of bondspersons was a huge blow to the slave economy of Missouri, a blow from which the state never recovered. In southwest Iowa just across the border from Missouri, Amity College in College Springs was closed because so many students left to serve in the Union Army. The buildings of this college were used to house the flood of fugitive slaves from Missouri.[17]

In this book the purpose has been to detail as many freedom escapes as possible along the liberty line on the western frontier of the United States. It would be impossible to describe every one of the thousands of escapes. However, it was our purpose to give the reader a sampling of how these escapes occurred and under what circumstances they occurred. Sometimes we had a few words from a slave advertisement, other times there was more of a complete narrative of the event. We tried to use as many accounts from the escaping bondspersons as possible and always gave, when there was a choice, the bondsperson's version of events or other Blacks who knew of the escape situation.

After much study of the conditions, in the slave states of Arkansas and Missouri there appears to have been no organized white Underground Railroad efforts. On occasion whites in these slave states offered assistance to the escaping bondspersons. However, more often than not it was free Blacks and their enslaved brethren who would give the escaping bondspersons aid and comfort in their escape attempts. The act of avoiding patrollers and other efforts to get out of the slave states and to move on down the line to freedom was mostly due to the individual efforts of the fleeing bondspersons. As is the case in situations like this very often the first step is the hardest step to take in the journey to freedom. As noted by Henry Bibb's quote at the beginning of this chapter, the bondspersons often had to leave family, friends and familiar surroundings and never got the opportunity to see these family members or friends or familiar surroundings again. And for this reason the bondspersons attempting to escape deserve most of the credit in their endeavor to find freedom.

The territory of Kansas was one of the hardest areas to escape from or through for the bondspersons in the United States but it became one of the most popular on the western frontier. Because of the shooting war going on between the pro-slavery and anti-slavery forces in Kansas the fleeing bondspersons had to try and escape across a war zone. Kansas had a number of reservations for Native Americans. Because almost all the "Indian Agents" put in these areas by the United States government were from southern slave holding states, these agents didn't want to see their reservations become hiding places for the escaping bondspersons. So, the fugitive slaves had to not only avoid getting caught up in a shooting war but great portions of the territory were off limits because they were on reservations for Native Americans where they might be captured. Also, career criminals like Jacob Herd, William Quantrill, Russ Hinds and the McGee brothers roamed the Kansas territory and the states of Missouri and Iowa looking to kidnap escaping fugitives so as to sell them in other slave-holding areas at a great profit.

Also, there were great distances that had to be endured on the western frontier. The land was sparsely settled and getting food and water could be a big problem. The more densely settled eastern portions of the United States offered more chances to find the necessities of life. The territories of Kansas, Nebraska and western Iowa had to be crossed by the bondspersons with few settlements. To the eager slave hunters this wide open country offered more chances for capture. Fortunately for the bondspersons by the mid to late 1850s Kansas, Nebraska and Iowa had a number of abolitionists more than willing to aid the escaping bondspersons at great peril to themselves.

Probably one of the most under-appreciated factors by chroniclers of the Underground Railroad in understanding the success or failure of escaping bondspersons was the amount of money they had with them when they escaped. The escaping freedom seekers that had money could often expect success in their attempt. However, the lack of money could often predict the defeat of any freedom attempt. Larry Gara said in his book *Liberty Line*, "Many people were reluctant or indifferent about returning runaway slaves."[18] If the freedom seeker had money with them for a meal or to pay to be ferried across a major river this could be enough to keep the free person from turning the bondsperson in for a reward. Oftentimes these bondspersons were greatly overcharged and it didn't take long for their travel funds to be depleted. However, money could buy forged travel papers and tickets on steamship lines, meals and countless other travel items.

Henry Bibb was a man who had tremendous intelligence and instincts about the world he lived in. He seemed to know just the right thing to do even if he had never been in the situation before. In his first attempt to escape from slavery he saved his money for the journey. He bought a new suit that he never wore until he was on his freedom route. This way, of course, his master had no idea how to accurately describe what Henry was wearing, which was one of the mainstays of the slave advertisements. Henry was a mulatto and knew that if he boarded the steamboat to Cincinnati he would do best to board the ship at dusk. He kept away from the lights, knowing his mulatto features would make it hard to distinguish him as a fugitive slave. While on board the steamship Henry spied a deckhand getting out of a hammock to go to work on his shift. Henry asked him if he could sleep in the hammock and the deck-hand said that he could, for 25 cents.[19] Henry gladly paid the sum and in this way was able to hide in plain sight on the steamship. However, the key here is that Henry had the 25 cents that provided him with a hiding place. When Henry was planning his flight to freedom there would have been no way he could have foreseen how important that 25 cents would be in his escape plot. Having never been on a steamship before Henry had no way of knowing the importance of hiding in that hammock. But because he had the money he was able to pull off this ruse and when everyone else had left the steamship in that Ohio port city Henry got up from his hammock and coolly walked off the ship.

Many times Underground Railroad stations couldn't escort bondspersons to the next site but they would give them money to help them on their journey. In Benjamin Drew's book *The Refuge: A North-side "View of Slavery"* and other interviews with successful escaping bondspersons a number of them stated they landed in Canada with only a small amount of money. This of course would imply that they began their journey north to freedom with a larger amount of cash and that this money was used to buy the necessities of travel.

The great historian John Hope Franklin has written that most of the escapees from slavery were young Black males in their teens or 20s. Almost three fourths of the advertised runaway slaves were of this gender and age in the years prior to the Civil War.[20] As we have stated before many of these runaway attempts were not for permanent freedom. Most of the time these runaway attempts were for temporary situations: visiting a loved one on another plantation, avoidance of punishment, just wanting to get away for a short period of time or to avoid certain work periods.

However, one wonders if the bondspersons who were successful in achieving permanent freedom, such as escapes to Canada or Mexico or to certain northern cities, were not successful in some part because they were able to accumulate money before their escape attempt. This money would be used to buy food, pay to be ferried across rivers and all the other unforeseen expenses that traveling across great distances can produce.

Some Underground Railroad stations on the western frontier such as Lawrence, K.T. and Tabor, Civil Bend, Denmark and Salem in Iowa would house, feed and then escort the bondsperson to the next station. Others would simply house and feed the bondspersons and the escapees were on their own to find the next stopping point. Of course some bondspersons managed to make it to freedom without using these stations at all. Having money would be very useful if the bondsperson, usually without the aid of a map and only following the North Star, was lost or was not able to make connections with sympathetic farmers. Since Kansas, Nebraska, and Iowa for all practical purposes didn't allow free or slave Black people to live in these areas at this time it was very unlikely that the escaping bondspersons could find aid and comfort from any Black person. Although in Iowa Black people like John Williamson, the Garner family and the Pyles family did yeoman's service in helping escaping bondspersons, the truth of the matter was that there were so few Black people living in these areas that help from this quarter was unlikely.

Although opportunities for slaves to earn money were very limited there were some slim chances. Relatives who worked as wait staff on steamboats or in upscale restaurants and hotels—be they slave or free—often received tips that could be given to relatives who wished to escape. Slaves who could have businesses such as basket-making, food preparations or other such enterprises could accumulate cash. However, this was dependant on the "master's" wishes and the number of hours worked. If one was working 12 to 14 hours a day it would be doubtful these opportunities would be realized.

If a bondsperson worked as a skilled laborer such as a leather worker and maker of shoes and saddles, they would often receive tips if they did outstanding work. The same could be said of carpenters, cabinet makers, musicians, blacksmiths, wagon or wheel-makers or other such craftspeople. The masters of these craftspeople were always paid first but many times the white customers would "tip" the slaves for very fine work done. Even fieldworkers were sometimes given money when they did outstanding work. On the hemp plantations of Missouri some more progressive masters paid on a "piece work" basis that allowed slave workers who produced more opportunities to earn cash. Thus, the accumulation of a travel fund could mean the difference between success or failure for an escapee whose main goal was permanent freedom in Canada or Mexico.

Even if the bondsperson escaped on a spur of the moment situation with no cash reserves, opportunities to make money could sometimes be obtained on the road, such as bartering labor for food. There were some instances where the bondspersons worked all or part of the way to freedom by stopping to work. This, of course, was very dangerous if slave hunters were in the neighborhood.

Henry Bibb found how difficult these employment opportunities could be when on the run. When he successfully escaped out of the deep slave south to Portsmouth, Ohio, he found himself out of money so he began working at the American Hotel in Portsmouth as a bellman at so much a month and tips. At the end of the month the hotel owner, probably realizing Henry was a fugitive slave, refused to pay him. Bibb worked himself out of the situation by receiving tips for the "free" boot shining he was to perform for each of the hotel guests. Bibb ended up making more from these tips than the salary the hotel owner was going to pay him.[21] Many of the bondspersons who escaped slavery from Missouri and Arkansas did so by using their employment on steamships and so needed little help from the white Underground Railroad until they reached Cincinnati or some other northern port city. However, those who traveled overland often paid for meals and other necessities but a number who escaped needed help from the white Underground Railroad in the north.

Living off the land is often a romantic notion but many whites or Blacks lacked the skills or equipment to be successful at this. Also, the great distances the bondspersons from the frontier had to travel overland, often a thousand miles, made this proposition a very difficult reality.

Larry Gara, in his ground-breaking book *Liberty Line: The Legend of the Underground Railroad*, first published in 1961, made the point that many bondspersons received little help from the white "Underground Railroad." He also pointed out that the white Underground Railroad was not as organized and was run in a more haphazard way than expressed by previous historians. However, in Gara's preface to his 1996 reprint edition he states, "Were I to write the book again, I would give more recognition to the abolitionists, many who risked a great deal to help escaping slaves."[22]

On the western frontier these white abolitionists made it possible for many of the bondspersons to successfully escape. However, this does not tell the whole story. Many bondspersons who, as stated before, worked on the steamships needed little help from the western frontier Underground Railroad and were more likely to be helped by free or fellow enslaved Blacks. Many of the bondspersons who worked long and extra hours to accumulate travel funds or who worked on their way to freedom needed only minimal help in escaping from slavery.

The runaway slave advertisements in the Missouri and Arkansas newspapers had many similarities. They would usually describe the bondspersons physical appearance, the clothes they were wearing when they escaped and any personality traits they might have that would make them stand out or any property such as a horse or firearm they might have obtained. Also, any possible destination, if known, would be stated, such as "Charles' wife was recently was sold to a master in Arkansas and he may be heading to that location."

There were several notable differences between the slave advertisements in Missouri and Arkansas. One of the most interesting was the fact that bondspersons in Arkansas were more likely to dress or act as if they were Native Americans. This obvious ruse was for a planned escape that would take them into the Indian Nations of what we now call Oklahoma. Since the Native American slave owners had the reputation of treating their bondspersons better this was an obvious destination for the slaves of Arkansas. The Seminoles in particular treaded their bondspersons more like tenant farmers than slaves. The Seminoles were often accused of "stealing" slaves from other environments but in reality a number of these bondspersons probably escaped into the Seminole territories for better treatment and a chance to accumulate property and gain advantage from their own labor. From the runaway slave advertisements in Missouri, we can see that this ruse of dressing like a Native American was used but not nearly to the extent to which it was attempted by Arkansas bondspersons.

Many times slaves would escape from an area such as Arkansas to a region like the Indian Nations. Their idea was that their present masters were very cruel. They would take their chances with a new "master." Once they were caught in the Indian Nations many times their old masters would not want to go to the expense of bringing them back and paying for the runaway's incarceration. Oftentimes the old masters would sell the runaway at a discount to save the expense of bringing them back to their original plantation. Thus the runaway would take the gamble with a new Native American master who had the reputation of promoting a more humane brand of slavery.

To the bondspersons of Arkansas and the Indian Nations wanting permanent freedom they many times were as likely to head southward into Mexico as they would go to the north into Canada. Although prior to 1850 and the passage of the brutal Fugitive Slave Act of 1850 some of the bondspersons from these areas may have headed to a northern city in the United States. Although the numbers of bondspersons in the Indian Nations probably never exceeded 8,000 or 9,000 it would appear as if the Cherokee bondspersons were more apt to head to the north, (although a number did look to the Rio Grande for freedom), while the Seminole, Creek, Choctaw and Chickasaw runaways seeking permanent freedom would many times head for the south into Mexico. It also may be noted that the Cherokee slaves seeking freedom might not only have wanted out of bondage but there is considerable likelihood they wanted to get away from the Cherokee civil war between the "Pins" and other Cherokee members. Oftentimes slaves would be killed by Pins as retribution for past murders of Pins or the pilfering of their property.

The path to freedom was often different in 1840 than in 1860. While many northerners thought it wrong in the 1840s for slaves to leave their masters, by the late 1850s many in the north felt the bondspersons were justified in leaving this horrible institution. While many of these people were not active on the Underground Railroad they would be more apt to look the other way if they saw a bondsperson escaping. They might be willing to feed an escaping bondsperson if they could be paid for the meal.

By the late 1850s the Missouri slave advertisements indicate that large groups of slaves were escaping; Arkansas slave advertisements did not reflect this phenomenon. It might be noted that the collection of Arkansas slave advertisements that have not been destroyed from the late 1850s were mostly sheriff's advertisements noting that runaways had been captured and that the slave owner would have to pay for their slaves' incarceration. It could be this was also happening in Arkansas, large number of slaves escaping in groups as in Missouri, but for whatever reason these advertisements did not survive to be microfilmed.

It should also be noted that even from the early slave advertisements in the 1840s and before in Arkansas it was not usual to see that an Arkansas slave had a firearm with them. In Missouri it was unusual for these early advertisements to note a runaway with a firearm but later advertisements from the 1850s noted this fact. Several reasons could be responsible for this. Arkansas even as a state had a reputation for being a lawless place filled with dangerous people and a rugged environment. The escaping bondsperson may have felt it prudent to take a firearm with them. Missouri, with three times the population, may have seemed a more settled area. However, after the Kansas territory opened in 1854 with all the violence in that territory the bondspersons from Missouri may have felt they needed firearms to protect themselves if they were passing through the area.

Mention of escapes by using steamboats as a means of travel was fairly common in both states in these advertisements and other articles and books. Most of the bondspersons of Arkansas and many in Missouri were immigrants to the states where they were held in slavery. The bondspersons many times had experience in traveling on steamships. Even if the fugitive bondsperson was escaping overland sometimes they would travel following the main rivers of the time — the Mississippi, Arkansas and Missouri Rivers. Most of the settlements were along these rivers and while the danger of being captured was greater so were the chances of finding food and water.

Very often the language of these slave advertisements included words like "fugitive slave" or other words to signify a law-breaker. We certainly feel that anyone held in bondage or anyone treated like a slave has every right to attempt to escape such a situation. There was a notion at this time in the world that determined that if one were to attempt to kidnap you into slavery or that if someone held you in a condition of slavery you had every right to use even deadly force to extricate yourself from that situation. Such laws didn't exist in the United States at that time however, this writer believes these escaping bondspersons had every right to exercise this right in freeing themselves or their spouses, children, family members, or friends from this horrible institution.

Considering the oral traditions of the Underground Railroad it is only natural that many legends have surfaced about the Underground Railroad on the western frontier. Many of the conductors were reluctant to write down anything about these escapes as they were doing something illegal. Anyone living in these states who has a secret hiding room in an older house usually has a story of these clandestine rooms being used to hide runaway slaves. However, a quick examination as to when the house or structure was built will usually put these stories to rest.

Because the phrase "underground" is used many people believed the escaping bondspersons traveled all the way to Canada via an underground tunnel! Many recognized sites on the Underground Railroad have tales of the area being laced by underground tunnels. However, these stories are just that — stories. In 1993 in Ohio 17 known Underground Railroad sites that were reputed to have underground tunnels for escape at these structures were examined using sophisticated equipment. No tunnels were found at any of these sites that had been known to house runaway bondspersons.[23]

In Tabor, Iowa, there had long been rumors that the town was honeycombed by underground tunnels. However, these rumors could quickly be put to rest. Most of these tall tales of underground tunnels honeycombing the town, especially through the town's spacious city park, said that these tunnels led to the houses of the leading townspeople and the college buildings. However, the college buildings were not built until well after the Civil War when the need for these tunnels was well past.

George Gaston's was one of Tabor's most involved citizens on the Underground Railroad. His granddaughter Etta stated there "never was a tunnel between ... my grandfather's G.B. Gaston's house or anywhere else for helping slaves escape."[24] Historical architects and historians from the State Historical Society of Iowa and officials from the National Park Service have tried to verify any traces of tunnels in Tabor or at the Todd house but it is obvious none ever existed. This author has gone through the some 2,000 surviving documents at the Todd House Museum and elsewhere on Tabor's Underground Railroad days and has found no mention of any tunnels of any kind. These papers do mention hiding bondspersons in spare bedrooms, attics, basements or outbuildings but never in tunnels. However, this does not prevent newspapers at much later dates from running outrageous and inaccurate stories of underground tunnels, always with no verifiable proof of their existence.[25]

The home of the Rev. John Todd. This was the scene of many Underground Railroad escapes. The National Park Service and various state historical societies try to provide advice on maintaining sites such as this with historical architects. With sophisticated equipment they try and find artifacts from the Underground Railroad days on the grounds around these sites. They also try and detect any tunnels on the property. So far the Todd House has yielded no indication there were ever any tunnels near the house or in the multi-acre park across the street from it (courtesy Todd House Museum and Tabor Historical Society, Tabor, Iowa).

Fiction writers are often guilty of doing insufficient research or no research at all and perpetuating the myths of underground tunnels. One author even used Tabor as a backdrop for a ridiculous story of the town being honeycombed with underground tunnels.

Not far from Tabor, Iowa, in Nebraska City, Nebraska, is a place that over the years has claimed to be an Underground Railroad stopping place at John Brown's Cave. This cave at times has been expanded into a tunnel so that tourists can go through it. Now the John Brown Cave is attached to the Mayhew Cabin. The Mayhew Cabin has great historical value. Allen and Barbara Mayhew, residents of this rustic log cabin before the Civil War, housed runaway bondspersons.

Barbara Mayhew's brother John Kagy was a major player in the Underground Railroad and the abolitionist activities on the western frontier and helped to build the cabin. Their father Abraham Kagy, who had a place a few miles outside of Nebraska City, was also a well-known figure in the abolitionist and Underground Railroad movement in the area. Nebraska City was an important place for escaping bondspersons on the western frontier as it was the major crossing point of the Missouri River into western Iowa.

However, the John Brown Cave or tunnel has a very checkered history. Again, this author has never been able to find any credible mention of the cave or tunnel in the literature of the time as a hiding place for runaway bondspersons. A newspaper article appearing on April 14, 1890, in the *Nebraska City News* states that the so-called "John Brown's cave" was actually used for a wine cellar. E.F. Mayhew, the son of Allen and Barbara Mayhew, made this claim and as the Mayhews grew grapes and made wine this seems to be a credible story. Mayhew even stated that many sightseers to the area who thought they were seeing "John Brown's cave" were being "gulled."[26]

However, there were also unsubstantiated legends among the bondspersons. At some point these events probably did happen, but not in the numbers proposed in these tales. There were stories of ropes being tied between two trees on routes taken by the slave patrollers who were looking for escaping slaves. These patrollers would then be "clothes lined" by this and knocked off their horses. Other stories were told of slave patrollers with their horses' tails being tied together and thus unable to properly chase the escaping bondsperson.

Writing about the escaping bondspersons, the liberty line or the Underground Railroad is often difficult because of the sometimes implied or overt racism displayed. Many white participants of the Underground Railroad saw themselves to be the main players in the saga and the escaping bondspersons to be mere fringe participants. Some abolitionists at the time even advocated the racial superiority of the white race. One of the most notable of these incidents was when Dr. Doy of Kansas refused to eat at the same table as the bondspersons he was trying to help liberate.[27]

Although Frederick Douglas' autobiography sold well before the Civil War interest in the Underground Railroad and the brave exploits of the escaping bondspersons waned after the Civil War. Books about the battles and the white participants of that epic struggle captured the imagination of the United States. The stories of the Black soldiers in the Civil War or the struggles of escaping bondspersons before the Civil War were not of interest to a majority of Americans right after that epic struggle.

In 1898, Wilbur H. Siebert wrote his remarkable book *The Underground Railroad from Slavery to Freedom* and somewhat rekindled interest in that institution. One the one hand as a historian Siebert is to be congratulated for getting these stories from white abolitionists before they died. On the other hand Siebert is to be chastised for not getting the story from the Black participants on the liberty line. In Siebert's book the Underground Railroad is an almost completely white undertaking with little assistance from the escaping bondspersons.

However, was Siebert just a reflection of his times? *Plessy v. Fergurson* was passed in 1896, setting up the American version of apartheid—separating the races with the phrase "separate but equal."[28] The races were separated but nothing was ever equal. The so-called "Jim Crow" laws were in effect. The frightening thing about this period is that it was often the federal government and the intelligentsia of America that were supporting American apartheid. Woodrow Wilson as president of Princeton University put stumbling blocks so that Black students couldn't apply for admission. He was an admirer of pre–Civil War slavery and the Ku Klux Klan. The federal government began the practice of not hiring Blacks to governmental positions during Wilson's first term. Wilson even segregated the nation's capital. He also made sure the federal government didn't intervene in the various states from supporting segregationist "Jim Crow" laws.[29]

During the period after the Civil War Englishman Herbert Spencer was a best-selling author and the most famous and most influential philosopher in the English-speaking world of his time. Spencer coined the phrase "survival of the fittest" and espoused ideas that some races were inferior to others. Other writers and philosophers of this era wrote of the idea of racial superiority. Racism was out in the open and was institutionalized in the schools. In the school book *History of the Phillipines* [sic] published in 1899, Uncle Sam is on the front cover of this book balancing some half-human, half-animal-like, dark-skinned creatures for the world to see. These dark-skinned somewhat humanoid forms are trying to weigh Uncle Sam down but he will not let them. The message here is obviously about the supposed racial superiority. This wasn't some racist pamphlet distributed by the Ku Klux Klan in the deep south but was a school textbook published by a firm in Chicago, Illinois, meant to go all over the United States both north and south![30]

What was also disturbing about the racism of this time was that it wasn't just uneducated white people promoting this point of view but it was also the educated white establishment who espoused this theme of apartheid and racial inferiority. Unfortunately some of those who wrote of the Underground Railroad activities seemed to support these racist viewpoints. The white abolitionists sometimes even wrote as if the escaping fugitive slaves were getting in the way of the narrative, not understanding the important work the white conductors were doing. In most of these accounts the whites writing of these escapes never understood that their part of a particular escape was just a mere fraction of the complete journey, sometimes over one thousand miles, the fugitive bondsperson had to make.

Some of the white historians during this period who wrote of the Underground Railroad were of the opinion that no Black person would have ever escaped without the help of a white person. This idea was espoused by William Elsey Connelley, the long time head of the Kansas State Historical Society. Connelley was writing about the raid on the Morgan Walker place in Missouri by Quantrill and the unsuspecting Quakers. At the very end two of the Quakers are hiding out and one of them is very badly wounded. A bondsmen stumbles upon their camp and discovers they have stolen a hog and a horse. The one Quaker pleaded with the Black man to get a wagon and said that the Quakers will take him to Kansas with them. When the Black man tells his "master" of their hiding place Connelley lashes out in his book at the bondsman saying, "his stupidity and the instinct of his people in their servitude made him decide ... treachery to those in distress who would give him liberty."

What Connelley doesn't seem to realize is that the bondsman could have easily been accused of the robbery of the horse and hog. The Black man was already sent looking for the missing hog. Also, news of the raid had spread all over the white and Black worlds of western Missouri. The plan Quantrill had talked the Quakers into was idiotic, it was driven by greed and its overall lack of common sense was breathtaking. Why would this Black man want to throw his lot in with this group that had absolutely no chance of success? However, apparently Connelley thought the only chance this Black man or any Black person would have for freedom was to throw their lot in with a group of white abolitionists no matter how badly their plans were thought out.[31]

In Cecil Turton's well-done, unpublished master's thesis, he writes that two bondsmen escaped from Westport, Missouri, with horses near the Kansas border. After the two got over the Kansas line they came into contact with some white abolitionists. The abolitionists gave them employment harvesting the wheat crop. The owner of the two bondsmen found his escapees. However, Turton calls the bondsmen "ignorant" for taking employment so close to their Missouri home. However, Turton knew nothing of the details of the escape or what the bondsmen had been told by the abolitionists in Kansas. When the bondsmen "master" tried to take them back to Missouri the Kansas abolitionists blocked them and didn't even allow the Missourian to take back their horses. The escape was pulled off successfully and the reason for Turton's derogatory name-calling is puzzling and disappointing.[32] What is even more bewildering is that Wilbur H. Siebert was Turton's advisor on this work and why didn't Siebert spot this unnecessary insulting language?

The WPA Federal Writer's Project was a wonderful concept in trying to get the slaves' point of view in the 1930s before these former bondspersons passed away. However, mostly white writers were used and many had no knowledge of Black history or even knowledge of the Civil War. Many follow-up questions were missed. These interviewers for the most part were writers and not historians. Some wrote the articles as if they were doing a fluff piece for a newspaper's Sunday supplement. In some cases it was obvious the interviewer had a racial agenda. Hannah Allen, a former bondswoman, was interviewed in Fredericktown, Missouri. The interviewer said, "Being a Negro, she naturally does not take life seriously...."[33] Unfortunately, there are other stereotyped comments by these interviewers. However, many of the Arkansas FWP interviews were well done, especially those by a Black man, Samuel S. Taylor.

Fortunately, in 1961 historian Larry Gara wrote his ground-breaking book *The Liberty Line: The Legend of the Underground Railroad*. He forced historians to take another look at some of the legends of the Underground Railroad. He especially encouraged historians to realize that the main participants in the Underground Railroad saga were not the white abolitionists but the courageous bondspersons whose stories had been in some cases long ignored.

Chapter Notes

Chapter 1

1. Under its bill of rights, the Lecompton Constitution, Section 23, stated that free Negroes were not allowed to live in the territory of Kansas. Section VII allowed slavery. There were three separate votes on the Lecompton Constitution which allowed slavery. They were on December 21, 1857, January 4, 1858, and August 2, 1858. On the final ballot the Lecompton Constitution was voted out. Finally, in October of 1859 the Wyandotte Constitution was voted in by an almost two to one margin. The Wyandotte Constitution did not allow for slavery. Punishment and imprisonment was allowed in the Kansas Territory for the mere possession of abolitionist material under the Lecompton Constitution. The Kansas Territory was following most other slave states in not allowing even abolitionist literature to be distributed in the state without hefty penalties. Both the Lecompton and Wyandotte Constitutions are located at the Kansas State Historical Society online. Paul Finkelman's *Slavery in the Courtroom: An Annotated Bibliography of American Cases* (Washington, D.C.: Library of Congress, 1985, 164–165) tells of the case *United States v. Crandall*. Reuben Crandall was a physician from the north who moved to Washington, D.C., in 1835 when slavery was allowed in the District. While unpacking his belongings someone asked to read an abolitionist pamphlet he saw among Crandall's things. Across the pamphlet was written "please read & circulate." The borrower left the pamphlet at a shop and forgot about it. The pamphlet was found and was traced back to Crandall. Among the five counts Crandall was charged with was "the intent to excite sedition and insurrection among slaves." Francis Scott Key, author of the "Star Spangled Banner," was the prosecuting attorney at the trial. Crandall spent eight months in jail but a jury found him innocent and he was freed from his Kafka-like experience.
2. Allan Nevins, *Ordeal of Union, Vol. 2: A House Dividing* (New York: Scribner's, 1947), 153–154.
3. Richard J. Hinton, *New York Times*, June 10, 1899. Review of Thomas W. Higginson's book. Hinton was a veteran of the border warfare in Kansas.
4. John Armstrong, *Reminiscences of Slave Days in Kansas*. This information was gathered by Zu Adams, an employee of the Kansas State Historical Society, in 1895. Reminiscences located in the Kansas State Historical Society.
5. Document in the Kansas State Historical Society detailing the life of John E. Stewart. It is believed that Stewart wrote this document somewhere around 1856. Hereafter cited as "Stewart document."
6. John Todd, *Early Settlement and Growth of Western Iowa or Reminiscences* (Des Moines, Iowa: Historical Department of Iowa, 1906), 55. The page numbers used here are from the version of this book reproduced by the Tabor Historical Society. Hereafter cited as "Todd book."
7. Cecil Turton, unpublished master's thesis, "The Underground Railroad in Kansas, Nebraska, and Iowa" (Ohio State University, 1935). The thesis was approved by Ohio State University professor Wilbur H. Siebert, pioneer writer and researcher of the Underground Railroad. 36. Hereafter cited as "Turton."
8. Reminiscences of Mrs. James Burnett Abbott of De Soto, Kansas, on September 1, 1895. This information was gathered by Zu Adams, an employee of the Kansas State Historical Society. Located in Kansas State Historical Society. Richard B. Sheridan, editor and compiler, *Freedom's Crucible: The Underground Railroad in Lawrence and Douglas County, Kansas, 1854–1865: A Reader* (Lawrence, Kansas: Division of Continuing Education, University of Kansas, 1998), 37–39. Hereafter cited as "Sheridan."
9. Wilbur H. Siebert, *The Underground Railroad from Slavery to Freedom* (1898; reprint, Mineola, New York: Dover Publications, 2006), 347. Hereafter cited as "Siebert."
10. "Letter from a Border Ruffian," *St. Louis Intelligencer*, Jan. 22, 1856. Reprinted in the *Burlington* (Iowa) *Hawk Eye* newspaper, date unknown, author's collection.
11. *Herald of Freedom* (newspaper Lawrence, Kansas Territory), June 6, 1855.
12. Letter to Dear Friends from O.E.L. (Learnard) written May 23, 1856. Located at the Kansas State Historical Society. Hereafter cited as "Learnard letter."
13. Transcription of the David Rice Atchison speech made shortly before Lawrence, Kansas Territory, was sacked on May 21, 1856. This resides in the Kansas State Historical Society archives. According to a note on the top of page made later by R. (Richard) J. (Josiah) Hinton (author of *John Brown and His Men*), "this report was made for me by or under the direction of Lt. Gov. (Dr.) Root (Joseph Pomeroy Root, subsequently elected the state's first lieutenant governor under the Wyandotte Constitution), who was a prisoner, heard & reported the speech."

14. Learnard letter.
15. South Carolina "Palmetto Guards" banner and its history, located in the Kansas State Historical Society's archives.
16. Jay Monaghan, *Civil War on the Western Border 1854–1865* (New York: Bonanza Books, 1955), 56–58. Hereafter cited as "Monaghan."
17. Letter to Eli Thayer, Esq. from George Washington Brown on June 4, 1856 while Brown was being held prisoner by pro-slavery men.
18. *Burlington* (Iowa) *Hawk Eye* undated newspaper article, author's collection.
19. Pro-slavery banner in the Kansas State Historical Society archives used by pro-slavery men on the raft where they put the Reverend Pardee Butler. Oswald Garrison Villard, *John Brown 1800–1859: A Biography Fifty Years After* (Boston and New York: Houghton Mifflin Riverside Press Cambridge, 1910), 110. Hereafter cited as "Villard." The Greeley mentioned on the flag was of course well-known Eastern abolitionist Horace Greeley. Greeley was the long-time editor of the *New York Tribune*, the most influential anti-slavery newspaper in America.
20. Letter to F.G. Adams from Isaac Maris dated July 22, 1895. F.G. Adams was employed by the Kansas State Historical Society and requested information from Maris concerning the activity of escaping slaves in Kansas.
21. Monaghan, 17.
22. Letter to Thaddeus Hyatt from John E. Stewart, Wakarusa, Kansas, dated December 20, 1859. Hereafter noted as "Stewart letter."
23. Stewart document.
24. Stewart letter.
25. Sheridan, 47.
26. Stewart letter.
27. Author's notes on a visit to the Adair Cabin in Osawatomie, Kansas, and a tour by the site's able administrator Grady Atwater.
28. Letter to the Rev. S.S. Jocelyn from S.L. Adair, Osawatomie, K.T., dated October 15, 1855.
29. William Cutler, *History of the State of Kansas* (Chicago: Andreas' Western Historical Publishing, 1882–1883), 565.
30. Letter to Zu Adams from S.L. Adair dated September 16, 1895. Zu Adams was an employee of the Kansas State Historical Society who was gathering information about the "slavery days" in Kansas.
31. Villard, 262.
32. Letter to Amos Lawrence from Thaddeus Hyatt dated February 11, 1857, telling of poor economic conditions in Kansas due to the drought and its consequences. Letter from Ladies of Orange, N.J., to Sir (Thaddeus Hyatt) dated October 20, 1856. Telling of aid they had raised to be sent to Kansas. These were but two of the many letters sent to Thaddeus Hyatt telling of poor conditions in Kansas for settlers and for the aid that had been raised for them. In 1860 Kansas suffered another severe drought which required the attention of Thaddeus Hyatt and his National Kansas Committee. Letters from S.C. Pomeroy to Thaddeus Hyatt dated November 2, 5 and December 3, 1860. Also, letter from A. Venard M.D. to Thaddeus Hyatt dated October 3, 1860. These were a few of the many letters Hyatt received on the severe drought of 1860 and the desperate conditions it created among the settlers, including cholera and malnutrition. All these letters reside in the Kansas State Historical Society.

33. *New York Times*, July 27, 1901. Obituary of Thaddeus Hyatt. Hereafter cited as "Hyatt, NYT."
34. Hyatt, NYT. Edgar Langsdorf, "Thaddeus Hyatt in Washington Jail," Kansas Historical Quarterly, August, 1940 (Vol. 9, No. 3), 228–239.
35. *Ibid.*
36. Letter to Gen. Thomas W. Higginson in Worcester, Massachusetts, from Sam Tappan, Lawrence, Kansas Territory, dated January 24, 1858.
37. Martha Parker and Betty Laird, *Soil of Our Souls: History of the Clinton Lake Area Communities* (Overbrook, Kansas: Parker and Laid Enterprises, 1980), 75.
38. John Doy, *The Narrative of John Doy of Lawrence Kansas: A Plain Unvarnished Talk* (New York: Thomas Holman, 1860), 20. Hereafter cited as "Doy."
39. Richard Cordley, "Lizzie and the Underground Railroad," *Pioneer Days in Kansas* (New York: Pilgrim Press, 1903), 122–136.
40. Letter to F.B. Sanborn, Esq. from E(Ephraim) Nute of Lawrence, K.T., dated March 22, 1859. Letter located in the Kansas State Historical Society.
41. Turton, 42.
42. Letter to unknown from Ephraim Nute of Lawrence, K.T., dated February 24, 1859. Hereafter noted as "Nute letter."
43. Doy, 93–94.
44. Turton, 42.
45. Nute letter.
46. Letter to Friend (Franklin B.) Sanborn from E.B. Whitman of Lawrence, K.T., dated April 30, 1858.
47. Letter to Zu Adams, an employee of the Kansas State Historical Society, from Thos. R. Bayne Williamstown, Kansas, dated September 11, 1895. The letter was in response to Miss Adams request for information about "slavery days" in Kansas. Bayne had been a slave owner and also stated, "the northern people don't now under Stand what Slavery was and never will."
48. Reminiscence of Marcus Lindsay Freeman, a former bondsman from the Kansas Territory. Freeman was a bondsman of Thomas Bayne. The paper was prepared by Zu or F.G. Adams in 1895. Located in the Kansas State Historical Society.
49. Albert Castel, *Civil War in Kansas: Reaping the Whirlwind* (Lawrence: University Press of Kansas, 1997), 42. Originally published as: *A Frontier State at War: Kansas 1861–1865* (Ithaca, NY: Cornell University Press, 1958). The new publication has a new preface and textual corrections. Hereafter cited as "Castel, *Kansas*."
50. Letter to George L. Stearns from James Montgomery, Mound City, K.T., dated November 27, 1860.
51. Turton, 35.
52. Letter to Dear Friend (George L. Stearns) from Dr. C.R. Jennison, Mound City, K.T., dated November 28, 1860.
53. Doy, 26.
54. *Ibid.*, 37–38.
55. *Ibid.*, 51–52.
56. Letter to unknown from Ephraim Nute, Lawrence, K.T., dated February 14, 1859.
57. Nute letter.
58. Sheridan, 23. Mr. James B. Abbott, leader of the group that freed Dr. Doy, read his account of the Doy affair on January 15, 1889, at a meeting of the Kansas State Historical Society.
59. Doy, 106–107.
60. *Ibid.*, 110–116.
61. Holland Wheeler, "Quantrill a Suspicious Loafer," *Kansas Historical Collection*, VII (1901–1902), 224–226.

62. Letter to H.V. Beeson from Judge Thomas Robert, Paola, Kansas, May 16, 1881. This letter is in the book of William Elsey Connelley, *Quantrill and the Border Wars* (New York: Pageant Book, 1956), 87. Connelley was the long time secretary of the Kansas State Historical Society. The Connelley book was originally published by the Torch Press in Cedar Rapids, Iowa, in 1910. Connelley was an extremely active director of the KSHS. This is a very important book as Connelley reproduced much primary historical material on this subject that has been lost or misplaced. According to historian Albert Castel, Connelley received much of his data from W.W. Scott, a schoolmate of Quantrill's who was going to write a book on him but just got to the stage of gathering the material for the book before Scott passed away. Connelley came into possession of the material and added many interviews and other helpful material. This information was published in this book. Unfortunately much of Scott's original material has been lost, but fortunately it was reproduced in Connelley's book. Hereafter sited as "Connelley."

63. Sheridan, 16.

64. William A. Settle, Jr., *Jesse James: Was His Name or Fact and Fiction Concerning the Careers of the NOTORIOUS JAMES BROTHERS of Missouri* (Columbia: University of Missouri Press, 1966), 26–27.

65. John P. Burch, *Charles W. Quantrell: A True History of His Guerrilla Warfare on the Missouri and Kansas Border During the Civil War of 1861 to 1865, as Told By Captain Harrison Trow* (Vega, Texas: J.P. Burch, 1923), 21

66. Margaret Wulfhuhle, "Kanwaka," in Martha Parker and Betty Laird, *Soil of Our Souls: History of the Clinton Lake Area Communities* (Overbrook, Kansas: Parker and Laird, 1980), 81–82.

67. Connelley, 128–120. Duane Schultz, *Quantrill's War: The Life and Times of William Clarke Quantrill, 1837–1865* (New York: St. Martin's, 1996), 53–54.

68. Connelley, 117.

69. Connelley, 117–121.

70. *Ibid*.

71. Albert Castel, *William Clarke Quantrill: His Life and Times* (New York: Fredrick Fell, 1962), 33. Hereafter cited as "Castel, *Quantrill*."

72. Connelley, 110. Sheridan, 20.

73. Castel, *Quantrill*, 35.

74. Connelley, 140–143.

75. Letter to Dear Friends Redpath & Hinton from L.F. Parsons, Osawatomie K.T., Dec. 1859. Located in the Kansas State Historical Society. Both Richard J. Hinton and James Redpath wrote biographies of Brown. In this letter Parsons, who had fought with Brown in Kansas, noted that both had requested information from him about Brown, probably for use in their books.

76. Edward E. Leslie, *The Devil Knows How to Ride: The True Story of William Clarke Quantrill and His Confederate Raiders* (New York: Random House, 1996), 71–72.

77. Connelley, 149–152.

78. *Ibid.*, 157.

79. Castel, *Quantrill*, 38. Connelley's book, written in a more genteel time, states on page 158 that Lipsey "fell from the porch with a charge of balls in his thigh." Castel's book, published in 1962, was permitted to correctly say Lipsey was hit in the "groin."

80. Connelley, 174–175.

81. *Ibid.*, 176.

82. Letter to Quintus E. Atkins, Esq., Racine, Wisconsin, from John Todd, Tabor, Iowa, Jan. 19, 1857. Todd reported that on the morning of January 18, 1857, the temperature was 28 degrees below zero and that the year before he had recorded a daytime temperature of 24 degrees below zero. The Springdale Quakers from Iowa would have been living in the Hawkeye state at that time and must have been aware of what the December–January temperatures could potentially be and the fact that at those temperatures traveling at that time would have been deadly to everyone involved.

83. Sheridan, 53.

84. Turton, 30.

85. *Doniphan* (K.T.) *Crusader of Freedom*, May 17, 1858.

86. Gray's Doniphan County History (Bendena, Kansas: Royalcroft, 1905), Part 2, Chapter V, 56. Extracts from an address of Daniel Webster Wilder at Wathena, Kansas, July 4, 1884. This custom still exists in Doniphan County, Kansas, as the author has eaten square Free-State, Black Republican pie in Doniphan County.

87. Letter to George L. Stearns from Joseph Gardner, May 29, 1860.

88. Sheridan, 61–66,144–149.

Chapter 2

1. *Manchester, England, Examiner Time*, August 5, 1854. This newspaper is part of the University of Detroit's Mercy Black Abolitionist Archive. It is protected under copyright laws.

2. Frederic Bancroft, *Slave-Trading in the Old South* (Baltimore, Maryland: J.H. Furst, 1931), 136–137.

3. *Missouri Slave Narratives: from the Federal Writers' Project, 1936–1938* (Bedford, Massachusetts: Applewood Books in cooperation with the Library of Congress). The Library of Congress reproduced these interviews exactly as originally typed by the Federal Writers' Project (FWP) interviewers. These interviews were of still living former slaves living in the state of Missouri from 1936 to 1938. Interview with Harriet Casey by J. Tom Miles in Fredericktown, Missouri, 74. Hereafter this interview will be noted as "*Missouri FWP*, Casey." The reader may wish to consult the preface for a further explanation of the various sources of these Federal Writers' Project Slave Interviews used in this books. Hereafter any interviews taken from Missouri in the Applewood Books will be noted as "*Missouri FWP*."

4. Doy, 59–61.

5. Federal Census of 1840, Federal Census of 1850, Federal Census of 1860, Section on population.

6. Harrison Anthony Trexler, *Slavery in Missouri, 1804–1865* (Baltimore, Maryland: John Hopkins Press, 1914), 12. Hereafter cited as "Trexler."

7. *Missouri FWP*, 24. Interview with Charles Baker about his mother Jane Baker who grew up in slavery and died at age 103. Charles Baker was the brother to Dayse Baker, the principal of what was known at that time as the "colored" Douglass School in Farmington, Missouri.

8. *Missouri FWP*, 6. Interview with Betty Abernathy in Cape Girardeau County, Missouri.

9. Benjamin Drew, *The Refugee: A North-Side View of Slavery* (Reprint, Reading, Massachusetts: Addison-Wesley, 1969), 124. Originally published in 1856 by John P. Jewett and Co., Cleveland, Ohio. Hereafter cited as "Drew."

10. Fugitive Slave Act (1850), Sections 1, 2, 3, 4.
11. *Ibid.*, Section 5.
12. *The Liberator*, July 19, 1861.
13. Stanley W. Campbell, *The Slave Catchers: Enforcement of the Fugitive Slave Law, 1850–1860* (Chapel Hill: University of North Carolina Press, 1970), 157. Hereafter cited as "Campbell."
14. *Ibid.*, 42.
15. *Ibid.*, 188.
16. Fugitive Slave Act (1850), Section 7.
17. Missouri Statesman, October 24, 1851.
18. "Trial of Henry W. Allen U.S. Deputy Marshal for Kidnapping in Syracuse, New York," *Syracuse* (New York) *Daily Journal*, 1852. Hereafter cited as "Allen Trial."
19. "'That Laboratory of Abolitionism, Libel, and Treason': Syracuse and the Underground Railroad," an exhibition of the Special Collections Research Center, Syracuse University Library. "The Jerry Rescue and Its Aftermath," digital edition.
20. *Ibid.*
21. *Boston Liberator*, October 10, 1851.
22. *Voice of the Fugitive*, December 2, 1851. This newspaper is part of the University of Detroit's Mercy Black Abolitionist Archive. It is protected under copyright laws.
23. Ralph Volney Harlow, *Gerrit Smith, Philanthropist and Reformer* (New York City: Henry Holt, 1939), 299.
24. Campbell, 156.
25. Allen Trial.
26. Letter to John Thomas, Esq., Syracuse, New York, from Gerrit Smith, Peterboro, New York, August 27, 1859. Letter resides in the Syracuse University Library.
27. Octavius Brooks Frothingham, *Gerrit Smith: A Biography* (New York City: Putnam's, 1878), 245–246.
28. United States ex rel. *Garland v. Morris*, Case No. 15,811, District Court D. Wisconsin, 1854. April 1854.
29. *Ibid.*
30. Laws of Missouri, 1836–1837, 3. Approved February 1, 1837, by Governor Lelburn W. Boggs.
31. Alphonso Wetmore, *Gazetteer of the State of Missouri* (St. Louis: 1837), 113–117. Hereafter cited as the "Gazetteer."
32. *Ibid.*
33. *Kansas City Star*, October 29, 1899.
34. Trexler, 120. Trexler gives Muldrow's first name as John instead of William as do some other historians. However, all local Marion County accounts of events give his name as William Muldrow. Also, there are records in Marion County, Missouri, of a William Muldrow from Philadelphia, Missouri, and his birth date and death date would seem to fit with these events. Trexler used a long distance account of the events in Marion County by a correspondent of the *New York Journal of Commerce* which was quoted in the Fourth Annual Report of the American Anti-Slavery Society. This same narrative was also found in the *Quarterly Anti-Slavery Magazine* for July of 1837. Perhaps this distant correspondent was not familiar with Muldrow's correct first name.
35. *Gazetteer*, 113–117.
36. Walter Williams, ed., *History of Northeast Missouri*, Vol. I (Chicago–New York: Lewis Publisher, 1913), 457.
37. Minnie M. Brashear, *Mark Twain, Son of Missouri* (Chapel Hill: University of North Carolina Press, 1934), 70–72. F.H. Soney, a local expert on Twain, stated that there were no murders in Marion City; another feature of the story had a house being blown up by dynamite, which never happened in this town. It is obvious that this story of Twain was pure fiction but it did deal with some of the underlying violence associated with slavery in Missouri at this time.
38. Collection of Illinois State Historical Library, Illinois Historical Publications, *Governor's Letter Book*, Vol. II, 66, footnote 1.
39. *Ibid.*, 71.
40. Trexler, 121. Harriet C. Frazier, *Runaway and Freed Missouri Slaves and Those Who Helped Them, 1763–1865* (Jefferson, North Carolina: McFarland, 2004), 132. Hereafter cited as "Frazier."
41. *Missouri Federal Writers' Project Slave Narratives*, digital edition on the Library of Congress American Memory website. Interview with Emma Knight in Hannibal, Missouri, 219. Hereafter the Library of Congress digital editions of the *Missouri Federal Writers' Project Slave Narratives* will be cited as "*Missouri FWP* D.E."
42. Trexler, 121. Frazier, 132.
43. *Marion County Palmyra Whig*, May 20, 1853.
44. *Missouri Courier*, November 10, 1853.
45. E.A. Perkins, *History of Marion County*, 218–220.
46. *Palmyra Weekly Whig*, October 23, 1856.
47. *Keokuk* (Iowa) *Argus*, May, 1846.
48. Interview with William Black in Hannibal, Missouri, *Missouri FWP*, 33.
49. *Hannibal Messenger*, August 26, 1854. Reprinted in the *Columbia Statesman*, September 1, 1854.
50. Fred W. Lorch, "Biography of Orion Clemens," *Palimpsest* Vol. X, October 1929, No. 10, 353–388.
51. Thomas C. Buchanan, *Black Life on the Mississippi: Slaves, Free Blacks and the Western Steamboat World* (Chapel Hill and London: University of North Carolina Press, 2004), 136. Hereafter cited as "Buchanan."
52. *Missouri Republican*, October 9, 1847.
53. *Arkansas State Democrat Herald*, May 15, 1840.
54. Drew, 255.
55. *Southern Shield* (Arkansas), January 29, 1842.
56. Trexler, 184.
57. William Wells Brown, *William W. Brown: An American Slave Written by Himself* (London: Charles Gilpin, 1850), 13–15. Hereafter cited as "William W. Brown." Google digital edition.
58. *Ibid.*, 22.
59. *Ibid.*, 26.
60. Joseph C. and Owen Lovejoy, *Memoir of the Rev. Elijah P. Lovejoy; Who Was Murdered in Defense of the Liberty of the Press at Alton, Illinois, Nov. 7, 1837* (New York: John S. Taylor, 1838), 291. This edition has an introduction by John Quincy Adams, former president and anti-slavery activist. Google digital edition.
61. William W. Brown, 82–83.
62. *Ibid.*, 102–104.
63. William E. Farrisson, "William Wells Brown in Buffalo," *The Journal of Negro History*, Vol. XXXIX, No. 4, October, 1954.
64. *Ibid.*, William W. Brown, 110.
65. *Ibid.*, William W. Brown, 107.
66. *Liberator*, September 1, 1848.
67. William Wells Brown, *Clotel; or, The President's Daughter: A Narrative of Slave Life in America* (London: Partridge & Oakley, 1853).
68. Campbell, 67.
69. *Ibid.*, 68–69.
70. Doy, 62–63.

71. Galusha Anderson, *The Story of a Border City During the Civil War* (Boston: Little, Brown, 1908), 182–187. Hereafter noted as "Anderson."
72. *Voice of the Fugitive*, October 10, 1851. This is part of the University of Detroit's Mercy Black Abolitionist Archives. It is protected under copyright laws.
73. *Voice of the Fugitive*, August 27, 1851. This is part of the University of Detroit's Mercy Black Abolitionist Archives. It is protected under copyright laws.
74. *Columbia* (Missouri) *Statesman*, September 29, 1855.
75. *Missouri FWP* D.E. Interview with Hattie Mathews, Farmington, Missouri, 250. *Missouri FWP* D.E. Interview with Charlie Richardson by Bernard Hinkle, Joplin, Missouri, January 27, 1938. Hereafter noted as "*Missouri FWP* D.E. Richardson."
76. *Columbia Statesman*, October, 24, 1856.
77. Trexler, 176.
78. *Missouri FWP*. Interview with George Bollinger, Cape Girardeau, Missouri, 42.
79. Drew, 131–132.
80. *Columbia Statesman*, June 23, 1848.
81. *St. Louis Argus*, July 26, 1839.
82. *Columbia Statesman*, September 12, 1851.
83. Trexler, 148.
84. Biographical Directory of the United States Congress: Thomas Hart Benton.
85. Missouri State Archives, "Crack of the Pistol: Dueling in 19th Century Missouri: Benton-Lucas Duel," Missouri Digital Heritage, Missouri Office of the Secretary of State.
86. Thomas Hart Benton, *Thirty Years View: A History of the Working of the American Government 1820 to 1850, Part Two* (New York, Boston: D. Appleton, 1856), 620. Google digital edition.
87. Theodore Roosevelt, *Thomas Hart Benton* (Boston & New York: Houghton Mifflin, 1886), 349. Hereafter cited as "Roosevelt."
88. Trexler, 136.
89. John F. Kennedy, *Profiles in Courage* (New York, Evanston, and London: Harper & Row, 1964), 110.This memorial edition had a foreword by Robert F. Kennedy. Hereafter cited as "Kennedy."
90. Roosevelt, 339.
91. Kennedy, 116–117.
92. Don E. Fehrenbacher, *The Dred Scot Case: Its Significance in American Law and Politics* (Oxford, New York: Oxford University Press, 1978), 425–426. Hereafter cited as "Fehrenbacher."
93. Official Web Site of Benton County, Arkansas, Section on History of the County: www.co.benton.Ar.us/ (last visited October 5, 2008). *Encyclopedia of Arkansas History & Culture*, section on Benton County.
94. Edward G. Mason, ed., *Early Chicago and Illinois* (Chicago: Fergus Printing, 1890), 110.
95. Letter to Sally Atkins from Arthur Atkins, Chicago, Illinois, June 3, 1851. Letter located at the Todd House Museum, Tabor, Iowa.
96. *Columbia Statesman*, July 25, 1851.
97. *Missouri FWP*. Interview with Rachael Goings, Cape Girardeau, Missouri, 121.
98. *Missouri FWP* D.E. Interview with Madison Frederick Ross, Commerce, Missouri, 299–300.
99. *Missouri FWP* D.E. Interview with Delicia Patterson, St. Louis, Missouri, 270–273.
100. *Oklahoma Slave Narratives: A Folk History of Slavery in Oklahoma from Interviews with Former Slaves from The Federal Writers' Project 1936–1938* (Bedford, Massachusetts: Applewood Books in cooperation with the Library of Congress). The Library of Congress reproduced these interviews as they were originally typed by the Federal Writers' Project interviewers. These interviews were of still living former slaves who were residing in the state of Oklahoma from 1936 until 1938. Interview with Esther Easter, Tulsa, Oklahoma, 88–90. Hereafter any of these former slave interviews taken from the Oklahoma edition of the Applewood Books will be noted as *Oklahoma FWP*.

Chapter 3

1. *Missouri FWP* D.E. Interview with Charlie Richardson by Bernard Hinkle, Joplin, Missouri, January 27, 1938, 292.
2. Campbell, 87–88.
3. *Ibid.*, 89.
4. *Frank Leslie's Illustrated Newspaper*, New York, June 27, 1857.
5. Fehrenbacher, 1–2.
6. *Frank Leslie's Illustrated Newspaper*, New York, June 27, 1857.
7. Fehrenbacher, 421.
8. John Anderson was born Jack Burton. Because of his life on the run as a fugitive slave who had killed a white man in self-defense to secure his freedom, he changed his name several times. John Anderson is the name he is most commonly known by and for clarity of his story that is the name that will be used throughout this narrative.
9. *Columbia Statesman*, October 7, 1853. This newspaper incorrectly spells Digges' name as "Diggs."
10. *Missouri Statesman*, October 28, 1853.
11. Frazier, 112–113.
12. Robin W. Winks, *The Blacks in Canada: A History* (Carleton Library Series, 2003), 175. Hereafter cited as "Winks."
13. Patrick Brode, *The Odyssey of John Anderson* (Toronto: Osgoode Society for Canadian Legal History, University of Toronto Press, 1989), 59, 61.
14. *Ibid.*, 123. Frazier, 121–122.
15. *Columbia Statesman*, December 19, 1856. Reprinted from the *Huntsville Citizen*.
16. *Columbia Statesman*, April 28, 1854.
17. *Columbia Statesman*, August 14, 1857.
18. *Weekly Anglo-African*, January 14, 1860. This is part of the University of Detroit's Mercy Black Abolitionist Archives. It is protected under copyright laws.
19. *Chicago Tribune*, January 4, 1860. *Ottawa: Old and New, A Complete History of Ottawa, Illinois*. Published locally by the *Republican-Times* of Ottawa, Illinois, 1912.
20. *Columbia Statesman*, May 22, 1857.
21. Drew, 196.
22. John Hope Franklin & Loren Schweninger, *Runaway Slaves: Rebels on the Plantation* (Oxford: Oxford University Press, 1999), 158–159. Hereafter cited as "Franklin & Schweninger."
23. *Missouri FWP*. Interview with Richard Bruner, Nelson, Missouri, 59–60.
24. Recorder of the Office of the County Records of Saline County, Missouri.
25. *Marshall Daily Democrat-News*, May 9, 1938.
26. *Ibid.*, December 26, 1978.
27. *Columbia Statesman*, November 11, 1853.

28. *Ibid.*, July 23, 1857.
29. *Columbia Tribune*, May 20, 2007.
30. *Palmyra Whig* item published in the *Columbia Statesman*, June 24, 1853.
31. *Batesville (Arkansas) News*, January 30, 1840.
32. *Columbia Statesman*, September 23, 1853.
33. *Ibid.*, October 27, 1854.
34. Drew, 122–123.
35. *Columbia Statesman*, August 7, 1857.
36. *Arkansas Advocate*, June 27, 1842.
37. *Columbia Statesman*, January 20, 1854.
38. *Ibid.*, March 24, 1854.
39. Drew, 209–211.
40. *Missouri FWP* D.E. Casey, 73.
41. Henry Clay Bruce, *The New Man: Twenty-Nine Years a Slave, Twenty-Nine Years a Free Man* (1895; reprint, Lincoln, University of Nebraska Press, 1996), 41.
42. *Ibid.*, 39–40.
43. *Ibid.*, 33.
44. *Ibid.*, 37–38.
45. *Ibid.*, 69.
46. *Ibid.*, 34.
47. *Ibid.*, 108.
48. Biographical Directory of the United States Congress: Blanche Bruce.
49. *Columbia Statesman*, October 31, 1856.
50. *Ibid.*, September 11, 1857.
51. Terrell Dempsey, *Searching for Jim: Slavery in Sam Clemens' World* (Columbia: University of Missouri Press, 2003), 169. Hereafter cited as "Dempsey."
52. Trexler, 179.
53. Dempsey, 173.
54. James Franklin Hopkins, *A History of the Hemp Industry in Kentucky* (Lexington: University of Kentucky Press, 1951), 97.
55. Miles Eaton, "The Development and Later Decline of the Hemp Industry in Missouri," *Missouri Historical Review*, 43, July 1949, 352.
56. Turton.
57. *Richmond (Missouri) Weekly Mirror*, February 16, 1855.
58. *St. Joseph Commercial Cycle*, September 28, 1855. Trexler, 204.
59. Melton A. McLaurin, *Celia: A Slave* (Athens: University of Georgia Press, 1991), 48.
60. *New York Times*, August 15, 1855.
61. Frazier, 91.
62. University of Kentucky: Notable Kentucky African Americans Database Website. Section on Underground Railroad, Conductors, Escapes. The site was last visited on April 4, 2009, and had been updated at that date.
63. *Platte Argus* (Missouri), April 16, 1855. Reprinted in the *New York Times*, April 26, 1855.
64. McFarland letter, date unknown, on the slave shackle. McFarland's slave shackle and letter are located at the Kansas State Historical Society.
65. Turton, 48.
66. Letter to John Todd, Tabor, Iowa, from E. Fraser of Boarman and Fraser Real Estate Brokers and General Gents in Kansas City, Missouri, November 15, 1860. Monaghan, 119.
67. Monaghan, 136.
68. *Missouri FWP* D.E. Interview with Ellaine Wright, 378.
69. *Ibid.*
70. E.F. Ware, *The Lyon Campaign in Missouri: History of the First Iowa Infantry* (Topeka, Kansas: Crane, 1907), 190–191, 217, 252.
71. *Missouri FWP* D.E. interview with Marilda Perry, Montgomery City, Missouri, 278.
72. *Ibid.*, 280.
73. Anderson, 178–181.
74. *The War of the Rebellion: A Compilation of the Official Records of the Union and Confederate Armies*, Washington, D.C., Government Printing Office, 1880, Series 1, Vol. III, 390. Hereafter cited as "*War of the Rebellion.*"
75. *Ibid.*, 419–423.
76. *Ibid.*, 466–469.
77. *Ibid.*, 477, 485.
78. Roy P. Basler, ed., *Abraham Lincoln: His Speeches and Writings* (1946; reprint, Cambridge, MA, New York City: Da Capo, 2001), 613–615. Hereafter cited as "*Abraham Lincoln: Speeches and Writings.*"
79. *War of the Rebellion*, Series 1, Vol. III, 59–560.
80. *Missouri FWP* D.E. Interview with Gus Smith in Rolla, Missouri, 321.
81. *Liberty Tribune*, date unknown, but the public notice is dated May 9, 1862.
82. *Liberty Tribune*, date unknown, but the public notice is dated May 23, 1862.
83. Wiley Britton, *The Civil War on the Border 1861–1862* (New York, London: Putnam's, 1891), 147–148. Hereafter cited as "Britton." Ian Michael Spurgeon, *Man of Douglas Man of Lincoln: the Political Odyssey of James Henry Lane* (Columbia: University of Missouri Press, 2008), 185–187. Hereafter cited as "Spurgeon." Castel, *Kansas*, 53–55.
84. Britton, 179. Castel, *Kansas*, 55–56. Britton, a Union man, still had a racist viewpoint regarding the bondspersons in Missouri. Britton couldn't believe some of the bondspersons would leave their masters where they had been "well-treated."
85. *Columbia Statesman*, October 25, 1925.
86. *Ibid.*, February 21, 1862.
87. Trexler, 237.
88. Spurgeon, 233–236.
89. Castel, *Kansas*, 94.
90. *Missouri FWP*. Mary A. Bell, St. Louis County, Missouri, interviewed by Grace W. White, 25–30.
91. *Missouri FWP*. Interview with Louis Hamilton in Fredericktown, Missouri, 145.
92. *Missouri FWP*. Interview with James Monroe Abbot Cape Girardeau, Missouri, 3.
93. Spurgeon, 236–237.
94. *Missouri FWP* D.E Interview with Dave Harper in Montgomery City, Missouri, 166–168.
95. Castel, *Kansas*, 126–133.
96. *War of the Rebellion*, Series 1, part 1, Vol. XXII, 580.
97. Daniel O'Flaherty, *General Jo Shelby: Undefeated Rebel* (Chapel Hill: University of North Carolina Press, 1954), 193.
98. Monaghan, 299.
99. *Ibid.*, 312.
100. *Missouri FWP*. Interview with Charles Gabriel Anderson in St. Louis, 20–22.
101. *Missouri FWP* D.E. Interview with Joe Higgerson in Sedalia, Missouri, August 12, 1937, 178.
102. Trexler, 206–207.
103. *History of Boone County, Missouri* (Cape Girardeau, Missouri: Ramfre Reprint, 1970), 349.
104. Western Historical Manuscript Collection of the State Historical Society of Missouri, *The Payne-Broad-*

well *Family Papers, 1803–1903*, Biographical Sketches Payne Family, 2–3. Hereafter noted as "Payne-Broadwell Papers."

105. John C. Crighton, *A History of Columbia and Boone County* (Columbia, Missouri: Computer Color-Graphics, 1987), 242.

106. Missouri State Archives Digital Heritage: *Missouri's Provost Marshals Papers 1861–1866*.

107. Material provided to me by Lynn Handy, a local historian from Fremont County, Iowa. In a letter to the author dated February 22, 2007, Mr. Handy noted that his father had attended school with some of the later generations of the freed bondspersons of Moses U. Payne.

108. Payne-Broadwell Papers, 3.

109. *Missouri FWP*. Interview with Robert Bryant in Herculaneum, Missouri, 61–63.

110. *Missouri Statesman*, May 27, 1864.

111. Missouri State Archives Digital Heritage: *Guide to African-American History*, section on Governor Thomas C. Fletcher.

112. *Missouri FWP*. Interview with Peter Corn in Herculaneum, Missouri, 87–89.

Chapter 4

1. W.E.B. DuBois, *John Brown* (Philadelphia: George W. Jacobs, 1909), 194–195. Hereafter cited as "DuBois."

2. Lord Richard Acton and Patricia Nassif Acton, "Chapter Four," in Bill Silag, ed., *Outside In: African-American History in Iowa 1838–2000* (Des Moines: State Historical Society of Iowa, 2001), 61.

3. Jessie Carney Smith, ed., *Notable Black American Women Book II* (Thomson Gale, 1995), 535.

4. Hallie Q. Brown, *Homespun Heroines and Other Women of Distinction* (New York: Oxford University Press, 1992), 34–35.

5. Mrs. Lawrence C. Jones, "The Desire for Freedom," *Palimpsest*, 8 (May 1927), 153–154. Mrs. Lawrence C. Jones was the granddaughter of Charlotta Gordon MacHenry Pyles.

6. *Ibid.*, 154–157.

7. *Ibid.*, 157–158.

8. *Ibid.*, 158–161.

9. O.A. Garretson, "Traveling on the Underground Railroad in Iowa," *Iowa Journal of History and Politics*, XXII (July 1924), 446. Hereafter cited as "Garretson."

10. Charles L. Blockson, *The Underground Railroad: First-Person Narratives of Escapes to Freedom in the North* (New York: Prentice Hall, 1987), 189.

11. Fort Madison (Iowa) *Plain Dealer*, May 27, 1857, and July 11, 1862.

12. Garretson, 427–428, 446.

13. Louis Thomas Jones, *The Quakers of Iowa* (Iowa City: State Historical Society of Iowa, 1914), 138, 188–189.

14. G. Galin Berrier, "Chapter Three," in Bill Silag, ed., *Outside In: African-American History in Iowa 1838–2000* (Des Moines, State Historical Society of Iowa, 2001), 50. Hereafter cited as "Silag: Berrier." Garretson, 430–432.

15. Jacob Van Ek, "Underground Railroad in Iowa," *Palimpsest* 5 (May 1921), 140–141. Hereafter noted as "Van Ek." Silag: Berrier, 50–51. Garretson, 432–433.

16. Finkelman, 79.

17. Silag: Berrier, 51. Garretson, 434–435. Van Ek, 141–142.

18. Finkelman, 79–80.

19. Louis Pelzer, *Augustus Caesar Dodge* (Iowa City: State Historical Society of Iowa, 1908), 143–146.

20. Garretson, 426.

21. Turton, 72.

22. *Voice of the Fugitive*, July, 2, 1851. This is part of the University of Detroit's Mercy Black Abolitionist Archives. It is protected under copyright laws.

23. Garretson, 451.

24. *Appanoose County History* (Chicago: Western History, 1878), 373.

25. *Ibid.*, 373.

26. Turton, 75.

27. Todd book, 22, 36.

28. Turton, 45.

29. *Ibid.*, 48.

30. Richard J. Hinton, *John Brown and His Men* (Funk and Wagnalls, 1894), 458.

31. William E. Connelley, "The Lane Trail," *Collections of the Kansas State Historical Society*, Vol. 13 (1913–1914), 269–270.

32. *Nebraska City News*, November 20, 1858. *Nebraska City News*, December 24, 1859. *Nebraska City News*, November 10, 1860.

33. *Nebraska News*, January 30, 1858.

34. File on S.F. Nuckolls located at the Morton-James Library in Nebraska City, Nebraska, Call# 1926–1927. Hereafter cited as "Nuckolls."

35. Williamson was living in Council Bluffs, Iowa, at the time of the Census of 1860. The person taking the census was an assistant marshal and as such had the power to arrest Williamson, Reed and the other man if they were not free Blacks or mulattos but in fact fugitive slaves. However, Williamson was well-known and apparently well-respected in Council Bluffs, as he had been in Tabor and Civil Bend, and apparently the assistant marshal either felt everything was in order or he sympathized with Williamson and his companions' plight.

36. *Nebraska City News*, December 4, 1858.

37. Todd book, 61.

38. *Nebraska City News*, November 27, 1858.

39. *Nebraska City News*, December 4, 1858. Todd book, 61.

40. Todd book, 61.

41. Lowel Blikre, "Phase 1 Intensive Survey of Seven Potential Historical Archeological Properties in the Civil Bend Vicinity, Benton Township, Fremont County, Iowa," prepared for the State Historical Society of Iowa, 12.

42. Fremont County Clerk's Office, Court Case No. 30, *Henry Garner v. S.F. Nuchols* [sic], etc. March Term District Court, 1859. Bob and Gertrude Handy, *Some Day: A Tale of Civil Bend by the River* (Interstate Publishers and Printers, 1973), 43.

43. Nuckolls, 1928.

44. Todd book, 62.

45. *Des Moines Valley Whig* article published in the *Nebraska News*, undated.

46. *Nebraska City News*, undated article in the Todd House Museum Archives.

47. *Nebraska City News*, November 24, 1860.

48. *Fremont Herald* undated article in the Todd House Museum. The *Fremont Herald* claimed it was non-partisan and published in Fremont County, Iowa. John Todd did not believe this. He could not locate its

offices in Fremont County, Iowa, and the paper certainly wasn't non-partisan. Todd believed the *Herald* was being published by the *Nebraska City News*, N.T., and attempted to pass it off as a "local" paper in Iowa.

49. *Nebraska City News*, November 24, 1860.
50. James Patrick Morgans, *John Todd and the Underground Railroad: Biography of an Iowa Abolitionist* (Jefferson, NC: McFarland, 2006), 95. Hereafter cited as "Morgans."
51. Todd book, 62. Morgans, 95.
52. *History of Fremont County, Iowa* (Iowa Historical Society, Iowa Historical Company, 1881), 393, 394, 519. Morgans, 95. I have tried to find the outcome or particulars of this historical case that some say was the first time in the state of Iowa that a Black man brought suit against a white man. I found mention of this court case and a description of the filing of this case as I described in footnote 41 in this chapter in the Todd House Museum Archives. The Handys also mention the trial in their book, *Some Day*, but give no particulars except what is mentioned here. *The History of Fremont County* is normally a very reliable source; however, they only mention the case to praise Judge Sears but give no information as to the outcome or details of the trial. My son, Patrick Morgans, went looking in the bowels of the Fremont County Courthouse in Sidney, Iowa, to find any court records on the trial but was not able at that time to locate any information. My daughter, Meredith Joy Kuehler, an attorney, has looked for any legal description of this historical trial in any law books or legal software available to attorneys but has not been able to find any information.
53. File on Alexander Majors located at the Morton-James Library in Nebraska City, Nebraska, 1691. *New York Times* obituary for Alexander Majors, January 16, 1900.
54. Federal Census, 1860, Otoe County, N.T., mss. Family #20, including census of slaves.
55. *Nebraska City News*, June 30, 1860.
56. Todd book, 60.
57. Letter to Q.F. Atkins, Racine, Wisconsin, from Martha Todd and her son James Todd, Tabor, Iowa, December 25, 1856. Hereafter cited as "Letter Martha Todd, Dec. 25, 1856."
58. Ibid.
59. Todd book, 65–66.
60. Letter Martha Todd, Dec. 25, 1856.
61. Jules Ables, *Man on Fire: John Brown and the Cause of Liberty* (New York: Macmillan, 1971), 114, 147. Hinton, 60. Morgans, 7–8. Todd book, 69, Villard, 270, 274.
62. Silag: Berrier, 53.
63. Turton, 53–54. *Des Moines Capital*, May 7, 1924. A humorous story occurred in Montgomery County, Iowa, shortly after the Civil War. The county seat was transferred from Frankfort to Red Oak. The old wooden courthouse in Frankfort was literally moved by a team of oxen to Red Oak. However, a snowstorm blew up while moving the courthouse, creating white-out conditions, and the men moving the courthouse barely made it home to ride out the storm. When they came back they couldn't find the courthouse building! After much searching, the wooden structure was found but afterwards jokes about the missing courthouse were common in Montgomery County.
64. Silag: Berrier, 49. Garretson, 447–449.
65. *Iowa State Register Morning Edition*, partial date of 1887. This was the forerunner to the *Des Moines Register*.
66. *Jasper County Record*, July 1, 1926.
67. Ibid. *Ohio History* (Ohio Historical Society, 1921), 466–472. Villard, 682–683. R.J. Hinton and some others have mistakenly stated that Coppoc was one of the Springdale Quakers conned and killed in William Quantrill's Morgan Walker raid described in Chapter 1.
68. Charles E. Payne, *Josiah Bushnell Grinnell* (Iowa City: State Historical Society of Iowa, 1938), 27–28.
69. Ibid., 30–31.
70. L. F. Parker, *History of Poweshiek County* (Chicago: S.J. Clarke, 1911), 222.
71. Letter to Leonard F. Parker, Grinnell, Iowa, from Amos Bixby, Boulder, Colorado, May 16, 1887. Copy of this letter in author's files.
72. Irving B. Richman, *John Brown Among the Quakers and Other Sketches* (Des Moines: Historical Department of Iowa, 1894), 21, 23, 32.
73. Turton, 80.
74. Ibid., 82.
75. Van Ek, 135.
76. Turton, 99. Lucas was interviewed by Wilbur H. Siebert.
77. Letter to J.Q. Anderson (Dear Brother) from J.G. (Jeremiah G.) Anderson, January 14, 1859. J.G. Anderson was one of John Brown's men who went on the raid with him into Missouri and later to Harpers Ferry. Hereafter cited as "Anderson letter."
78. Villard, 367.
79. Stephen B. Oates, *To Purge This Land with Blood: A Biography of John Brown* (New York: Harper & Row, 1970), 262–263. Hereafter cited as "Oates." Villard, 372–374. Oates describes Hutchison as a correspondent for the *New York Times*. William Hutchison wrote a letter to *New York Times* editor Henry J. Raymond complaining that he was not running any of his articles about Kansas. Raymond, in a letter of September 18, 1857, told correspondent Hutchison that too many of his articles were one-sided, slanted towards the free-state side, and that was why they were not being run. It is not known for sure if in December of 1858 Hutchison was still a correspondent for the *Times* or for the *Tribune*.
80. Villard, 380.
81. Anderson letter.
82. Oates, 262–263. Villard, 376–377. *Nebraska City News*, February 12, 1859.
83. Letter to Col. James Redpath from William F. Creitz of Holton, Kansas, dated December 17, 1859. Redpath wrote one of the first legend-building biographies of John Brown.
84. Ibid. *Nebraska City News*, February 12, 1859. The pro-slavery Nebraska City newspaper despised Brown and gave wild estimates of the number of his men with him as being 75.
85. DuBois, 95. This was freeman Samuel Harper's account of the trek north to Canada with John Brown.
86. Villard, 383.
87. *Nebraska City News*, February 12, 1859.
88. A photocopy of the original resides in the Todd House Museum Archives.
89. F.B. Sanborn, *The Life and Letters of John Brown, Liberator of Kansas and Martyr of Virginia* (Boston: Roberts Brothers, 1891), 488.
90. Record on Public Meetings in Tabor, Iowa, Maria Gaston's Reminiscences, 101–102.
91. Villard, 386.
92. Ibid., 388.
93. Silag: Berrier, 56–57.
94. Todd book, 67.

95. *Taylor County* (Iowa) *Tribune*, October 4, 1860. Morgans, 102.
96. *Page County* (Iowa) *Herald*, November 9, 1860. Reprinted from an undated newspaper article from the *St. Louis Democrat.* Hereafter cited as "*Page County Herald.*" Todd book, 66.
97. *Page County Herald.*
98. *Ibid.*
99. Catharine Grace Barbour Farquhar, "Tabor and Tabor College," *The Iowa Journal of History and Politics*, October, 1943, 362.
100. Todd book, 67.
101. *New York Times*, August 31, 1860.
102. Glen Noble, *John Brown and the Jim Lane Trail* (Broken Bow, NE: Purcells, 1977), 107. Hereafter cited as "Noble."
103. *Ibid.*, 106.
104. *Nebraska City News*, February 20, 1857.
105. Letter to Thaddeus Hyatt, address unknown, from A.D. Searl, Tabor, Iowa, August 21, 1856. Morgans, 111.
106. *Nebraska City*, Nebraska *News* April 14, 1890.
107. Noble, 109.
108. *Nebraska City News,* December 5, 1857.
109. Noble, 107.
110. Alice Lockwood Minick, "Underground Railroad in Nebraska," *Proceeding and Collections of the Nebraska State Historical Society* Second Series Vol. 2 (Lincoln, Nebraska: State Journal Company Printers, 1898). Gaston Manuscript. This material in the Gaston Manuscript was gathered by W.E. Gaston, son of James Gaston, erstwhile conductor on the Underground Railroad in Tabor, Iowa. They were recollections of the Gaston, Cummins and Townsend family pioneers and their children and early events in the town of Tabor. Addenda, 11.

Chapter 5

1. *Autobiography of Sir Henry Morton Stanley* (New York: Houghton Mifflin, Riverside Press, 1909), 146–148.
2. Harry S. Ashmore, *Arkansas: A Bicentennial History* (New York: W.W. Norton, 1978), 54. Hereafter cited as "Ashmore."
3. 1860 United States Census.
4. Francis Newton Thorpe, ed., *The Federal and State Constitution, Colonial Charters, and Other Organic Laws of the States, Territories, and Colonies now or heretofore forming the United States of America*, House Document No. 357, 59th Congress 2nd Session (7 volumes; Washington, D.C. 1909), Volume I, 268–286.
5. George E. Lankford, ed., *Bearing Witness: Memories of Arkansas Slavery Narratives from the 1930's WPA Collections* (University of Arkansas Press, 2003). Interview by Mrs. Florence Angermiller with Harry "Jim" Johnson of Pearsall, Texas, telling of his days as a slave in Arkansas, 11–12. Hereafter cited as "Lankford, Johnson." Any other interviews from this book will be noted by Lankford and the interviewee's name and any other information.
6. Lankford. J.E. Boone, Little Rock, Arkansas, interviewed by Samuel S. Taylor, 398. Taylor, in keeping with the "genteel" times of the 1930s, didn't use the word "ass," but just put in a dash. It is very obvious that this was the word Boone used in his interview. Samuel S. Taylor was the only fulltime Black writer working on the FWP in Arkansas and his interviews were head and shoulders above the rest.
7. Both the WPA interviews of the Federal Writers' Project in *Bearing Witness* edited by George E. Lankford and the interviews from the Federal Writers' Project of *Arkansas Slave Narratives* often mention the fear and the excessive cruelty that the Arkansas slave patrols produced. In reviewing many of these interviews it was obvious that one of the standard questions asked the interviewees was about the presence of the slave patrols. A lot of the respondents to that question mentioned the savage beatings or whippings the slave patrols had administered to their relatives or someone they knew and the fear these patrollers produced.
8. *Arkansas Slave Narratives: from the Federal Writers' Project, 1936–1938* (Bedford, Massachusetts: Applewood Books in cooperation with the Library of Congress). These interviews many times were the same as in the Lankford book. However, because Applewood Books used copies of the same typed pages as the original interviews sometimes they are easier to read and any notes made by the interviewer can be seen. Hereafter these will be cited as "*Arkansas FWP.*" Nancy Anderson from West Memphis, Arkansas, interviewed by Irene Robertson, 50–51.
9. *Arkansas FWP.* Lucretia Alexander, Little Rock, Arkansas, interviewed by Samuel S. Taylor, 34. Hereafter cited as "*Arkansas FWP,* Alexander." Lankford book, Plomer Harshaw, Muskogee, Oklahoma, interviewed by Ethel Wolfe Garrison, 6. Hereafter cited as "Lankford Harshaw."
10. Buchanan, 38. Buchanan's well researched and well written book contains one assumption that I believe to be incorrect. He mentions that Arkansas had only 144 free Blacks in 1860. Buchanan attributed this to the lack of any large city in Arkansas. A more reasonable explanation would be the execution of the Expulsion Act of 1859, which stated any free Blacks in the state by the next year would be made slaves. By 1860 most of the free Blacks had fled the state of Arkansas for good reason.
11. Buchanan, 24.
12. *Arkansas Gazette*, July 28, 1841, August 16, 1841, December 8, 1841, March 2, 1842.
13. Siebert, 65.
14. Calvin Fairbank, *Rev. Calvin Fairbank During Slavery Times: How He "Fought the Good Fight" to Prepare "the Way"* (1890; reprint, New York: Negro University Press, 1969), 34, 39, 42, 48. Hereafter cited as "Fairbank."
15. Fairbank, 35–36.
16. *Ibid.*, 38.
17. *Ibid.*, 42.
18. *Ibid.*, 44.
19. Into the Fiery Furnace: Anti-Slavery Prisoners in the Kentucky State Penitentiary 1844–1870 <http//www.ket.org/underground/research/Prichard.htm> (last visited August 30, 2007). The article and the website are the work of James M. Prichard, senior archivist of the Kentucky Department of Libraries.
20. Levi Coffin, *Reminiscences of Levi Coffin*, New York (1876; reprint, Arno Press and *The New York Times*, 1968), 284–292. Hereafter cited as "Coffin."
21. Fairbank, 46.
22. Coffin, 719–726.
23. Buchanan, 39.
24. Drew, 179–180.
25. Buchanan, 104.

26. Ashmore, 68–69.
27. Drew, 90–91
28. Ibid., 85–92.
29. *Arkansas Gazette*, May 30, 1839.
30. *Washington, Telegraph* (Washington, AR), May 3, 1848.
31. Buchanan, 108.
32. Drew, 128–131.
33. Buchanan, 106, 118.
34. *Arkansas Gazette*, May 29, 1844. *Arkansas State Democrat Herald*, July 10, 1840.
35. *Arkansas State Democrat Herald*, May 15, 1840. *Democratic Star*, October 12, 1854.
36. Henry Bibb, *Narrative of the Life and Adventures of Henry Bibb: An American Slave Written by Himself* (New York: published by the author, 1849), 15. Google digital edition. Hereafter cited as "Bibb."
37. Ibid., 43.
38. Ibid., 48–51.
39. Ibid., 105.
40. *Voice of the Refugee*, February 26, 1851. This newspaper article is a part of the University of Detroit's Mercy Black Abolitionist Archive. It is protected under copyright laws.
41. Walter Johnson, *Soul by Soul: Life Inside the Antebellum Slave Market* (Cambridge, Massachusetts: Harvard University Press, 1999), 2–3.
42. Bibb, 110–113.
43. *Arkansas Gazette*, September 2, 1840.
44. Bibb, 134.
45. Ibid., 137.
46. Ibid., 143–144.
47. Ibid., 149.
48. Ibid., 152–153.
49. Ibid., 167–169.
50. Ibid., 172–173.
51. S. Charles Bolton, *Fugitives from Injustice: Freedom-Seeking Slaves in Arkansas, 1800–1860*, internet publication of the National Park Service's "National Underground Railroad Network to Freedom," 23. Hereafter cited as "Bolton–NPS."
52. DuBois, 120–121. Frederick Douglas, *Life and Times of Frederick Douglas, His Early Life, as a Slave, His Escape from Bondage, and His Complete History to the Present Time* (Hartford, CT: Park, 1881), 284. Electronic version by the University of North Carolina, Chapel Hill. Hereafter cited as "Douglas."
53. Samuel Ringgold Ward, *Autobiography of a Fugitive Negro: His Anti-Slavery Labours in the United States, Canada, and England* (Toronto, London: John Snow, 35 Paternoster Row, 1855), 17–25. Electronic version by the University of North Carolina, Chapel Hill.
54. Bernell E. Tripp, "Mary Miles Bibb: Education and Moral Improvement in the 'Voice of the Fugitive.'" Paper presented at the Annual Meeting of the Association for Education in Journalism and Mass Communication (76th, Kansas City, MO. August 11–14, 1993), 3–5. Hereafter cited as "Tripp paper."
55. Douglas, 286.
56. Gara, 149.
57. *Voice of the Fugitive*, January 1, 1851. This newspaper article is a part of the University of Detroit's Mercy Black Abolitionist Archive. It is protected by copyright laws.
58. *Voice of the Fugitive*, February 26, 1851. This newspaper article is a part of the University of Detroit's Mercy Black Abolitionist Archive. It is protected by copyright laws.
59. *Voice of the Fugitive*, June 17, 1852. This newspaper article is a part of the University of Detroit's Mercy Black Abolitionist Archive. It is protected by copyright laws.
60. Tripp paper, 23–24.

Chapter 6

1. *Oliver v. Weakley et al.*, Case No. 10,502, Circuit Court, Third Circuit, 18 F. Cas. 678; 1853, October, 1853, Term.
2. *Van Metre v. Mitchell*, Case No. 16,865, Circuit Court, W.D. Pennsylvania, 28 F. Cas. 1036; 1853, October 1853.
3. 1860 Census (population).
4. Orville W. Taylor, *Negro Slavery in Arkansas* (Fayetteville: University of Arkansas Press, 2000), 59. Hereafter cited as "Taylor."
5. *Arkansas Gazette*, June 24, 1840.
6. *Southern Shield*, March 20, 1840.
7. *Arkansas Gazette*, June 17, 1840.
8. Ibid., July 20, 1842.
9. The Foster Memorial AME Zion Church in Tarrytown, New York, is recognized as a part of the National Park Service's "Road to Freedom" program. Their website details Amanda Foster's work in Arkansas. *http://www.cr.nps.gov/nr/travel/underground/ny5.htm* (last visited on March 24, 2007).
10. *Arkansas Gazette*, June 3, 1840.
11. Ibid., November 3, 1841.
12. Ibid., November 10, 1841.
13. Ibid., August 21, 1844.
14. *Arkansas Advocate*, June 7, 1841. *Arkansas Gazette*, July 3, 1844. *Arkansas Gazette*, May 31, 1849.
15. *Southern Shield*, February 5, 1842 & May 31, 1850. *Arkansas Gazette*, May 20, 1853.
16. Franklin & Schweninger, 78.
17. Lankford, Harshaw, 6.
18. Taylor, 215.
19. Lankford, Alexander, 414.
20. Taylor, 102.
21. Ibid., 105–106.
22. Lankford. Joe Ray interviewed by Ethel Wolfe Garrison, Muskogee, Oklahoma, 143.
23. *Arkansas FWP*. Miss Irene Robertson interviewed by Fannie Alexander at Helena, Arkansas, 30.
24. Taylor, 108.
25. Arkansas Slave Narrative; from the Federal Writers' Project, 1936–1938. These interviews were taken directly from the Library of Congress' American Memory website. Hereafter interviews taken directly from this site will be noted as *Arkansas FWP* D.E. Interview with Pauline Howell in Brinkley, Arkansas. Vol. II , Part 3, 342.
26. *Arkansas FWP* D.E. Interview with Ellen Cragin, Little Rock, by Samuel S. Taylor. Vol. II Part 2, 42–44.
27. *Arkansas FWP* D.E. Interview with Ella Johnson, Little Rock, Samuel S. Taylor. Vol. II, Part 4, 77.
28. Lankford. Katie Rowe interviewed by Robert Vinson Lackey at Tulsa, Oklahoma, 146.
29. Ibid., 145.
30. *Arkansas Advocate*, July 25, 1842. *Arkansas Gazette*, August 21, 1844. *Arkansas Gazette*, July 8, 1845.
31. *Arkansas Gazette*, August 17, 1842.
32. Ibid., September 7, 1842.
33. Ibid., April 26, 1843.

34. *Arkansas Advocate*, May 15, 1843.
35. *Washington Telegraph*, June 13, 1843.
36. Ibid., January 15, 1845. *Arkansas Gazette*, December 1, 1845.
37. Drew, 236–237.
38. Taylor, 213–214.
39. *Washington Telegraph*, September 10, 1845.
40. *Arkansas Gazette*, September 15, 1845. *Arkansas Gazette*, October 13, 1845. *Arkansas Gazette*, May 29, 1847. *Arkansas Gazette*, September 27, 1850.
41. Taylor, 220.
42. *Arkansas Gazette*, April 3, 1847. *Arkansas Gazette*, July 22, 1847. *Arkansas Gazette*, July 24, 1858. *Arkansas Gazette*, August 14, 1858.
43. *Washington Telegraph*, May 3, 1848.
44. Ibid., June 20, 1849.
45. Winks, 172.
46. Ibid.
47. Roman J. Zorn, "An Arkansas Fugitive Slave Incident and Its International Repercussions," *Arkansas Historical Quarterly*, 16 (Summer 1957), 139–149.
48. Roman J. Zorn, "Criminal Extradition Menaces the Canadian Haven for Fugitive Slaves, 1841–1861," *Canadian Historical Review*, Vol. 38 Number 4 (1957), 291.
49. Winks, 172–173.
50. *Arkansas Gazette*, August 9, 1850. *Arkansas Gazette*, October 11, 1850.
51. Ibid., January 31, 1851. Ibid., February 7, 1851.
52. Bolton–NPS, 16.
53. Franklin and Schweninger, 210.
54. J. Blaine Hudson, *Fugitive Slaves and the Underground Railroad in the Kentucky Borderland* (Jefferson, NC: McFarland, 2002), 36.
55. *Arkansas Gazette*, January 31, 1851. *Arkansas Gazette*, July 4, 1851. *Washington Telegraph*, October 10, 1853. *Arkansas Gazette*, February 8, 1850. *Arkansas Gazette*, December 29, 1845.
56. *Arkansas FWP*, 78–83. Lankford, 90–94. Interview of Joseph Samuel Badgett, Little Rock, Arkansas, by Samuel S. Taylor.
57. *Arkansas Gazette*, June 6, 1851, *Arkansas Gazette*, August 12, 1840, *Batesville* (Arkansas) *News*, September 15, 1842.
58. *Chicago Daily Tribune*, December 12, 1853.
59. George and Willene Henrick, eds., *Fleeing for Freedom: Stories of the Underground Railroad as told by Levi Coffin and William Still* (Chicago: Ivan R. Dee, 2004), 91–92. Hereafter cited as "Henrick."
60. Steve Weisenburger, *Modern Medea: A Family Story of Slavery and Child-Murder from the Old South* (Hill & Wang, 1999), 72. Hereafter cited as "Weisenburger."
61. Ibid., 71.
62. Henrick, 97.
63. *Provincial Freeman*, April 5, 1856. This newspaper article is a part of the University of Detroit's Mercy Black Abolitionist Archive. It is protected by copyright laws.
64. Ibid.
65. Weisenburger, 243–244.
66. *Provincial Freeman*, October 13, 1855. This newspaper article is a part of the University of Detroit's Mercy Black Abolitionist Archive. It is protected by copyright laws.
67. *Arkansas Gazette*, March 7, 1851.
68. Ibid., December 30, 1844.
69. Ibid., March 7, 1851.
70. Lankford, R.C. Smith interviewed by Mrs. Jesse R. Ervin Alderson, Oklahoma, 393.
71. Lankford, Scott Bond interview, town and interviewer unknown, 77.
72. *Arkansas Gazette*, April 4, 1851.
73. Ibid., July 25, 1851. *Democratic Star*, November 16, 1854.
74. Ibid., April 9, 1852.
75. James L. Penick, *The Great Western Land Pirate: John A. Murrell in Legend and History* (Columbia, Missouri & London: University of Missouri Press, 1981), 56.
76. *Arkansas Gazette*, April 15, 1840.
77. Ibid., December 2, 1840.
78. *Arkansas Gazette*, August 27, 1852. The last two items appeared in the same edition of the *Arkansas Gazette*, September 10, 1852.
79. Ibid., June 24, 1853.
80. *Arkansas Gazette*, September 1, 1854. *Arkansas Gazette*, October 13, 1854. *Democratic Star*, September 21, 1854. *Democratic Star*, May 3, 1855. *Washington Telegraph*, July 28, 1858.
81. *Arkansas Gazette*, April 9, 1855.
82. *Arkansas Gazette*, March 7, 1857. *Arkansas Gazette*, August 7, 1858. *Arkansas Gazette*, January 1, 1859.
83. Lankford. Callie Washington interviewed by Carrie Campbell, Coahoma County, Mississippi, 416–417
84. Lankford. Peter Brown interviewed by Irene Robertson, Helena, Arkansas, 262.
85. *Arkansas Gazette*, March 26, 1859.
86. Ibid., March 31, 1860.
87. The Official Records of the Union and Confederate Armies. Report of Brigadier Samuel R. Curtis U.S. Army Commanding Army of the Southwest. Report written by Curtis at the Headquarters of the Army of the Southwest, Cross Timbers, Arkansas, April 1, 1862. Imaging of the report done by the Library of Congress.
88. *War of the Rebellion*, Series 1, Vol. 22, Part 1, Chapter 39, p. 69.
89. *Arkansas Gazette*, November 20, 1862.
90. Ibid., July 4, 1863. *Washington Telegraph*, January 4, 1865.
91. *Washington Telegraph*, September 9, 1863.
92. Anderson, 280–283. In a letter to General McClernand, on August 12, 1863, Lincoln writes to the general who wanted Lincoln to reinstate him to Grant's command. Lincoln states, "I can not give you a new command, because we have no forces except such as already have commanders. I am constantly pressed ... to give commands respectively to Frémont, McClellan, Butler, Sigel, Curtis, Hunter, Hooker.... I have no commands to give them." *Abraham Lincoln: Speeches and Writings*, 717–718. Curtis, who has been largely forgotten as an effective Union commander, was too good to keep out of the fray and was given command of the Department of Kansas on January 16, 1864.
93. *Abraham Lincoln: Speeches and Writings*, 689–690.
94. Letter to John Todd, Tabor, Iowa, from David Todd, Pine Bluff, Arkansas, June 6, 1864.
95. Letter to John Todd, Tabor, Iowa, from his sister Mary Sloan, Harrisburg, Pennsylvania, August 11, 1864.
96. Letter to John Todd, chaplain of the 46th Iowa Regiment, Memphis, Tennessee, from David Worcester, Island 63 below Helena, Arkansas, August 31, 1864.
97. Monaghan, 298–299.
98. Lankford. Molly Finley interviewed by Irene Robertson in Honey Creek near Mesa, Arizona, 24.

99. Lankford. Mary Ann Brooks interviewed by Mrs. Bernice Bowden in Pine Bluff, Arkansas, 420–421.
100. Bolton-NPS, 74–75.
101. Lankford. Johnson, 12.

Chapter 7

1. Todd book, 44.
2. Johnson and Spence, eds., *The Expeditions of John Charles Frémont, Vol. 1, Travels from 1838 to 1844* (Urbana, Chicago and London: University of Illinois Press, 1970), 283.
3. *Southern Shield*, July 23, 1842. *Arkansas State Democrat Herald*, November 13, 1840.
4. *Washington Telegraph*, September 27, 1854.
5. Morgans, 8. Todd book, 59.
6. Letter to Q.F. Atkins from Jonas Jones, Tabor, Iowa, Sept. 5, 1854. Located at the Todd House Museum Archives, Tabor, Iowa.
7. Morgans book, 9. Todd book, 59.
8. Deacon Adams, "Tabor and the Northern Excursion: Deacon Adams' Own Story." *The Annals of Iowa*, 3rd Series, Vol. 23 (October 1955), 130.
9. *Ibid.*, 131.
10. Tabor Public Meetings. These are records of the early town meetings and various reminiscences of the towns' early pioneers. The town of Tabor, Iowa, was deeply involved in the Underground Railroad and in efforts to keep slavery out of the territory of Kansas. Reminiscences of Samuel H. Adams, 103.
11. Robert Gaston family papers. Gaston's family was one of the pioneer families in Tabor, Iowa, and was deeply involved in the Underground Railroad. This item is from a 1903 undated newspaper article in the *Tabor Beacon*. Hereafter noted as "Robert Gaston's papers."
12. Handy, 39.
13. *Ibid.*
14. William Still, *The Underground Railroad* (New York: reprint of original by Arno Press and the *New York Times*, 1968), 548–549.
15. *Ibid.*
16. *Ibid.*
17. *Ibid.*
18. *Ibid.*, 550.
19. Quintard Taylor, *In Search of the Racial Frontier: African Americans in the American West 1528–1990* (New York, London: W.W. Norton, 1998), 83. Hereafter cited as "Quintard Taylor."
20. *Ibid.*, 86.
21. Siebert, 25. Gara, 27.
22. *Born in Slavery: Slave Narratives from Federal Writers' Project, 1936–1938. Texas Narratives*, Volume XVI part 2, 132. This is from the Library of Congress American Memory website. Interview with Felix Haywood in San Antonio, Texas. Haywood further stated that after the Civil War he went to Mexico to look around but came back to the United States. Haywood's interview is one of the highlights of the Federal Writers' Project's slave interviews. He was in his 90s and blind but his mind was sharp, his language was vivid, and his story was instructive.
23. Alwyn Barr, *Black Texans: A History of African Americans in Texas, 1528–1995* (Norman: University of Oklahoma Press, 1996), 30. Hereafter cited as "Barr."
24. Ronnie C. Tyler, "Fugitive Slaves in Mexico," *The Journal of Negro History*, Vol. LVII, No. 1, January, 1972. 1. Hereafter cited as "Tyler."
25. Barr, 26.
26. *Ibid.*, 29.
27. This incident has become commonly known as the "Cherokee slave revolt." However, it technically was not a revolt, insurrection or uprising. More accurately it was a large slave escape. However, unlike most escapes by bondspersons, this resulted in armed clashes between Native Americans and enslaved African Americans. We have chosen to call it by its most commonly known name of "Cherokee slave revolt."
28. Daniel F. Littlefield, Jr., *Africans and Seminoles: From Removal to Emancipation* (Westport, Connecticut, and London: Greenwood Press, 1977), 80. Hereafter cited as "Littlefield, *Seminoles*."
29. Daniel F. Littlefield, Jr. and Lonnie E. Underhill, "Slave 'Revolt' in the Cherokee Nation, 1842," *American Indian Quarterly*, Vol. 3 No. 2, Summer 1977. 121–123. Hereafter cited as "Littlefield and Underhill."
30. *Born in Slavery: Slave Narrative from the Federal Writers' Project, 1936–1938, Oklahoma Narratives Volume XIII*. Digital edition. These were taken from the Library of Congress' American Memory website. Morris Shepard interview Fort Gibson, Oklahoma, 287–288, 290. Hereafter these Oklahoma digital edition slave narrative will be cited as "*Oklahoma FWP D.E.*"
31. *Oklahoma FWP* D.E. Kizlah Love interview, Colbert, Oklahoma, 192, 194.
32. Clara Sue Kidwell, *The Choctaws in Oklahoma: From Tribe to Nation* (Norman: University of Oklahoma Press, 2008), 32–33.
33. Taylor, 220.
34. Aaron Mahr Yanez, "The UGRR on the Rio Grande," *CRM* No. 4 (1998), 43–44.
35. Daniel F. Littlefield, Jr., *Africans and Creeks: From the Colonial Period to the Civil War* (Westport, Connecticut, and London: Greenwood, 1979), 200. Hereafter cited as "Littlefield, *Creeks*."
36. Kenneth W. Porter, "The Seminole in Mexico," *The Hispanic America Historical Review*, Vol. 31, No. 1 (Feb. 1951), 18–19. Hereafter cited as "Porter Seminole." Susan A. Miller, *Coacoochee's Bones: A Seminole Saga* (Lawrence: University Press of Kansas, 2003), 168. Hereafter cited as "Miller." Quintard Taylor, 60. Tyler, 8.
37. Porter Seminole, 7.
38. *Ibid.*, 35.
39. Miller, 173.
40. Phillip Thomas Tucker, "John Horse: Forgotten African-American Leader of the Second Seminole War," *The Journal of Negro History*, Vol. 77, No. 2, (Spring, 1992), 74–75.
41. *Ibid.*, 80.
42. *Ibid.*, 79.
43. Tyler, 5. Miller, 148.
44. Tyler, 10.
45. United States Congress, Senate, "Indian Affairs, Laws and Treaties," Senate Document No. 452, 57th Congress, 1st Session (Washington, 5 Vols., 1903–1941) Vol. II, 149–151, 493–496.
46. Anne Hodges and H. Wayne Morgan, *Oklahoma: A Bicentennial History* (Nashville, American Association for State and Local History, 1977), 30.
47. Annie Heloise Abel, *The American Indian as Slaveholder and Secessionist* (Lincoln, Nebraska, and London: University of Nebraska Press, 1992), 2. Hereafter cited as "Abel."

48. J.B. Davis, "Slavery in the Cherokee Nation," *Chronicles of Oklahoma*, Vol. 11, No. 4 (December, 1933), 1068.
49. Wyatt F. Jeltz, "The Relations of Negroes and Choctaw and Chickasaw Indians," *The Journal of Negro History*, Vol. 33, No. 1 (January 1948), 31.
50. Littlefield and Underhill, 128. Littlefield, *Seminole*, 103–104.
51. *Oklahoma Slave Narratives: A Folk History of Slavery in Oklahoma from Interviews with Former Slaves from the Federal Writers' Project 1936–1938* (Bedford, Massachusetts: Applewood Books in cooperation with the Library of Congress). Polly Colbert interview, Colbert, Oklahoma, 33. Hereafter cited as "*Oklahoma FWP*."
52. *Oklahoma FWP*, Nancy Rogers Bean interview, Hulbert, Oklahoma, 13. Hereafter cited as "*Oklahoma FWP*, Bean."
53. Kenneth W. Porter, "Notes Supplementary between Negroes and Indians," *Journal of Negro History*, Vol. xviii (July 1933), 289, 307.
54. *Oklahoma FWP*, Mary Grayson interview, Tulsa, Oklahoma, 117.
55. Lankford. Victoria Taylor Thompson interviewed by Ethel Wolfe Garrison, Muskogee, Oklahoma, 20.
56. Littlefield, *Creeks*, 136.
57. *Oklahoma FWP*, Nellie Johnson interview Tulsa, Oklahoma, 155–158. Hereafter cited as "Johnson interview."
58. *Arkansas Gazette*, August 13, 1852 and *Arkansas Gazette*, October 29, 1852 for Granderson. *Arkansas Gazette*, January 21, 1853 for William.
59. Littlefield, *Seminoles*, 200.
60. Abel, 41–42.
61. *Ibid.* Ironically the Reverend Kingsbury's son, also named Cyrus, a layman, remained in the territory and became a Union supporter when the Civil War erupted.
62. *Ibid.*, 62.
63. William H. Seward, "Freedom in the New Territories," March 11, 1850, U.S. Congress, Senate, *Congressional Record*, 31st Congress, 1st Session, App., pp. 260–269.
64. Abel, 290–295.
65. Patrick Minges, ed., *Black Indian Slave Narratives* (Winston-Salem, North Carolina: John F. Blair, 2004). Chaney Richardson interviewed by Ethel Wolfe Garrison in Fort Gibson, Oklahoma, October, 1937. *Oklahoma FWP*, interviews, 50–51. Hereafter cited as "Minges *Oklahoma FWP*."
66. *Oklahoma FWP*, Lucinda Davis interview, Tulsa, Oklahoma, 53–55. Hereafter cited as "*Oklahoma FWP* Davis."
67. *Arkansas Gazette*, December 27, 1850;
68. *Ibid.*, June 25, 1859.
69. Littlefield Creeks, 164.
70. Gaston Manuscript located in the Todd House Museum Archives in Tabor, Iowa. This manuscript with its addenda is material gathered by W.E. Gaston, son of James Gaston, a veteran of the Tabor Underground Railway. This manuscript contains information on the early history of Tabor, Iowa, and its abolitionist and Underground Railroad activities and its help in keeping slavery out of Kansas. Most of the residents of Tabor had attended Oberlin College in Oberlin, Ohio. This college was a bastion of abolitionists and many of its graduates became involved in the Underground Railroad. The manuscript contains recollections of the Gaston, Cummings and Townsend family pioneers and their children. Addenda 6, 9, 10 and 12. Hereafter cited as "Gaston Ms."
71. *Oklahoma FWP*, Bean., 13.
72. Abel, 23.
73. *Provisional Congress Journal*, vol. i, 244.
74. Monaghan, 209–210.
75. *War of the Rebellion*, Series 1 Vol. 3, 690–692.
76. *War of the Rebellion*, Series 1 Vol. 13, 489–490.
77. Author's notes and material from the Creek Council House Museum in Okmulgee, Oklahoma. Gary Zellar, *African Creeks: Estelvste and the Creek Nation* (Norman: University of Oklahoma Press, 2007), 45.
78. Minges, *Oklahoma FWP*, Chaney McNair interview in Vinita, Oklahoma, by Annie Faulton in June of 1939, 42–43.
79. Minges, *Oklahoma FWP*, Moses Lonian interview in Vinita, Oklahoma, by James R. Carseloway in July 1937, 56–61.
80. Monaghan, 252–253.
81. *War of the Rebellion*, Series 1, Vol. 22 (Part 1), 447–448.
82. *Oklahoma FWP*, Davis, 59–61.

Chapter 8

1. Bibb, 47.
2. *Nebraska City News*, November 20, 1858.
3. William Gilpin, *Mission of the North American People, Geographical, Social and Political* (Philadelphia: J.B. Lippincott, 1873), 202.
4. *Washington Post*, May 31, 1995.
5. "Act to Punish Offences Against Slave Property" passed by the Legislative Assembly of Kansas Territory on August 14, 1855. Also, "Kansas Bogus Legislature.org" <http://kansasboguslegislature.org/legis/slavery.html> (last visited May 15, 2009). Kansas State Historical Society.
6. Monaghan, 61–63. Villard, 148–165. Kansas State Historical Society online, "Wyandotte Constitution."
7. Turton, 99.
8. Bayne letter.
9. *Kansas City Star*, July 2, 1905. Trexler, 204. Turton, 43.
10. 1860 Federal Census.
11. *Ibid.*
12. *Abraham Lincoln: Speeches and Writings*, 335.
13. Trexler, 204.
14. *Ibid.*, 206.
15. Quintard Taylor, 93.
16. Lecompton Constitution, Kansas State Historical Society.
17. Blockson, 190.
18. Gara, 57.
19. Bibb, 49.
20. Franklin and Schweninger, 210.
21. Bibb, 170.
22. Larry Gara, *The Liberty Line: The Legend of the Underground Railroad* (Reprint, Lexington: University Press of Kentucky, 1996), Preface XII.
23. Larry Gara, "An Epic in Unites States History," *Underground Railroad*, produced by the Division of Publications, National Park Service, Washington, D.C., 12.
24. *Tabor Beacon*, Centennial Issue, July 23, 1952.
25. *Council Bluffs Nonpareil*, August 26, 1926.

26. *Nebraska City News*, April 14, 1890.
27. Doy, 37–38.
28. *Plessy v. Ferguson*, 163 U.S. 537 (1896) No. 210.
29. Douglas A. Blackmon, *Slavery by Another Name: The Re-Enslavement of Black Americans from the Civil War to World War II* (Anchor Books, 2009), 357–358.
30. Marshall Everett, *History of the Phillipines: Young People's Edition* (Chicago: J.S. Ziegler, 1899).
31. Connelley, 175.
32. Turton, 48.
33. *Missouri FWP*. Interview with Hannah Allen, Fredericktown, Missouri, 8.

Bibliography

Letters

Adair, S.L. (Osawatomie, K.T.), to the Rev. S.S. Jocelyn, October 15, 1855.

Adair, S.L., to Zu Adams, September 16, 1895.

Anderson, J.G., to J.Q. Anderson (Dear Brother), January 14, 1859.

Atkins, Arthur (Chicago, Illinois), to Sally Atkins, June 3, 1851.

Bayne, Thos. R. (Williamstown, Kansas), to Zu Adams, September 11, 1895.

Bixby, Amos (Boulder, Colorado), to Leonard F. Parker (Grinnell, Iowa), May 16, 1887.

Brown, George Washington, to Eli Thayer, Esq., June 4, 1856.

Creitz, William F. (Holton, Kansas), to Col. James Redpath, December 17, 1859.

Fraser, E. of Boarman and Fraser Real Estate Brokers and General Agents (Kansas City, Missouri) to John Todd (Tabor, Iowa), November 15, 1860.

Handy, Lynn (Percival, Iowa), to author (Council Bluffs, Iowa), February 22, 2007.

Hyatt, Thaddeus, to Amos Lawrence, February 11, 1857.

Jennison, Dr. C.R. (Mound City, K.T.), to "Dear Friend" (George L. Stearns), November 28, 1860.

Jones, Jonas (Tabor, Iowa), to Q.F. Atkins, September 5, 1854.

Ladies of Orange, N.J., to Sir (Thaddeus Hyatt), October 20, 1856.

Learnard (O.E.L), to "Dear Friends," May 23, 1856.

Maris, Isaac, to F.G. Adams, July 22, 1895.

McFarland to Kansas State Historical Society, no date. Letter is about McFarland slave shackle.

Montgomery, James (Mound City K.T.), to "Dear Friend" (George L. Stearns), November 28, 1860.

Nute, E. (Ephraim) (Lawrence, K.T.), to F.B. Sanborn, Esq., March 22, 1859.

Nute, Ephriam (Lawrence, K.T.), to "unknown," February 14, 1859.

Nute, Ephraim (Lawrence, K.T.), to "unknown," February 24, 1859.

Parsons, L.F. (Osawatomie, K.T.), to Dear Friends Redpath & Hinton, December, 1859.

Pomeroy, S.C., to Thaddeus Hyatt, November 5 and December 3, 1860.

Searl, A.D. (Tabor, Iowa), to Thaddeus Hyatt, August 21, 1856.

Sloan, Mary (Harrisburg, Pennsylvania), to John Todd (Tabor, Iowa), August 11, 1864.

Smith, Gerrit (Peterboro, New York), to John Thomas, Esq. (Syracuse, New York), August 27, 1859.

Stewart, John E. (Wakarusa, K.T.), to Thaddeus Hyatt, December 20, 1859.

Tappan, Sam (Worcester, Massachusetts), to Gen. Thomas W. Higginson, January 24, 1858.

Todd, David (Pine Bluff, Arkansas), to John Todd (Tabor, Iowa), June 6, 1864.

Todd, John (Tabor, Iowa), to Quintus E. Atkins Esq. (Racine, Wisconsin), Jan. 19, 1857.

Todd, Martha, and her son James Todd (Tabor, Iowa) to Q.F. Atkins (Racine, Wisconsin), December 25, 1856.

Venard M.D., A., to Thaddeus Hyatt, October 3, 1860.

Whitman, E.B. (Lawrence, K.T.), to "Friend" (Franklin B.) Sanborn, April 30, 1858.

Worcester, David (Island 63 below Helena, Arkansas), to John Todd (Memphis, Tennessee), August 31, 1864.

Newspapers Footnoted in the Book

Arkansas Advocate (Little Rock, Arkansas)
Arkansas Gazette (Little Rock)
Arkansas State Democrat Herald
Batesville News (Arkansas)
Burlington Hawk Eye (Iowa)
Chicago Daily Tribune
Chicago Tribune
Columbia Missourian
Columbia Statesman (Missouri)
Columbia Tribune (Missouri)
Council Bluffs Nonpareil
Democratic Star (Arkansas)
Des Moines Capital
Doniphan Crusader of Freedom (Kansas Territory)
Examiner Time (Manchester England)
Fort Madison Plain Dealer (Iowa)
Frank Leslie's Illustrated Newspaper (New York)

Fremont (Iowa) Herald (believed to be published by Nebraska City News in Nebraska Territory)
Herald of Freedom (Lawrence, Kansas Territory)
Iowa State Register Morning Edition
Kansas City Star
Keokuk Argus (Iowa)
Jasper County Record (Newton, Iowa)
The Liberator (Boston, Massachusetts) *New York Times*
Liberty Tribune (Missouri)
Marion County Palmyra Whig (Missouri)
Marshall Daily Democrat-News (Missouri)
Missouri Courier (Hannibal)
Missouri Republican (St. Louis)
Missouri Statesman (Columbia)
Nebraska City News
Nebraska News (Nebraska City)
Page County Herald (Clarinda, Iowa)
Palmyra Weekly Whig (Missouri)
Platte Argus (Missouri)
Provincial Freeman (Windsor, Toronto, Chatham Ontario, Canada)
Richmond Weekly Mirror (Missouri)
Southern Shield (Arkansas)
St. Joseph Commercial Cycle
St. Louis Argus
St. Louis Intelligencer
Syracuse Daily Journal (New York)
Tabor Beacon (Iowa)
Taylor County Tribune (Iowa)
Voice of the Fugitive (Sandwich [now Windsor] Ontario, Canada)
Washington Post
Washington Telegraph (Arkansas)
Weekly Anglo-African (New York)

Documents, Court Cases, Websites and Miscellaneous Items

Abbott, Mrs. James Burnett. Reminiscences of Mrs. Abbott of the Underground Railroad days in Kansas, dated September 1, 1895. Kansas State Historical Society.
"Act to Punish Offences Against Slave Property" passed by the Legislative Assembly of Kansas Territory on August 14, 1855. Also, Kansas Bogus Legislature.org <http://kansasboguslegislature.org/legis/slavery.html> (last visited May 25, 2009). Kansas State Historical Society.
Arkansas Slave Narratives from the Federal Writers' Project, 1936–1938. These interviews were taken directly from the Library of Congress' American Memory website.
Armstrong, John. Reminiscences of slave days in Kansas by John Armstrong. Located in the Kansas State Historical Society.
Atchison, David Rice. Transcript of Atchison's speech before the sacking of Lawrence, Kansas Territory, on May 21, 1856. The transcript resides in the Kansas State Historical Society.
Author's notes on visit to the Adair Cabin in Osawatomie, Kansas.

Author's notes and material from the Creek Council House Museum in Okmulgee, Oklahoma.
Benton County, Arkansas, Official Website. Section on "History of the County" <www.co.benton.Ar.us/> (last visited October 5, 2008).
Biographical Directory of the United States Congress online: Thomas Hart Benton. <http://bioguide.congress.gov/biosearch/biosearch.asp>
Biographical Directory of the United States Congress online: Blanche Bruce. <http://bioguide.congress.gov/biosearch/biosearch.asp>
Blikre, Lowel. "Phase 1 Intensive Survey of Seven Potential Historical Archeological Properties in the Civil Bend Vicinity, Benton Township, Fremont County, Iowa," prepared for the State Historical Society of Iowa. April 2005.
Bolton, Charles S., *Fugitives from Injustice: Freedom-Seeking Slaves in Arkansas, 1800–1860.* Internet publication of the National Park Service's "National Underground Railroad Network to Freedom."
Federal Census for 1840, 1850, 1860.
Foster Memorial AME Zion Church in Tarrytown, New York, is recognized as a part of the National Park Service's "Road to Freedom" program. Their website details Amanda Foster's work in Arkansas <http://www.cr.nps.gov/nr/travel/underground/ny5.htm> (last visited March 24, 2007).
Freeman, Marcus Lindsay. Reminiscence of Marcus Lindsay Freeman, a former bondsman in Kansas. Located in the Kansas State Historical Society.
Fremont County Clerk's Office, Court Case No. 30 *Henry Garner v. S.F. Nuchols* [sic], etc., March Term District Court, 1859. Transcribed from a written summation of this court case found in the Todd House Museum Archives.
Gaston Manuscript and Addenda. The material in this manuscript was gathered by W.E. Gaston, son of James Gaston, erstwhile conductor on the Underground Railroad in Tabor, Iowa. They were recollections of the Gaston, Cummins and Townsend family pioneers and their children and early events in the town of Tabor, Iowa. Tabor, Iowa, was deeply involved in the Underground Railroad and other abolitionist activities.
Gaston, Robert, family papers. The Gaston family was deeply involved in the Underground Railroad in Tabor, Iowa.
Handy, Lynn. Material given to the author from Lynn Handy on Moses U. Payne and Payne family.
"Into the Fiery Furnace: Anti-Slavery Prisoners in the Kentucky State Penitentiary 1844–1870" <http//www.ket.org/underground/research/Prichard.htm> (last visited August 30, 2007). This article and the website are the work of James M. Prichard, Senior Archivist of the Kentucky Department of Libraries.
Laws of Missouri, 1836–1837, 3. Approved February 1, 1837, by Governor Lelburn W. Boggs.
Lecompton Constitution of Kansas. Kansas State Historical Society online.
Life and Times of John E. Stewart by John E. Stewart. Document in the Kansas State Historical Society believed to have been written by Stewart around 1856.

Majors, Alexander file located at the Morton-James Library in Nebraska City, Nebraska.
Mathews, Dale. Mathews family papers. The Mathews family was involved in the Underground Railroad in Tabor, Iowa.
Missouri Slave Narratives from Federal Writers' Project, 1936–1938. Digital Edition on the Library of Congress' American Memory website.
Missouri State Archives. "Crack of the Pistol: Dueling in 19th Century Missouri: Benton-Lucas Duel." Missouri Digital Heritage, Missouri Office of the Secretary of State.
Missouri State Archives Digital Heritage: *Guide to African-American History, Section on Governor Thomas C. Fletcher.*
Nuckolls, S.F. file located at the Morton-James Library in Nebraska City, Nebraska.
Official Records of the Union and Confederate Armies. Report of Brigadier General Samuel R. Curtis U.S. Army Commanding Army in the Southwest. Report written by Curtis at the Headquarters of the Army of the Southwest, Cross Timbers, Ark., April 1, 1862. Imaging of this report done by the Library of Congress.
Oklahoma Slave Narratives: from Federal Writers' Project, 1936–1938. Digital Edition on the Library of Congress' American Memory website.
Oliver v. Weakley et al. Case No. 10,502 Circuit Court, Third Circuit, 18 F. Cas. 678; 1853, October, 1853, Term.
Payne-Broadwell Family Papers, 1803–1903. Western Historical Manuscript Collection of the State Historical Society of Missouri. Biographical Sketches Payne Family.
Plessy v. Ferguson, 163 U.S. 537 (1896) 163 U.S. 537 Plessy v. Ferguson No. 210
Records of Public Meetings in Tabor, Fremont County, Iowa. Section on Maria Gaston's Reminiscences and section on Samuel Adams' Reminiscences.
Records of the Recorder of the Office of the County Records of Saline County, Missouri.
Seward, William H. "Freedom in the New Territories," March 11, 1850, U.S. Congress, Senate, Congressional Record, 31st Congress, 1st Session, App., pp. 260–269.
Syracuse University Library. "That Laboratory of Abolitionism, Libel, and Treason: Syracuse and the Underground Railroad." The Jerry Rescue and Its Aftermath, digital edition.
Texas Slave Narratives from Federal Writers' Project, 1936–1938. Digital Edition on the Library of Congress' American Memory website.
Tripp, Bernell E. "Mary Miles Bibb: Education and Moral Improvement in the 'Voice of the Fugitive.'" Paper presented at the Annual Meeting of the Association for Education in Journalism and Mass Communication, (76th Kansas City, Mo. August 11–14, 1993).
United States ex rel. *Garland v. Morris,* Case No. 15,811, District Court D. Wisconsin, 1854, April 1854.
United States Congress, Senate, "Indian Affairs, Laws and Treaties," Senate Document No. 452, 57th Congress, 1st Session. Washington, 5 Vols., 1903–1941, Vol. II.
University of Kentucky: Notable Kentucky African Americans Database Website. Section on Underground Railroad, Conductors, Escapes. This site was last visited on April 4, 2009, and had been updated on that date.
Van Metre v. Mitchel, Case No. 16, 865, Circuit Court, W.D. Pennsylvania, 28 F. Cas. 1036; 1853, October 1853.
Wheeler, Holland. "Quantrill a Suspicious Loafer," Kansas Historical Collection, VII (1901–1902), 224–226.
"Wyandotte Constitution." Kansas State Historical Society online.

Books

Able, Annie Heloise. *The American Indian as Slaveholder and Secessionist.* Lincoln: University of Nebraska Press, 1992.
Ables, Jules. *Man on Fire: John Brown and the Cause of Liberty.* New York: Macmillan, 1971.
Adams, Nehemiah. *A South-Side View of Slavery.* Savannah: Beehive, 1974.
Anderson, Galusha. *The Story of a Border City During the Civil War.* Boston: Little, Brown, 1908.
Appanoose County History (Iowa). Chicago: Western History, 1878.
Arkansas Slave Narratives from the Federal Writers' Project, 1936–1938. Bedford, Massachusetts: Applewood Books in cooperation with the Library of Congress.
Ashmore, Harry S. *Arkansas: A Bicentennial History.* New York: W.W. Norton, 1978.
Bancroft, Frederic. *Slave-Trading in the Old South.* Baltimore: J.H. Furst, 1931.
Barr, Alwyn. *Black Texans: A History of African Americans in Texas, 1528–1995.* Norman: University of Oklahoma Press, 1996.
Basler, Roy P., ed. *Abraham Lincoln: His Speeches and Writings.* 1990. New York City: Da Capo, 2001.
Bayliss, John F., ed. *Black Slave Narratives.* New York: Macmillan, 1970.
Benton, Thomas Hart. *Thirty Years View: A History of the Working of the American Government 1820–1850, Part Two.* New York, Boston: D. Appleton, 1856. Google digital edition.
Bibb, Henry. *Narrative of the Life and Adventures of Henry Bibb an American Slave Written by Himself.* New York: published by the author, 1849. Google digital edition.
Blackmon, Douglas A. *Slavery by Another Name: The Re-Enslavement of Black Americans from the Civil War to World War II.* New York: Anchor Books, 2009.
Blockson, Charles L. *The Underground Railroad: First-Person Narratives of Escapes to Freedom in the North.* New York: Prentice-Hall, 1987.
Brashear, Minnie M. *Mark Twain, Son of Missouri.* Chapel Hill: University of North Carolina Press, 1934.
Britton, Wiley. *The Civil War on the Border 1861–1862.* New York: Putnam's, 1891.
Brode, Patrick. *The Odyssey of John Anderson.*

Toronto: Osgoode Society for Canadian Legal History, University of Toronto Press, 1989.
Brown, Hallie Q. *Homespun Heroines and Other Women of Distinction.* New York: Oxford University Press, 1992.
Brown, William Wells. *William W. Brown, an American Slave Written by Himself.* London: Charles Gilpin, 1850. Google digital edition.
Brown, William Wells. *Clotel; or, The President's Daughter: A Narrative of Slave Life in America.* London: Partridge & Oakley, 1853. Google digital edition.
Bruce, Henry Clay. *The New Man: Twenty-Nine Years a Slave, Twenty-Nine Years a Free Man.* Lincoln: University of Nebraska Press, 1996 (reprint).
Buchanan, Thomas C. *Black Life on the Mississippi: Slaves Free Blacks and the Western Steamboat World.* Chapel Hill: University of North Carolina Press, 2004.
Burch, John P. *Charles W. Quantrell, A True History of His Guerrilla Warfare on the Missouri and Kansas Border During the Civil War of 1861 to 1865, as Told by Captain Harrison Trow.* Vega, Texas: J.P. Burch, 1923.
Campbell, Stanley W. *The Slave Catchers, Enforcement of the Fugitive Slave Law, 1850–1860.* Chapel Hill: University of North Carolina Press, 1970.
Castel, Albert. *William Clarke Quantrill: His Life and Times.* New York: Frederick Fell, 1962.
Castel, Albert. *Civil War in Kansas: Reaping the Whirlwind.* Lawrence: University Press of Kansas, 1997.
Coffin, Levi. *Reminiscences of Levi Coffin.* 1876. Reprint, New York: Arno Press and the New York Times, 1968.
Connelley, William Elsey. *Quantrill and the Border Wars.* New York: Pageant Book, 1956.
Cordley, Richard. *Pioneer Days in Kansas.* New York: Pilgrim, 1903.
Crighton, John C. *A History of Columbia and Boone County.* Columbia, Missouri: Computer Color-Graphics, 1987.
William Cutler. *History of the State of Kansas.* Chicago: Andreas' Western Historical Publishing, 1882–1883.
Dempsey, Terrell. *Searching for Jim: Slavery in Sam Clemens' World.* Columbia: University of Missouri Press, 2003.
Douglas, Frederick. *Life and Times of Frederick Douglas, His Early Life, as a slave, His Escape from Bondage, and His Complete History to the Present Time.* Hartford, Connecticut: Park Publishing, 1881. Digital version by University of North Carolina.
Doy, John. *The Narrative of John Doy of Lawrence Kansas: A Plain Unvarnished Talk.* New York: Thomas Holman, 1860.
Drew, Benjamin. *The Refugee: A North-Side View of Slavery.* Reading, Massachusetts: Addison-Wesley, 1969.
DuBois, W.E.B. *John Brown.* Philadelphia: George W. Jacobs, 1909.
Everett, Marshall. *History of the Phillipines: Young People's Edition.* Chicago: J.S. Ziegler, 1899.
Fairbank, Calvin. *Rev. Calvin Fairbank During Slavery Times: How He "Fought the Good Fight" to Prepare "the Way."* Chicago: R.R. McCabe, 1890. Reprint, New York: Negro University Press, 1969.
Fehrenbacher, Don E. *The Dred Scott Case: Its Significance in American Law and Politics.* New York: Oxford University Press, 1978.
Finkelman, Paul. *Slavery in the Courtroom: An Annotated Bibliography of American Cases.* Washington, DC: Library of Congress, 1985.
Franklin, John Hope. *From Slavery to Freedom: A History of Negro American.* New York: Alfred A. Knopf, 1967.
____, and Loren Schweninger. *Runaway Slaves: Rebels on the Plantation.* New York: Oxford University Press, 1999.
Frazier, Harriet C. *Runaway and Freed Missouri Slaves and Those Who Helped Them, 1763–1865.* Jefferson, North Carolina: McFarland, 2004.
Frothingham, Octavius Brooks. *Gerrit Smith: A Biography.* New York City: Putnam's, 1878.
Fugitive Slave Act of 1850. American Historical Documents 1000–1904. Harvard Classics. New York: P.F. Collier, 1938.
Gara, Larry. *The Liberty Line: The Legend of the Underground Railroad.* Lexington: University Press of Kentucky, 1961, 1996.
Gilpin, William. *Mission of the North American People, Geographical, Social and Political.* Philadelphia: J.B. Lippincott, 1873. Google digital version.
Gray's Doniphan County History. Bendena, Kansas: Royalcroft, 1905.
Handy, Bob, and Gertrude Handy. *Some Days: A Tale of Civil Bend.* Hamburg, Iowa: Interstate, 1973.
Harlow, Ralph Volney. *Gerrit Smith, Philanthropist and Reformer.* New York: Henry Holt, 1939.
Henrick, George, and Willene Henrick, eds. *Fleeing for Freedom: Stories of the Underground Railroad as told by Levi Coffin and William Still.* Chicago: Ivan R. Dee, 2004.
Hinton, Richard J. *John Brown and His Men.* New York: Funk and Wagnalls, 1894.
History of Fremont County, Iowa. Iowa Historical Society, Iowa Historical Company, 1881.
Hodges, Anne, and H. Wayne Morgans. *Oklahoma: A Bicentennial History.* Nashville: American Association for State and Local History, 1977.
Hopkins, James Franklin. *A History of the Hemp Industry in Kentucky.* Lexington: University of Kentucky Press, 1951.
Hudson, J. Blaine. *Fugitive Slaves and the Underground Railroad in the Kentucky Borderline.* Jefferson, North Carolina: McFarland, 2002.
Jackson, Donald, and Mary Lee Spence, eds. *The Expeditions of John C. Frémont, Vol. 1, Travels from 1838 to 1844.* Urbana: University of Illinois Press, 1970.
Johnson, Homer Uri. *From Dixie to Canada: Romance and Realities of the Underground Railroad.* Buffalo, New York: 1894.
Johnson, Walter. *Soul by Soul: Life Inside the Antebellum Slave Market.* Cambridge, Massachusetts: Harvard University Press, 1999.
Jones, Louis Thomas. *The Quakers of Iowa.* Iowa City: State Historical Society of Iowa, 1914.

Kennedy, John F. *Profiles in Courage*, Memorial Edition. New York: Harper & Row, 1964.

Kidwell, Clara Sue. *The Choctaws in Oklahoma: From Tribe to Nation*. Norman: University of Oklahoma Press, 2008.

Lankford, George E., ed. *Bearing Witness: Memories of Arkansas Slavery Narratives from the 1930's WPA Collections*. Fayetteville: University of Arkansas Press, 2003.

Leslie, Edward E. *The Devil Knows How to Ride: The True Story of William Clarke Quantrill and His Confederate Raiders*. New York: Random House, 1996.

Littlefield, Daniel F., Jr. *Africans and Creeks: From the Colonial Period to the Civil War*. Westport, CT, and London: Greenwood, 1979.

_____. *Africans and Seminoles: From Removal to Emancipation*. Westport, CT, and London: Greenwood, 1977.

Lovejoy, Joseph C., and Owen Lovejoy. *Memoir of the Rev. Elijah P. Lovejoy, Who Was Murdered in Defense of the Liberty of the Press at Alton, Illinois, Nov. 7, 1837*. New York: John S. Taylor, 1838. Google digital edition.

Mason, Edward G., ed. *Early Chicago and Illinois*. Chicago: Fergus Printing Company, 1890. Google digital edition.

McCarthy, Timothy Patrick, and John Stauffer, eds. *Prophets of Protests: Reconsidering the History of American Abolitionism*. New York: New Press, 2006.

McLaurin, Melton A. *Celia, a Slave*. Athens: University of Georgia Press, 1991.

Miller, Susan A. *Coacoochee's Bones: A Seminole Saga*. Lawrence: University Press of Kansas, 2003.

Minges, Patrick, ed. *Black Indian Slave Narratives*. Winston-Salem, North Carolina: John F. Blair, 2004.

Missouri Slave Narratives from the Federal Writers' Project, 1936–1938. Bedford, Massachusetts: Applewood Books in cooperation with the Library of Congress.

Monaghan, Jay. *Civil War on the Western Border 1854–1865*. New York: Bonanza, 1955.

Morgans, James Patrick. *John Todd and the Underground Railroad: Biography of an Iowa Abolitionist*. Jefferson, North Carolina: McFarland, 2006.

Nevins, Alan. *Ordeal of the Union, Vol. 2, A House Dividing 1852–1857*. New York: Scribner's, 1947.

Oates, Stephen B. *To Purge This Land with Blood: A Biography of John Brown*. New York: Harper & Row, 1970.

O'Flaherty, Daniel. *General Jo Shelby: Undefeated Rebel*. Chapel Hill: University of North Carolina Press, 1954.

Ohio History. Ohio Historical Society, 1921.

Oklahoma Slave Narratives from the Federal Writers' Project 1936–1938. Bedford, Massachusetts: Applewood Books in Cooperation with the Library of Congress.

Ottawa: Old and New, A Complete History of Ottawa, Illinois. Ottawa, Illinois: Republican-Times Publishers, 1912.

Parker, L.F. *History of Poweshiek County* (Iowa). Chicago: S.J. Clarke, 1911.

Parker, Martha, and Betty Laird. *Soil of Our Souls: History of Clinton Lake Area Communities*. Overbrook, Kansas: Parker and Laid Enterprises, 1980.

Payne, Charles E. *Josiah Bushnell Grinnell*. Iowa City: State Historical Society of Iowa, 1938.

Pelzer, Louis. *Augustus Caesar Dodge*. Iowa City: State Historical Society of Iowa, 1908.

Penick, James L. *The Great Western Land Pirate: John Murrell in Legend and History*. Columbia: University of Missouri Press, 1981.

Perkins, E.A. *History of Marion County* [Missouri]. St. Louis: publisher unknown, 1884.

Richmond, Irving B. *John Brown Among the Quakers and Other Sketches*. Des Moines: Historical Department of Iowa, 1894.

Roosevelt, Theodore. *Thomas Hart Benson*. Boston: Houghton-Mifflin, 1886.

Sanborn, F.B. *The Life and Letters of John Brown, Liberator of Kansas and Martyr of Virginia*. Boston: Roberts Brothers, 1891.

Settle, William A. *Jesse James: Was His Name or Fact and Fiction Concerning the Careers of the NOTORIOUS JAMES BROTHERS of Missouri*. Columbia: University of Missouri Press, 1966.

Sheridan, Richard B., ed. *Freedom's Crucible: The Underground Railroad in Lawrence and Douglas County, Kansas, 1854–1865: A Reader*. Lawrence: Division of Continuing Education, University of Kansas, 1998.

Siebert, Wilbur H. *The Underground Railroad from Slavery to Freedom*. Reprint, New York: Macmillan, 1898.

Silag, Bill. *Outside In: African-American History in Iowa 1838–2000*. Des Moines: State Historical Society of Iowa, 2001.

Smith, Charles Edward. Unpublished thesis, *The Underground Railroad in Iowa*. Northeast Missouri State College, 1971.

Smith, Jessie Carney, ed. *Notable Black American Women Book II*. Thomson Gale, 1995.

Spurgeon, Ian Michael. *Man of Douglas Man of Lincoln The Political Odyssey of James Henry Lane*. Columbia: University of Missouri Press, 2008.

Stanley, Henry Morton. *Autobiography of Sir Henry Morton Stanley*. New York: Houghton Mifflin: Riverside, 1909.

Still, William. *The Underground Railroad*. Reprint, New York: Arno Press and the New York Times, 1968.

Switzer, William. *History of Boone County, Missouri*. Cape Girardeau, Missouri: Ramfre Reprint, 1970.

Taylor, Orville W. *Negro Slavery in Arkansas*. Fayetteville: University of Arkansas Press, 2000.

Taylor, Quintard. *In Search of the Racial Frontier: African Americans in the American West 1528–1990*. New York: W.W. Norton, 1998.

Thorpe, Francis Newton, ed. *The Federal and State Constitutions, Colonial Charters, and Other Organic Laws of the States, Territories, and Colonies now or heretofore forming the United States of America, Volume I*. Washington, DC: Government Printing Office, 1909, 7 Volumes.

Todd, John. *Early Settlement and Growth of Western Iowa or Reminiscences*. Des Moines: Historical Department of Iowa, 1906.

Trexler, Harrison Anthony. *Slavery in Missouri, 1804–1865*. Baltimore: Johns Hopkins University Press, 1914.
Turton, Cecil. "The Underground Railroad in Kansas, Nebraska, and Iowa." Unpublished master's thesis, Ohio State University, 1935.
Villard, Oswald Garrison. *John Brown 1800–1859: A Biography Fifty Years After*. Boston: Houghton Mifflin, 1910.
The War of the Rebellion: A Compilation of the Official Records of the Union and Confederate Armies. Washington, DC: Government Printing Office, 1880.
Ward, Samuel Ringgold. *Autobiography of a Fugitive Negro: His Anti-Slavery Labours in the United States, Canada, and England*. Toronto: John Snow, 35 Paternoster Row, 1855. Digital version, University of North Carolina.
Ware, E.F. *The Lyon Campaign in Missouri: History of the First Iowa Infantry*. Topeka: Crane, 1907.
Weisenburger, Steve. *Modern Medea: A Family Story of Slavery and Child-Murder from the Old South*. New York: Hill & Wang, 1999.
Wetmore, Alphonso. *Gazetteer of the State of Missouri*. St. Louis, 1837. New York: C. Keemle, Harper & Brothers. Google digital edition.
Williams, Walter, ed. *History of Northeast Missouri, Vol. 1*. Chicago: Lewis Publisher, 1913.
Winks, Robin W. *The Blacks in Canada: A History*. Carleton Library Series. Montreal: McGill–Queen's University Press, 2003.
Zellar, Gary. *African Creeks: Estelvste and the Creek Nation*. Norman: University of Oklahoma Press, 2007.

Periodical Articles

Abing, Kevin. "A Holy Battleground: Methodist, Baptist, and Quaker Missionaries Among Shawnee Indians, 1830–1844." *Kansas History*, Summer 1998.
Adams, Deacon (Samuel H.). "Tabor and the Northern Excursion: Deacon Adams' Own Story." *The Annals of Iowa*, 3rd Series, Vol. 23 (October 1955).
Andreas History of Kansas *Collections of the Kansas State Historical Society*, XV (1923).
Braund, Kathryn E. Holland. "The Creek Indians, Blacks, and Slavery." *The Journal of Southern History*, Vol. 57, No. 4 (Nov. 1991).
Connelley, William E. "The Lane Trail." *Collections of the Kansas State Historical Society*, Vol. 13 (1913–1914).
Davis, J.B. "Slavery in the Cherokee Nation." *Chronicles of Oklahoma*, Vol. 11, No. 4 (December 1933).
Eaton, Miles. "The Development and Later Decline of the Hemp Industry in Missouri." *Missouri Historical Review*, 43 (July 1949).
Farquhat, Catharine Grace Barbour. "Tabor and Tabor College." *The Iowa Journal of History and Politics* (October 1943).
Farrisson, William E. "William Wells Brown in Buffalo." *The Journal of Negro History*, Vol. XXXIX (October 1954).
Frazee, George. "An Iowa Fugitive Slave Case, 1850." *Annals of Iowa*, 3d Series 6 (April 1903).
Garretson, O.A. "Traveling on the Underground Railroad in Iowa." *Iowa Journal of History and Politics*, XXII (July 1924).
Harnack, Curtis. "Underground Railroad." *The Iowan Magazine* (June-July 1956).
Jeltz, Wyatt F. "The Relations of Negroes and Choctaw and Chickasaw Indians." *The Journal of Negro History*, Vol. 33, No. 1 (January 1948).
Jones, Mrs. Lawrence C. "The Desire for Freedom." *Palimpsest Magazine*, 8 (May 1927).
Langsdorf, Edgar. "Thaddeus Hyatt in Washington Jail." *Kansas Historical Quarterly*, Vol. 9, No. 3 (August 1940).
Lewis, Lloyd. "The Man Historians Forgot." *Kansas Historical Quarterly*, Vol. 8, No. 1 (February 1939).
Littlefield, Daniel F., and Lonnie E. Underhill. "Slave 'Revolt' in the Cherokee Nation, 1842." *American Indian Quarterly*, Vol. 3, No. 2 (Summer 1977).
Lorch, Fred W. "Biography of Orion Clemens." *Palimpsest Magazine*, Vol. X, No. 10 (October 1929).
Minick, Alice Lockwood. "Underground Railroad in Nebraska." *Collections of the State Historical Society*, Second Series Vol. 2. Lincoln, Nebraska, State Journal Co. Printers.
Porter, Kenneth W. "Notes Supplementary between Negroes and Indians." *Journal of Negro History*, Vol. XVIII (July 1933).
_____. "The Seminole in Mexico." *The Hispanic American Historical Review*, Vol. 31, No. 1 (Feb. 1951).
Todd, J. (James) E. "John Brown's Last Visit to Tabor." *Annals of Iowa*, (April–July 1898).
Tucker, Phillip Thomas. "John Horse: Forgotten African-American Leader of the Second Seminole War." *The Journal of Negro History*, Vol. 77, No. 2 (Spring 1992).
Tyler, Ronnie C. "Fugitive Slaves in Mexico." *The Journal of Negro History*, Vol. LVII, No. 1 (January 1972).
Van Ek, Jacob. "Underground Railroad in Iowa." *Palimpsest Magazine*, 5 (May 1921).
Yanez, Aaron Mahr. "The UGRR on the Rio Grande." *CRM*, No. 4 (1998).
Zorn, Roman J. "An Arkansas Fugitive Slave Incident and Its International Repercussions." *Arkansas Historical Quarterly*, 16 (Summer 1957).
_____. "Criminal Extradition Menaces the Canadian Haven for Fugitive Slaves, 1841–1861." *Canadian Historical Review*, Vol. 38, No. 4 (1957).

Index

Abbott, Elizabeth Ann Watrous 9–10
Abbott, James 9–10, 23, 110, 114, 186
Adair, Rev. Samuel 15
Adams, Samuel H. 98, 164
Amity, Iowa 104–105, 189
Anderson, Rev. Galusha 55–56, 81
Anderson, John 2, 66–67, 148
Anthony, Dan 19–20
Arkansas 1–2, 3, 5–6, 13, 20, 26, 49–50, 61, 66, 70–71, 80, 84, 87–88, 100, 119–129, 133–161, 163, 166, 168, 169, 172, 176–178, 184, 186, 190, 192–194, 198
Arkansas River 119, 124, 127, 146, 148
Armstrong, J.H.B. (Iowa) 97
Armstrong, John (Kansas) 8
Atchison, David Rice 10–13, 16
Atchison, Kansas 13, 103, 145

Beecher's Bibles 7, 12
Benton, Sen. Thomas Hart 59–61, 189
Bibb, Henry 3, 41, 56, 97, 129–138, 176, 186, 190–192
Bibb, Mary Miles 137–138
Blanchard, Dr. Ira 8, 98–100, 113, 115–117, 165
Boonville, Missouri 17, 50, 71, 84, 87
"Border Ruffians" 10–12, 34
Bounty hunters see Slave hunters
Brown, Frederick 15
Brown, Jason 15
Brown, John 8, 15–16, 25, 29, 90, 98–99, 104, 106, 108–115, 187–188, 196
Brown, John, Jr. 15–16
Brown, Owen 15–16
Brown, William Wells 2, 36, 50–55, 108

Bruce, Blanche 2, 74
Bruce, Henry Clay 2, 72–74
Butler, Pardee 13, 28
California 1, 36, 39, 45, 103, 123, 125, 163, 165–167, 179, 186
Canada 1–3, 13–14, 16, 18–21, 24, 29–34, 38, 42, 46, 48–50, 52–54, 56–58, 62, 67–68, 71–72, 78–79, 92, 96–97, 99, 101–102, 106, 108, 112, 114–115, 118, 123, 125–126, 128–131, 134–138, 140, 143, 146, 149–150, 152–155, 159, 165, 178, 181–182, 189, 191–193, 195
Cape Girardeau, Missouri 38
Cherokees 3, 29, 100, 106, 134–136, 142, 155, 157, 169–171, 175–185, 193–194; slave revolt 169–170
Chicago, Illinois 14, 34, 40, 42, 62, 64, 66, 68–69, 77, 94, 99, 101–102, 108, 115, 152, 189
Chickasaws 3, 171, 175–176, 178–179, 182, 185, 193
Choctaws 3, 143, 146, 151, 155, 157, 170–172, 175–176, 178–179, 182, 185, 193
Cincinnati, Ohio 49, 53, 68, 122–123, 128, 130–131, 137, 152–154, 191–192
Civil Bend, Iowa 8, 33, 90, 98–102, 107, 111, 113, 115–118, 165, 181, 191
Civil War 5, 20, 21, 25–26, 30, 32–33, 38, 43, 47, 54–55, 57, 63, 69, 73–74, 76–89, 93, 97–99, 105–106, 117, 123–124, 145, 155, 158–161, 167, 174, 179, 180–182, 184–185, 188, 191, 195–198
Clarke, Ann 8
Clemens, Samuel see Twain, Mark
Cleveland, Ohio 53–54, 99, 108
Coffin, Levi 123–124, 153

College Springs, Iowa see Amity, Iowa
Columbia, Missouri 37, 56, 58, 71
Congregational 9, 15, 55, 92–93, 104, 106, 160, 178
Coacoochee 172–174
Council Bluffs, Iowa 1, 100, 103, 116–117, 186
Creeks 3, 169–172, 174–178, 180, 182–183, 185, 193

Daggs, Ruel 94–95
Daniels, Jim 109–112
Davis, Lucinda 180, 185
Dean, John 25, 27–28, 30, 31, 32
Denmark, Iowa 92–94, 107, 191
Dickens, Charles 44–45
Douglas, Frederick 136–137, 196
Douglas, Stephen A. 6–7, 45, 79
Douglas County (Kansas) 9, 17
Doy, Dr. John 19, 21–24, 34, 37, 55, 196

Eliza (escaped slave) 99–102, 107
Emancipation Proclamation (Lincoln) 73, 160
Emancipation Proclamation in Missouri 88
England 36, 55, 67, 124, 149–150, 176

Fairbank, Rev. Calvin 121–124
Falls City, Nebraska 117
Fayetteville, Arkansas 134, 155, 159
Federal troops see Union Army
Fisher, Charles 18–19
Fort Gibson 142, 170, 175–176, 180
Frémont, John C. 61, 81–84, 162
Fugitive Slave Act of 1793 95–96
Fugitive Slave Act of 1850 7, 18–20, 39–40, 43, 54, 60, 64, 95, 101, 105, 127, 137, 181, 193

219

Galesburg, Illinois 62, 94
Gardner, Joseph 23, 34–35
Garner, Henry 101–102, 115–117, 192
Garner, Margaret 152–154
Garner, Maria 115–117, 192
Garrison, William Lloyd 7, 92
Gaston, George 98, 100, 103–104, 113–116, 181–182, 195
Gaston, Maria 98, 113–114,
Glenwood, Iowa 100, 181
Great Britian *see* England
Greeley, Horace 15, 106
Grinnell, Iowa 29, 62, 106–108, 114–115
Grinnell, Josiah B. 106–107, 115

Hackett, Nelson 3, 66, 148–149
Hannibal, Missouri 43–44, 50, 75
Harper, Samuel 90, 110–112
Harpers Ferry, Virginia 15–16, 20, 42, 104, 106, 109, 115, 118
Hart, Charles *see* Quantrill, William
Haywood, Felix 162, 168
Helena, Arkansas 141, 143–145, 159–160
Henry, William *see* Rescue, Jerry
Herd, Jacob 21, 24–26, 115–117, 190
Hitchcock, George 103–104
Holton, Kansas 8, 13, 15, 21, 33, 111, 112
Horse, John 172–175
Hurd, Jacob *see* Herd, Jacob
Hyatt, Thaddeus 14–15, 17

Independence, Missouri 1, 31
Indian Nations 1, 3, 5–6, 109, 134, 136, 143–144, 147, 155, 162–163, 168–169, 171–176, 178, 180–182, 184, 186, 193
Iowa 1–2, 5–6, 14, 16, 21, 28, 32, 46–47, 73, 76, 79, 87–88, 90–98, 100–101, 106–108, 111, 114, 116–118, 162, 165, 167, 186, 189–190, 195
Iowa City, Iowa 16, 108, 114–115

Jackson County (Missouri) 33–34, 84
"Jayhawkers" 21, 25, 29–31, 161
Jennison, Charles R. 20–21, 29, 79, 83–84, 109–110, 187
"Jerry Rescue" 2, 40–42, 46, 55
Johnson, Harry "Jim" 119–120, 161

Kagy, Abraham 8, 99, 118, 196
Kagy, John 8, 29, 99, 109–110, 115, 118, 187, 196
Kansas 2–3, 5–29, 31–35, 37, 41, 50, 58–59, 68–69, 74–79, 83–86, 98–100, 103–104, 106, 108–111, 115, 117–118, 159, 162, 167, 181, 183–190, 191, 194, 196–198
Kansas City, Missouri 19–20, 63, 79, 85
Kansas-Nebraska Act of 1854 6–7, 14, 60, 64, 99, 186, 189

Lafayette County (Missouri) 30, 59, 68, 75, 187
Lane, James 24, 33, 83–84, 86, 117–118
Lawrence, Kansas 2, 10–13, 17–27, 29, 31, 35, 62, 86, 107, 110, 114, 191
Leavenworth, Kansas 19, 24, 27, 33, 73–74, 88, 111, 182
Lecompton, Kansas 8, 12, 17
Lecompton Constitution 5,
Lewis, Iowa 29, 62, 103–104, 165, 181
Lexington, Missouri 37, 68, 78, 83, 103
Liberty Party 41, 43, 45
Lincoln, Abraham 48, 79, 82–84, 87, 99, 105, 160–161, 179, 189
Linn County (Kansas) 18–19
"Little Dixie" 2, 58, 64, 75, 98
Little Rock, Arkansas 121–123, 125, 127, 129, 133, 140, 142, 146, 147, 151, 156–159, 161, 180
Lizzie (escaping bondswoman) 17–18
Lucas, George W.S. 188

Majors, Alexander 102–103
Marion County (Missouri) 2, 40, 43–47, 50, 69, 75, 106
Marshall, Missouri 37, 69
"Mascogos" 168, 172, 174
Mayhew, Allen 99, 118, 196
Mayhew, Barbara 99, 118, 196
Mexico 6, 125, 140, 143, 146, 159–160, 162–163, 168–170, 172, 174, 191–193
Minick, Alice Lockwood 118
Minnis, William 121–123
Missouri 1, -3, 5–8, 10–11, 13, 18–41, 43–48, 50–52, 54, 56–95, 97–98, 100, 105–107, 109–112, 114–117, 119–121, 124–125, 127–128, 135, 146, 148, 152, 160–161, 165–167, 173, 177, 181, 184, 186–190, 192–194, 197–198
Missouri Compromise of 1820 7, 36
Missouri River 13, 16–17, 48, 62, 73, 75, 79, 98, 100–101, 103–104, 111, 115, 118, 128, 163–165, 181
Mitchell, "Uncle Tom" 106
Montgomery, James 19, 20–21, 79, 106, 109–110, 187
Muldrow, William 43–45

National Kansas Committee 14, 16
Nebraska 5, 7, 13–14, 29, 33, 41, 76, 79, 87, 91, 98–100, 103, 108, 114–115, 117–118, 167, 181, 186, 188, 190, 191
Nebraska City, Nebraska 9, 62, 99–102, 111, 117, 163–165, 167, 196
New England Emigrant Aid Company 11
Nucholls, Steven Friel 99–101, 107, 115–117
Nute, Rev. Ephraim 18–22

Oberlin College 15, 98, 103, 107, 123, 160, 178
Ohio 24–25, 28, 31, 49, 53, 64, 91–92, 96, 98, 108–109, 122–123, 134, 136, 146, 152–153, 163–164, 188, 192, 195
Oklahoma 5–6, 29–30, 100, 117, 136, 162, 171–173, 175–177, 185–186, 193
Ontario Province, Canada 38, 41, 57, 66, 68, 71, 128
Osawatomie, Kansas 15, 29–30, 109–111

Parker, L.F. 107
Payne, Mose U. 71, 87–88
Pease, Williamson 125–126
Perrysburgh, Ohio 131, 135
Pine Bluff, Arkansas 127, 148, 159–160, 180
Pinkerton, Allan 115
Platt, Elvira 98
Pyles, Charlotta Gordon MacHenry 91–92, 192

Quakers 28–33, 53–55, 68, 92–94, 105, 107–108, 137, 166, 197, 198
Quantrill, William 18, 24–33, 86, 190, 197, 198
Quincy, Iowa 103, 165
Quindaro, Kansas 8

Red Oak (Frankfort), Iowa 103–105
Reed (Reid), Thomas 100, 102
Republican Party (Republicans) 15, 48, 61, 71, 82, 102, 111, 161–162
Richardson, Chaney 179–180
Richardson, Charles 57, 64
Riley, William 18–19, 22
Robinson, Dr. Charles 11
Rowe, Katie 139, 145

St. Joseph, Missouri 19, 21, 23–24, 37, 39, 50, 77, 83, 103, 113, 116, 167
St. Louis, Missouri 37–38, 40, 42, 48–49, 51–52, 55–57, 59,

65–66, 68, 70, 75, 79, 81–82, 84, 87–88, 91, 116, 124, 135, 140
Salem, Iowa 92–96, 107, 191
Scott, Dred 60–61, 65–66, 121
Seminoles 3, 171–176, 182–183, 185, 193
Shepard, Morris 170–171
Simpson, Napoleon 5, 33–35
Slave catchers *see* Slave hunters
Slave hunters 8, 14, 26, 28
Springdale, Iowa 28–30, 108–109, 115
Stevens, Aaron 90, 110–111, 115, 188
Stewart, John E. 9, 14–15, 23–24, 27–28, 34, 162, 187
Stowe, Harriett Beecher 92
Stringfellow, John H. 12, 187, 189
Syracuse, New York 2, 40–42

Tabor, Iowa 9, 15–17, 29, 33, 62, 76, 88, 90, 98–104, 106–107, 109, 113–116, 118, 162, 164–165, 181–182, 191, 195–196
Texas 6, 20, 39, 59, 63, 79, 87, 134, 146, 149, 154–155, 159–163, 168–169, 171–174, 178, 180, 182, 185
Todd, Rev. John 9, 79, 98, 100, 102–104, 113, 162, 195
Topeka, Kansas 8–9, 15, 33, 62, 99, 110
Toronto, Canada 66
Trowbridge, Deacon Theron 92–93
Turner, Pastor Asa 92–93
Twain, Mark 45–46, 48, 79

Union Army (troops) 12, 26, 32, 38, 56, 63, 73–74, 79–88, 97, 106, 145, 160–161, 182–185, 189

Wabaunsee County (Kansas) 7–8
Walker, Sheriff Sam 17, 27, 31
Walton or Walter *see* Bibb, Henry
Ward, Rev. Samuel Ringgold 41, 136–137
Warren, John 128
Washington D.C. 12, 16–17, 39, 59, 74, 99, 161, 182, 184
Wild Cat *see* Coacoochee
Williamson, John 99–100, 102, 115–116, 192
Wyoming, Nebraska (river crossing) 99, 118

www.ingramcontent.com/pod-product-compliance
Ingram Content Group UK Ltd.
Pitfield, Milton Keynes, MK11 3LW, UK
UKHW052313030125
452830UK00014B/254